TO KILL NATIO[N]

TO KILL NATIONS

American Strategy in the Air-Atomic Age and the Rise of Mutually Assured Destruction

Edward Kaplan

CORNELL UNIVERSITY ITHACA AND LONDON

First published 2015 by Cornell University Press
First paperback printing 2020

Library of Congress Cataloging-in-Publication Data

Kaplan, Edward, author.
To kill nations : American strategy in the air-atomic age and the rise of mutually assured destruction / Edward Kaplan.
pages cm Includes bibliographical references and index.
ISBN 978-0-8014-5248-2 (cloth : alk. paper)
1. Nuclear warfare—Government policy—United States—History—20th century. 2. Nuclear weapons—Government policy—United States—History—20th century. 3. Air warfare—Government policy—United States—History—20th century. 4. Air power—United States—Philosophy—History—20th century. 5. United States. Air Force—History—20th century. 6. United States. Air Force. Strategic Air Command—History—20th century. 7. United States—Military policy. 8. Strategic forces—United States—History—20th century. 9. Strategy—History—20th century. 10. Cold War. I. Title.

UA23.K344 2015
355.02'17097309045—dc23

2014029090

ISBN 978-1-5017-5204-9 (paperback)

Contents

Preface

I became interested in the paradoxes of nuclear strategy during the early 1980s. To a high school student keenly interested in history, news reports of the SS-20 and Pershing II missile deployments in Europe created fascination about a weapon whose existence deterred its use. The two world wars of the twentieth century were filled with technological advances used without restraint. How did nuclear weapons come to be not only unused but unusable? My interest received a new twist a decade later. In the mid-1990s, the US Air Force (USAF) began the Aerospace Basic Course, which, like the Marine Corps program that inspired it, trained new lieutenants in the fundamentals of the Air Force mission and indoctrinated them into their service. I wondered: Why, with fifty years of Air Force heritage to call on, did we choose to ape Marine Corps methods for forging service identity? The answer seems clear: from their first days in uniform, Marines embody their mission and identity. Early Air Force history shows self-confidence, defined by strategic bombing. What happened to that clear sense of mission? As an officer and an instructor at the Air Force Academy charged with introducing cadets to military history and their service, these questions became important personally and professionally.

Reflection on cultural images deepened my disquiet. Iconic images of World War II instantly recognizable to the public appear in American history books. The flag raising at Iwo Jima is synonymous with the Marine Corps. The mushroom cloud over Nagasaki is equally iconic, but produces unease. Where the Marines chose that flag raising as their memorial for World War II, the Air Force avoided its most recognizable image, instead opting for an abstract sculpture which suggests the missing man formation. One service is at home with its past while the other avoids it.

Movies reflect the absence of a clear USAF self-image. Immediately following the Second World War, Hollywood mirrored the public's comfort with the armed services. *To Hell and Back* (1955), *Patton* (1970), and *Saving Private Ryan* (1998) embody an all-conquering US Army led by a charismatic general and everyday GIs struggling to survive and return. *Sands of Iwo Jima* (1949), *A Few Good Men* (1992), and *Flags of Our Fathers* (2006) promote the Marines. The Navy is well represented by such films as *The Caine Mutiny* (1954), *The Hunt for Red October* (1990), and even *Top Gun* (1986). Pro–Air Force images were common in films through the early 1960s—*Twelve O'Clock High* (1949), *Strategic Air Command*

(1955), and *A Gathering of Eagles* (1963) come to mind. However, by and after the middle of that decade, the Air Force is parodied unintentionally in movies like *Iron Eagle* (1986) and intentionally in *Dr. Strangelove* (1964).

This last movie illuminates the fate of Air Force identity. Those early movies depict a service defined by strategic bombing in the nuclear age and comfortable in that role. They are almost unknown now. While the Navy could use F-14s buzzing the tower in *Top Gun* in a recruiting commercial today, Jimmy Stewart looking skyward at a B-36 is only a curiosity for a film class.

Dr. Strangelove, though, is a classic. Its characters, frightening and absurd, mock public figures like Herman Kahn and Curtis LeMay. What makes the story line bizarre, and characters like General Buck Turgidson laughable and terrifying, is its contrast with the conviction of the director and his audience that nuclear war cannot be won. We know this fact. The characters do not. Why is Turgidson funny and frightening? Was he, and the USAF with him, always so out of step with reality, or had something changed between 1945 and 1964? The answer is definitively that something *had* changed: the American understanding of and preparation for nuclear war.

Addressing so large a topic was not something I could do on my own. First, and foremost, I would like to thank my advisor, John Ferris, as well as Holger Herwig, Stephen Randall, and James Keeley for their counsel and guidance. Hew Strachan generously reviewed the final work and provided essential guidance. I must thank Colonel Mark Wells for giving me the opportunity to seek graduate education and to return to the classroom at the Air Force Academy. Any historian learns to praise dedicated archivists. I had the great fortune of meeting many professionals during my research. Finally, thanks to my wife, Leigh, and to my parents, whose encouragement always was freely given and warmly welcomed.

TO KILL NATIONS

Introduction

PREVAIL

Air power as we know it now can kill a nation.

—Colonel Grover Brown, "Concepts of Strategic Air War," 1951

In November 1958, senior officers of the US Air Force were disappointed in their president.[1] In the Zone of the Interior Commanders' conference at Patrick Air Force Base in Florida, a center developing a new generation of weapons intended to strike the USSR with unprecedented speed and power, the agenda was short and the mood dark. The Thor missile launch intended as its "special event" was aborted. The main presentation, by the commander of Air Forces in the Pacific, Gen. Lawrence Kuter, expressed frustration about the Second Taiwan Straits Crisis. American ships and aircraft had deterred the Communist Chinese as they shelled Nationalist-held islands, he argued, but the USAF had deployed slowly to the region, alarmingly slower than another rival, the Navy.

Even worse was what he called a "public information problem." The president told Kuter to refrain from immediately using nuclear weapons if war started, although a decade of planning was "predicated on nuclear warfare with high quality weapon systems to thwart the massive manpower and quantities of materiel available to the Communist Bloc." Kuter lamented the failure "to convince our own government that to counter the Chinese Communist threat nuclear weapons must be used."[2] Gen. Thomas White, the Air Force chief of staff, proclaimed Kuter's talk "the finest I have heard in many a long year!" He supported his fellow Airman's views on nuclear weapons and national leaders. Both men agreed that President Eisenhower did not understand the importance of using nuclear weapons to counter the Communist Chinese threat. He had failed because he feared nuclear war.

These were serious charges from experienced officers. During the Second World War, Kuter was for a time the youngest general, a principal author of the plan for strategic bombardment of the Axis, and had commanded in both Europe and the Pacific. After the war, he led Air University, the Air Force's intellectual center. White had a similarly distinguished career, rising through the ranks to command the USAF in 1957. These officers were not outliers; they held and shaped the core beliefs of their service. They represented a form of nuclear thinking that gripped the Air Force for a generation after 1945: air-atomic strategy.

To today's reader, it is easy to dismiss this exchange as a vaguely horrifying real-life version of *Dr. Strangelove*. Viewed in hindsight, White and Kuter appear to be virtually interchangeable with their fictional counterparts Jack D. Ripper and Buck Turgidson: either dangerously irresponsible or outright maniacs. Viewed within the context of the times, however, their exchange of views on nuclear war becomes much harder to dismiss as Strangelovian. The purpose of this book is to provide that context.

Air-atomic strategy grew from prewar doctrine, tempered by blood in the skies over Germany and Japan and driven by the potential of the atomic weapon. Airmen believed that these new weapons would overcome indecisive wartime efforts with conventional explosives. Targets could be destroyed with certainty in one strike, industries wrecked in a day, and countries annihilated. Airpower could be unleashed.

These developments matter to the study of airpower and nuclear strategy. They are an overlooked, but vital, story because their subject is nothing less than the killing of nations. The weapons built to destroy and protect are with us today but are thought of as fundamentally unusable—when they are thought of at all. The apparent stability of the nuclear contest between the superpowers after the Cuban Missile Crisis has become, in the popular imagination, the natural, right, and only way of conceiving of nuclear weapons.

While the first two conclusions are true, the last is wrong and dangerous. It is possible for a power to think of nuclear weapons as eminently usable, and the first two decades of the nuclear age demonstrate how that was, and could be again. In the air-atomic era, ideas for employing nuclear weapons grew from classical airpower theory that aimed at the destruction of the enemy's industrial economy, altered by wartime failure to realize quick victory. Air-atomic targeting, and the operational plans it built, categorized targets as components of industrial systems, as in World War II. As Soviet nuclear forces became a threat, air-atomic strategy replied on prioritizing the destruction of those forces on the ground—an offensive-defense. Victory was still possible. The internal logic of air-atomic theory was sound, even as it became a prescription for national suicide. The logic was compelling enough to build the Strategic Air Command (SAC) into the dominant arm of the US military, with hundreds of bombers, each carrying more firepower than dropped by all the air forces in the Second World War.

For twenty years, air-atomic strategy existed independently of the declaratory policies enunciated by American civilian leaders. These policies were not harmonious. When the White House changed declaratory policy, air-atomic operational plans altered only gradually, sometimes reluctantly, in the direction civilian leaders wanted. When declaratory policy finally turned against air-atomic thought—most fundamentally its central tenet that victory in nuclear war was possible—SAC and the Air Force struggled to keep those ideas alive and succeeded for several years. The power of air-atomic ideas and the shape of the military it drove made the outcome of that shift from seeking victory to seeking stability far from preordained. The same logic can drive today and tomorrow's nuclear powers.

The growth of air-atomic strategy also drove the organization from which it emerged. Atomic weapons first enabled airpower and the Air Force, and then enslaved them. The USAF grew from a service charged with, but incapable of carrying out, an atomic offensive, to become the most powerful military force in history. It became wedded to a strategy that by 1965 could cause national annihilation. Even with today's GPS-guided weapons, the idea of strategic airpower still struggles in the shadow of the unrestrained violence its advocates prepared to launch in the air-atomic age.

Today's Air Force has revived the idea of strategic attack, but with precision rather than blunt force. This was essential to restoring the service's self-identity, as is willful amnesia about its own past. The modern USAF wants to distance itself from the time in which its core ideas were challenged and defeated. Meanwhile, nuclear weapons remain under the control of the Air Force but are a neglected backwater whose past distracts from the bright future. While nuclear strategy has continued to evolve since the 1960s, the idea of stability, not victory, remains at its core.

Before victory became impossible, it was plausible. Strategic Air Command could have destroyed the USSR throughout the air-atomic period, while the latter could scarcely strike back at first. The casualties would have been horrendous in the Soviet Union and its allies, while its retaliatory capacity was small. Yet it was growing, and sooner or later could hammer the United States. American decision makers rejected—hardly even considered—the only means to forestall this danger definitively, preventive war. Eisenhower was right to fear nuclear war, and even more so were his successors. Kuter and White, and their air-atomic strategy, were sensible in 1945, and only gradually did their ideas for seeking victory with nuclear weapons become unworkable in the face of Soviet nuclear power.

Yet, even as "victory" came to mean national destruction, air-atomic thought retained its internal logic for its acolytes. The best way to defend the United States from Soviet nuclear attack was to strike quickly, so reducing the assault, and if possible, blocking it by catching Soviet forces before their launch. For this threat to deter an attack in the first place, moreover, SAC had to be visibly willing to use unrestrained violence. If SAC's leaders seemed as though they would hesitate at the critical moment, or to lack faith in their solution to Soviet nuclear power, the strategy would fail. To use a contemporary analogy, they were dedicated to winning a game of "Chicken" by throwing the steering wheel out of their car as it hurtled down the road toward the Soviets.

Only outside intervention broke the spell of air-atomic thought and imposed a new strategy on American nuclear forces. This blow crippled the policy of the USAF. Its leaders regarded those decisions as disastrous, yet they obeyed their civilian masters. Only in *Dr. Strangelove* did generals launch nuclear attacks for what they perceived as the good of the nation.

Several schools of scholarship have analyzed early nuclear strategy while missing key parts of the context that gives them meaning. Histories of airpower focus on operations in Europe, Korea, and Vietnam.[3] Given this emphasis, strategic airpower poses a problem. Nuclear air operations did not occur, only preparation for them and the deterrent they created; they are a "latent direct" use of direct airpower, to use one historian's taxonomy.[4] Between 1945 and 1991, the greatest forces in history never fought each other, and so achieved their purpose. Historians, naturally attracted to topics with concrete events to study, ignore the methodologically difficult topic of latent air-atomic power. Such works can become Whiggish histories of precision airpower, ignoring an era when raw violence replaced precision. The existing literature nonetheless richly describes airpower's evolving role in conflict and informs my discussion of the origins of air-atomic theory. In turn, the air-atomic era fills in the gap of latent airpower history in the two decades following the Second World War.

A second literature stems from deterrence theory, including works of strategists and histories of nuclear strategy. This genre provides a guide to understanding modern nuclear theory centered on a nuclear force sufficient to deter conflict through the threat of punishment, rather than one designed to compel an enemy through violence. Indeed, this literature not only studies this idea, its early examples gave birth to it. Those early works are vital to understanding why air-atomic strategy was flawed in its final years. However, they ignore the historical roots of nuclear strategy, which lie in conventional ideas about airpower and wartime experience. The thoughts of the military services on nuclear matters before 1965 are overlooked or demonized. In the air-atomic period, victory with atomic weapons went from being probable, to plausible, to impossible.[5]

Reconsidering those decades before the nuclear taboo made seeking victory through atomic airpower unthinkable, and attempting to understand them would enrich these works. The internal logic of air-atomic strategy, as it slid from promising victory to threatening Armageddon, illuminates the origins of modern nuclear strategy. The extensive literature on the fragility of command and control in the 1980s speculated on the difficulty of operating in a transnuclear environment. Understanding how the military planned to prevail when command and control (C2) in the midst of a nuclear war was thought to be unnecessary could enlighten how the military might operate if more sophisticated C2 failed. Similarly, comprehension of air-atomic thought could also inform analysis of contemporary nations in an analogous position to the United States in the 1950s, with an effective nuclear monopoly threatened by a rival with potential nuclear capability. A more complete perception of the nuclear past, however uncomfortable, can inform our present.

As these genres stand today, histories of airpower ignore nuclear weapons; meanwhile, studies of nuclear strategy, nuclear policy, and national security ignore airpower. In both schools, Kuter, White, and nuclear airpower are irrelevant. In the second, these officers also are cavemen, unenlightened and dangerous.

In the third genre, many social scientists use nuclear strategy during the early Cold War as material for case studies. These authors superbly inform on narrow topics such as weapon procurement, while also building frameworks for understanding dimensions of the development of nuclear strategy. However, like their counterparts who write about the development of strategy as a whole, their abstract approaches lead authors to reject military positions, sometimes dismissed as stemming from "cold war battle fatigue." Officers such as Kuter and White were men for whom "we ought to feel a measure of responsibility, and of compassion, [whom] we asked to live apart in a terrible world that never was."[6] The air-atomic period gives these works an expanded historical grounding for theory and the potential to refine conclusions.

Finally, in diplomatic and strategic histories of the 1950s, airpower appears only as a tool of power. These works establish the international and domestic contexts in which air-atomic strategy thrived and then struggled. However, some works get the military details wrong but most ignore them. Often, the term *strategic bombing* conjures images from the Second World War to explain nuclear forces during the twenty years that followed the end of the war. Other authors write as though the logic of Assured Destruction dominated nuclear planning in the 1950s, when the United States retained a huge superiority over the USSR, which drove its policy. Kuter and White are lost in the clutter of presidential press conferences and NSC meetings, at most serving as the obedient executors of Eisenhower's will. The relationship between the views of these men, the areas where they agreed and differed, and the reasons why they did so, are overlooked, and with them fundamental elements of American strategy. Understanding the air-atomic age will restore the military details, which matter very much in this case. They help explain the (illusory) mismatch between national and military strategy. In fact, it was essential to have them visibly at odds for the deterrent to work at all.[7]

These schools all miss a matter that is important to each of them: the rise and fall of air-atomic power in the early Cold War. It emerged in 1945, was transformed by the growth of American and Soviet nuclear arsenals, and finally was superseded by a new strategic approach that substituted stability for victory.

The evolution of nuclear strategy and the evidence about it cannot be presented as a chronicle, because events and people intersect in important ways on many paths that would be tangled in a simple narrative. The evolution of air-atomic ideas is best understood in its own terms and its own words, taking great caution to avoid anachronistic judgments. This is the story of the most important organizing ideas of key institutions and the beliefs of the leaders of those institutions, and then how these beliefs interacted with one another and changed with time. Deterrent theory and atomic plans shifted over the years in reaction to the pressures of American and Soviet technology. Ideological struggle between the armed services, fought in a vicious bureaucratic arena, molded forces and weapons. National policymakers tried to bend the military to their ideas of security policy, and vice versa. All three levels of analysis—airpower and its weapons, military services and their ideologies, and political leadership and its policies—must be examined side-by-side for the picture to snap into focus. Since national policy was the dominant factor in steering American nuclear strategy, presidential administrations are the logical organizational unit.

The eight thematic chapters that follow are grouped into three chronological sections. The first covers the Truman administration and ends with the Korean War. Chapter 1 addresses the historical antecedents of air-atomic theory. Preatomic airpower theory combined with atomic weapons was the basis of the new age. Chapter 2 examines declaratory US policy on nuclear weapons through Korea, the role of atomic weapons in plans, the relationship between the two, and the pursuit of victory in nuclear war. Chapter 3 focuses on the disruption caused to other services, chiefly the Navy, by the rise of the Air Force on the back of its new strategy, and atomic weapons.

The second section of three chapters moves into the Eisenhower administration. Chapter 4 documents the "fantastic compression of time" that forced the timescale for decision on the use of nuclear weapons from months in 1950 to hours in 1960. The combination of an offensive Soviet nuclear threat and new technology, particularly missiles, forced dramatic changes in methods and strategy, ushering in the late air-atomic age. This period featured the malignant growth of air-atomic forces as they absorbed funding and attention from all other forms of military power. Chapter 5 examines the interaction of national policy under the Eisenhower administration with the new nuclear reality, in plans for nuclear war and through real world crises. Eisenhower used air-atomic forces to "safeguard his country" through "cleverness, indirection, subtlety, and downright deviousness."[8] Chapter 6 recounts the continued clashes between the Air Force and its sister services whose new ideas, including finite deterrence and stalemate, threatened its predominance.

The final section addresses the rethinking of nuclear strategy by the Kennedy administration and its defense secretary, Robert McNamara. Chapter 7 examines the evolution of nuclear strategy, with an emphasis on multiple options and civilian control of the execution of war plans. The final stage of this evolution, Assured Destruction, transformed the goal of nuclear strategy from victory to stalemate, and superiority to sufficiency. Chapter 8 addresses the impact of these new ideas on the Berlin and Cuban Missile crises, plans for nuclear warfare, weapons for future war, and the USAF.

During the first twenty years of the Cold War, SAC was created, with weapons able to destroy the USSR and ideas to do exactly that. At first, SAC could achieve these aims with little danger to the United States, but that outcome soon became unlikely, and later threatened to become impossible. Before that day arrived, responsible leaders forced change on SAC and ended the air-atomic era. But for twenty years, the idea of seeking victory with nuclear weapons was the core of American security. This is the story of that idea.

1

ANTECEDENTS

The air-atomic concept that drove American air strategy for the two decades after World War II did not spring into being fully formed. Rather, like any complex body of thought, it emerged from several wellsprings. Although the genealogy of airpower ideas can be traced back to antiquity, this chapter's purpose is more modest. It will show the links between airpower thinking before 1939, subsequent wartime experience, and the first postwar conceptions of atomic warfare. This entire span of ideas was within the living memory of the postwar Air Force's generals and senior thinkers, and formed the context into which they placed the atomic bomb. While the first airpower theorists made fundamental contributions, the clear and abstract thought developed during the immediate prewar years, particularly in the Air Corps Tactical School, reinforced by personal experience in the skies over Europe and Japan, had the most profound and direct effect on these leaders. In turn, they integrated the new atomic weapon into an existing framework of theory and hard-won experience, creating the air-atomic idea.

The Roots of Airpower Theory

Compared to its land and naval cousins, airpower theory is in its infancy. Bookshelves are packed with studies of the development of airpower doctrine over time, but the influence of three primary thinkers can be most readily discerned in postwar US Air Force (USAF) theory: Giulio Douhet, Billy Mitchell, and the Air Corps

Tactical School (ACTS).[1] Douhet's abstract theorizing, while not a direct source of postwar thought, contains several important concepts that illuminate it. While both he and Mitchell are perhaps best understood as "prophets" of airpower rather than as sources of wartime practice, the ACTS officer staff were the immediate predecessors of American wartime theory and the progenitors of air-atomic strategy. These thinkers derived their ideas by generalizing from their experiences during the First World War.

Giulio Douhet, the Great War Italian infantry officer, conceived of a separate role for airpower, independent of land and naval forces. He was a pioneer in forging airpower strategy as an independent branch of military theory. Douhet's general ideas were molded by the particular experience of static warfare between Italy and Austria. He believed airpower could protect Italy from future devastation by attrition. Land war was doomed to produce grinding static fronts, because technology had given the defender a decisive advantage. Airpower was freed from this deadlock by its ability to pass over the opposing army. In his 1921 book, *The Command of the Air*, Douhet outlined a short and decisive air-centered war. Fleets of bomb-laden "battle planes" would seek out and destroy the enemy. In an era before radar, he concluded that the only effective defense against aerial attack was the destruction of bombers at their home bases. After this exchange of blows, a victor would emerge, whose surviving bombers could roam at will over the enemy's cities. With command of the air established, Douhet hoped the enemy nation would sue for peace.[2]

If the enemy government failed to do so on its own, or its populace did not exert sufficient pressure to force this comparatively bloodless end to hostilities, Douhet's bombers would "*inflict the greatest damage in the shortest possible time*" (emphasis in original).[3] However, the ability of airpower to strike any target did not mean that every target should be struck. He identified six major sets of targets for attack: industry, transportation, infrastructure, communication nodes, government buildings, and most important, popular will. This demonstrates his basic notion that, in industrial warfare, conflict extended beyond the armed forces to societies.[4]

The dominant air force would damage the recalcitrant enemy as much as possible in the shortest time. Douhet prescribed area attacks using high explosives and incendiary bombing to destroy structures and poison gas to maximize casualties. Thus the enemy would quickly surrender because of the prospect of destruction, or inability to resist, following the obliteration of his industry and national morale. In Douhet's grim calculus, a short brutal conflict was cheaper to both sides than a repetition of the Great War. "These future wars may yet prove to be more humane than wars in the past in spite of all, because they may in the long run shed less blood."[5]

The relationship between Douhet's thinking and that of the US Air Force in the late 1940s is difficult to establish directly. However, his name is commonplace in the work of civilian strategists such as Bernard Brodie and in the criticisms leveled at air-atomic strategy by the Navy. By the late 1940s, Douhet's ideas became an integral part of the framework in which the atomic bomb was debated. The huge destructive potential of the new weapon made Douhet's previously unrealizable thinking seem to be within reach. The siren call for independent airpower to attack an enemy's centers of power and force capitulation was irresistible, as were the notion that the only defense was offense and the concept of "vital centers," whose destruction would compel an enemy's surrender.

Billy Mitchell's turbulent history serves as the second major influence on the air-atomic idea. His conviction that an independent Air Force should conduct independent air operations with the goal of independent results was a living memory for senior air officers in 1946. As Mark Clodfelter writes, Mitchell's ideas were rooted in bureaucratic political realities and the vestiges of progressivism. Mitchell, like turn-of-the-century social activists, believed in the reforming power of technology. From an organizational standpoint, he held that only an independent Air Force could understand and apply the revolutionary changes in warfare wrought by the air weapon. An Air Force imprisoned within the Army never could reach its full potential.[6]

Although Mitchell differed from Douhet in believing that air-to-air combat was a viable means to gain air superiority, he shared the basic beliefs in paralyzing the enemy through attack on his vital centers and that attacking cities would cause fewer casualties than attritional land combat. Intriguingly, he used the progressive movement's language of order and efficiency to promote airpower to the public during his fruitless campaign for interwar independence.[7] Through the use of modern technology, war could be made more efficient, achieving military objectives for a lower overall cost in lives, both friendly and enemy.[8] The idea of efficient airpower, implicit in Douhet, struck a chord that echoed throughout the nuclear air age.

Simultaneously, and in sympathy with Mitchell's campaign for independence, was the third major influence—the Air Corps Tactical School. Its ideas about targeting the fragile "industrial web" of an industrial opponent drove wartime Air War Plans Division-1 (AWPD-1) and Air War Plans Division-42 (AWPD-42) and postwar targeting plans. The Combined Air Force 1925–6 text stated that air attack aimed to undermine the enemy's will to resist. Airpower was inherently an offensive weapon; defense was wasteful and futile. These early ideas diverged from Douhet and Mitchell in the 1930s with the introduction of the concept of high-altitude precision daylight bombing (HAPDB). The origins of HAPDB can be tentatively traced back to the systematic approach to strategic bombing promoted by a Royal Air Force officer, Lord Tiverton. According to one historian, Maj. Edgar Gorrell and William Sherman "appropriated" Tiverton's concepts of the "industrial fabric" and "key nodes," making them into what became identified as a uniquely American style of strategic bombing theory.[9] Reasoning from examples in the American economy, ACTS hypothesized that a modern industrial economy was like a spider's web, with raw materials and goods flowing from point to point. While some nodes of the web were unimportant, others (e.g., ball bearings, oil) were essential to the integrity of several further strands. Identifying and destroying these critical nodes on which the economy depended would unravel the entire structure. Precise and devastating attack on the critical nodes would wreck enemy resistance while minimizing civilian deaths. This concept had the additional organizational benefit, in the fight for Air Force independence, of making airpower a scarce commodity to be carefully conserved. It could be used only against the most important targets, not squandered on support of the Army.[10]

Although its formal theory for the application of strategic airpower was elaborate, the ACTS acknowledged that the underlying logic was straightforward. Haywood Hansell, primary author of US wartime plans, summarized as a syllogism: modern nations needed industry to wage war, aircraft could penetrate any air defense and destroy any target, therefore air warfare could destroy an enemy's ability to wage war. Hansell also credited ACTS with creating principles for target selection. Attacks must make the maximum possible contribution to the offensive and should be sufficient to prevent a target's reconstitution while conserving enough bombers to carry through with the campaign.[11]

Douhet, Mitchell, and ACTS provided several ideas critical to understanding the atomic era. Most fundamental was the notion that properly applied airpower should operate independently and could be decisive. Exactly what constituted proper application was hotly contested, but almost all airpower advocates shared the basic idea of independent and decisive airpower. Furthermore, airpower promised efficient defeat of an enemy in a short time, with only a fraction of the resources required in 1918. All these thinkers firmly believed that the bomber was the answer to static land warfare. Finally, the ACTS idea of targeting a fragile industrial economy took hold with great force.

Plans and Outcomes in Europe

These prewar ideas, most directly those developed at ACTS, fed into wartime plans. Hansell holds that without the preparation of doctrine at ACTS, the first operational plan, AWPD-1, could not have been written in July 1941. It established target systems consistent with the prewar thinking: German electrical power, transportation, oil, and morale. Secondary targets included air bases, aircraft factories, aluminum plants, and magnesium plants. Ranking far below those targets were other military objectives.

The first major revision of the war plan, AWPD-42, written in the bleakest days of the Stalingrad campaign when a Soviet collapse seemed imminent, changed the priorities. The German air force, submarine building yards, and transportation moved to the top of the list, followed by the old standards of electrical power, oil, aluminum and its derivatives, and rubber. The final Combined Bomber Offensive plan, written and approved in the spring of 1943, changed the target list again, placing the German aircraft industry, ball bearings, and oil at the top of an expanded list. Despite the exigencies of war, plans always emphasized industrial targets based on the ACTS targeting syllogism.[12]

The 1945 US Strategic Bombing Survey (USSBS) assessed the effectiveness of this targeting in damaging the German war effort. Several historians, notably Gentile and MacIsaac, have described the survey as a flawed study used to promote service agendas, usually Air Force independence, but also at times the Navy's policy. Gentile charges that the survey's authors deliberately distorted the study by phrasing questions in terms of the effectiveness of the attack on industry, rather than probing the impact on morale. In fact, the survey reflected typical organizational behavior. Its authors defined the effectiveness of bombing in terms embedded in the routines of wartime air operations: industrial targets damaged and the effects on military production, measured in units of weapon systems and aggregated indicators such as gross domestic product. Whether the airpower advocates who framed the questions were consciously or unconsciously biased, and no matter the validity of their conclusions, they pushed air (and nuclear) strategy along the track they favored.[13]

After a thorough ground survey, research, and extensive statistical analysis, the USSBS concluded that strategic bombing attacks had badly disrupted key industries. Compared to its peak, aviation gasoline production fell by 90 percent and other oil-based products by half by December 1944. Attacks on transportation reduced rail car loading by three-quarters, over five months of attacks in 1944. Steel production fell by 80 percent in only three months. Compounding the cost of the lost industry, 20 percent of the German nonagricultural labor force became tied down in repair and reconstitution. The survey further found that German armament production underwent accelerated collapse in early 1945. Armament output in March 1945 was less than half of its July 1944 peak. According to the USSBS authors, 90 percent of this decline was due to bombing.[14] Particularly notable about these statistics was the relatively late effect of the bombing. The survey's authors repeatedly noted that most bombing sorties took place after mid-1944. Thus the decisive attack took place only after several years of buildup.

The USSBS reflected what airpower advocates believed the war's experience had shown them. Though controversial, these figures led the survey's authors to several conclusions, framed as signposts for future operations, which bolstered prewar ideas about strategic bombing. First, and most important, the prime tenet of airpower theory—that it could have independent decisive effect—was reinforced. "Even a first class military power . . . cannot live long under full-scale and free exploitation of air weapons over the heart of its territory." After noting that air superiority, or even supremacy, was a prerequisite to a successful campaign, a hard-won practical lesson, the authors acknowledged that attacks on morale (nearly impossible to measure) had been less than successful. The German populace had shown surprising resiliency under air attack, that the authors attributed to the "power of the police state over its people," which "cannot be underestimated." The survey also reinforced the idea of careful target selection, the need for persistent reattack, good target intelligence, and finally, the necessity of maintaining a technological edge.[15] While the USSBS's conclusions do not reflect current views regarding the effectiveness of strategic airpower in the Second World War, they do demonstrate how contemporary airmen thought about the experience. The USSBS's authors and their Air Force readers believed that the study was accurate and its conclusions sound, even if modern students hold that the Combined Bomber Offensive's (CBO) effects were complex and indecisive. Their contemporary beliefs, not today's historical understanding, drove the evolution of air-atomic theory.

Beliefs about the importance of the command of the air had been reinforced, as had the idea that airpower's unique contribution to modern war was to attack the industrial web. The conclusion that the United States had, on balance, executed a sound strategic bombing campaign, was reinforced by comparison to Axis failures. A lead author of the survey later stated that Germany had failed in the Battle of Britain because it failed to concentrate forces, efficiently employ the forces that it did commit, or keep losses to a level where it could sustain a campaign.[16] Even the Germans held that airpower's decisiveness had been proven. In 1946, Generaloberst Alfred Jodl wrote that in the next war "air forces . . . will play a decisive role."[17]

Incendiary Improvisation

Airpower in the Pacific War was similarly decisive but applied in different ways. As with Germany, the attacks on Japan initially were motivated by prewar ideas, which focused on critical industry, but unlike Germany that target was abandoned. Early B-29 attacks proved disappointing. Unexpected weather combined with the dispersed nature of Japanese industry to frustrate attacks. In March 1945, Maj. Gen. Curtis LeMay, a veteran of the European air war, decided to "knock [the Japanese] out of the war." LeMay's plan aimed to maximize disruption through shock and the willingness to use civilian casualties as a means to disrupt Japan economically and politically.[18] The resulting attacks reduced Japan's oil refinery capacity by 83 percent, aircraft engine plants by 75 percent, airframe plants by 60 percent, and wrought similar results in other war-critical areas. Overall industrial output fell to 40 percent of its 1944 peak within a few short months, half a million civilians were slain. LeMay later wrote that "the effectiveness on the Japanese war machine and on the Japanese population was intensified because of the rapidity with which each assault followed the previous one."[19] To him and other airpower advocates, these results validated compressing a strategic air attack into the shortest time possible.

The Pacific strategic bombing survey reached conclusions that reinforced the earlier European report. Control of the air was essential to the campaign's success, even though full control was never established. "Heavy, sustained, and accurate attack against carefully selected targets is required to produce decisive results." The report's authors concluded that their survey "supports the findings in Germany that no nation can long survive the free exploitation of air weapons over its homeland."[20]

In addition to reinforcing earlier conclusions about strategic bombing, the Japanese campaign also demonstrated that indiscriminate attacks could have decisive effect. Maj. Gen. John Montgomery, Twenty-first Bomber Command deputy for operations and then a member of the Pacific survey, said of the technique of maximum shock, "when you bomb a target, put enough against it where you don't have to come back. If you prolong by . . . spreading out the attack, you give the enemy additional time to calculate what he wants to do to resist you. When you are moving as fast as we were moving, they don't have a chance."[21]

The destruction of Hiroshima and Nagasaki made the largest impression, concluded the Pacific survey team, but "it is the Survey's opinion that certainly prior to 31 December 1945, and in all probability prior to 1 November 1945 [the target date for the invasion of Kyushu], Japan would have surrendered even if the atomic bombs had not been dropped." A member of the survey team later recalled that a senior Japanese official told them, "'The decision to get out of the war, would have been taken without the atomic bomb and before the invasion because we could no longer stand the level and intensity of the air attacks we were getting.'"[22] It was intense air bombardment, rather than some unique effect of the atomic bomb that forced Japanese capitulation.

New Weapons and Proven Ideas

The atomic weapons were effective less because of the damage they caused than the short time in which they had done it. After receiving reports of the damage inflicted by the Hiroshima weapon, airmen showed great enthusiasm, too much for some tastes. Army Chief of Staff Marshall rebuked Spaatz and LeMay on 8 August 1945 because, "you and General LeMay are being widely quoted in papers . . . to the effect that our present Army is not necessary for the further prosecution of the war . . . and that the future of Armies has been decidedly curtailed."[23] The atomic weapon, amplified by the rapid destruction of Japan's cities, had not only "brought the war to an end fast," but generated enthusiasm for strategic airpower's future. More broadly, it reinforced the idea that a major force able to reach targets could produce major results.

Notably, both the European and Japanese operations were carried out free from the interference of Axis strategic air campaigns. Although German (and to a lesser extent Japanese) fighters defended against Allied attacks, neither power waged a simultaneous campaign against Allied industry or bomber bases. In its formative experience in thinking about and waging strategic air campaigns, the USAF was trying to destroy an opponent's industry. This molded its thinking during the early nuclear age.

In 1945, strategic bombing theory, as interpreted by the Air Force and reflected in official reports, showed great consistency with prewar thought. It sought decision in the same places, directly through attacking industry and the enemy's ability to resist, and indirectly through assaulting his will to resist. The biggest problem was the need to deploy a decisive force able to strike enough targets to disrupt a system beyond repair. To a large extent, as LeMay later stated, the question was "one of plain and simple numbers. There was no radical change in tactics or anything else. In the early days we just didn't have enough airplanes to do the job. . . . We simply did not have an air force there to do the job well."[24]

As both USSBS reports concluded, the problem of insufficient numbers—really, of firepower—eventually was solved by sending more aircraft. The atomic bomb promised a different solution. Rather than increasing the number of bombers, the new weapon magnified the firepower of each bomber. The USSBS thought the effect of one atomic bomb equivalent to that caused by 220 conventionally armed B-29s.[25] The atomic bomb played to that most essential of airpower's promises, efficiency. In addition to typical early twentieth-century American ideas about progressive efficiency, air-atomic thinking embraced technological optimism. As the early air-atomic force developed, its proponents sought to build "better" weapons, with an implicit definition that they would fly higher, faster, and further.

According to LeMay, "it was the technical superiority of our forces that provided the basis for our strategic advantage in the years following World War II."[26]

A 1946 report on the tests at Bikini Operation Crossroads emphasized the cost effectiveness of atomic weapons. Gen. Thomas Power, later the chief of Strategic Air Command, and previously LeMay's operational commander during the Tokyo fire raids of March 1945, said that the basis of air operations was the comparative cost of conflict to the United States and the enemy. In a conflict between industrial powers, if one side could wage war more cheaply than the other, it stood a better chance of winning. Cost "can be measured in terms of . . . the ability to wage war. If the cost balance is tipped in our favor, it is within the realm of possibility that the enemy may be beaten to its knees and will capitulate."[27] Power continued that the destructive power of the new weapon alone "had reduced the cost of eliminating an enemy's war potential," and that its psychological aspects might even exceed the physical ones.

Col. Dale Smith, writing in the Air Force's semi-official journal, *Air University Quarterly Review*, assessed the impact of the weapon in similar terms. The new weapon potentially changed the focus of targeting from systems of specific industries to entire industrial economies. He anticipated the destruction of all the enemy's critical industrial systems simultaneously, which would paralyze and kill the opposing nation, "just as surely as a man will die if a bullet pierces his heart and his circulatory system is stopped."[28]

If the weapon's power made it effective as a strategic weapon, scarcity made it unsuited for tactical use. Power told Truman that "the employment of the Atomic Bomb and the realization of its tremendous insidious power has become a matter of national policy."[29] This was an updated version of the prewar notion that the scarcity of airpower meant it must be husbanded for use against an enemy's most vital points, not wasted on the battlefield. Once again, this claim reinforced the organizational argument for independence.

Another defining characteristic of the atomic bomb, setting it apart from wartime experience, was a comparative lack of defense. The first SAC commander, Gen. George Kenney, told the chief of staff, General Spaatz, that "in this modern age, and most probably increasing in the future, the offense, particularly because of its capability for retaliation, is not only the best but is the only defense." Major General Anderson, commandant of the Air War College in 1947, lectured that defense was futile in the age of atomic weapons and jet aircraft. "You won't be able to fight them in the air, we'll go back to counter-artillery work."[30] If Douhet's ideas had seemed to be invalidated by the failed air attacks on Schweinfurt, Germany, Hiroshima had given them new life.

The atomic weapon was well suited to overcome the perceived shortcomings of strategic bombing in the just finished war. To airmen frustrated by the long build-up from AWPD-1 to the decisive period in Europe and the Pacific, the atomic bomb promised a decisive force at the outbreak of hostilities. "The present Army Air Force M-Day plan calls for an Air Force in being capable of striking a lethal blow at the enemy. This plan is capable of execution in force only through the most effective employment of the Atomic Bomb."[31] This execution would be rapid, decisive, and efficient. Arguments about discrimination or precision were not made.

The atomic bomb was revolutionary in many ways, yet strategic airpower practitioners added it to their prewar ideas and wartime experience in an incremental fashion. Thirty years later, when asked how he "conceived of warfare" before 1950 when he was assigned to the Air University, General Burchinal said, "We were reviewing history at that point. We weren't looking ahead; we were looking back and seeing what happened, and teaching from what happened—the basic lessons, that sort of thing."[32]

The characteristic firepower of the new atomic weapon, 220 B-29s in one bomb, reinforced old ideas. It is telling that the USSBS authors conceptualized the new weapon in multiples of the old. So, too, targeting focused on the enemy's industry, following in the ACTS mindset. Gen. Hoyt Vandenberg told the House Armed Services Committee in 1949 that disruption of the production of war equipment will affect a nation's capacity to wage war. Since the industrial organization of any nation at war must operate at peak loads, this disruption can lead to a condition where production capacity will not sustain the required effort.[33]

The strategic air campaign sought to paralyze the enemy through massive shock, a prospect made more realistic by the new weapon, but hardly a new concept. As with wartime experience, campaigns were seen as a one-way operation waged against an enemy that could not do the same. As important for airmen as the direct military role was the fact that the atomic bomb strengthened their primary argument for organizational independence from the Army. A scarce resource that had to be applied against carefully selected targets, far from the front lines, required expertise that could not be efficiently provided by an air arm subservient to ground forces.

The emerging air-atomic ideas also were amoral, to the extent that their authors considered moral implications at all. During World War II, the ethical implications of conventional air attack could not be measured and were largely ignored by those executing them.[34] They associated morality more in the decision to use force, than in its use. When they did consider moral issues, it was in terms of the length of a war rather than its conduct. LeMay later wrote, "We just weren't bothered about the morality of the question . . . I think it's more immoral to use less force than necessary, than it is to use more. If you use less force . . . you are protracting the struggle." As Sahr Conway-Lanz notes, intent was a key issue in assessing the moral implications of atomic use.[35] To air-atomic advocates, like American conventional commanders in Korea and Vietnam, civilian deaths were tragic, but unavoidable. If civilians died incidentally to an effort to end a war immediately, that was permissible.

That the atomic bomb was placed into a historical and experiential context is precisely what one would expect of an organization like the Air Force. It was unlikely to have abandoned its notions about what airpower could do. Organizations rarely conduct a wholesale review of their basic standard operating procedures unless they undergo a major trauma such as a military defeat. Since the application of airpower against industry was the defining idea behind the USAF's World War II's campaigns, those campaigns were judged successful, even decisive. The USAF would not just suddenly stop believing that victory was possible, when even more potent weapons were at hand. The bomb fit already existing ideas and procedures for employing airpower. Immediately after the Second World War, the USAF saw the A-bomb not as the apocalyptic weapon it later became but as a better means to execute a proven body of strategic thought.

Air-atomic ideas flowed in an uninterrupted stream from prewar theory and wartime experience. Airmen believed that their prewar doctrines had been validated in the heat of battle.[36] The precise role of the atomic bomb, and its balance with conventional forces in a future independent Air Force, were unclear, but that weapon fell squarely into their existing conceptual framework. A 1946 board led by General Spaatz, soon to be the first chief of staff of the Air Force, described the atomic bomb as just an additional weapon that had not altered the basic concept of strategic airpower. Air-atomic ideas were part of a "vision of total war that had developed out of the whole experience of the twentieth century. . . . atomic weapons simply made the great war of the future more destructive and total."[37]

2

DECLARATION, ACTION, AND THE AIR-ATOMIC STRATEGY

In 1956, Paul Nitze, author of NSC-68 and former chief planner at the State Department, wrote an article in *Foreign Affairs* about nuclear strategy, which introduced a useful distinction between two forms of policy. "Declaratory policy," the public face of nuclear strategy, consists of the nation's announced nuclear stance. "Action policy" is how a nation actually prepares to carry out nuclear strategy. These policies are distinct, often uncoordinated, and relevant for that fact.[1] This chapter addresses both types of policies, and their intersection with air-atomic ideas.

The most important test of a military theory is its use in wartime. The air-atomic theory, while thankfully not proven in conflict, was tightly integrated into early postwar plans against the Soviet Union. This chapter will outline the plans written by the Joint Chiefs which, unsurprisingly, were patterned on the recently completed war, and on the central role of the air-atomic offensive within them. Next it will examine the function of strategic air attack in the Air Force's war plans, which conformed closely to the Joint Chiefs' expectations. Then it will consider how the Air Force and other government bodies assessed its ability to carry out the strategic air offensive plans. Finally the chapter will see how plans for atomic war fit within national strategy.

Outline for War

The Joint Chiefs of Staff (JCS) wrote war plans after 1945 as it had been done during the war. Through its subcommittees, the JCS constructed standing plans, coordinated across the services, which served as a basis for wartime action. Significantly, from an organizational perspective, these plans also were the foundation of budgeting.

The postwar planning process involved close interservice cooperation from the outset. Differing concepts of what would be necessary for successful prosecution of a war would—and did—clash during the procedure. The resulting plans can be read as a judgment of which ideas about modern war were most acceptable to the nation's military experts. Planning on national levels was firmly linked to the operational level. Although the realities of planning at lower levels could cause a divergence in equipment, training, and other factors, this hampered execution only in minor ways.

The earliest plans, before the NSC-68 buildup, were rooted in tight budgets. This sometimes made the distance between paper plans and reality uncomfortably large. Thus, in writing his 1947 report on the role of airpower in the postwar world, future secretary of the air force Thomas Finletter was briefed by the Joint Staff. After Finletter and his associates admitted they could not understand the plan, the Army chief of staff, Dwight Eisenhower, told his colleagues, "Gentlemen, these five civilian gentlemen who are here are just patriotic American citizens trying to do something they've been asked to do by the President. I think we really owe it to them to tell them that there is no war plan."[2] Since the Pincher series was well developed by this point, in effect Eisenhower told Finletter there was no realistic plan. To acknowledge Eisenhower's point about feasibility, however, does not deny the role of the plans as an arena for the competition of strategic ideas.

Although the emergency plans evolved over time, their overarching outlines remained largely the same, as did the role of the strategic air offensive within them. From the start, the JCS recognized Soviet preponderance in land forces as a central fact in the next war. In January 1945, before the Second World War even ended, the Joint Staff projected that the Soviets, while deficient in naval and strategic airpower, could overrun Europe to the English Channel, most of the Middle East, and parts of Asia contiguous to the USSR. Only in the Western hemisphere, Japan, North Africa, and India, could the United States stop a Soviet advance.[3] In the face of this overwhelming force, the United States and its allies would have to retreat, ceding control of central Europe and withdrawing to a defensive position in Italy or possibly Spain.[4]

From this basis followed planning for a three- (or, in later plans, four-) phase war, which mirrored the one just past. The only offensive action during the first phase was an air-atomic one, supplemented by operations to secure bases from which medium bombers could attack Soviet targets. Later, after mobilization, US forces would reenter Europe, destroy Soviet power, and enforce surrender terms in a conflict well within a traditional use of military force.

Plan Offtackle (later renamed Shakedown), the plan for a war starting in December 1949 to be fought with existing forces, illustrates contemporary planning and the role of the strategic air offensive. It defined national war objectives, and the overall strategic concept of the operation, in classic Clausewitzian terms, as imposing "the war objectives of the United States upon the USSR by destroying the Soviet will and capability to resist, by conducting a strategic offensive in Western Eurasia, and a strategic defensive in the Far East."[5] To carry out this concept, Allied forces would, in priority order: defend the Western Hemisphere, secure areas required for operations, conduct the strategic air offensive "against the vital elements of the Soviet war-making capacity," halt the Soviet offensive, mobilize Western offensive forces, aid Allies, and exploit any psychological weaknesses of the USSR or its satellites.[6] Soviet operations were expected to be simultaneous attacks on Western Europe, the Near and Middle East, bombing of the United Kingdom, limited operations in the Far East, air attacks on North America, operations against Allied sea communications, and widespread sabotage. Once the Red Army occupied the Channel ports, the planners expected intensified attacks on the Britain, together with campaigns against Scandinavia and Spain, and attempts to disrupt Allied counter-operations.[7]

After detailing the essential defensive tasks, Offtackle stated that "a strategic air offensive with atomic and conventional bombs will be initiated at the earliest possible date subsequent to the outbreak of hostilities. This offensive will be aimed at vital elements of the Soviet warmaking capacity and at the retardation of Soviet advances in western Eurasia."[8] The war would have four phases. The first, from the outbreak ("D") to D+3 months, would contain most of the air-atomic offensive. The next nine months would see a continuation of the air offensive while other forces attempted to halt the Soviet advance, build up in remaining footholds, and awaited mobilized forces. From D+12 to D+24 months, air offensives would continue while mobilized forces prepared for reentry into Europe. The remainder of the war, including the liberation of Europe and eventual victory, fell into a fourth phase, from D+24 onward.[9]

First-phase air operations, aimed at targets designed to disrupt enemy industry and to retard the advance of Soviet troops, would strike JCS-designated targets. Carriers would "support the strategic air offensive to the extent of their capabilities."[10] In the second phase of the war, the tasks of the strategic air offensive would depend on accomplishments in the initial period. Offtackle's planners explicitly denied that the air offensive alone could inflict enough damage to allow reentry into Europe. Hence renewed attack on already damaged systems, to prevent their recovery, and destruction of additional unspecified ones, would continue until the Western powers could take the offensive. The planners also anticipated that the changing ground situation might bring additional sensitive targets within reach. Targets to slow the Soviet advance must still be attacked, given the conservative damage expectations for the initial offensive.[11]

Offtackle only sketchily outlined the second year, and third phase, of the war. As in the second phase, the air offensive would service "target systems previously attacked," and other targets as they became available. The requirement to retard the Soviet advance would have abated, and the targeting focus would shift to "best create favorable conditions for the Allies' return to the Western European continent."[12] In the final phase of the war, starting at D+24 months, "the major portion of the strategic air effort will be directed against targets the destruction of which will result in the greatest and most timely reduction in the capabilities of Soviet armed forces in Europe." No doubt, the planners envisioned something akin to the heavy and medium bombers' support of Overlord. Although the plan addressed in general terms the need for ground operations within the Soviet Union proper, the role of strategic airpower was not mentioned.[13]

Strategic Air Offensive

The air-atomic offensive was central to all these plans, from the earliest Pincher series to Offtackle. The atomic bomb was a way to intensify the strategic air offensive and bring the war to a close earlier.[14] On D-Day, the JCS anticipated it would be the only possible offensive action. During the first months of operations, it would take the leading role, with ground and sea forces subordinated. As an Air Force planner at the Joint Strategic Plans Committee (JSPC) in 1946 told a Navy colleague,

> In view of the fact that we are incapable of successfully engaging the enemy ground forces, our initial attacks must be by air. In order to prosecute air action the Air Forces must have predetermined targets; they must have bases to permit their craft to reach the targets; we must plan to secure the necessary bases; you must plan to keep the sea lanes open; we must establish and deploy land forces to hold the bases.[15]

The air offensive's function was to buy time for mobilization and the ground offensive. It would "destroy the Russian ability to wage war."[16] The JSPC, conscious of the fate of previous invasions of Russia, expected the atomic campaign to avoid a repetition of those disasters. They expected to "concentrate on first destroying Russia's power to wage war and [then on occupying] only certain areas necessary for control."[17]

As these goals imply, the strategic air attack was in line with recent experience and existing theory. The targeting terminology developed toward the end of this period illuminates the relative priorities of the different systems. The traditional attack on the industrial web acquired the shorthand term of disruption, or "Delta." Attacks against enemy troops to slow their advance across Europe were termed retardation, or "Romeo." The third and final category, attacks on Soviet atomic offensive forces, was known as blunting, or "Bravo." The very use of these designations shows how the destruction of an individual target was tied to a particular objective, rooted in airpower theory. Thus the aim was to disrupt an industrial target so as to undermine the enemy's war-waging ability, rather than under the later term *countervalue*—to destroy some valuable aspect of the enemy's economy for an indeterminate reason. These aims were uses of force in the traditional sense: to bend an opponent to American will. The language of targeting categories was loaded with history and planner's experience, embedded in the routines and categories of airpower theory and practice.

These plans outlined the role of the strategic air offensive but did not designate specific targets. In other words, which targets, or sets, should be struck to disrupt Soviet industry? In November 1945, a Joint Intelligence Committee (JIC) study estimated that the twenty most profitable objectives for atomic attack were "mixed industrial areas containing the highest proportion of research and development centers, specialized production facilities, and key government or ministry personnel."[18] These targets would "exploit the maximum capabilities of the weapon, produce the quickest, most direct, and certain effects on the Soviet Union's immediate offensive capabilities" and latent offensive power. More succinctly, they must be the most efficient targets. Notably, such targeting did not promise decision but instead simply to weaken Soviet military power from within. This was not the Douhetan vision of attacking the enemy's will to resist, but the ACTS plan for disrupting the industrial web. It was the product of ACTS-trained and wartime-tested commanders, applying their experience to a new enemy. The USAF was acting as any successful organization does, applying proven ideas to new problems. A Douhetan will-breaking goal in 1946 would have been as abrupt a shift of the underlying strategy as Assured Destruction's abandonment of victory proved to be later.

Examination of these twenty items shows what made a target suitable. The planners deemed only three characteristics as relevant for inclusion in the summary list: population, area, and major industries. The industrial targets are listed by their significance to the systems of production: Sverdlovsk does not just have a large tank factory, it produces 9 percent of all tanks. The targets are the industrial systems spread between cities, with the cities essentially just aiming points.

Driving this efficient selection of targets was the scarcity of the weapon. A December 1945 study assumed that only twenty to thirty weapons would be available.[19] In fact, probably unknown to those planners, even fewer weapons

TABLE 1 Extract of target list from JIC 329

CITY	ESTIMATED POPULATION	APPROX AREA (SQ MI.)	INDUSTRIAL/STRATEGIC IMPORTANCE
Moscow	4,000,000	110.0	Primary center for scientific research and development and capital of the USSR, its important industries include: 13% of plane output, 43% of truck output, 2% of steel output, 15% of copper output, machine building, oil refinery, ball-bearing plant, electronics and electrical equipment.
Gorki	644,000	13.5	Important center for bacteriological research and a major industrial center for: 11% of plane output, 24% of tank output, 45% of gun output, 43% of truck output, oil refinery, machine building, radio equipment.
Kuibyshev	500,000	12.6	Bacteriological research center, important industries include: 22% of plane output, gun manufacture, oil refinery, ball-bearing plant, machine building.
Sverdlovsk	500,000	20.2	9% of tank output, 11% of gun output, 1% of steel output, machine building, tire plant, ball-bearing plant. Also has a bacteriological institute.

Source: "JIC 329/1," reproduced in Steven Ross and David Rosenberg, *Long Range Planning*, vol. 1 (New York: Garland, 1990).

were at hand. One writer estimates the upper limit of bombs at twelve by late 1945, fifty by 1947, and one hundred fifty by 1948. Another states that only twenty-nine weapons were available by mid-1947.[20] In any case, there were few bombs while limited production of fissionable material prevented any major increase in the foreseeable future. Their scarcity also drove planners to rely on conventional bombing when the stockpile was exhausted.

The selection of industrial targets in urban settings based on efficiency criteria had other notable causes and effects. From an organizational standpoint, their selection was predictable. Industry in urban areas was the target in both theaters of the Second World War and viewed as the key to victory. To abandon such targets would have been unusual. They were embedded in the organizational routines, tools, and training of the planners. The JCS planners did consider and discard other targeting schemes to prevent Soviet moves against the Western hemisphere. They rejected the most obvious target, the Soviet armed forces, because "strategic weapons have been shown to be ineffective against initial front-line strength."[21] From an Air Force perspective, such a campaign would become tactical support. The Soviet transportation system was, in theory, an excellent target set for disrupting industrial output and military operations, but not in practice. Unlike a concentrated transportation system with chokepoints like those of Germany and Japan, Soviet transportation was dispersed. No atomic bomb could inflict enough damage to the Soviet war machine to justify its use on a single transportation target.[22] Industry and command and control made the most sense within the existing targeting framework. An attack on "end product facilities supporting those forces that pose the greatest menace would probably pay the greatest profits."[23] Although attacks on governmental control would not cause decisive results, because Allied ground forces could not exploit the resulting chaos, "the ability of the atomic weapon to destroy concentrations of personnel is one of its outstanding features and should therefore be exploited."[24]

Moreover, although cities provided a usefully compact mass of industrial and governmental control targets, they were selected essentially because information about the Soviet Union was too sketchy to locate anything else of value. As the 1946 Plan Pincher noted, "The scarcity of detailed intelligence and the availability of the atomic bomb serve to point up industrial urban areas as a suitable target system. Cities can be used in this study to establish in general the location of the Soviet industry."[25]

By 1948, the plans incorporated a phase of intelligence gathering into the air campaign. Area targets would be struck first, while simultaneous reconnaissance filled in targeting gaps for later exploitation, particularly for transportation and hydroelectric power installations.[26]

Starting with Offtackle in 1949, later plans added an additional category of targets: those required to retard a Soviet advance (Romeo). Its authors recommended that the subordinate SAC plan should be rewritten "to conduct a strategic air offensive . . . [to destroy] the vital elements of the Soviet war-making capacity and [to retard] Soviet advances in Western Eurasia."[27] This switch in plans was enabled by the growing weapon stockpile. The 1949 decision to accelerate the production of fissile material opened new target categories, while the limits to intelligence left troop concentrations as the only set of large, potentially knowable, targets beyond urban areas. "Based upon the increased number of bombs available, the current concept for the atomic offensive, now being prepared contemplates class A damage to vital Soviet industries . . . [and] to retard Soviet offensives and their employment if practicable for the destruction of the atomic offensive capabilities of the USSR."[28] The number of targets for the air offensive expanded from 20 in the initial 1945 list to 104 urban centers during the 1950

Plan Offtackle. Still, just before the Korean War, targeting was largely as it had been at the start—focused on urban areas and the war-supporting industries within them.[29]

Offtackle shows several important characteristics of the role of strategic air offensive in early war plans. That offensive was second in priority only to the defense of the Western Hemisphere, and the only offensive action that would be carried out from the start of the conflict, and throughout it. This is perhaps the central distinction between postwar plans and the course of World War II. The ability of an air-atomic force to launch an offensive without months of buildup was a new element in otherwise conservative plans. Yet the plans imply at every stage that attacks on industry and enemy troops would create conditions for further joint operations. The mechanism for generating those effects was equally familiar to the World War II veterans. The conservatism of the plans disturbed one senior Air Force planner on the JCS who "suggested that the present concept is too much like that of the last war and that we should not be misled by precedent."[30] Until the Korean War, however, plans remained conservative. Their most radical part was essentially orthodox, applying the lessons of prewar and wartime doctrine and experience, just doing so with more force in less time. Atomic airpower allowed one bomber to deliver 220 B-29 equivalents in a single raid, but that unit of measurement remained backward looking. Again, given the resource constraints in the late 1940s, there was no other way to carry out the offensive. To duplicate the decisive effects of conventional bombers of 1944–45 would require similarly sized fleets. In January 1946, the JCS realized that practice could not be replicated. "The air forces that will be available are too small to permit decisive results to be obtained by the employment of high explosive bombs or incendiaries alone. . . . The only weapon which the United States can employ to obtain decisive effects in the heart of the USSR is the atomic bomb delivered by long-range aircraft."[31] Yet, as the actual plans showed, the decisive effects were too elusive for the conservative JCS planners to rely on.

The JCS plans tied directly into the Air Force's and SAC's ideas for the strategic air offensive. While the JCS directed the campaign, the Air Force and SAC had to carry out the plans. By early 1950, the Air Force had a detailed plan to carry out the JCS-directed offensive, but not the ability to do so.

In 1947, Gen. George Kenney, SAC's first commander, proposed a "strategic concept" for carrying out the air offensive more radical than anyone else was willing to accept. He believed the atomic bomb was a far more decisive weapon than the JCS thought, because he drew starker conclusions from the same factor which separated the air-atomic idea from earlier concepts of strategic airpower—the compression of time. He told the commander of Air University,

> When we consider that 100 atom bombs will release more foot pounds of energy than all the TNT bombs released by all the belligerents of World War II combined from September 1939 to August 14, 1945 and that that effort could be put down in a single attack, it is evident that the long drawn out war is out of date. . . . No nation, including our own, could survive such a blow.
>
> A war in which either or both opponents use atomic bombs will be over in a matter of days. . . . Bombing of targets which will affect enemy production in a few months is meaningless. . . . The air force that is superior in its capability of destruction plays the dominant role and has the power of decision. . . . The advantage accruing to the aggressor who makes a surprise attack has become so great that it can almost be considered decisive.[32]

Kenney's thinking went far beyond the state of doctrine in 1947. It reflected the same creativity that had marked his time as MacArthur's air commander in the Southwest Pacific during 1943–44 and transferred to the strategic level his own operational experiences in using intelligence and ruthless counterforce tactics to smash a small, but competent, enemy air force. The idea that the era of industrial bombing was past came a decade too soon, and was not in keeping with Air Force policy, although it hints at creativity within the Air Force. It took the critical idea of time compression further than was normal for the late 1940s, but Kenney still believed that victory through the application of strategic airpower was possible.

Mainstream Air Force doctrine about strategic airpower in this period was close to that found in the JCS plans, not surprisingly, given the coupling of planning within the JCS and services. Above all, they agreed on the principal target set, industry in urban centers. An Air Force plans section study in 1946 declared that if mechanized warfare continued to be predominant, then industry would remain the focus of targeting for strategic air attack.[33] In 1948, Vice Chief of Staff Hoyt Vandenberg, told the secretary of the air force that atomic bombs should be used only against targets of "sufficient size and importance" to Soviet warmaking capacity, and that most such targets were in cities.[34] Maj. Gen. Charles Cabell, director of Air Force Intelligence, lectured Air War College students that the Soviet warmaking economy was remarkably concentrated and therefore vulnerable to atomic attack. Fewer than two dozen cities accounted for three-quarters of production.[35] As far as Kenney was concerned, to strike those cities was unavoidable, because military targets were within them. In 1974, when asked if there was any way to "fight a clean war," he replied simply—"No."[36]

The Air Staff selected targets methodically. In late 1948, Gen. Robert Walsh, recently transferred from his previous assignment as USAF chief of intelligence in Europe, outlined the process to students at the Air War College. To strike the "vital elements of the Soviet warmaking capacity," the large number of potential targets had to be reduced to a "practical minimum." By collecting and organizing raw data to determine the locations of important political, economic, and military centers, this process identified 210 urban areas. Of those, the Air Staff selected 70 for destruction in priority order, with an eye to physical and psychological effect. Intriguingly, Walsh noted that the major Ukrainian centers of Kiev and Kharkov, which would have been included in a raw target list, were omitted. "Tentative conclusions by our psychologists point to the desirability of winning the Ukrainians to our side. While we explore this facet further, we are not including Ukrainian installations in the list for atomic fire." This consciousness of ethnic differences in nuclear targeting is reminiscent of debates thirty years later. Most important, though, according to Walsh, was the need to strike targets as rapidly and simultaneously as possible and over a wide area. The physical effects of a dispersed maximum shock attack would be complemented by the psychological impact:

> It is important that the first attack be a heavy one. . . . [The] total effect is greatly increased by selecting targets from within widely scattered areas; [to exploit] the waves of fear, rumor, and tall tales which emanate through refugees from an attacked area. Here the waves from separate shocks come together, there is a great confusion and therefore, in effect, another disturbance.[37]

Gen. Curtis LeMay emphasized a different reason for a heavy initial attack—to prevent Soviet defenses from learning SAC tactics. "We are trying to avoid being forced into any piecemeal attack to provide training for the Russian defenses. When we go in we intend to go in from enough directions and in enough strength to make it effective." At this point, though, LeMay did not anticipate that Soviet defenses could seriously disrupt his first wave of attacks.[38] The tactics for the strategic air offensive were a mix of proven techniques from Europe and the Pacific, adapted to a new enemy and technology. Five or six bombers would support a single A-bomb carrier to the target.[39] The key to offensive tactics was saturating Soviet defenses.[40]

Operational factors also shaped the selection of cities for targeting. The same air defenses LeMay believed to be manageable were made so by changing mission profiles. Bombers would go in high, fast, and at night or in bad weather, using radar to find their targets. In turn, this made small or concealed targets more difficult to find. Given limited information on war materiel stockpiles, "This all adds up to a capability of SAC to locate and bomb with an acceptable assurance of success industrial targets in urban areas and prominent, well defined individual installations such as oil refineries and other manufacturing sites."[41]

This industrial targeting, with elements of physical destruction and psychological distress, was consistent with historical experience and JCS planning. As LeMay told the National War College in 1950, "The best support we can give the European allies is to make sure that something important collapses behind the Russian Army."[42] Implicit in that statement was opposition to the retardation mission. While conscious of the effect of his campaign on the Red Army, LeMay believed the Romeo mission was an ineffective use of limited atomic resources. A 1974 interviewer asked about how the retardation mission affected SAC's plans starting in 1950, when it was added by the JCS. After a telling moment of confusion when he had to be reminded that "retardation" meant supporting the theater commander, he dismissed it as "a tactical mission."[43]

The end of this period also saw debate between advocates of two contending targeting frameworks, vertical and horizontal. Vertical targeting grouped targets by function, in a model similar to that used in the European theater: power generation, petroleum, and armored vehicle production, for example. This approach guided one of the JCS's first detailed targeting lists in 1949, focused on the electrical power generation target set. When LeMay rejected the targets as being difficult to find, recognize, and hit, a major fight occurred between the Joint Staff and Air Force targeteers. The replacement plan, adopted by 1951, used a horizontal targeting approach. It aimed to destroy as much industry as possible with a given weapon in one area, systematically prioritizing industry obliteration of which would maximize "destruction and damage to attain the strategic war aim of disruption."[44] Horizontal targeting attempted to avoid wasting any destructive power from scarce weapons. By December 1951, the accepted plan used 231 weapons against 200 aiming points ("designated ground zeros") in 104 cities, which it hoped would destroy major portions of critical Soviet industries, such as 90 percent of aircraft assembly, 65 percent of combat ship building, 74 percent of iron production, and 88 percent of tank production. An Air Force targeteer told Air War College that horizontal targeting was not area bombing and was not aimed at morale. "We are not interested in the area type of attack that the British did on the Germans, burning down towns . . . we are not interested in population as such."[45] Both horizontal and vertical targeting measured success in terms of the percentage of distinct target systems destroyed. The argument was about efficiency, not of ends, nor the means to reach them.

Even with his clearly stated preferences, LeMay acknowledged the JCS's central role in integrating SAC into the overall war effort. He told one questioner after a speech that "our targets are assigned by the Joint Chiefs of Staff. I am just the man who destroys the target."[46] However true this sentiment, the outcome of debates over issues such as horizontal targeting and the relative priority of retardation show that the mechanics of selecting targets for strike came increasingly under SAC's control, even if the JCS exercised overall influence.

Closing the Capability Gap

How to deliver weapons to targets was LeMay's decision. He aimed to do so as quickly as possible. In November 1948, soon after taking control of SAC, LeMay stated his goal to Vandenberg. SAC would become capable of delivering 80 percent of the entire US atomic stockpile in one mission.[47] Within weeks of LeMay's declaration to Vandenberg, senior leaders met at the "Dualism" conference held at Air University. Writing to Gen. Lauris Norstad, LeMay summarized their conclusions with respect to weapon delivery. "We propose to develop the capability to deliver in one mission all the stockpile made available to us."[48] This idea was hardly isolated to LeMay; it had widespread acceptance among senior members of the Air Force. Vandenberg himself, several months before LeMay took over SAC, told Secretary of the Air Force Stuart Symington this basic principle of strategic air warfare. "Atomic weapons should be used at the earliest practicable date and in the greatest possible mass after the outbreak of war with the USSR to enhance the psychological and perhaps decisive effect which will be produced by great destruction in a very short period of time. Delay . . . will permit the USSR to increase the effectiveness of her defenses."[49] Of course, to cope with rapidly evolving technology and techniques, the SAC commander alone should decide the timing and tactics of the attack. The concomitant of such arguments, of course, was that SAC must be a far larger organization in peacetime than would be necessary for a slower and more phased campaign. Thus it must be a far more costly force, with obvious repercussions on military budgets.

The existence of plans does not always equate to the capability to execute them. That was the case in the late 1940s. Firm ideas about the application of strategic airpower in war collided with the realities of resource constraints, demobilization, and equipment limitations. SAC was not prepared to carry out the war plan with any efficiency until 1950 at the earliest. To some degree, the JCS realized the distance between the paper plans and real capability. During the 1946 discussions leading up to Plan Pincher, Air Force Gen. Frank Everest acknowledged that "there would not be enough planes at any time in the near future for operations from all the bases indicated on the charts in the paper."[50] Taken together with

Eisenhower's comment quoted above, senior generals clearly understood how planning at that time was merely exercises on paper.

When LeMay took control of SAC in October 1948, he immediately assessed its capability. On being told that crews were doing a fantastic job of radar bombing, a skill that LeMay knew from experience was difficult even in good conditions, he grew skeptical. His suspicions were confirmed when he looked closely at their techniques. To his dismay, from only fifteen thousand feet crews were bombing reflectors placed in the radar-clutter free Gulf of Mexico. As their wartime targets would be attacked at night from forty thousand feet in rough terrain that would strain radar bombing skills, the training results were grossly misleading. The first step toward improving SAC's performance was to gauge accurately what its crews could do in a realistic mission. LeMay chose Wright-Patterson Air Force Base in Dayton, Ohio, as the target for this first major exercise. To simulate the inaccurate maps of many Soviet targets, he gave the bomber crews 1930s era charts. As LeMay suspected, because of equipment failures when taken up to actual operational altitudes and gaps in training the crews utterly failed to accomplish the mission. Everything that could go wrong, did. Not one crew would have bombed the target successfully.[51] Of 303 runs made at the target, the circular error probable was 10,100 feet, outside the effective radius of a Hiroshima-sized weapon. LeMay told Vandenberg, "At the present time we do not have one unit manned and trained to an acceptable state of efficiency."[52]

LeMay agreed with a report by Charles Lindbergh on Air Force proficiency, which concluded that "actual striking power . . . is much lower than its numerical strength and materiel quality indicate." The SAC commander's prescription was a straightforward increase in basic proficiency. Pilots had to be free to concentrate on their flying skills, and not be distracted by additional duties, as had been standard under LeMay's predecessor. Crews had to improve their basic skills, especially bombing accuracy. All this had to be done through rigorous and accurate simulated missions.[53]

Not surprisingly, SAC's technical incapacity was matched by the lack of a realistic war plan. Kenney had assigned crews to targets, which they were trained to hit, but had given them only a rudimentary sketch of routes, target identification, and so forth.[54] On reviewing the plans, LeMay said,

> As far as I was concerned, SAC didn't have a war plan. This didn't worry me very much, because they didn't have any capability for war anyway. They may have had something in the file about go and take the high ground around Gettysburg or something of that general nature, but a war plan as I understood it, what targets you were going to destroy, and

> what the timing was going to be, and where you were going to do it from, and what outfit was going to do it, and all these details, no, they didn't have anything like that.[55]

Even as his staff hammered out workable procedures, other problems emerged. During a review of the logistics to support his Emergency War Plan, LeMay discovered that the airlift essential for moving his command to overseas wartime bases was already allocated to other missions. In July 1949, the Military Air Transport Service reported that only 80 of the necessary 105 C-54 transports would be available in the first three days of mobilization. Without this airlift, SAC would be delayed in carrying out the offensive. LeMay pleaded with Vandenberg to recognize the importance of the strategic air offensive through sufficient logistical support. "My entire plan is dependent upon the provision of this airlift."[56]

Central to improving SAC's efficiency was measuring performance. LeMay instituted what would become a hallmark of SAC culture through the command's life: the SAC Management Control System (MCS). He and his staff created the first version of the MCS in July 1949 as "a method of evaluating the efficiency of SAC bombardment wings within the limits of available resources." The initial rating scheme gave overall scores in resources and performance, with subareas totaling 1000 points, giving a weighted rating to the performance of each bomber wing. It measured factors ranging from personnel assigned versus authorized and AWOL rates to in commission aircraft and radar bombing accuracy. All of these subareas were weighted and combined to create scores that were tracked every month for comparison across wings. Although the system changed over time, the Taylorian approach made clear to subordinate commanders what counted: readiness to execute operations without delay.[57] LeMay consciously placed his "units on a competitive basis, and by tabulating those items that earmark an outfit good or bad . . . I constantly [compared] our units and their commanders."[58] Combined with a change in attitudes that war always was a real possibility, which fit with the air-atomic idea that forces must be ready to strike instantly, and through regular exercises, LeMay brought SAC rapidly to a much higher degree of readiness than it had attained under Kenney.

The results were indisputable. By October 1949, less than a year after the Dayton test, LeMay told Vandenberg that one B-36 group had won a bombing competition with a circular error probable (CEP) of 441 feet on a visual drop and 1,031 feet on radar drops. LeMay was particularly gratified by the realism of the competition, which

> heavily penalized equipment malfunctions. A crew which failed to drop any bomb, either visual or radar, on the assigned target by reason of malfunction or misidentification did not receive a score as a crew, nor did

> its accomplishments contribute to the aggregate score of its group. After reaching the initial point there were no dry runs allowed except for legitimate weather aborts on visual runs only. Consequently, many visual drops were made with ten to twenty seconds [*sic*] sighting run and a good number of the radar runs were made under turbulent thunderstorm conditions.[59]

The performance of this group reflected the general improvement across the command. A January 1950 evaluation, similar to the Dayton test, simulated 84 bombing runs against Offutt Air Force Base in Omaha. The accuracy was vastly increased, down to an average CEP of 4,635 feet, rapidly approaching the desired standard of 3,000 feet. LeMay attributed the improvement to better procedures, mission briefings, target materials, increased training time, and more modern equipment. He assessed the command as "75% effective," citing several lessons learned from the previous year's experience. Most important, aircraft commanders had taken personal responsibility for their crew and aircraft's performance. That, combined with basic tactics proven to be feasible, and refined in-flight refueling procedures, led him to be pleased with the state of the command on the eve of the Korean War.[60]

Naturally, the improvement was not complete in all areas. The constant exercising was designed to show flaws, and did so. During one simulated mission in 1950, the 301st Bomb Group sent fourteen bombers and fourteen tankers on a transoceanic attack. When the bombers attacked simulations of their wartime targets, the results were disappointing: Stalingrad would have remained undamaged, Kuybyshev would have been hit only by half the planned number of weapons, and only Saratov would have been struck as programmed. The commander of the exercise attributed most of the problems to mechanical failures with the supporting tankers and in some bombing equipment. Yet exercises such as these ensured that failings were not hidden, but instead frankly discussed and dissected to improve operations.[61]

In these first few years, LeMay and his staff also identified communications as a key limiting factor in executing the war plan. Communications, command, control, and intelligence (C3I) was the basis for coordinating the execution of the war plan, just as it was for any military operation. A successful campaign would require not only issuing orders for attacks, but also receiving bomb damage assessments, ordering restrikes, coordinating logistics for damaged bombers, and the multitude of other requirements, both seen and unforeseen. Without a strong communications network, the tightly coordinated strike force would quickly unravel. The postwar Air Force, with new global responsibilities, had inherited a patchwork of telephone, teletype, and radio circuits with which to work in peace, crisis, and wartime. During one trip to a base in Sacramento, California, LeMay sent a message to Omaha that took longer to arrive than he did, having lain in the SAC communications center for twenty-seven hours. During exercises, messages took six hours to be relayed to destinations.[62] In February 1950, he told the vice chief of staff that SAC's communications were so primitive that he had to rely on commercial telephone relays during crises. "I consider this weakness to be one of the most important 'soft spots' in our ability to carry out our war plan today."[63] Inadequate communications could not sustain an air strategy coveting tightly coordinated strikes to inflict maximum damage in minimum time.

Even with these limitations, the trend in SAC's operations was clear—it was a force daily becoming better able to execute its mission as defined in the Air Force's war plans. The USAF's 1950 Emergency War Plan (EWP 50) divided the future war into four phases, closely tied to the JCS parent, Offtackle. In the first three months, an initial air offensive would be completed while "essential defensive tasks" were undertaken, Navy antisubmarine warfare aided as necessary, the Soviet offensives impeded, and mobilization begun. The strategic air offensive and the defensive tasks in North America would continue in the second phase from D+3 months to D+12. Airpower would help to halt Soviet advances in Asia, reduce the effectiveness of Soviet forces, and otherwise "enhance" the allied military position. Phases three and four continued the air offensive and prepared for reentry into Western Europe.[64]

The strategic air offensive aimed to provide "maximum contribution toward the disruption of the vital elements of the Soviet war-making capacity"—Delta—and, "the retardation of Soviet advances in Western Eurasia"—Romeo. More specifically, its objectives were "the disruption of the Soviet industrial system, the elimination of the political and administrative controls of the Soviet Government, the undermining of the will of the Soviet people and government to continue war, and the disarming of the Soviet armed forces." The planned target systems included oil installations, power plants, submarine construction, aviation fuel production, lead plants, aeroengine plants, armored and motor vehicle manufacturing, synthetic ammonia, and other industries as identified. The plan required 286 bombs for these attacks, with 6 more held in reserve to strike Soviet atomic energy facilities, all supplemented by attacks with conventional high explosives.[65]

The plan specified how, if successful, these operations would affect the war. Destruction of Delta targets would stop critical war-supporting industries by cutting their electric power, disrupting related, but less critical, industries, and "by the chaos and possible panic occasioned by the industrial damage, the disruption of urban services, the interference with control channels, and the insecurity and fear on the part of the people."[66] This was a classic attack on the industrial web.

In a decidedly more conservative tone, reflecting the air-atomic disdain for attacking military forces directly (and inefficiently), EWP 50 addressed the second half of the campaign. The destruction of Romeo targets would not directly stop the Soviet offensive, but rather starve their forces of momentum by denying fuel, engines, vehicles, and other necessities for a mechanized army. Inability to replace losses, disruption of mobilization, and "perhaps" morale "will force the Soviet High Command to reevaluate their strategic situation and make decisions which will have an immediate though unpredictable effect on current military operations."[67]

By mid-1950, LeMay viewed SAC's ability to carry out the offensive optimistically. Where the initial phase of the offensive was to last three months, LeMay told an Air War College audience that he expected to deliver SAC's portion of the stockpile within three weeks.[68] Furthermore, the 25 percent losses anticipated in EWP 50 were less a realistic expectation than a necessity for logistical plans. Presumably, LeMay was showing the conservatism of an experienced wartime commander who knew that he would need reserves to cope with unforeseen contingencies. LeMay claimed that many targets could be struck more cheaply and overall losses would not exceed 10 percent.[69]

The Air Force plans for a strategic air offensive in the late 1940s and early 1950s were consistent with earlier ideas of using airpower for independent effect. Timing was a central measure of the plan's effectiveness. World War II campaigns were thought effective only once a sufficient force had been built, and correctly used only when attacks were compressed into the shortest possible time—effecting maximum shock. Even with atomic bombs and a well-trained force to deliver them, the vision of a nation-breaking force was still in the future. The most optimistic projections forecast weeks or even months until a campaign could show effects. Part of the limitation was technological. Despite their power, atomic bombs were not a panacea. Unlike fusion bombs, fission weapons were easily comprehensible in terms of previous experience, which reflects the limits to their power.

The other limitation was in number of aircraft. The Air Force director of plans and operations, Maj. Gen. Samuel Anderson, warned Symington in February 1950 of the gap between the demands of an extended campaign and the reality of a force just beginning to recover from years of shrinking budgets and manpower. His staff calculated that strategic operations could be sustained through the first year of war for only four groups of bombers. This strength would allow the delivery of the initial stockpile, but greatly complicate follow-on atomic and conventional attacks. Although mothballed B-29s could ease this problem, they would suffer greater attrition than more modern aircraft and support sustained effort by only two more groups, for a total of six. Until production caught up to attrition eighteen months into the war "our capability will steadily decline. At no time during this period will our capability be more than fifty percent of that required to perform the tasks demanded of Air Force strategic bombers."[70]

The JCS and Air Force understood, and tried to quantify, the gap between plans and reality. Before the Korean War, there were three studies of the atomic bomb's effectiveness in a war against the USSR. Starting in 1948, first the Air Force, then an ad hoc committee created by the JCS, and finally the newly formed Weapons Systems Evaluation Group, studied the strategic air offensive. Although the assessments used different and increasingly sophisticated methodologies, they reached the same general conclusions: the assault probably would succeed as planned, causing heavy but uncertain physical damage to Soviet industry, but with unpredictable and possibly counterproductive psychological effects. These estimates were in line with more conservative Air Force and JCS predictions. Estimates of physical damage counted only that caused by blast, routinely dismissing fire. Planners believed that thermal damage was too unpredictable and subject to widely variable weather conditions to be relied on for destroying targets.[71]

The first two major studies of the prospects of the strategic air offensive stemmed from an October 1948 order by the secretary of defense to evaluate "the chances of success of delivering a powerful strategic air offensive against vital elements of the Soviet war-making capacity as contemplated in current war plans."[72] The JCS 1952 series examined the penetration of Soviet defenses. JCS 1953, also known as the Harmon Report, assessed the effect of a successful air offensive. The Weapons Systems Evaluation Group Report Number 1 (WSEG 1) followed up these reports, after dissatisfaction with them.

JCS 1952/1, authored largely by the Air Force and submitted in December 1948, concluded that the strategic air offensive could succeed.[73] It determined that urban industrial concentrations, oil, transportation, and electric power, were the best target systems to accomplish the offensive's objectives, with cities having the highest priority. Their destruction should cripple the Soviet armed forces and "could well lead to Soviet capitulation." The authors concluded that the concentration of industry and governmental targets permitted "efficient use of atomic bombs," since the seventy largest urban centers contained most critical industry, including 78 percent of armaments, 94 percent of motor vehicles, 99 percent of tanks, 75 percent of Soviet oil refining capacity, and 80 percent of the aviation gas refineries.[74]

JCS 1952/1 projected that attacks on these targets would reduce Soviet industrial output by more than 50 percent. The necessary target materials on the seventy top cities would be ready by February 1949, with information on the remainder of the 210 urban targets and 2,100 more independent targets being prepared as rapidly as possible. Thus SAC would have sufficient information to attack most important target systems. Furthermore, JCS 1952/1 projected that within eight months of a war's start, intelligence would be adequate to attack two remaining target systems, transportation and hydroelectric power.[75] In carrying out this initial campaign, SAC would lose roughly one-quarter of its forces, but even so "ample capability still remains for the delivery of the entire stockpile of atomic bombs."[76]

The report concluded that "a powerful, strategic air offensive against vital elements of the Soviet war-making capacity could be delivered as planned." The risks in execution, most notably attrition and the safety of overseas medium bomber bases, were substantial but would not jeopardize the offensive. This confident report was not universally accepted. The chief of naval operations agreed that a strategic air offensive should be in the Emergency War Plan (EWP), but not that it could be delivered as planned. The risks dismissed by the Air Force authors were acceptable "for present planning purposes only." He urged a joint evaluation of the problem.[77]

This concern led to a broader effort led by two senior officers from each service, the Harmon Report, submitted in May 1949.[78] It examined the planned two-stage offensive under then-current plan Trojan. In the first fourteen days of the war, the Harmon Report estimated that the most important thirty cities, on which there was sufficient intelligence, could be attacked without further reconnaissance. While that was underway, information could be gathered on the remaining forty cities about which targeting data were incomplete. Evidently, the authors of JCS 1952/1 had been overoptimistic in estimating that the target folders for the first seventy cities would be ready by February 1949. The second stage of the offensive would be complete thirty days into the war, when the available stockpile would have been expended.

Through a mathematical model based on statistical deviation, the Harmon committee reached mixed conclusions about the offensive. Overall, industry would be reduced by between 30 and 40 percent.[79] All aviation fuel production likely would be knocked out, as would three-quarters of the rest of Soviet refining capability, indicating that petroleum, oil, and lubricants (POL) was the most lucrative target for atomic bombardment. Steel production would fall by 45 percent, rubber by 57 percent, aircraft assembly by 59 percent, aircraft engine production by 68 percent, machine tools by 24 percent, but electric power generation by only 1 percent. In addition the attacks would destroy 320 square miles of Soviet cities, 13 percent of the total urban area of the USSR, with superficial damage caused to 840 square miles, or 35 percent, of the rest.[80] This damage would kill 2.7 million people and "vastly complicate" the situation for the remaining 28 million in the 70 target cities, with substantial but indecisive (and perhaps counterproductive) psychological effects.[81] While civil and military control would be disrupted, the Soviet citizenry would not turn against the government.

Instead, citing Second World War precedent, Harmon predicted that the populace would unite in the face of the destruction. Inevitable, but temporary, chaos in the attacked areas probably would increase absenteeism at industry, but not decisively. Soviet troops at the front were unlikely to suffer psychologically from the attacks on their cities, unless they were suffering military reverses.[82]

The military effects of this disruption of Soviet industry were in line with the plan's predictions. The initial Soviet advance into Western Europe would not be halted, but the reduction of POL would hamper the army's mobility, while reducing the tempo of sea and air operations. The depletion of basic equipment stocks and logistic disruption would further curtail activity. Soviet generals would have to make important decisions under "difficult circumstances."[83] The air offensive would "facilitate greatly the application of other Allied military power with prospect of greatly lowered casualties"—exactly its envisioned role.[84]

The members of the Harmon committee unanimously adopted the report. When the JCS submitted it to the secretary of defense, however, they outlined some reservations, which generally showed they thought its conclusions conservative. The JCS believed that the conclusion that industrial capacity would be reduced by between 30 and 40 percent was misleading. The body of the report (vice the summary) detailed that selected target systems such as POL would be far more heavily damaged. The JCS also believed that shock would slow recuperation and rejected the negative estimation of psychological effect as being only "informed opinions on an admittedly abstruse and controversial matter."[85]

Vandenberg further wanted the wording on psychological effects changed to reflect their status as opinions and to conclude that "this situation may well cause a high degree of absenteeism and disorganization in industries essential to the war effort. This would force a modification of Soviet invasion plans, and, in time, adversely affect the morale of the Soviet armed forces."[86] Not surprisingly, Admiral Denfeld vigorously rejected these suggestions, which "would detract from and to a large extent, destroy the value of the entire report."[87]

While the JCS 1952/1 and Harmon reports were being written, an independent body was chartered to carry out precisely these kinds of detailed assessments. The Weapons Systems Evaluation Group (WSEG) emerged at the end of 1947 as the brainchild of Vannevar Bush, director of the wartime Office of Scientific Research and Development. Its role to evaluate new weapon systems was hammered out over the next year, leading to its establishment in early 1949, under Lt. Gen. John E. Hull. Its first task was to evaluate the air offensive.[88]

Hull's group produced a report in February 1950 that was generally positive about the prospects for a strategic air offensive. WSEG 1 had a narrower focus than either JCS 1952/1 or Harmon, examining delivery of weapons to targets, but not their effects on the Soviet economy. Unlike Harmon, which assessed the seventy urban centers in Plan Trojan, Hull used the updated Offtackle offensive on 104 urban centers with a projected force of 570 medium bombers, mostly operating from the United Kingdom, and 54 heavy bombers flying from the continental United States. The B-50s and B-29s would hit 51 percent and 35 percent of the targets respectively, while B-36s struck only 14 percent. Consistent with actual SAC plans, the core of the attack was compressed into thirty days, with all sorties delivered within ninety days.[89]

The report concluded that the stockpile could be delivered under most circumstances, with between 70 percent and 85 percent of atomic bomb carriers reaching their targets. Given an accuracy of three thousand feet CEP on radar bombing with the largest weapon in the arsenal, WSEG estimated that two-thirds of bombed industry would be damaged beyond repair. A Hiroshima-sized weapon would inflict that level of damage on half the targets, but the remainder would be repairable. SAC would lose one-third of its force during a night bombing campaign, and 50 percent during daylight bombing, far higher losses than the USAF anticipated.[90]

WSEG identified logistics as the major obstacle to carrying out the campaign. Attrition and lack of supplies meant that only the atomic offensive could be carried out, not concurrent conventional attacks. Three problems stood out: the availability of overseas medium bomber bases, overtaxing of airlift during a crisis, and insufficient stocks of aviation fuel at forward operating bases. These shortcomings, together with "grave deficiencies" in intelligence on Soviet defenses, led Hull's group to recommend a reevaluation of Offtackle.[91] Nonetheless, they concluded that the atomic portion of the offensive largely could be delivered as planned and cripple Soviet industry.

LeMay interpreted the results as a validation of SAC, in contrast to earlier skepticism about the study. When an officer on the WSEG team had approached LeMay at the start of the study requesting assistance and bearing a letter stating that he represented the secretary of defense, LeMay crumpled up the letter, threw it at the officer and exclaimed, "I will have none of this." After WSEG submitted its report, LeMay complimented the officer for the "fine job you did on that report" and recorded in his Commanding General's Diary for 9 May 1950 that WSEG reported that "SAC is ready to do its job."[92]

The role of strategic airpower in the plans of the early air-atomic age was very much like that of preatomic days. The new weapon was treated as an incremental improvement on earlier weapons. Joint and Air Force planners fit this new but fundamentally understandable weapon into an existing doctrinal framework. Strategic airpower sought victory by attacking the enemy's industry and causing massive damage in a short time. If that did not cause immediate surrender, the strain on Soviet logistics would guarantee eventual victory. The plans were as conservative as the ideas behind them, reflecting the victorious experience of their authors. The new weapon promised to better realize prewar ideas because the "decisive force" would be available at the outset, but the end was to repeat what was viewed as the successful conclusions in both theaters—enemy industrial collapse. By 1950, SAC was well prepared to carry out at least the atomic portion of that campaign.

Air-Atomic Containment

Action policy was firmly rooted in air-atomic ideas but that does not necessarily mean declaratory policy was as well. The degree to which these matters were synchronized was critical for the continuation of air-atomic ideas. National policy could provide a friendly environmental niche in which the air-atomic idea would thrive, a neutral one in which it had to struggle against other conceptions of national security, or a hostile one in which it might be snuffed out. Determining how friendly national policy was requires examination of basic national security policy, and two specific nuclear issues: preauthorization for use and the decision to research thermonuclear weapons.

The first relevant set of papers, the Basic National Security Policies (BNSP), hammered out in the National Security Council, were overarching statements of foreign policy and security strategy. The United States only began to create formal national security strategies after 1947. Though the Eisenhower administration first used the term BNSP, Truman's NSC-20 and NSC-68 served the same function. John Gaddis, in *Strategies of Containment*, divides strategies like those articulated in the BNSPs into two loose categories: symmetrical and asymmetrical. The first type meets threats with similar types of force. Nuclear forces are used to counterbalance nuclear forces, conventional against conventional, and unconventional against unconventional. Asymmetrical strategies attempted to contain Soviet power by playing American strengths against Soviet weaknesses. Although these policies were unique in varying ways, the basic distinction between the two categories is a useful organizing idea. Each Cold War administration generally took one outlook or the other, except Truman's, whose 1948 NSC-20 reflected an asymmetrical approach to the Soviet threat, and 1949 NSC-68 a symmetrical one.

The NSC-20 series shows the imprint of George Kennan, its primary author. Kennan's ideas, first expressed in the "Long Telegram" of 1946, focused on containing Soviet power in the long term. He believed that the military threat to the United States could be managed as long as additional industrial centers—such as those Western Europe and Japan—remained out of the Soviet orbit. Moscow's pressure against the West would be met with "counter-pressure," defined as primarily ideological and economic, rather than military. Since communism exploited social and economic upheaval, it could not take hold without desperation as a growth medium. Once restabilized and revitalized, Europe and Japan could independently resist Soviet political subversion, communism's spread would be checked, and the Soviet system would be forced to change from within.[93]

Although Kennan focused on the peaceful challenge and defeat of the Soviet threat, he did address its military aspects. In 1946, he expressed broad agreement with air-atomic concepts. Consistent with his belief that the United States could not match Soviet land forces, he told the Air Force chief of staff, General Spaatz, that any conflict against the Soviet Union would be "an air war in the strictest sense of the term." Sounding like an orthodox airpower theorist, Kennan suggested that Soviet industry was particularly vulnerable to strategic bombing due to its concentration. He estimated that the destruction of about ten vital targets would incapacitate the Soviet Union.[94] As the author of containment policy in the Cold War, Kennan set the terms of the debate in a way no one else did. That he accepted the role of the atomic bomb in an air-atomic framework shows that national policy was compatible with air-atomic theory from the start.

Kennan's ideas won policy approval in the NSC-20 series. Most of NSC-20/1, the first major report, addressed the wider issues of peacetime containment of the Soviet threat. Chapter 5, "The Pursuit of Our Basic Objectives in Time of War," discussed policy alternatives if peaceful measures were to fail. The United States could not repeat the total war of 1941–45 against the USSR. NSC-20/1 rejected the occupation of the Soviet Union or unconditional surrender as wartime objectives. Soviet leaders were more likely to accept a compromise peace than surrender. Imposition of a democratic system on Russia after a Soviet defeat would fail because "the psychology and outlook of a great people cannot be altered in a short space of time at the mere dictate or precept of a foreign power, even in the wake of total defeat and submission." Hence, NSC-20/1 concluded, absolute assertion of American will on Soviet territory was unattainable and any final settlement must be politically negotiated.[95]

Having defined the limits to American power, NSC-20/1 stated the positive aims that the American government should seek in wartime. Very much like the peacetime strategy of containment, which used political and economic means to limit communist influence to where it already existed, in wartime the first goal would be to destroy Russian military influence outside Soviet borders. American military power should also disrupt the mechanisms by which the Communist Party exported subversion to the West and assure Soviet military helplessness. A peace settlement with a defeated Soviet regime would eradicate its external military and political influence. To do that, enough Soviet military-industrial potential would be razed to prevent a postwar Communist government from threatening war again. Furthermore, any settlement should create economic dependence on the outside world, liberate national minorities, and guarantee the free flow of people and ideas into and out of Russia.[96] This plan extended the conviction that Soviet power would collapse naturally if prevented from spreading. In peacetime, Soviet influence would be limited to its already existing area and its expansion resisted. In wartime, it would be reduced to Russia and deprived of tools for invasion or subversion.[97]

This image of war was largely compatible with existing ideas about strategic airpower. Denying the Red Army the essentials of large-scale war fighting was essential to destroying the Soviet ability to export its ideology by force. A successful air-atomic campaign would eviscerate the Red Army's industrial support. A Soviet military paralyzed by a lack of fuel and replacement weapons could not threaten neighbors. Since NSC-20/1 rejected the occupation of the Soviet Union, guerrilla resistance was irrelevant and immobilized Soviet forces would be impotent. Other goals stated in NSC-20/1, such as promoting separation in non-Russian parts of the USSR, might be helped by careful targeting, which avoided industry in these potentially rebellious areas.

One part of NSC-20/1, however, conflicted in part with an air-atomic campaign. To encourage the disintegration of Soviet power, NSC-20/1 emphasized the need not to antagonize the civilian population through the infliction of "inordinate hardship and cruelties."[98] Although this warning came with the caveat, "within the limits of military feasibility," that statement acknowledged that a heavily armed nation like the Soviet Union could be defeated only through major damage. Especially given Kennan's comments to Spaatz, NSC 20/1 accepted a strategic air campaign—despite its attendant civilian casualties—as a necessity.

NSC-30, which examined a public declaration on the use of atomic weapons, illuminates the Truman administration's policy regarding their use. In December 1948, Vannevar Bush asked Secretary of Defense Forrestal to consider whether in crisis or war, the United States might hesitate, or use atomic bombs too late. He asked whether a public statement explicitly stating that the United States would use atomic weapons might enhance deterrence.[99]

Vandenberg resisted such a debate. He told Symington that even if the NSC's decision was favorable, it would merely reinforce planning that already assumed that atomic weapons would be used. Any other conclusion would create problems. To defer any decision about use until the circumstances of a war were clear would "hamstring our vital planning for every future contingency in a most insecure world." The Air Force would face particular problems if the NSC decided that atomic weapons would be used only in retaliation for Soviet strikes.[100] Instead the atomic offensive must be launched immediately and robustly to cripple Soviet war-making capacity and enable victory.

The NSC expressed its position in NSC-30 of September 1948. The decision to employ atomic weapons was of "the highest priority," but since the circumstances would prevail when a war broke out was unpredictable, "a prescription preceding diagnosis could invite disaster." A preannounced declaration would unnecessarily constrain American options. Nothing could be gained from a public statement of American policy, while the Soviets might exploit any perceived hesitation about atomic use. Thus the military shall "be ready to utilize promptly and effectively all appropriate means available, including atomic weapons."[101] This decision could hardly have supported the strategic air offensive more. It favored the use of atomic weapons. Indeed, if an atomic offensive was the only measure the military could take in war, there would be almost irresistible pressure to do so.

The Truman administration shifted to a different national security strategy in the wake of a Soviet atomic test and Mao's victory over Nationalist China. NSC-68, the fruit of a joint State and Defense Department study, was the brainchild of Paul Nitze, who later emerged as an important nuclear strategist. NSC-68 advised a "perimeter defense," because the international situation had deteriorated and further losses could not be accepted. Rather than meeting Soviet thrusts with selective responses, emphasizing asymmetrical American strengths, NSC-68 recommended challenging Soviet military force with American military force. In contrast to NSC-20/1's concern that American resources were limited, NSC-68 claimed that a properly managed American economy could spend whatever was required on the military. NSC-68 emphasized the military aspect of power and rejected negotiations until the balance of power shifted in America's favor.[102]

The role of atomic weapons, barely mentioned in NSC-20/1, was central to NSC-68. American atomic capability could deliver a "serious blow against the war-making capacity of the USSR." That attack would be necessary for victory but not sufficient—a conclusion in line with the JCS plans.[103] Soviet atomic capability was the changed factor. NSC-68 forecast that the Soviets might be tempted to attack Europe if they thought a successful assault against the United States was possible. It prescribed a buildup of air, ground, and sea strength to "put off the day" that a Soviet surprise attack could succeed and reduce US dependence on atomic weapons. At the same time, NSC-68 acknowledged that only "overwhelming atomic superiority and . . . command of the air" might deter the USSR from using atomic weapons or launch a surprise attack. So, the United States must build up atomic forces as rapidly as it did conventional ones.[104]

In that it called for a massive buildup of conventional forces, NSC-68 did not strongly favor the air-atomic approach. It rejected the arguments of air-atomic advocates that airpower was the most efficient and the only affordable approach to American security. Reliance on mobilizing latent strength, the basis of JCS plans, was unacceptable in the NSC-68 conception of security. It also implicitly questioned the ability of the strategic air offensive to buy time for conventional mobilization and prepare the ground for those forces by hollowing out the Soviet military. Its concern that a surprise attack could eliminate SAC further questioned underlying assumptions of the strategic air doctrine. Still, a military based around NSC-68's ideas could carry out an air-atomic offensive, if the buildup of atomic forces was accomplished as prescribed.

Between 1947 and 1950, the role of the strategic air offensive in basic national security policy was mixed, but still compatible with the visions of NSC-20/1 and NSC-68. The goals of NSC-20 coincided with those of the air-atomic advocates: so, too, its recognition of limited American resources and fundamental frugality. NSC-68, while less supportive of the air-atomic idea, still found ample room for it under the enlarged tent of American military strength. Unlike later versions of symmetrical containment, NSC-68 did not favor conventional forces so far as to treat the use of atomic weapons as unacceptable.

Notably, neither declaratory policy, nor air-atomic concepts, advocated preventive war. Preventive war means attacking a nation because it may be a threat at some time in the future, in contrast to preemptive attack, the launching of an attack to forestall one already underway. Preventive war is a strategic decision; preemption is an operational one. As several historians have written, Truman and Eisenhower, as well as air-atomic advocates, seriously discussed preventive war with different degrees of openness. They sensed that the American atomic arsenal was a "wasting asset" that would lose its value when the USSR developed a deliverable atomic capability.[105] Nonetheless, Truman and Eisenhower rejected prevention as impractical, given the costs of occupying a devastated Soviet Union, and incompatible with American values.[106] When some airpower advocates, such as Gen. Orvil Anderson, crossed the line from preemption to prevention, Truman immediately fired them.[107] For his part, LeMay later denied that he had advocated prevention during this period. "We knew for a fact that it would be possible to curtail enemy expansion if we challenged them in that way. Some of us thought it might be better to do so then, than to wait until later. . . . I never discussed what we were going to do with the force we had, or what we should do with it [SAC], or anything of that sort."[108] Whether LeMay, speaking twenty years after the start of the Cold War, was entirely truthful is uncertain, but national policy on preventive war, and the fate of air-atomic advocates who tried to undermine it, were crystal clear. Several historians doubt LeMay's restraint, citing for instance, his arrangement to have the Atomic Energy Commission transfer atomic weapons to SAC in an emergency, independent of a presidential directive.[109] Such measures do not necessarily presage preventive war. Rather, they straddle the line between preemption and prevention in a way compatible with air-atomic thinking. Preparation to retaliate with the greatest degree of force and coordination required the rapid transfer of weapons. In the event of a decapitation attempt, the scenario envisioned by LeMay's agreement with the AEC, SAC could still reply quickly, disarming the Soviets and perhaps terminating the war.

There was tension for air-atomic advocates, and other military professionals, in the debates over striking first. Prevention and preemption, though distinct concepts, are active. They use force to seek victory. By contrast, deterrence is negative; the use of force is failure. Preemption at the operational level, serving a deterrent strategy, may have been the only viable course, but it was a frustrating one, if the vocal advocates of prevention were voicing a deep-seated unease, which seems to be the case.

The Truman administration faced another decision about atomic issues that affected the strategic air offensive, whether to build the hydrogen bomb. While the administration could have set policies that complicated an air-atomic offensive, or ignored its special requirements, it chose a declaratory policy compatible with the strategic air offensive.

Soon after NSC-30, the NSC debated whether the United States should seek the "super," or thermonuclear, weapon. The position of each major player in this debate was largely framed in terms of the air-atomic offensive. In an internal assessment, the Air Force's planning chief argued that the super would be efficient. Where current war plans called for up to fourteen atomic bombs to hit a single city—with the attendant bombers and escort aircraft—one or two thermonuclear weapons would have the same effect. Fewer bombs and aircraft would be required, and could work in less time, thereby increasing shock. The increased damage would complicate repair but might perhaps have additional psychological effects.[110] Essentially, these arguments related the super to atomic weapons exactly as the latter had been compared to conventional weapons. They were more powerful, but fit into the same conceptual framework.

The Joint Chiefs shared these views. They added that thermonuclear weapons would increase flexibility in planning, making attacks on some tactical targets economical. Destruction of major concentrations of troops or materiel, on the scale of the Normandy landings or Stalingrad would have called for several fission weapons, but they could be eliminated with one super.[111] The massive damage caused by the super's blast and thermal effects would completely disrupt the transportation, utilities, and industry of urban areas, and threaten societal cohesion. They would be more effective against Bravo targets than fission weapons, because hydrogen bombs would destroy an airfield and supporting infrastructure, and prevent its use for an extended period. Again, they would wreck some targets that were difficult to attack with the smaller fission weapons, such as large areas with dispersed industry, widely separated air objectives, troop concentrations, hardened bunkers, and critical but imprecisely located targets. The super's larger firepower would also make any target hit unsalvageable, preventing any need for reattack, and create more "bonus" damage to adjacent areas.[112] "These considerations, aside from operational factors, establish a military requirement for super bombs."[113]

Even Senator Brien McMahon, chairman of the Joint Committee on Atomic Energy, couched his support for the super in terms of the strategic air offensive. In November 1949, he told Truman that one super could destroy 150 square miles, which would take twenty-three fission weapons. This efficiency would free fission weapons for use against other targets, including tactical ones. Like Air Force supporters of the super, McMahon expected attacking with a single large weapon would increase the "shock and demoralization, psychological and otherwise, that follow from concentrating an offensive within the shortest possible space of time."[114]

Naturally, LeMay anticipated the prospect of an improved weapon. In the earliest stages of the decision process, he was told by a colleague assigned to the secretary of defense's office, "Look, Curt, I've just been to a briefing, and there is no question that you are going to get a bomb that's so goddamned big that it will change the whole aspect and picture of the thing." The officer later recalled, "old Curt rubbing his gut. This was just right up his alley."[115]

Not only did the NSC decide in favor of building the super, but the key players framed the decision entirely in terms of the air-atomic offensive. The weapon would be built because it was an efficient way to destroy Soviet industry, with the potential of more shock.

These policy decisions at the national/declaratory level were important in the formation and influence of the air-atomic idea. When declaratory and action policy are unsynchronized, a host of potential problems emerge, from peacetime budget fights where both sides talk past each other, to more serious misunderstandings in wartime. In the immediate postwar period, though, the top levels of America's security establishment created national policies that had ample room for an atomic strategic air offensive. The commitment of national leaders to air-atomic power is attested to by the approval of expansion of the Air Force to 143 wings, from 95, in 1952.[116] Gaps in this linkage diminished over time as national policy evolved to meet and embrace air-atomic concepts. The major documents of the period make the same assumptions about the relationship of strategic airpower, enemy industry, and ultimate victory as did Air Force thinkers. Before the Korean War, the air-atomic idea floated with the current of national policy. It was a military strategy perfectly suited to a national strategy of security through military strength.

3

FINDING A PLACE

By 11 October 1949, the B-36 hearings of the House Armed Services Committee had been filling the meeting chamber and headlines for two months. The first phase had featured intense scrutiny of the procurement of the B-36, America's largest bomber. That aircraft, just entering service after a troubled development process, had been helped—so charged an anonymous document submitted to Republican Congressmen—by corruption. The allegations pointed to Air Force Secretary Symington, but also implicated senior USAF officials, and questioned the value of their bomber and strategy. That phase, which exonerated Symington and the procurement process, wrapped up with the revelation that the author of the anonymous document was a Navy Department civilian. Yet five of the seven investigatory items on the agenda remained. The second phase of the hearings examined the air-atomic idea and national security. On 11 October, a parade of Navy officers testified about their service, the Air Force, and the atomic bomb. Commander Tatom's comments reflected the tone of the hearings. He told congressmen that if an atomic bomb were detonated at one end of the runway at National Airport, a person standing at the other end, 6,500 feet away, would be unhurt.[1] That a distinguished Naval officer would tell Congress something so patently false, and that the Navy would put him in front of Congress and the nation to say it, testifies to the service's desperation in the fight against its new rival. These issues can be understood only in the context of the struggle between the Navy and the Air Force, as the latter sought a place in the national security structure. Central to this struggle were the atomic bomb and the air-atomic idea.

This chapter will examine the air-atomic strategy and the organizational struggles it fueled. The structure for national security policy changed dramatically with the National Security Act in July 1947. "Unification," as the creation of a single Defense Department was known, created an independent Air Force and placed all three services under the direction of the secretary of defense. This development was bound to annoy a service that coveted its autonomy as much did the Navy. Ominously, not only was the Air Force placed into the security structure as a coequal to the Army and Navy, but it threatened to seize the latter's position as America's first line of defense. The basis of the Air Force's power was the air-atomic idea. It became the central issue around which revolved interservice fights in war planning and budgeting, culminating in the B-36 hearings. The struggle between the two services was one between different and largely incompatible conceptions of national security.

The chapter will conclude by assessing an event that bridged the early and late air-atomic periods. The Korean War saw the move from nuclear scarcity to nuclear plenty, from a desire to target industry to a fear of enemy airpower, and to a massive increase in the conceived scale of the air offensive. The Air Force that entered Korea was ready to be one part of a joint team; that that emerged was well along the path to becoming, in the words of Colin Gray, "our [entire] team, not only its leading player."[2] Yet this war also illustrated political and operational problems that would cripple the USAF's ability to control the rules of the game.

A Seat at the Table

Air Force leaders had pursued independence and equality with the other services as an institutional goal for decades. Achievement of this aim depended on the existence of a mission no other service could perform. In the interwar years, the idea of strategic bombardment alone had not been enough to convince the government to grant the USAF the autonomy enjoyed by the Royal Air Force. Instead, bodies like the Baker Board had granted it semi-autonomy within the Army. Perceptions of the success of the strategic air campaigns in the Second World War, combined with the atomic bomb, assured the Air Force's independence in 1947. During 1946, in its run up to the unification debates, the then Army Air Force defined its postwar mission as threefold: "(1) To gain and maintain air superiority. (2) To destroy the *war potential* of an enemy in accordance with strategic plans. (3) To seek out and destroy all types of enemy forces" (emphasis added).[3] Given the conviction that offensive airpower alone could effectively provide air superiority, both missions were rooted in the air-atomic strategy.

Explicitly defining the missions of each service was central to the unification process. In earlier eras, splitting mission responsibilities had been comparatively easy, with the waterline an easily recognized boundary. In 1947, though, airpower's great strength—flexibility—hampered easy delineation. Should a single air service control all aircraft, or should each service maintain its own aircraft to conduct service-specific missions? There was no unambiguous solution, but the services had to find some rough agreement. After meetings between the Joint Chiefs at Key West, Florida, and Washington in March 1948, the JCS published the first in a series of directives delineating the service missions.

The Key West agreement made the Air Force "responsible for strategic air warfare." Among its collateral functions was the interdiction of enemy seapower, antisubmarine warfare, and aerial mine laying. The Navy, in addition to its traditional roles of destroying enemy naval forces and suppressing enemy commerce, was assigned the primary mission of gaining sea supremacy and authorized to "conduct air operations as necessary for the accomplishment of objectives in a naval campaign." Its collateral functions further expanded the Navy's potential role, directing that it be "prepared to participate in the over-all air effort as directed by the Joint Chiefs of Staff."[4] Defense Secretary Forrestal issued a clarification which, while directing the Navy not to use its assigned missions as a justification for building a strategic air force, "agreed it should not be denied the air [capability] necessary to accomplish its mission." He reiterated that the Navy had stated that it did not intend to build a separate strategic air force, while the Air Force did not want to control carrier aviation.[5] Although the agreement traced the borders of service responsibility, it contained loopholes large enough to pass an aircraft carrier, or a B-36, through.

Primacy of the (Air) Offensive

One such issue was the primacy of the strategic air offensive. In the run up to unification, General Doolittle told the Senate Military Affairs Committee that air superiority must be established before any other operations could be launched.[6] Once air superiority was established, the United States could not afford to delay taking the offensive. To do so would only invite the enemy to strike first. General Arnold, again, told Air Force generals in 1945 that control of the air was no longer an "auxiliary operation."[7] Spaatz informed Congress "the time lag is gone." In the next war the United States would not have time to mobilize.[8] Quoting the Strategic Bombing Survey, Eisenhower reminded a congressional committee of the link between control of the air and exploitation through strategic attack, noting "no nation can long survive the free exploitation of air weapons over its homeland."[9]

Eisenhower's statement reflected a major but easily ignored element of the interservice debate. The Army remained largely neutral, and slightly favorable to the USAF. From the perspective of Army officers, unification was a blessing: instead of forcing air and armored officers to argue over which would receive the greater share of (limited) Army funding, it ensured that the USAF would argue for its share with the Navy too. While the Army would suffer from the USAF's budgetary success of the next fifteen years, it did better than it would have done with the USAF as the viper next to its bosom. Thus, in 1948–49, the Army supported USAF missions and also helped it to fight the USN. From the early 1950s, however, the Army again would engage the USAF on grand strategic issues, occasionally cooperating with the Navy. From 1958, the Army would join the Navy in a full-blooded attack on SAC. Meanwhile, the sheer coincidence that LeMay had been a subordinate to Eisenhower in the European theater may have eased civil-military relations in the 1950s.

If airpower contributed to victory in a necessary and independent way, still it was part of a larger effort. In 1946, Norstad briefed the president that the "Ground-Sea-Air" team remained important. Although the balance between the three might change, all would remain necessary.[10] Gen. Orvil Anderson, senior Air Force representative on the Strategic Bombing Survey and later head of Air University, expected future wars to follow a phased course similar to World War II. Although airpower would dominate the first phase, the other services had key roles to play.[11] Air Force leaders did not argue that airpower alone was decisive, but rather that it must be addressed first. It was necessary, but not sufficient, to victory.

Inseparable from the idea that the air war must be the first priority in a future conflict was the need to eliminate duplication of effort. Only the efficient application of airpower by a single Air Force could achieve air superiority and conduct a successful air offensive. In his testimony before Congress, Doolittle emphasized that every dollar should be spent to provide the maximum possible security. The combination of a unified Defense Department and autonomous Air Force was the only way to do so.[12] Airpower could exist for other functions under the control of other services, such as fleet support, but, as Norstad held in 1946, "the ultimate and over-all responsibility for air power [must be] vested in a single service."[13]

The sentiments of Air Force generals were reinforced by the president's Air Policy Commission, better known as the Finletter Commission. At Truman's direction, the board comprehensively examined American aviation with an eye to the needs of national security. Its report, published in 1948 as *Survival in the Air Age*, underlined the requirements for an independent Air Force. Its conclusions were much in line with air-atomic strategy. The Finletter Commission reasoned that, whereas a naval threat could not reemerge for many years, an air threat might do so sooner. After nodding toward the need for a defensive force able to block an air attack against the United States, Finletter's report demanded units "capable of dealing a crushing counteroffensive blow on the aggressor."[14] That force, threatening a counterattack of "utmost violence," would deter an aggressor. As the unnamed aggressor might be able to use atomic bombs in mass by 1953, the Air Force must be capable of deterrence and counterattack by that date. The extant Air Force of fifty-five groups must be increased to at least seventy, supplemented by twenty-seven National Guard and thirty-four Air Reserve groups. With fighters for defense and seven hundred heavy bombers, this was in line with the program the Air Force had been promoting for several years.[15] To create this minimum required combat force before 1953, the report recommended that Air Force appropriations be increased from $2.85 billion in FY 1947–48 to $4.15 billion in 1948, $5.45 billion in 1949, and upward at the same rate until 1953. Army appropriations would remain static, while the Navy increased at slower rate than the Air Force, with its additional funds focused on upgrading to naval aviation.[16] Nonetheless, "we can no longer follow our traditional procedure of relying entirely on the Navy as our force in being in peacetime." Finletter's recommendations show both the placement of airpower as an independent military instrument and the displacement of the Navy from the center of national defense and its budget.[17]

Finletter's report, and unification itself, came during one of the periodic troughs in the cycle of American military budgets. As Samuel Huntington remarked in *The Common Defense*, during the postwar era military policy moved from resting on mobilization to deterrence. The immediate postwar years fell into the earlier model, which demanded the rapid disbanding of the mobilized forces. The Army fell from more than 8 million soldiers on VJ day to under 2 million by July 1946, and the Air Force from 218 combat groups on VJ day to 109 by 1 January 1946. The Navy lost half its personnel by March 1946.[18] The military budget from FY 1947 to FY 1950 also reflected the traditional rapid demobilization. Actual spending on defense for FY 1947 totaled $14.4 billion, $11.7 billion in FY 1948, $12.9 billion in FY 1949, and stayed steady at $13 billion in FY 1950, before the Korean War and the impact of NSC-68.[19] The FY 1945 budget had been $80 billion.[20]

Naval Anxiety

Resource constraints amplified the Navy's need to compete for funding, but above all it was anxious over its role. The Air Force threatened to displace a service that had led American military policy since Mahan's day and had just concluded an epic victory in the Pacific. The air-atomic idea was the key ground on which the Navy would resist the Air Force's advance. In 1947, Rear Admiral Daniel Gallery, the assistant chief of Naval Operations (Guided Missiles), outlined the reasoning behind the Navy's organizational fight over the next two years. Gallery forecast that World War III would be quite different from World War II, primarily because of strategic bombing amplified by the atomic bomb. This essentially was a nautical version of the air-atomic strategy following from the US Navy's use of massed carriers against Japanese land targets in 1944–45. The Navy must possess this potentially decisive force. Gallery reasoned that transoceanic atomic bombing was impractical with current technology, whereas the Navy's carriers were a mature platform from which to launch it, because intercontinental range was built into the ship rather than the aircraft. A carrier-based offensive had the additional advantages of eliminating requirements to seize and supply overseas bases for medium bombers, and would be far harder for Soviet bombers to locate and attack. "It seems obvious that the next time our Sunday Punch will be an Atom Bomb aimed at the enemy capitals or industrial centers and that the outcome of the war will be determined by strategic bombing. . . . I think the time is right now for the Navy to start an aggressive campaign aimed at proving that the Navy can deliver the Atom Bomb more effectively than the Air Forces can." The Air Force would be relegated to continental defense.[21]

Gallery's memorandum demonstrates that both services acted from similar motives. Just as the USAF was adapting its successful wartime strategy to a new era, so too was the Navy. Both services realized that the stakes were high, because each relied on constant research and development and ongoing capital investment to maintain its military capability and future political influence. Major investment was required to buy the bombers and aircraft carriers that would make the services effective in five, ten, and twenty years. A prolonged funding drought not only would erode that capability in the mid-term, but also could weaken future arguments for long-term investment. It would always be easier to urge continuation of a current capability than to gain support for reviving an "obsolescent" one.

The Air Force brass would not have been surprised by Gallery's views. Indeed, the Navy already was seeking to dominate the budget by gaining control of the Mediterranean part of the war plan. In October 1946, Maj. Gen. George McDonald, the USAF intelligence chief, warned Spaatz that the Navy had launched a coordinated press, radio, and speaking campaign, which sought to "indoctrinate" the Navy line into "public informers" who would then evangelize the Navy's message. That message was "beautiful." Eliminate the Army from defense of the Mediterranean, then "argue that carrier air power can dominate the Mediterranean and you have Navy and Air merged into one service claiming the budget—NAVY."[22] Later, McDonald warned the chief of staff that Naval intelligence officers working with Air Force targeteers in the Pentagon had been "more or less awkwardly researching the target files of the Twelfth and Fifteenth Air Forces without asking the Air Force officer sitting next to them for assistance," so to build a case that carriers could operate in the Mediterranean.[23]

For decades, the Navy had played the leading role in armed diplomacy for the United States and expected this role would continue. As a naval officer working on Admiral Stark's staff told an Air Force colleague, "The Navy alone projects American power overseas, [and] that Air Power did not begin until the atomic bomb on Hiroshima."[24] By contrast, some USAF officers believed that airpower could replace warships as a symbol of American resolve. As the Navy carried out its traditional function when battleships and a carrier battle group visited Turkey at the height of the 1946 crisis, so Arnold sent a B-29 on an around-the-world flight to demonstrate the Air Force could "show the flag" as well as the Navy—and more economically.[25] The next year, he mused, four hundred B-29s flown into the US occupation zone in Germany could be a potent instrument of foreign policy.[26] Something similar occurred during the Berlin Airlift, which the supporters of airpower held proved that it could assume an instrumental diplomatic role. LeMay called the Air Force the best "big stick" in the modern world.[27] *Air Force* magazine crowed that the airplane had supplanted the gunboat.[28] Was the carrier next?

The Navy had an ambiguous relationship with the new weapon. As Gallery's memo shows, some influential officers wanted to place the bomb at the center of a resurgent Navy's war fighting. Yet other points of view were present in the Navy's thinking about the bomb. Bernard Brodie, later a prominent nuclear strategist, compiled a contemporary study of the Navy's attitude toward the atomic bomb, based on interviews with naval officers. Brodie does not note for whom he performed the study, but the degree of Navy cooperation is impressive. Although the Navy did not publish an official statement on the new weapon, Fleet Admiral Nimitz, the commander of naval operations (CNO), reviewed and approved Brodie's synthesis. Because of his expertise and access, Brodie's views can be taken as an authoritative illumination of the service's opinions on the issues central to its disputes with the USAF.[29]

According to Brodie, the Navy wished to prepare for three contingencies: peacetime operations involving police functions requiring precision, a one-sided atomic war, and a conflict where both sides had atomic weapons. The latter situations were complicated because technological change in the mid-term, which Brodie said was "fifteen years," would dramatically alter the required forces.

The Navy justifiably thought seapower superior to airpower for the first mission, because the visible presence of major warships in an area had greater deterrent effect than distant and invisible atomic bombers. In the transition from peace to the two wartime states, the Navy denied that the absence of a Soviet surface navy made warships obsolete. Rather, they still must defeat Soviet submarines and support traditional logistical and amphibious roles, where the Navy's bombardment power remained irreplaceable. In the atomic era, Naval officers believed they required a combination of carrier groups, amphibious forces, escort craft, and submarines (eventually to be outfitted with new bombardment weapons, presumably guided missiles).

This large surface Navy also must deprive the enemy of bases near US territory, which was a vital defensive role, since the only contemporary method of atomic attack required B-29 type bombers with limited range. "Push-button" warfare would not emerge before the mid-term, because intense research was required to extend rocket technology to intercontinental ranges while carrying bulky atomic weapons. Meanwhile, the Navy dismissed large subsonic (Air Force) aircraft operating without fighter escort from extreme distance, as an ineffective way to deliver scarce atomic bombs, because of the rapid improvement of air defenses, represented by guided missiles and jet fighters. Future offensive forces instead would rest on high-speed, short-range aircraft and evolutionary developments of the V-2 that could be placed on submarines or surface ships. Outlying bases would provide both protection against long-range aircraft and staging points for deep attacks into enemy territory.

Meanwhile, the Navy contended, surface fleets would survive or evade atomic attack as they carried out their missions. "Active" defense using fighters and shipborne antiaircraft guns would cripple attacking bombers and scarce atomic weapons, making such attacks unthinkably wasteful. "Passive" defense, tactical dispersion of ships and design changes, would further reduce the effectiveness of any bombs that did penetrate active defenses. Cities, not navies, were vulnerable to atomic attack.

Brodie noted that the Navy's case relied on the assumption of continued atomic scarcity. Long-range bomber aircraft and attacks against the fleet were dismissed as wasteful of the scarce resource, yet given the increased effectiveness of atomic bombs over conventional weapons, raids could be effective despite suffering greater losses than had been acceptable in 1944. If the atomic attack on Hiroshima equaled 210 B-29s then, using the 1945 criteria of a 10 percent loss rate, twenty-one aircraft lost was acceptable on a conventional raid of that size.[30] If atomic bombs became more plentiful, more aircraft could be lost so long as they struck the targets. Ultimately, Brodie believed, even if 90 percent of bombers were destroyed, the 10 percent that penetrated could inflict sufficient damage to justify the mission. If 500 atomic weapons could reach an enemy's industrial potential, a nation with 5,000 of them could absorb a 90 percent loss and achieve victory.

Furthermore, if those weapons cost only $1 million each, victory would have been cheap. These two scenarios showed that the Navy's presumption of weapon scarcity was unreliable and misleading. Attacks even with B-29s might be effective with heavy losses. Therefore, surface fleets could be vulnerable. If the Navy's arguments were right, the Soviets would have to make attacks on its carriers a top priority. Even more, if the arguments about scarcity fell, so too did most of the USN's critique of the limits to USAF policy.

While forward US bases were essential as launching points for invasion, Brodie thought the Navy grossly overestimated its ability to detect or intercept long-range bombers. He feared it was ignoring problems like large vulnerable bases and concentrated naval-essential industry, and new ideas. His conclusion, which could have applied to the Air Force's generals as well, was that

> it is pertinent to point out that any military organization, especially after a great war in which it has fought with brilliant success, tends to feel an enormous vested interest in the experience which it has acquired with so much pain and labor. It is not likely to feel spontaneous sympathy with the suggestion that the experience may be of very diminished applicability for the future.[31]

The Navy's position on atomic bombs showed the same conservatism as the Air Force's. Where the Air Force integrated it into an already existing strategic bombing framework, the Navy placed it in existing ideas about distant bases, amphibious warfare, shore bombardment, and the ability of carrier-based aviation to conduct strategic bombing on land. The Navy showed self-serving biases in its projections of the technological future. For example, jets were automatically thought to favor the defender, but that ignored the offensive potential of the technology. A high-altitude supersonic or even high subsonic bomber would be an elusive target, especially for short-ranged interceptors. There was no reason to believe that aviation technology would automatically favor the defense, but there may well have been good reason to believe that it would aid the vastly more experienced USAF over its rival. As important, the Navy overemphasized the potency of short-range weapon systems, missing the long-range potential of both aircraft and missiles.

Although not every Navy officer who testified at the B-36 hearings took the same approach, most did not oppose the atomic weapon per se but instead attacked the strategic bombing doctrine to which it was attached. Seen from a broader organizational perspective, the different Navy positions on the atomic bomb converge into a single attack on the Air Force's possession of the new weapon. Discrediting either half of the air-atomic equation would, the naval attackers hoped, restore their service to preeminence.

While Brodie was analyzing the Navy's position on atomic weapons, the Navy pushed to determine the Air Force's view. In July 1948, when asked whether the Navy should be allowed to use atomic bombs, Symington sent a policy memorandum that rankled the naval establishment. The Navy should use atomic weapons only against targets related to normal naval missions the Air Force could not attack. Given the weapon's scarcity, only targets of the "greatest strategic significance" should be attacked. Given the Air Force's focus on industry as the most efficient, and most significant, target, it is difficult to imagine the Air Force agreeing that many ordinary naval targets would demand atomic weapons. Moreover Symington stated, should the Navy develop an air offensive capability, it must be under Air Force control, because the strategic air offensive was its primary mission under the Key West agreement. Thus, Symington concluded, the Navy should develop an atomic delivery capability only if all three services had sufficient resources for all of their primary and secondary missions, or atomic weapons became less scarce.[32]

No matter what a naval officer thought of the air-atomic idea, his vision included large ships of some sort. Like aircraft, warships had to be planned for and constructed over several years. The Navy would face major problems in wartime if its combat vessels were not already built. This tension heightened the problems between the Air Force and Navy. Both needed to have most of their wartime strength available on the first day of the next war, yet the financial situation constrained resources for premobilization tasks. Only those functions that absolutely must be executed on the first day of war could receive adequate funding. Thus, the air-atomic idea, with the emphasis on launching a decisive force at the outbreak of war, meant a small Navy. That idea must die if the Navy was to live. The battleground for the Navy's fight was the planning process and the underpinnings of the air-atomic idea.

Tension Boils Over

The interservice tension was manifested across the Pentagon, especially in the top echelon of Navy leadership. By 1948, vice chief of Naval Operations and future JCS chairman, Admiral Arthur Radford, had gained a reputation within the Air Force for his strong opposition to its strategy. In November 1948, Symington told Forrestal that Radford "believes much of the future of the Navy lies in these attacks against the Air Force."[33] In October, the Navy's chief told a budget meeting of the JCS that his service "has honest and sincere misgiving as to the ability of the Air Force successfully to deliver by relatively low-performance bombers, deep into enemy territory in the face of strong Soviet air defenses, and to drop it on targets whose locations are not even accurately known."[34] Secretary of the Navy John Sullivan also attacked the Air Force mission. Symington alleged that Sullivan deliberately misquoted Spaatz during a meeting with Forrestal. Where Spaatz had said decisive bombing could not be mounted from US bases alone, Sullivan quoted him as saying the Air Force was incapable of sustained bombing.[35]

An earlier conflict had been waged over the Pacific Report of the US Strategic Bombing Survey. Both services approached that survey aware of its political implications. The Navy even feared it might lose control of carrier aviation to the Air Force. Rear Admiral Ralph Oftsie, who later played a prominent role in the B-36 hearings, led the Naval Analysis Division of the Pacific Survey while Maj. Gen. Orvil Anderson, later commandant of Air University, retired for advocating preventive war, led the Military Analysis Division. From the start, the divisions bickered over the report's scope. Oftsie directed his division to study

> all prior operations which brought us within striking range of the Japanese homeland, and without which there would have been no successful conclusion of the war. . . . The result of the Survey's effort . . . may well be the basis for the major decisions respecting our post-war national security. This may include the form of our military-naval organization, the relative "weight" of our respective armed forces.[36]

When Anderson argued that a study of the entire Pacific War was beyond the survey's charter, he was overruled. The two divisions went separate ways, writing reports that reflected their services' interests. Each believed the other's report was biased, each with some truth. Oftsie's staff accused Anderson's personnel of minimizing the role of carrier aviation in attacking Japan and distorting the superiority of air over naval power. Anderson's division retorted that the Naval Division had written less about the effects of strategic bombing on Japan than a paean to carrier task forces. As each side grew angrier, its draft reports became more partisan. Anderson's report bluntly concluded, "Airpower dominated its own element. Airpower dominated naval warfare. Airpower dominated ground warfare." Although each team objected to the publication of the other's report in the USSBS, both eventually were printed as supporting reports.[37] This bureaucratic infighting devalued the final reports and strengthened the extreme views each side had of the other's motives and integrity. The USSBS fight was cause and symptom of hostility.

Planning was central to that fighting because it was the nexus of war-fighting ideas and budgets. The major disagreement was over responsibilities in the Mediterranean, the focus of the Pincher plan. The Navy's struggle to put the carrier at the center of the atomic offensive and thereby of defense policy—and budget—encountered intense resistance. During the initial formulation of Pincher, which depended on securing Egypt and operating against the USSR from the Eastern Mediterranean, the JCS debated the carrier's role. In June 1946, Navy captain Matthias Gardner observed that the US and Royal Navies would have overwhelming surface and airpower, which any offensive must exploit. In line with the Air Force's position on airpower, Air Force Brig. Gen. Frank Everest agreed the initial effort against the Soviet Union must be undertaken by airpower based on land and at sea. He doubted, however that carrier-based aviation could strike vital Soviet centers. Not until 1949 would the Navy have a purpose-built atomic, bomb-carrying aircraft, the North American AJ Savage, with a combat radius of only 700 nautical miles (NM). Thus aircraft on a carrier in the Barents Sea, 1,200 NM from Moscow, or the Aegean, 1,500 NM away, could launch only one-way missions. Beyond the morale problems inherent in such attacks, to sustain an offensive would be difficult with these aircraft.[38] Even more: since the AJ was still on the drawing boards, the Navy lacked any aircraft able to strike the vast Soviet interior. As Hap Arnold rhetorically asked Symington, "What can a Navy do against Russia?"[39]

At another planning meeting, the Navy and Air Force representatives argued over control of the antisubmarine warfare (ASW) mission. Gardner wanted the Navy to control all sea-based aircraft conducting ASW, while Everest wished all aircraft performing the same mission to be under the same command. Since that threatened the loss of Navy autonomy, Gardner denounced the idea of dividing responsibility based on the type of landing gear an aircraft had. Everest found the shoreline an equally absurd border. When Gardner noted the Navy had aircraft and crews prepared for the mission, but the Air Force did not, Everest concluded that agreement was impossible because of fundamental differences between the two services. Gardner retorted that the Navy was compromising on some fundamental principles but the Army was conceding far less, and the Air Force nothing at all. Planning was grinding to a halt over interservice issues.[40]

One Air Force representative on the JSPC noted that when a subordinate admiral had his staff begin to plan for sea-based operations against Soviet airpower in the North Sea, the CNO "discouraged" the concept. If naval airpower was inefficient in the North Sea with British bases nearby, it would be less effective and more expensive in the Mediterranean.[41]

By 1948, during discussions over Bushwacker, the splits widened and become more formalized. Arguments were limited to the Mediterranean but still covered the strategic air offensive and the role of the carrier. In one split decision, the Navy argued that fast carrier task forces could launch atomic and conventional attacks that would saturate enemy defenses and distract Soviet bombers and fighters from other operations. The Air Force retorted that carrier task forces were a wasteful duplication of assets, while exposing them to Soviet attack was not justified by their small offensive force.[42] In March 1949, on the eve of the B-36 hearings, the Navy continued its efforts to make carrier task forces equal in the initial strategic air offensive. It wanted NSC-20/4 to direct an immediate strategic air offensive against not just "Soviet war making capacity," but also other "suitable targets of the Soviet Powers." Both the Air Force and Army opposed the change.[43]

As difficult as the Navy's role would have been with the new carrier, it was even more difficult without, as a series of exercises held in 1950 at the Naval War College showed. An observer reported that in one exercise, a judge ruled that two Soviet atomic bombs on the densely packed bridgehead of an amphibious invasion force had implausibly inflicted only "light damage." In another exercise simulating operations in the Eastern Mediterranean, however, more than one hundred Soviet aircraft attacked three carriers. Although the Soviets lost many bombers, the judges decided that in *this* case the carriers *had* been destroyed. The exercises demonstrated a key weakness of carrier in the atomic age, vulnerability in "enclosed waters." Soviet reconnaissance aircraft could find them while avoiding protective fighters. As carrier-borne attack aircraft had limited range, they had to maneuver close to the coast where they were vulnerable. An otherwise effective antiaircraft formation was vulnerable to an attack by high-altitude aircraft with atomic bombs.[44] The conclusion was clear: the carrier force that had assaulted Japan was ill-suited to an atomic campaign.

In 1950, when a student at the National War College asked LeMay what carriers would do in the strategic air offensive, he replied he had recently asked the naval officer on his staff to examine that issue: whether, for example, carrier aviation could provide fighter escort for bombers coming in from the North Sea. He was told that sea was too shallow for carriers to operate. SAC bombers operating in the Mediterranean similarly were out of luck; carriers must operate in the western half of the sea, taxing the range of their aircraft. LeMay asked whether submarines could pick up ditched aircrew. Since it would take twenty days to get submarines on station, by which time LeMay expected most of the offensive to be over, they would be of little help. He told his questioner, "To be perfectly frank with you, I don't know what the Navy is going to do when the war starts."[45] The CNO, Admiral Sherman, asked the chairman of the JCS to tell LeMay "privately and informally, that his statement, if made, is considered by the Joint Chiefs of Staff as unfortunate and inopportune."[46]

Attempts to insert carriers into the strategic air offensive offended air-atomic advocates' notions of efficiency and their attempt to control the atomic stockpile. After the war, an interdepartmental organization, the Armed Forces Special Weapons Project (AFSWP), linked the services and the Atomic Energy Commission, the custodian of atomic weapons. Among other responsibilities, AFSWP was responsible for training and weapon assembly.[47] In March 1948, the USAF chief of staff recommended that operational directives for AFSWP come solely from the Air Force, because it alone had atomic weapons. Clearer lines of authority would speed the delivery of atomic weapons to SAC in a crisis, reducing the time required to launch an offensive. The president's chief of staff, Admiral Leahy, rejected this request, because he believed the USAF wanted predelegated authority to use the weapons. Spaatz, in turn, asked that the USAF receive operational control of the AFSWP only when the president authorized an atomic offensive. The Army chief of staff, General Omar Bradley, and Spaatz, accepted modified wording that the AFSWP report to Spaatz on "all matters relating to the support of strategic air operations." The CNO, Admiral Louis Denfeld, rejected this change. Spaatz warned Forrestal that the Navy's opposition jeopardized not only the "rapid implementation of emergency war plans," but also command of the strategic air offensive.[48]

The two services also clashed over the definition of "balanced forces." The Navy argued that idea meant military spending should be divided evenly between the services. The Air Force retorted that strategic air offensive forces must take precedence in the budget because they had to be ready at the outbreak of war. It did not argue, however, that the Air Force should claim so much of the budget that the other services could not carry out their wartime roles. In 1945, Arnold told the Senate that "our security program must be balanced. The relative importance to our security of expenditures for the various arms must be considered on an overall basis."[49] In 1948, Symington told Forrestal that a balanced force was not man-for-man or dollar-for-dollar identical across the three services, but properly proportioned to carry out war plans.[50]

The last major interservice fight before the hearings was over the cancellation of the supercarrier, the USS *United States*. The carrier, radically different from wartime ships, weighed 65,000 tons and lacked an island. It was designed to launch and recover aircraft weighing 100,000 pounds, able to carry the atomic bomb. The Navy thought this vessel was a flexible instrument, able to launch moderate numbers of large aircraft with the most advanced weapons, or many smaller aircraft. According to Denfeld, the carrier was to be a "progressive improvement of naval capabilities," able to provide flexible firepower in many contingencies: sea control, antisubmarine warfare, mining, attacks on enemy forces in coastal areas, support of amphibious operations, and atomic attack, as directed by the JCS.[51]

Vandenberg told Forrestal that Denfeld's reasoning was wrong. The new ship with a few large bomber aircraft was useless for strategic air warfare or antisubmarine warfare. Bombers would only be exposed to air attack, while carriers could be struck by air, surface, and subsurface threats. Existing Air Force aircraft could best attack submarine bases, while the Navy's existing carriers could overwhelm the Soviet surface navy. The resources spent in buying and maintaining the carrier and its escorts could purchase far more bombers and bombardment capability.[52] Another contemporary concluded that five hundred B-36s (including bases) could be purchased for the cost of the USS *United States* and task force (not including supporting naval bases), which only included fifteen to twenty bombers.[53]

An article written after the B-36 hearing, but suppressed internally by the Air Force so as not to antagonize the Navy, concluded that carriers were uneconomical, vulnerable to attack, and "technologically out of phase." Contemporary carrier technology could not conduct the strategic air offensive. The USS *United States'* twenty bombers could launch merely five simultaneous atomic strikes, because accepted tactics demanded that other aircraft be dedicated to other roles like electronic countermeasures. At that rate, the carrier would take a year to accomplish what a land-based force could do in two weeks, despite the need to use maximum force in minimum time. The carrier also could not attack the real Soviet naval menace, submarines. At its core, asserted the author, the Navy's arguments ignored reality: a war against the Soviet Union would by geographic necessity be different from the Pacific War.[54]

Together with the content of war plans, Forrestal's cancellation of the USS *United States* confirmed the air-atomic orientation of national defense policy before the Korean War. The long campaign to expand the Navy's role in war plans and the budget died with the carrier, symbolizing the Navy's failure to adapt the atomic bomb to its mission. Despite its inability to sell a navalized version of the air-atomic strategy, the Navy continued to press for a broader role.

Air Force Exasperation

An internal Air Force study of the Navy's position just before the B-36 hearings illuminates the Air Force's view of the Navy and the hardening of its position. Its authors, colonels Ahring and Whisenand, working for the chief of staff, recommended a stronger Air Force public information campaign. It should follow the Navy's propagation of a "party line" and abandon its tolerant approach to military planning. Evolution had been accepted when revolution was needed. "The unsupportable and unrealistic theory of equality of land, sea and air forces was accepted— accepted because it walked on fewer toes and saved the faces of those responsible for the obsolete military machine with which we entered World War II."[55] Laden with "half-truth, untruth, distortion, and the reproduction of public records which have been deliberately altered," Navy tactics had crossed the line and required stronger Air Force counteraction.[56]

The authors identified five issues that "the admirals" had been using to discredit strategic airpower: distortion of the USSBS, testimony before the Eberstadt task force (formed by Secretary of Defense Forrestal to examine streamlining the Defense Department),[57] a public relations campaign by high-ranking officers, a history of the Pacific War that obscured the USAF role, and the portrayal of the cancellation of the USS *United States* as "an Air Force hatchet job."

The distortion of the bombing survey's results continued the fight that had occurred in its writing. The authors charged that an anonymous document (distinct from that which emerged at the B-36 hearing), written by a naval reserve captain, had been circulated to hundreds of newspapers in recent months. It deliberately misquoted the European survey to reverse its meaning and inserted parenthetical expressions to distort accurate quotes. It applied the survey's comments on the alleged ineffectiveness of RAF area bombing to the campaign as a whole, leaving readers to think the survey had concluded bombing was ineffective.[58]

A second Air Force study stated that the document was trying to impress six conclusions on their readers:

> First, that strategic bombing in war is illegal. Second, that "area bombing" and "strategic bombing" are interchangeable and synonymous terms. Third, that strategic bombing in World War II was a total failure [in] that war production actually increased under strategic bombing. Fourth, that only "tactical bombing" is effective. Fifth, that strategic bombing can never be conducted until air domination has been achieved. And sixth, the destructive power of the atomic bomb has been vastly over-rated—the atomic bomb is just another bomb.

To support that last point, the pamphlet alleged it would take eight hundred to a thousand atomic bombs to inflict damage equivalent to the Stalingrad campaign. This was a deliberate misquotation of a scientist who said that eight hundred to twelve hundred atomic bombs could inflict the same damage as the USSR had suffered in the entire war.[59]

Then, the colonels noted, the Navy portrayed the Okinawa campaign as proof carriers could dominate land-based airpower. Yet this claim ignored the role of USAAF bombers in striking Japanese airfields to slow Kamikaze attacks. Without this diversion of Air Force missions to support the Naval Task Force, the carrier attacks might have failed. By writing the Air Force out of that history, the Navy was turning the truth, the vulnerability of the carriers, into the opposite. In reality, said Ahring and Whisenand, the Pacific air war was won before November 1943, and land-based aircraft had scored 80 percent of the kills. When naval aviation reached Okinawa, they faced Japanese pilots with an average of only one hundred flying hours, who still put 40 percent of the carriers out of commission during 1944–45.[60] Whether Ahring and Whisenand's retort to the Navy's history is accurate is less important than the anger with which it was presented.[61]

The USAF, Ahring and Whisenand concluded, must recognize that its role and the air-atomic idea were not universally accepted. A fight must be waged within the government and public, through a concerted effort, led by a knowledgeable officer who could tell the "truth" about the Air Force's (and Navy's) record during World War II. Air Force leaders must enunciate a clear and uncompromising position, because national survival was at stake.[62]

The anonymous document that vexed Ahring and Whisenand was only one of several in circulation. Another that reached Republican congressmen and triggered the B-36 hearings alleged illegal tampering by Symington in the bomber's procurement. In exchange for contributions to Truman's 1948 election campaign, allegedly Symington ensured the purchase of a supposedly inadequate bomber. The Air Force was particularly irritated because the document drew on classified information that should not have been available outside the service. So sensitive was the B-36's poor performance that only two copies existed of the document that appeared to have been compromised. Norstad, the vice chief of staff, recalled that even the carbon copies had been destroyed. One copy was with the secretary or chief of staff, and the other in his safe. He asked the Office of Special Investigations (OSI), the Air Force's internal investigative force, to examine the situation. When the OSI commander argued that the locked safe in Norstad's secure office could have been opened, the vice chief insisted that was impossible. The OSI chief offered to break in himself. Two days later, he told Norstad the contents of a paper existed only in the safe, proving it could have been undetectably compromised. This convinced Norstad that the Navy had stolen the document.[63] True or not, this belief illustrates attitudes.[64]

Endgame

The anonymous document triggered the B-36 investigation, and the "Revolt of the Admirals." Although the investigation focused primarily on bomber procurement, the committee cast a wider net, including a study of "the effectiveness of strategic bombing to determine whether the nation is sound in following this concept to its present extent."[65] The air-atomic idea was on trial.

The first half of the investigation focused on the accusations of corruption. It closed when the committee uncovered the author of the anonymous document. Cedric Worth, a civilian employed in the Navy Department, admitted in open session to having written it, but unconvincingly claimed his superior (the undersecretary of the navy) knew nothing about the activity. He conceded that the accusations contained in the document, based on rumor, were false.[66] The hearings, however, continued to address the ideas of the strategic air offensive.

The Navy attacked the B-36 on many grounds: that it was technically incapable of the strategic air offensive mission, the Pacific War represented a proper concept for war, and the Navy had been shut out of the joint decision-making process. However, the core of its arguments directly attacked the ideas behind the strategic air offensive. They claimed strategic bombing was a flawed concept forced on the Joint Chiefs and was overemphasized to the detriment of other missions.[67] Had the Navy been able to convince the public or Congress any of these claims were true, it would have crippled the Air Force's position.

The Navy argued that unrestricted use of force was immoral; only precision bombing against military targets was acceptable, which constrained the use of any weapons. Accuracy, however, was impossible from high altitudes with an atomic bomb. Oftsie noted, correctly, that although strategic air warfare could encompass strikes against any part of an enemy society, in reality most targets were in cities.[68] Admiral Radford asked rhetorically, "Are we for or against mass bombing of non-combatants?"[69]

By contrast, dive bombing and low-altitude-level bombing—which current naval equipment could perform—minimized bloodshed while enabling the destruction of military targets. Indiscriminate bombing was counterproductive in the long term because it inevitably caused economic dislocation, requiring large infusions of American aid and increasing instability from which communism could grow. Oftsie, reflecting the thinking in NSC-20, testified that "a stable world economy may be impossible to achieve after another war if it [was] again attended by large scale destruction of the homes and cities of the belligerent nations."[70] Since the B-36 could conduct only high-altitude atomic bombing, it was incapable of precision attack and must cause the avoidable deaths of millions. It was an immoral, ineffective, and unsound weapon.[71]

The Air Force retorted with the classic air-atomic argument of efficiency: the initial atomic attack would shorten the war, increasing the chances of victory while reducing the cost. Success in modern war, Vandenberg argued, depended on the tight integration of war plans with industry, which was "vast, highly organized, and consequently vulnerable." Nations must operate their industries at peak loads to sustain a total war, and bombing could disrupt it. The ultimate goal of bombing was "crippling of the *sources* of enemy power—political, economic, and military—by direct attack" (emphasis in original).[72] To reject the only method of damaging the enemy's war potential, high-altitude atomic bombing, "deprives us of the opportunity of choking off enemy warmaking power at its source. It brings it about that the enemy's weapons have to be met and destroyed by our soldiers and tactical airmen while those weapons are shooting at them."[73] Symington, probably still incensed about the accusations of corruption made against him, remarked

> If war comes, we believe that the atomic bomb, plus the air power to deliver it, represent the one means of unleashing prompt crippling destruction on the enemy, with absolute minimum combat exposure of American lives. If it is preferable to engage in a war of attrition, one American life for one enemy life, then we are wrong. That is not our way. That is not the way in which the mass slaughter of American youth in an invasion of Japan was avoided. To whatever extent we can bring it about that weapons fashioned at Los Alamos, and carried in aircraft fashioned at Fort Worth, can destroy or diminish the power of an enemy to kill American soldiers, sailors and airmen, we are for pursuing that method.[74]

To Symington, the loss of civilian life was secondary to gaining the quickest victory possible, because that would save many American lives. War was immoral, not any particular method of waging it. Massive numbers of deaths were unavoidable in total war. The only solution was to shorten it as much as practicable. Anything less than maximum force would extend the war and its suffering for all parties. Finally, Vandenberg argued, the least brutal war is the one that is never fought. Strategic airpower was the most important and visible deterrent.[75]

The Navy argued that the air-atomic offensive was an Air Force concept forced on the Joint Chiefs without due consideration, with the Navy's position being ignored despite the need for consensus decision making. Indeed, the JCS really had not approved the idea of strategic air warfare with atomic bombs delivered by heavy bombers. Denfeld noted that the Weapons Systems Evaluation Group (WSEG) had just been established to assess the practicability of the strategic air offensive, which proved it was not universally accepted.[76] Radford stated that though congressmen could not do the kind of analytical work that WSEG did, "the big question that you have to decide up here is whether or not, by your conclusion, you approve of the strategic bombing blitz."[77] In effect, he told Congress, the new national defense machinery set up in 1947 could not judge the effectiveness of the air-atomic idea.

Air Force generals retorted that the strategic air offensive was a long-standing part of national war plans, which the Navy had supported. Strategic air bombardment had been embraced as a national strategy since Pearl Harbor. Wartime experience had been subjected to the USSBS's consideration, "the most thorough evaluation which any military operation has ever received." The Strategic Air Command, the only national force responsible for the strategic air offensive, took its operational orders directly from the Joint Chiefs, not its parent service. The JCS determined the target systems and targets, while WSEG, studied not only the air offensive, but many complex national defense problems.[78]

Finally, the Navy argued that the Air Force had overemphasized the strategic attack mission to the detriment of its other missions, while the B-36 had become a symbol of the "atomic blitz" theory of warfare, which promised cheap and easy victory. That was a dangerous illusion; there are no shortcuts in war. Oftsie warned, "Much emphasis has been placed upon the instant character of an offensive using atomic bombs. Among laymen this has produced an illusion of power."[79] Through this chimera, the Air Force had dangerously unbalanced the national defense. Unlike the USN, the USAF was inflexible. "It cannot be a useful part of the fighting team of all services which must stand ready to meet the potentially disastrous shock of an enemy's initial attack." By giving first priority to strategic bombing, the Air Force had created a force capable only of independent action, useless for supporting the other services. The exaggeration of the importance of strategic bombing had stifled acquisition of shorter ranged, but more flexible, jet bombers.[80]

Bradley retorted that neither the secretary of defense, the JCS, nor the Air Force war planners "believe we should depend solely on strategic bombing, or atomic weapons."[81] Rather, the capacity to conduct a strategic air offensive was a major deterrent to war, because it was based on a force-in-being. If deterrence failed, attacks on Soviet industry would reduce American losses and ensure eventual victory. USAF generals denied they had ever advocated cheap and easy war and noted the Joint Chiefs had determined the number of bombers needed. Even so, the number of B-36s in the Air Force was a small percentage of the inventory. In particular, Vandenberg denied that strategic bombing consumed a disproportionate share of the defense resources—"all eggs in one basket." Strategic Air Command operated less than one-third of the Air Force's total aircraft, and B-36s were only 5 percent of the total aircraft, flown by 4 percent of the personnel, and they could support ground troops if so ordered by JCS, which exercised direct control over targeting.[82]

Even casual observers saw the political content of the admirals' complaints. The premise that the Air Force had hijacked national defense policy was weak—to contend that the Joint Chiefs was a democratic organization working on unanimity, rather than a hierarchy supporting the secretary of defense, was unconvincing. Hierarchical structure formed the basis of the naval officer's experience throughout his career, as it does every American military service. Consensus building could never trump civilian supremacy in the unified military. Relations can be more or less amicable between the services, but they are peers, who must defer to higher authority. The wartime fight with MacArthur over Pacific strategy, with the ultimate resolution having to come from the president, shows that the Navy understood the process. The concern about the bluntness of the atomic offensive, that it inflicted too much damage, has a hollow ring. The Navy had not shied away from forms of economic warfare (blockade, unrestricted submarine warfare, or mining that damaged civilian as well as military targets) that targeted enemy societies.

Although the investigating committees rejected them, however, the USN's other premises had more substance. The idea that atomic bombing could lose the peace by destroying so much of the enemy's infrastructure that extremist ideologies could take root in chaos, leaving the United States to rebuild a devastated nation while combating insurgents, has a chillingly contemporary feel. This idea was doubly true if one assumed that only the United States would act this way, or feared that any atomic war would devastate both combatants. The admirals' complaint that the Air Force was concentrating unduly on the strategic air offensive also had a point. The balance between tactical and strategic bombers had changed dramatically in recent years, although less than what would prevail over the next decade. The admirals were pointing to a real trend, although putting more resources into strategic bombers arguably was correct at the time.

Of interest are a few assumptions on which both generals and admirals agreed. They spoke as though the United States would be the actor, not the object, of a strategic offensive. The references to Soviet capabilities lacked the edge of such discussions ten years later. The Navy did not focus on the vulnerability of US bases or bombers. The two services agreed on the general shape of the next war, which would be fought as a recognizable variant of World War II. Limited wars like Korea, let alone insurgencies like Vietnam, made no appearance.

The heart of the Navy's inability to convince the Congress and the public of its case was its lack of a viable alternative. Its arguments were negative attacks on the air-atomic idea, without a positive program to replace it. When confronting a heartland power, naval technology could not provide a convincing alternative to the intercontinental manned bomber. It would have been shocking had the Navy not vigorously fought to maintain its position. The admirals were in a fundamental sense correct: the Air Force was displacing them from the leading edge of American defense. To men who had formed their identities in the naval service, and seen their vision of war dramatically validated in Tokyo Bay, bowing to a different conception of security was asking too much. An Air Force observer at the Naval War College described naval officers as having five characteristics: "a strong identification with his service, professional pride, reliance upon authority, pride in rank, and relatively high educational attainment." These traits, combined with an intense respect for the traditions of the US and even the Royal Navy, combined to color attitudes toward the Air Force. Navy officers dismissed the new service as an "upstart and a fraud," that seemed an "inflated organization dealing in a rather unprofessional way with a lot of airplanes."[83] A service identified so strongly with tradition and with so recent a major victory was bound to fight vigorously to keep itself from being displaced.

The B-36 hearings had a decisive outcome. Admiral Denfeld was fired, following Secretary Matthews who had resigned on the cancellation of the USS *United*

States. It concluded the first round of Navy resistance to the Air Force, but it was only a setback, not a defeat. The Navy continued the struggle for control over the strategic offensive mission and still wanted, and would get in short order, its own capability for atomic delivery. The Navy's campaign, culminating in the hearings, influenced the Air Force as well. As the exasperated tone of Ahring and Whisenand's memoranda indicates, it may have hardened Air Force positions into even stronger support of the air-atomic offensive and a desire for vengeance. Not only had the Navy challenged the USAF, which required that the basics of the strategy be articulated, but it also had lost the argument. Congressional and public victory for their ideas must have felt like long-awaited validation.

The Air Force's reaction to the Navy's challenge provides an important lesson. The exasperation and defense showed the importance of organizational behavior. The Air Force did not react to strategic ideas alone. There were a few civilian critics of the air-atomic strategy even in the late 1940s. Some were prominent men, like Nobel Laureate and master of operational research, physicist P. M. S. Blackett. However, the Air Force did not feel compelled to counter their arguments publicly. Only when confronted with a threat against its newly won role, which if successful would have reduced the Air Force's budget and endangered its independence, did it vigorously react. The threat worthy of response was the one that threatened the budget and programs.

For the moment, that threat was gone. The new Air Force had placed itself in the national security hierarchy and, armed with the air-atomic strategy, had displaced the Navy from the leading edge. None of the three services was satisfied with its role, however, and fights continued. In the meantime, with the general war against the Soviet Union just over the horizon, the United States stumbled into a new kind of war, in which the strategic air offensive had little role.

Policy Confronts Reality in Korea

American involvement in Korea bridges the early and late air-atomic eras, and the Truman and Eisenhower administrations. The decisions then taken on atomic weapons set the stage for Eisenhower-era security policies and modes of decision making in subsequent crises. Strategic airpower had two phases in the Korean War. The first, from the outbreak of the conflict to mid-1952 featured a short strategic campaign, followed by large-scale uses of interdiction and tactical airpower. The second phase, starting in mid-1952 and lasting to the armistice, involved serious plans to extend the war to Manchuria, and possibly beyond.

The first campaign featured the USAF's traditional definition of strategic: industry. The enemy force-in-being was not a valid target for strategic airpower, only its potential. By August 1950, Maj. Gen. O'Donnell, commander of the Far East Air Forces (FEAF) Bomber Command, claimed that most North Korean industry had been destroyed, while attacks on Pyongyang had forced the communists to shift their government to Seoul.[84] In September, FEAF commander Lt. Gen. George Stratemeyer reported that the bombers had run out of targets. Everything on the initial list, which "represented the enemy's potential for making war on South Korea and on the forces of the United Nations," was destroyed.[85] The SAC official history recorded the strategic air campaign complete by 1 October. SAC units, subordinate to FEAF Bomber Command, had dropped 7,009 tons of bombs, 45 percent of which struck strategic targets, while the balance had supported land forces.[86] The campaign also proved the viability of SAC's mobility plan, which was central to the war plan.[87]

As the ground war ground on, the strategic campaign remained dormant. Two wartime USAF examinations agreed that after October 1950 airpower was purely a tactical affair. General Kenney, sent by Vandenberg to Korea to assess the air campaign, reported only on tactical operations. The "inflexible and stupid" North Korean Air Force knew little about aerial warfare. Despite this advantage, which threatened to inflate the USAF's self-confidence, the air campaign had many problems, ranging from insecure communications and poor coordination with the Navy to lazy bombing techniques that would fail against a "real anti-aircraft defense."[88] So, too, in January 1951 Lt. Gen. Glenn Barcus devoted just a few pages to the strategic effort. The five B-29 groups operating by 8 August gave a "significant bombing capability" to FEAF, which could not be fully used because of "the paucity of strategic targets in Korea, while the war potential of North Korean and Chinese forces resided outside Korean boundaries and was proscribed for attack." The bombers destroyed the few targets available, suffering fewer losses than against similar objectives during 1942–45. This success stemmed less from Bomber Command competence than North Korean incompetence, and B-29s had suffered unexpected difficulty against the MiG-15. Quantitative estimates of the effect of the strategic attacks on the ground campaign were impossible, but destroying the Wonson POL refinery had forced the Communists to bring in all their fuel from outside Korea, producing critical shortages for the North Korean Army (NKA) during battles along the Naktong River. When Barcus published his report, "the greatest difficult facing the B-29 units is the lack of suitable targets," which led FEAF inappropriately to use bombers to interdict rail lines.[89]

By *contemporary* definitions of "strategic," there were no viable targets in Korea after October 1950, but many outside the peninsula. The reconstituted North Korean Army and the Communist Chinese depended on logistics leading back to factories in Manchuria and the USSR. As Vandenberg told Congress, "strategic air power should go to the heart of the industrial centers to become reasonably efficient. Now, the source of the materiel that is coming to the Chinese Communists and the North Koreans is from Russia. Therefore, hitting across the Yalu, we could destroy or lay waste to all of Manchuria and the principal cities of China if we utilized the full power of the United States Air Force."[90]

Vandenberg tempered that conviction with what became a constant Air Force refrain: to destroy Manchurian industry would weaken SAC through attrition until it could not fight the USSR. "While we can lay the industrial potential of Russia today [to] waste, in my opinion, or we can lay the Manchurian countryside [to] waste, as well as the principal cities of China, we cannot do both."[91] Even in July 1950, Vandenberg warned Stratemeyer that the "considerable cost" of diverting B-29s to Korea could be justified only by their use against vital targets.[92] Soon, O'Donnell warned LeMay that Vandenberg's fears were being realized. FEAF, following MacArthur's direction, had set mission priorities in "exactly the wrong order," with close air support first, followed by air superiority, interdiction, and only last oil and industry. His direct advice to LeMay: "My only recommendation to you is—for God's sake!—never let a SAC unit go under a theater command again."[93]

In December, after the Chinese intervention, Vandenberg recommended that the Eighth Army be withdrawn and Korea abandoned, and the war continued by sea and air action against Manchurian industry. According to Assistant Secretary of State Dean Rusk, Vandenberg feared that Chinese intervention was a prelude to a larger war that the Soviet Union would start by summer. If so, time "would not work in our favor since we would not improve our ground potential significantly but would in that period have given the Soviets a chance to produce additional atomic bombs. He did not say specifically, but the implication was that it would be better for us to precipitate hostilities at an early date in order to prevent further USSR atomic buildup."[94] Here, Vandenberg walked a fine line between using his bombing capacity efficiently and weakening SAC's Emergency War Plan (EWP) mission. For his part, LeMay held that to divert any more bombers from SAC would cripple the national atomic capability.

After the immediate crisis of Chinese intervention passed, FEAF continued to clamor for more SAC bombers. Stratemeyer requested a strike by US-based B-36s on an unidentified North Korean target using tanker support. LeMay rejected this request for several reasons rooted in the need to keep SAC ready for EWP. Logistics would be difficult, because SAC already had too few spare engines, and must reserve its thirty-seven B-36s in service for wartime missions, because the rest were under repair or being upgraded.[95] Use of the B-36, identified with atomic bombs, might cause difficulties with allies.[96] A further request in June 1952 to assign SAC bombers to a non-SAC commander met the same rebuff. LeMay insisted that SAC forces must remain under the control of an organization cognizant of the EWP.[97]

As well as keeping tight control over SAC assets, and worrying that those in Korea were being used inefficiently, LeMay feared that any defeat could reduce the deterrent influence of SAC. During a daylight mission in October 1951, communist fighters intercepted eight B-29s, destroying three and damaging the rest. The bomber crews had become complacent, predictable and psychologically unprepared after months in which they had not been intercepted. Even worse, Bomber Command then scrubbed future daytime B-29 raids because no objectives justified the potential losses. Although B-29s could continue daytime missions, the cancellation was an "important propaganda victory for the enemy in that the ability of the US Air Force to operate its bombers during daylight hours was publicly discredited." As Communist Air Forces were developing a night intercept capability, LeMay feared a repetition of the same error. Heavy losses on a night-time raid, even if due to causes that could be corrected, would let the enemy "discredit the night bombing capability of the Air Force, in addition to its daylight capability, the entire concept and deterrent value of the Strategic Air Command would suffer."[98]

Korean operations also damaged SAC's deterrent and wartime capability when reserve pilots called back to active duty used a loophole to avoid serving, claiming a "fear of flying." In March 1952, LeMay issued an official policy letter addressing the issue. Since the start of the war, 129 officers had requested suspension from flying duty, stating they were afraid to fly. LeMay railed against this subterfuge. It displayed a "deplorable lack of the fine moral fiber and character demanded of a commissioned officer." Because SAC was the only effective force against the USSR, each crew carried grave responsibility. Those "are so heavy that we just can't afford to mollycoddle a few weak individuals who are unwilling to carry their fair share of the burden." Hence, all officers must fly on pain of court-martial.[99] LeMay told the Air Force personnel chief that the problem would snowball without such drastic measures.[100] This issue is indicative of the brittleness of SAC's strength during LeMay's early tenure, and his struggle to husband his resources for the main struggle against the USSR.

This draining of SAC strength was matched by reluctance to expand air attacks beyond Korea, so contradicting the core idea of strategic air doctrine—to attack enemy strength at its source. During the first two years of war, national policymakers considered and rejected escalation using conventional or atomic weapons. Thus, in July 1950, Secretary of State Acheson warned that expanding the war to China might bring in the USSR under the terms of their newly signed mutual defense treaty.[101] Later that month, the NSC considered that Manchurian targets could be attacked only after the PRC intervened.[102]

Time and again, when the NSC or JCS examined escalating horizontally, to attack Manchurian industry, or vertically, to use atomic weapons, they rejected the idea, because to do so would cause worldwide hostilities with the communist bloc, leaving Korea a tertiary theater which drained military resources from greater ones. In July 1950, the NSC directed that if major Soviet combat units became involved, "the U.S. should prepare to minimize its commitment in Korea and prepare to execute war plans."[103] The efficacy of escalation into China was doubtful as well, as bombing Manchuria would devastate the civilian population, but not slow the Chinese army. While transportation targets could be effective, "the results of air operations would be evidenced in the political, psychological, and economic fields with only indirect effects on the Chinese military capabilities."[104]

The diplomatic ramifications of escalation became apparent when Truman mentioned atomic weapons at a press conference on 30 November 1950. The British government had already expressed concern over horizontal escalation. Foreign Secretary Bevin advised the British ambassador to Washington that if China intervened, MacArthur should not expand the war outside Korea without permission from Truman, which should require "prior consultation between United States government and his Majesty's Government."[105] Not surprisingly, the Attlee government became alarmed when, in response to a question about the Chinese intervention, Truman replied there "always had been active consideration" of using the atomic bomb.[106] Acheson immediately sent clarifications to key embassies, saying that by law only the president could approve atomic attacks, which he had not done.[107]

Nonetheless, Prime Minister Attlee traveled to Washington for immediate consultations. The two leaders agreed "we do not wish to be bogged down in an all-out war with China" and that World War III should be prevented, or at least delayed. Truman hoped the conflict never would demand atomic bombing; he desired to "keep the Prime Minister at all times informed of developments which might bring about a change in the situation."[108] Attlee noted "we therefore do not want to bomb the industries in Manchuria and the various centers in China. As a matter of fact the Chinese get on without large industrial centers. In this respect they are like the Huns."[109]

This episode shows the limitations of air-atomic strategy in real conflict, in the first case where it emerged. Fears of horizontal and vertical escalation dominated every discussion of using strategic airpower against Manchuria. The consequences of conventional bombing, let alone atomic weapons, generated enough anxiety to demonstrate a major problem for both early and late air-atomic strategies: that it operated better as a threat than a tool.

As the war dragged on, the NSC and JCS again considered expanding the war by air attack on Manchuria. In March 1952, Vandenberg remarked, "In all of North Korea there are few targets worthy of the terrific punch that can be carried by medium and heavy bombers, and there is perhaps no target worth an atomic bomb. . . .

The industries of North Korea, and the ability of North Korea to support a war, [were] quickly destroyed in the early weeks of the conflict."[110] Chinese industry was a different matter. A July 1952 JCS paper concluded that the USSR and China were "extremely sensitive regarding the Manchurian industrial complex," while a threat to it could split the two communist powers.[111] In November 1952, Army Maj. Gen. Kenneth Nichols, chief of the Armed Forces Special Weapons Project, claimed that political benefits could accrue from using atomic weapons. The threat of precipitating a major war was worthwhile in order to convince enemy and ally that "we will utilize these powerful weapons whenever peace is disturbed."[112]

This was not idle speculation. During that month senior military leaders seriously considered atomic attack, with the goal of ending the war if the communists refused to sign an armistice. Their discussions reflected the military realities behind Eisenhower's political pledge to end the war in Korea. Gen. Mark Clark, overall commander in Korea, held that the only additional pressure his forces could deploy without reinforcements would be to extend the air war beyond the Yalu. Even if he received reinforcements, Clark planned first to smash enemy air and communication facilities in Manchuria and China before attacking on land. The air offensive would have two objectives: to disrupt support for communist forces in Korea and to divert enemy air forces from the front. This plan would require at least two more medium bomber wings.[113]

Whether the campaign would involve atomic weapons was a separate question. One Air Staff paper declared that "profitable atomic targets available in Manchuria are extremely limited. Sustained atomic operations, if confined to Manchurian targets, would result in the uneconomical expenditure of fissionable material" and risk escalation, with grave repercussions.[114] Nonetheless, Air Staff Intelligence assessed the required types and numbers of weapons to remove the PRC Air Force as a threat: that task demanded attacks on 203 air bases, requiring 190 35 KT bombs. To interdict Manchurian rail lines of communication involved attacks on rolling stock and repair facilities, and 37 more weapons. Known troop concentrations in Korea and Manchuria would need 4 more weapons and munitions storage another eight.[115]

The Chinese Communist Air Force (CCAF) topped this targeting list because it had become a formidable threat. In a miniature version of SAC's response to the Soviet offensive air threat in the Cold War, the immediate focus of a strategic air offensive changed from Manchurian industry to the CCAF. The Air Force plans chief advised Twining that "CCAF air offensive capability has now developed to the extent that success of either the CCAF or Allied Air Force in achieving air superiority may lie with the force that strikes the initial decisive blow."[116] The late air-atomic age had reached Korea, perhaps earlier than anywhere else.

Throughout the winter, as the new administration settled into the White House, the JCS argued over expansion of the war. In February, it produced a split paper on the objectives of an enlarged air campaign. The Army-Navy-Marine view called for an air offensive against Communist air bases in Manchuria, with follow-on attacks against lines of communication (LOCs). The plans were "indefinite as to purpose, extent and timing."[117] The Air Force proposed a more structured operation working in stages of increased pressure with reconnaissance followed by destruction of the CCAF and then interdiction of LOCs in Manchuria. The USAF also "more definitely states that destruction of the CCAF and interdiction of LOC's is more practicable with atomic weapons due to the inordinate tonnage of conventional bombs required and the attendant resulting attrition."[118] In the next month, the plans directorate reiterated to the JCS that the CCAF must be destroyed before any other "large scale attacks against China or Manchuria." This could most effectively be done with atomic weapons, although later missions could use either atomic or conventional weapons.[119]

By late March, the JCS adopted the Air Force's line, and late air-atomic thinking. JCS 1776 stated that atomic attacks would destroy CCAF bases quickly, something "especially desirable because of its increasing offensive threat to U.N. security."[120] The CIA estimated that the threat of destruction of Manchurian industry would force China to reach an armistice, although a simultaneous ground advance into North Korea might bring in Soviet aircraft. The use of atomic bombs would show determination, although that might not force Communist concessions and an armistice.[121]

By May, the plans were firming up. The USAF Plans chief recommended to the NSC that atomic weapons "should be used as an integral part of any offensive course of action which extends air operations beyond present limitations." The initial attack would require 138 bombs against fixed sites and a few more for transportation targets.[122] LeMay urged that the atomic portion of an attack precede any naval or ground action, to maximize security and surprise, while if atomic weapons were used bombers should revert to SAC control, a position with which the Air Staff agreed.[123] By the time the combatants signed the armistice on 27 July 1953, an air-atomic offensive, complete with centralized SAC control, had reached advanced planning. At least one postwar evaluation concluded that the threat of atomic attacks had produced the armistice. A 1954 internal Air Force document stated "there is good reason to believe that speculation as to US intentions to employ atomic weapons against China in Manchuria was largely responsible for the communist decision to agree to an armistice."[124] To the Air Force, this claim proved the diplomatic power of a threatened air-atomic offensive. It also strengthened Eisenhower's resolve to use SAC as a diplomatic tool to avoid war.

Like contemporary thinking about strategic airpower in the Second World War, however, these conclusions on the effectiveness of the atomic threat in hastening the signing of the armistice do not reflect current historiography. Most historians believe that the atomic threat was never clearly communicated to the Communist combatants by the Indian intermediaries. The conclusion of the war stemmed from a complex series of factors, most prominently the death of Stalin and subsequent power struggle in the Kremlin, unrest in Eastern Europe, and generalized fears of continued war, rather than a specific atomic threat.[125]

The Korean War demonstrates several points about strategic air thinking. The shift from early to late air-atomic thinking is evident in the differences between the contemplation of attacks on Manchurian industry in 1950, and the blunting offensive of 1953. Furthermore, the enemy was impressed by the general threat of atomic weapons, particularly when wielded by an administration that was vocally friendly to atomic use. A 1952 RAND study found the official Communist line minimizing the importance of the weapon had been ineffective with their troops, for whom the "mental image of the destructive powers of the A-bomb is exaggerated."[126] Misunderstanding of airpower extended to higher ranks of the Communist armed forces. In an August 1951 speech, Vandenberg told his audience that North Korean General Nam Il, during a "harangue" at the armistice table, expressed his outrage over the effectiveness of air attack in preventing a communist victory, mischaracterizing that use as "strategic" when in fact it was interdiction. "What we call 'strategic' air attack was scarcely used at all in Korea, because the real 'strategic' targets— the root sources of enemy war production— lay outside Korea."[127]

Despite grudging enemy praise, strategic airpower advocates viewed Korea with dissatisfaction. Inherent in early and late air-atomic views of strategic combat was the idea that unrestricted violence should be applied until a decision, the quicker, the better. A 1951 *Air University Quarterly Review* article claimed the Korean War had "heavily underscored the strategic doctrine of the USAF." It dragged on without decision because strategic airpower could not be applied against the enemy's sources of power, sheltered behind an inviolate border.[128]

Postwar Air Force opinion hardened around this idea. LeMay told a 1958 Naval War College audience that "we did not exploit our airpower in Korea. . . . [Our] objective was vague, our offensive was limited and our combat power was not employed to its fullest extent."[129] Similarly, in 1965, Twining told an interviewer that although tactical airpower did a "wonderful job," the sanctuaries prevented heavy bombers from "doing the job they could have done."[130]

Although the term was not used, the sensing of an idea of an "atomic taboo" frustrated the Air Force. Because strategic airpower and atomic weapons were inseparable in an air-atomic theory, hesitance to use atomic weapons or attack distant sources of enemy strength stymied both. Korea hinted at an inherent limit of an air-atomic strategy in limited wars. Horizontal escalation, attacks on targets in an expanded area, and vertical escalation, use of weapons of increased violence, had become one and the same.

The Air Force emerged from Korea much as it had from World War II. Its leaders were convinced that strategic airpower doctrine had been reinforced, even if the example was largely negative. And just as it had after V-J Day, it confronted a new strategic reality, this time created by thermonuclear weapons and a nascent Soviet air-atomic force. The institution's reaction was like that of most organizations convinced of their own success but faced with a new challenge. It was time to buckle down and work harder.

4

THE FANTASTIC COMPRESSION OF TIME

The most important change to the air-atomic strategy in the 1950s was the compression of time. The "time factor" forced SAC to act ever more rapidly: defensively so to escape destruction, offensively in order to achieve a meaningful victory. The timescale for decision shrank from months to days to hours. This had uncontrolled, uncontrollable, and unintended consequences. It led to one of the largest and most complex weapons procurements in history, and an unusual military situation. By the end of the 1950s, SAC was well positioned to launch a first strike, but not to absorb one. Its efforts to overcome this dilemma led it toward a razor edge of preparation and to ideas of preemption and a policy which required politicians to be willing to destroy the world on a hair trigger. Air-atomic strategy was no longer balanced with other forms of military power, but threatened to eat them alive. This chapter will examine the time factor itself, its impact on thinking within the Air Force, its consequences on planning for a campaign against the Soviet Union, and the perceived shape of future conflict.

The causes for the change in the time factor fall in two broad categories: Soviet strategic power and technological change. The rise of a Soviet air-atomic force able to target the United States put the timer in motion, while technological progress dialed in ever shorter time limits. Both categories are necessary but neither is sufficient on its own to explain the dramatic changes to air-atomic thinking during the 1950s. Only the combination of a hostile Soviet atomic threat and missile technology can account for the dramatic effects of the time factor.

Enemy in the Mirror

The fact of Soviet capability changed how the Air Force thought about strategic airpower in general war. By mid-1950, SAC compared Soviet ability to its own at its nadir in 1947.[1] In 1951, a CIA study reiterated SAC's estimate that the Soviets had just a crude attack capacity with the Tu-4 Bull, a Soviet copy of the US World War II–era B-29, as its only aircraft able to reach US targets. Except for Alaska and the area around Seattle, the Bull had to fly a near suicidal one-way mission to reach the continental US at all. A small Soviet stockpile, estimated at no more than 100 weapons by mid-1952, crippled SUSAC, or "Soviet Union SAC," contemporary shorthand for Soviet atomic capability, which was actually located in the Long Range Aviation (LRA) and, after 1959, the Strategic Rocket Forces (SRF).[2]

The same estimates addressed how the Soviets would use their limited means. Analysts agreed that SUSAC's best target would be American atomic forces.[3] The Soviets would apply classical Douhetan theory, directing an exchange of offensive blows until one side achieved superiority. The expectation of SUSAC's behavior was a mirror-image of what air-atomic advocates wanted to do themselves in the best of all possible worlds—launch a disarming surprise attack.

The threat posed by ordinary bombers, minuscule relative to what SAC could inflict, was still large in an absolute sense. The Air Force Plans chief told Congress in 1950 the Soviets could "knock out" SAC by the middle of 1951.[4] In December 1950, an NSC estimate projected that an attack in 1954 would inflict 3 million casualties and render homeless 7 million more.[5] With even a crude ability, the Soviet Air Force posed a serious threat.

The reality of Soviet capability in the 1950s was not nearly what the Air Force or the intelligence community feared. The Soviets were indeed racing as fast as they could in the nuclear arms race, but in the early years, their pace was slow. The Bull only reached operational units in large numbers at the time when the B-29 proved itself unable to cope with modern jet fighters in Korea. The bomber's short range and the Soviet Union's inability to place it at overseas bases near North America further crippled LRA's real-world capability. In 1953 the USSR had fewer than a dozen atomic bombs, while the US had over thirteen hundred; hence, Steven Zaloga concludes that "the shortcomings of the Soviet nuclear forces were so severe that it is doubtful that Stalin ever seriously considered their employment in a strike against the United States."[6]

A second generation of Soviet bombers fared little better after Stalin's death. The M-4 (Bison A) jet bomber, handmade in small production batches, had a range of only 5,500 miles. Only 33 aircraft were produced, nine crashed between 1955 and 1958, and the remainder were converted to tankers in the early 1960s. The M-6 (Bison B) featured an improved range, up to 9,300 miles with refueling, but its engines required major overhaul after only 100 hours of flying, drastically reducing their utility. At no time did the USSR have more than 60 Bisons in service of the 116 manufactured. In 1957, the Tu-95 (Bear) joined the Bisons. Although ultimately a very successful aircraft, the Bear's first few years were plagued by engine problems. Other issues further degraded the LRA's operations. Rather than fly nuclear armed sorties, as SAC did in the late 1950s, Soviet alert bombers were kept unarmed. The arming process could take two hours, because the weapons had to be transferred from KGB custody (until 1959) held on a separate part of bases.[7]

Despite these limitations, planners had to create forces fit to deal not with today's marginal enemy but tomorrow's dangerous one. The United States could not be sure of the technical flaws in Soviet aircraft and would have been unwise to assume its enemy was incompetent. Soviet deception aimed to exaggerate their strength, and their spectacular scientific success, ranging from the fast development of atomic and hydrogen weapons to Sputnik, forced US planners to treat Soviet nuclear power very seriously. While the LRA was fundamentally flawed in the 1950s, and according to Richard Rhodes far less effective than SAC as late as 1962, Soviet strategic forces did reach real parity by the late 1960s, although that was only evident in hindsight.[8] The problems in accurately estimating Soviet strategic capability and intentions were remarkably difficult. The continued inaccessibility of Soviet records keeps it so.[9] The opacity of any military development program, combined with a tightly closed society and an active deception program made for ambiguous intelligence. As John Prados points out, this left room for organizational biases to run rampant.[10] For the Air Force and SAC, convinced there was one best way to apply airpower, this meant a tendency to mirror-image their own capabilities and objectives. Thus SUSAC did not exist, yet it remains a more meaningful term than those who coined it in the 1950s thought, because it shows the source of their own fears much better than it does its real-world counterpart, the LRA.

Technology Accelerates the Clock

If the rudimentary Soviet bomber threat fixed the notion of a time frame in which action must be taken, then rapid technological advance drastically shortened the interval for action. Dangerous progress was made in the development of weapons and delivery systems. As Thomas Power told a civilian audience in 1959, the "fantastic compression of time—both warning time and reaction time—which has resulted from the rapid advances in military technology" posed a dramatic problem for SAC.[11]

The fusion bomb was the first major advance to accelerate the time factor. Air Force leaders recognized the new weapon as being qualitatively different from fission bombs. In 1955, LeMay told an audience that hydrogen weapons revolutionized the rate of war. "Years of war, as we once knew it, can now be capsuled [*sic*] into hours. All of the firepower of four World War II years can now be laid down between sunup and sundown."[12] This new scale of destruction changed fundamental notions of warfare. As Twining said, military principles had been rewritten: mass must be measured in megatons.[13] The prospects for offensive operations were clear. More powerful weapons were likelier both to destroy any particular target, and others in the same area. Fewer aircraft could have the same effect, just as one atom bomber could do the job of hundreds of conventional ones. The new weapon amplified the air-atomic principle of maximizing shock but also made the few Soviet bombers a greater threat. The offensive promise of the new weapons was also a defensive worry. Just as they increased SAC's potency, shortening the time needed for "decisive effect," they increased the threat to its aircraft.

Complementing changes in weapons were those in delivery systems. Aircraft technology underwent rapid improvement just after the war. Jet engines, swept wings, and electronics all enabled the manned bomber to fly higher and faster. Each new aircraft was aimed to penetrate Soviet defenses by flying above them or rapidly through them. LeMay's command diary recorded his confidence that technological progress should be pushed to extreme limits. "He didn't feel we should stop short of the highest performance possible."[14] SAC's aircraft embodied this principle. The most advanced version of the B-50, the premier medium bomber of 1950, could reach 30,000 feet and bursts of speed up to 340 knots.[15] Ten years later, the B-58 operated at 58,000 feet and 1,150 knots.[16]

These key characteristics of speed and altitude, with their implications for reaching targets faster (and of letting Soviet aircraft do the same to SAC bases) were further embodied in ballistic missiles. In abstract, missiles were the perfect advanced bombers, with unmatched speed and ability to evade defenses, although in reality they had technological frailties. However, the promise—and threat—of missile-delivered hydrogen weapons accelerated the time factor by another notch for both strategic offense and defense. Combined with the destructive power of thermonuclear weapons, the potential to inflict unsustainable shock through simultaneous destruction of many targets in a few hours deeply shaped airpower. However, these weapons did not enter service overnight. The offensive power and defensive problem grew, but incrementally. So, too, the reaction to them was conservative, adapting existing procedures by steps to cope with possibilities.

The change in the time factor took its most concrete form in the idea of "warning time," classified as being either "strategic" or "tactical." The former encompassed situations where a Soviet intent to attack was known days or weeks beforehand. The latter occurred only when an actual attack was underway. One form of warning might exist without the other. The worst case, with neither form, constituted a surprise attack. By 1954, a National Intelligence Estimate (NIE) concluded that the preparations for a major Soviet assault (defined as involving 850 aircraft) would give strategic warning of fifteen to thirty days.[17] The next year, the NSC published the first agreed list of "indicators and warnings" of a Soviet attack. The first of its three categories were unambiguous signs of imminent Soviet attack, effectively tactical warning, including items such as penetration of North American radar coverage, Soviet attacks on NATO allies, and large concentrations of Soviet submarines in American coastal waters. The second category showed that attack "probably" was imminent, including Soviet aircraft in a flight pattern able to reach North America, extensive preparation of long-range aircraft for offensive operations, delivery of an ultimatum under threat of attack, and attempts to assassinate American officials. Actions that could be a prelude to Soviet attack, or cause a crisis that would lead to one, made up the final and most ambiguous category of indicators. They ranged from Soviet ultimata to NATO or Japan, to setting up beacons to guide Soviet bombers to their targets in the United States, to distribution of weapons to American communists.[18]

The next year's NIE, through these firmed up indicators and better intelligence, anticipated a "generalized degree of warning" of up to six months before a maximum-effort Soviet attack. The growing problem was a surprise attack by a few aircraft. The 1955 NIE concluded that up to 250 aircraft could launch a surprise attack.[19] The 1957 NIE estimated that 300 Soviet aircraft, augmented by submarine-launched missiles, could do so.[20] By 1959, in JCS studies, submarine-launched ballistic missile attack had reduced the definition of acceptable tactical warning to only five minutes.[21]

Though SAC overestimated Soviet power at any point, these assessments became true with a lag of a few years. Every year, a larger and more sophisticated LRA (and SRF) gained an incrementally greater potential to attack with nothing more than tactical warning. This fact, combined with Soviet thermonuclear capability and more sophisticated aircraft and missiles, increased SAC's vulnerability to Soviet attack. That threat was recognized as early as 1953. The geographic scope of the danger gradually extended from SAC's bases overseas to all of them, including those in North America. Intercontinental and submarine-launched missiles dramatically increased the threat of a successful preemptive attack on SAC. A 1960 Air Force estimate, concluded that, depending on assumptions, between 100 and 430 missiles could disable SAC. Both cases placed unverifiable confidence in Soviet quality and grossly overestimated Soviet missile quantity.[22] However, the basic premise—that uninterceptable Soviet ballistic missiles were a grave threat to SAC airbases—is valid.

This situation was unique in the short history of strategic airpower. Despite appearing in Douhet's original vision, it was the first time that two strategic air forces would simultaneously and systematically attack one other, with both sides having the capability of inflicting decisive damage on the other. In 1940, for example, the German air campaign against Britain had concentrated on the RAF, which had not simultaneously and systematically struck back at the Luftwaffe. From that point, with tiny exceptions, until the end of the war, one side attacked and the other defended. By 1954, the time factor made SAC and SUSAC simultaneous object and verb.

The Air Force's reaction to the time factor was simple: stay ahead. Technologically, air-atomic advocates pushed weapon systems steadily forward. Ballistic missiles joined—but did not replace—higher and faster bombers from 1957. These improved weapons were essential to striking fast. Throughout the 1950s, SAC pared away at the time to launch a decisive attack. A 1952 editorial in *Air University Quarterly Review* stated, "We must, in a sense, take off when we hear the enemy warming his engines."[23] The essential idea was to hit the Soviets decisively before they could react. A similar ideal can be discerned in Col. John Boyd's later idea of staying inside the enemy's decision cycle. Unlike Boyd's idea, the late air-atomic campaign depended on maximizing shock to accomplish the mission. Rapid reaction and overwhelming firepower would win the day.

Just as the transition from conventional to early air-atomic strategy was incremental, so was the shift to the late air-atomic ideas. The set of measurements that showed the effectiveness of SAC could be maintained and intensified. Accuracies could become tighter, aircraft faster and more numerous.

The intensifying of the time factor shaped the broad ideas the Air Force held about airpower, and its operations plans and ideas about future warfare, as reflected in procurement of new weapon systems. Strategists claimed that the very nature of war had been altered by the foreshortened time frame; decisive victory or defeat would be achieved in a matter of hours. The key consistency between the early and late eras was that the goal remained victory and the primary tactic was the offensive-defense. That is, American lives would be preserved by disrupting the Soviet attack through SAC's own offensive. Ideally, it would destroy Soviet weapons at their source.

In a 1951 lecture, Col. George Brown, a member of the Air War College Faculty, outlined three distinct schools of strategic air thought. The most conservative thinkers, typified by Admiral Oftsie, thought airpower would be effective only when used against transportation and fuel systems. To attack industry more generally was pointless and immoral. The second group thought only industry was a suitable target, while airpower was one part of an extended joint effort, as outlined in the plans of the late 1940s. Brown told his audience that a third group saw the revolutionary potential of atomic firepower. "These people reason that air power as we know it now can kill a nation; that industrial destruction is only a part of possible results."[24]

The new factor in USAF thinking was the perception of airpower's decisive capability. While the mainstream of airpower thought always had recognized the decisive potential of airpower, actual plans had recognized that other services were needed to win the war. Airpower gutted the enemy's military-industrial potential and created conditions for traditional invasion and occupation. Airpower was all the United States could do until mobilization. Part of air-atomic age thinking rejected these ideas as conservative. Plans chief, Maj. Gen. Robert Lee, told a group assembled in 1953 to determine the Air Force's overarching objectives that airpower now was "the primary or decisive instrument of implementing national policy."[25] In this new environment, airpower acted because it must defend the United States by destroying Soviet strategic capability. Whereas in the past, if airpower had failed to act, the United States still could mobilize forces, in the late air-atomic era, it must act immediately to avoid instant defeat. If it succeeded, moreover, airpower would inflict such grievous harm as to achieve decisive victory. Defense meant attack. As the plans division advised in 1951, in the first thirty days of war, the USAF must simultaneously destroy Soviet bombers and industrial capability. If this task was done correctly "our ultimate military victory is assured," if not, "our ultimate military defeat is most probable."[26] The minimum capacity to achieve these aims was termed the "Survival Force." The initial air offensive force, and the units needed to defend and support it, comprised this essential organization. Every other element of the armed forces must take a lower priority, because "the principal threats to survival are air threats, and the survival tasks are air tasks."[27]

In this thinking, airpower had new offensive and defensive roles. In the early air-atomic age, airpower held the promise of destroying the enemy's military potential but could not stop its force-in-being. In the late air-atomic age, the Soviet center of gravity was redefined as SUSAC. Given its increased lethality, SAC held that once it accomplished the blunting and disruption objectives, it could defeat the Soviet Union automatically. Soviet ground forces could not move or live in such an environment. Lt. Gen. Lawrence Kuter, commander of Air University, wrote in *Air Force* magazine, "Surface forces may never again be able to mass and maneuver with virtual immunity from devastating air attack."[28] By the mid-1950s, strategic airpower advocates believed that airpower could destroy both the enemy's military potential and his force-in-being. During the 1955 fiscal year budget fight, the Air Staff declared "that the introduction of [fusion] weapons has changed the basic nature of war. The Air Force believes that both the enemy military force in being and the war sustaining resources can be effectively neutralized by air action."[29]

Several effects flowed from the conviction that war had fundamentally changed. The first was certainty that any general war must be atomic. Air Force leaders became convinced they must make national leaders share their conviction, because any hesitation to use atomic weapons in war could cause defeat. There would be no time to educate them during a crisis. As Chief of Staff Nathan Twining told the assembled Air Force generals in 1954,

> They just don't know—they just don't appreciate what this bomb is and what it can do; they just think they are horrible and drop the subject and won't discuss it—and that's about the situation in this world today, except in this country. Certainly if we ever depart from the fact that this is another munition, purely, we are going to use it when it is to the best interests of the United States to use it, we have lost this one.[30]

Instant Readiness

Another concomitant of these beliefs was the idea that traditional strategy and forces were useless. By 1960, the chief of long-range plans declared that "the success of any attempt to fight conventionally is questionable on the basis of staying power alone."[31] Spending on conventional forces was wasteful, because it detracted from the deterrent/survival force, yet still could not withstand the much larger Red Army. LeMay told the assembled generals at the 1956 Commander's Conference that "we are spending an enormous amount of money in National Defense, and we are spending half of it . . . on a military machine that I feel in 1958 will get licked in ten days."[32]

Mobilizing those conventional forces was equally wasteful. In 1953, the USAF plans chief declared the United States could no longer depend on mobilization.[33] This became official policy in the first basic Air Force doctrine manual, which affirmed "the conventional build-up phase subsequent to the initiation of hostilities and preparatory to taking the offensive may no longer be necessary and, in any event, can no longer be assured."[34] In the following year, Vice Chief of Staff Thomas White wrote that the "coming of age of the long-range bomber and the development of nuclear weapons have shredded the old timetables of military planning."[35] Senior planners realized this would be a major point of friction with the other services. Col. James Whisenand contrasted the "Airman's" view with that of soldiers and sailors whose "strategic thinking is dominated by the post

D-Day mobilization concept."[36] Another planner, Col. Robert Richardson, summarized the changed nature of war succinctly when he said that while success in preatomic (and early air-atomic) war depended on the forces and a mission, in the late air-atomic age, it also depended on posture. While the other services depended on building forces and shifting them into place, strategic airpower was the only facet of military power that could adequately be prepared to act instantly, to maintain the hair-trigger posture required for success in the new age.[37]

The tightening of the time factor also reinforced and subtly changed the offensive-defense strategy. The notion that airpower was an innately offensive weapon did not alter but the role of the offensive strike did. In early air-atomic thinking, airpower struck at the enemy's military potential. In late air-atomic strategy, the target was SUSAC and its threat. The offensive-defensive was more immediate in effect and in failure more devastating.

The obverse of reliance on offensive means of defense was a certainty that traditional means were futile. Given its fusion weapons and sophisticated delivery systems, SUSAC could not be stopped in the air, but only on the ground. A 1953 SAC/Air Defense Command (ADC) exercise pitted ninety-eight bombers against US targets over a two-day period protected by interceptors on alert. ADC intercepted just six aircraft.[38] A 1954 three-volume Air University study concluded that in the best case, active air defense, built with unlimited funds, could destroy only 30 percent of an attacking force.[39] Even if it destroyed 95 percent of incoming bombers, a few "leakers" could inflict unacceptable damage. Given the history of air defense these views were strong, despite SAC's gross overestimate of Soviet strength. In the years after the 1954 study, the steady improvement of Soviet bombers and missiles made defense even less plausible. The answer was clear in the real world, as well as the one Americans imagined. The nuclear offense would save more US lives than defense could do. In 1952, Twining told the Senate that because "a bomber attack, pressed home in force and with resolution, will always break through," a principal element of US air defense was "long range counterair attack . . . a function of our continental defense, [that] falls to the Strategic Air Command."[40]

Reliance on the offensive-defense had several effects. Because SUSAC, the primary target, always was mirror-imaged to behave as SAC, superiority over it must be maintained. If SUSAC gained parity with SAC, no offensive-defensive effort could be sufficient, yet just like SAC, SUSAC would develop as fast and far as it could. Reinforcing this idea was the reality that because of national policy, SAC would never begin hostilities, but must be prepared to act second, at best with tactical surprise and at worst a victim of it and yet somehow still smash SUSAC on the ground. Retired Lt. Gen. Ennis Whitehead summarized this effect in 1957. "We must continuously maintain forces much larger than [the] USSR does if we are to be able to destroy her with that portion of our forces which escape destruction should she conduct a surprise attack. Therefore we need not equality of our long range strike force but rather an overwhelming superiority."[41] Acceptance of the offensive-defense strategy also further tightened the time factor, by creating a positive incentive to strike quickly. SAC needed to scramble from its bases to avoid destruction, and to hit fast—indeed, first—so to perform its mission. Greater speed saved American lives. In 1956, Twining told the Armed Forces Staff College, "Every hour of every day that we shorten the air battle means thousands, perhaps millions, of American lives saved; and millions, perhaps billions, of our dollars saved."[42] LeMay tied the same idea to traditional airpower strategy when he told Georgetown students, "No military man likes to fight, and if he does get into a fight, he wants to get it over as soon as possible. To do that, you have to use the most efficient means at your disposal."[43]

Carrying out the offensive-defense strategy required a force-in-being, as had earlier industrial targeting, but SAC now fulfilled two roles. The nation's essential defensive force in wartime—the "survival force," was indivisible from the deterrent force of peace. As LeMay said, "The way to prevent global nuclear war is to be undeniably and convincingly ready to win it without question."[44] In 1956, SAC assigned the deterrent force several roles: to inflict unacceptable damage on an aggressor, be overawingly superior in size to the enemy's force, be able to "blanket" targets despite losses, and be inseparable from the wartime "survival force."[45] The deterrent power of the force-in-being grew directly from its war-winning potential. A force that could not win a war could not deter one.

This notion also assumed a meaningful victory could be won in nuclear war. The 1954 Air University study concluded that victory in the hydrogen age was the same as it had always been: to compel the enemy to submit to American political will. That objective could best be accomplished by denying an aggressor any chance of victory, a condition which historically occurred when its force-in-being was destroyed. In the nuclear air age, that situation placed the enemy "in a hopeless position because everything it desired to protect lay open to progressive destruction."[46] In striking contrast to McNamara's later definition of Assured Destruction, the study rejected the idea that defeat arose from the loss of some arbitrary proportion of American population or industrial strength.[47] American civilian losses simply were defined out of the equation. In public, even the most strident air-atomic advocates sometimes balked from calling the outcome of a nuclear exchange "victory," but their message remained the same: we must compel the enemy to do our will. In 1958, Power told a civilian audience that "in a nuclear war, there are no winners, only different degrees of losers. If such a war should be forced upon us, we could not escape much devastation and loss of life, even though we should be victorious in the end—that is, prevent the aggressor from forcing his will upon us."[48] What mattered was the position relative to the enemy at the end of the exchange. As White told an AP reporter in 1960, the nation with the better offense and defense will "come out relatively better off than the other fellow."[49] This definition of victory, the emphasis on winning it with the force-in-being, reinforced the necessity of superiority.

The doctrinal manuals published by the Air Force from the early 1950s captured the shifts in thinking. Until 1953, with the approval of Air Force Manual (AFM) 1-2, there was no official Air Force doctrine. AFM 1-2 was a good summary of early air-atomic thinking. It stressed attack on enemy industrial potential and other ideas that had been refined since 1945. However, its 1955 edition reflected the transition to late air-atomic thinking. Representative of this shift was a change from a focus on "air superiority," effectively a tactical term used, as during World War II, to denote the dominance of an air force in a theater, to one of "air control," which the 1955 AFM 1-2 defined as "achieved when air forces, in peace or in war, can affect the desired degrees of influence over other specific nations."[50] This explicit link between peace and wartime mirrored the continuity between deterrent and survival forces. Not incidentally, the language also implied a connection to the well-established idea of "sea control" long used by the Navy. Although it included the wartime air superiority function, air control was a more ambitious idea, demonstrating SAC's prominence in the new age.[51] It approached the RAF concept of "air control," the use of air forces to maintain imperial rule in overseas colonies.[52]

The two versions of AFM 1-2 also differed over the basic role of force in national affairs. The 1953 version rejected force as all but a last resort. "War is never the chosen instrument of United States national policy. Military force is the court of last resort, to be forcibly applied only after all other instruments of national policy have failed to avert the threat to the security of the United States." The 1955 update, however, described a continuous conflict between nations, in which "any elements of a nation's power, or all elements, may be used, as required, to gain its desired ends through courses of action which are consistent with its national policies" in war or peace.[53] As with the redefinition of air control, this phrasing was a deliberate updating of doctrine to reflect a new era. At any point along the continuum of conflict from deterrence to devastation, the United States might employ any instrument of policy, including armed force or atomic weapons. To justify the change, Kuter argued "it is possible that circumstances could come about in which the only choice would be between domination by the communists as one alternative and war, as the other. . . . Would it be acceptable for us to have doctrine which stopped short of this reality?"[54]

The continuities in these ideas were at least as important as were changing ideas about war and the role of strategic airpower. Even though the target had changed from enemy potential to actual strength, the offensive still was at the center of airpower theory. The need to strike as early as possible, crystallized in the survival force concept, was just an intensification of earlier plans for the strategic offensive. Most important, the central role of atomic weapons still was to gain victory over an opponent.

USAF officers shared one doctrine, but there was not uniform support for the unconstrained growth of late air-atomic strategic forces. In November 1957, when discussing the role of the Air Force in national security, its senior officers divided between LeMay, then vice chief of staff, and his successor as SAC commander, Gen. Thomas Power, and the commanders of nonstrategic units: Tactical Air Command (TAC), Air Material Command, North American Air Defense Command, and Pacific Air Forces. LeMay and Power believed that the Air Force must "provide military strength as a basis for diplomatic action through adequate long range air offensive power." Their opponents believed the Air Force should "provide *versatile* airpower so as to permit *flexibility* in national decision" (emphasis added).[55] To the SAC generals, offensive forces were to deter all wars: "Only intercontinental air offensive forces based in the United States and protected by suitable air defense forces, can win a general war and hence deter the Soviets from initiating such a war." To the tactical generals, offensive forces could be "the primary deterrent to general war" alone.[56] There was a place for nonstrategic "direct defense" forces, and the Air Force must meet the "requirements of strategic, air defense, and tactical missions." To meet these needs, the USAF must work with an Army sized to meet commitments such as NATO and a Navy with ten heavy carriers. LeMay and Power wanted the Army prepared only for "token deployment overseas," and otherwise "solely for civil defense," and a Navy with only antisubmarine aircraft and carriers.[57]

Both sides of this debate accepted the importance of airpower in modern war, but the non-SAC generals rejected the singular focus of their late air-atomic service. They doubted the utility of air-atomic forces at all levels of conflict, and perhaps their deterrent power. They directly questioned the size of the offensive strategic force, indirectly questioning the tenets of late air-atomic thinking. "SAC may be too large." Like critics in the other services, and the Kennedy administration, they saw the counter–air target system as the key problem, and possibly counterproductive. The non-SAC USAF generals show how late air-atomic ideas, and the costs associated with them, challenged the survival of all other forces.

These critics expressed their disagreement solely within the Air Force, seeking more resources for their own commands and trying to influence doctrine. Outside the organization, they presented a unified front. General White, the chief of staff, told the group that arguing inside the service was acceptable but "they must present a solid front" to outsiders. The Objectives Paper debate resulted in a status quo of maintaining viable nonstrategic air forces. Tactical Air Command would specialize in local wars while being prepared to participate in a strategic attack on the USSR, the USAF would maintain control of the air defense mission, and SAC would be "maintained and improved."[58] Senior Air Force leaders outside SAC disliked the air-atomic push to expand strategic forces and doubted the effectiveness of strategic airpower alone as a deterrent, but kept it in the family. Nonetheless, the inexorable logic driving the late air-atomic forces toward continued growth, based on the blunting mission, continued unabated.

From Ideas to Plans

Actual plans bridged general ideas about airpower and reality. As in the late 1940s, planning for war evolved incrementally from existing concepts over the course of several years. Thus the 1951 JCS war plan Pinecrest was a product of early air-atomic thinking. It identified war industry as the primary target of strategic air attack and projected a six-month attack. If Moscow refused to surrender, newly mobilized Western armies then would prosecute the war.[59] This plan, with progress measured in months marked the beginning of the transition to late air-atomic plans. The 1952 Air Force Emergency War Plan (AFEWP), presumably written to support Pinecrest's immediate successor, identified the target sets for the strategic air offensive as "destruction of known targets affecting the Soviet capability to deliver atomic bombs, destruction of vital segments of Soviet industry, and retardation of Soviet advances."[60] This shift from concentrating on disrupting Soviet industry (Delta) to blunting Soviet atomic forces (Bravo) was an important step in basic thinking. Again, it stemmed from the time factor.

As technological pressure and Soviet capability tightened the time factor, forces were planned to strike ever faster and harder. In target systems, LRA overshadowed enemy industry. Tactics shifted to enable a faster offensive, so to protect SAC and smash LRA. Matching the frantic pace of reaction and decision was an expanded scale of effort, facilitated by more delivery vehicles and more potent weapons.

Of the three major target systems, the one least affected by the time factor was retarding the advance of the Red Army (Romeo), simply because to the Army's chagrin, slowing down the Red Army always was a distant third in priorities. Bernard Brodie told an Air War College audience that, on a 1951 visit to the Pentagon, he had failed to find a reasonable definition of Romeo. Brodie asked an Army officer if, without a retardation campaign, it took sixty-five days for the Red Army to reach Spain, but with one it took seventy-five days, what was the point? The officer could only say the time would be used for demolition. Brodie concluded that the aim of the strategy was simply "retardation for a retardation period."[61] Romeo was nonsensical in the framework of strategic air thought, because it did nothing to damage the enemy's war potential or effective force-in-being—SUSAC.

An added obstacle to embracing Romeo was organizational. LeMay and NATO commander Lauris Norstad struggled in 1951 over authority to plan Romeo targets. Consistent with his position (and with eventually codified doctrine) on centralizing control over the offensive, the SAC commander wanted to manage selection of and attack on retardation targets. Norstad wanted that power for himself. Atypically, LeMay lost the fight.[62] By 1954, Air War College taught that, unlike the blunting and disruption missions, retardation was under the control of theater commanders.[63] Given the need for ever tighter control over and coordinated execution of the strategic campaign, it is hard to imagine another conclusion. Many Romeo targets, by their nature, could not be identified before hostilities. Other than setting aside some weapons for theater use, SAC could do little central planning.

The second target system, disruption of Soviet industry, had been the staple of strategic air attack plans since World War II and remained important in the late air-atomic era. The structure of Soviet industry, with clusters of important factories located away from population centers, simplified targeting. In 1951, the Soviet industrial system was divided into four categories, differentiated by the time that strikes against them would take to affect Soviet military capability. Targets such as oil fell into the first category, whose effects would be felt immediately, while attacks on others like the aircraft industry might be felt three to six months later. More basic heavy industry, such as steel and coke, fell into the six- to twelve-month time frame, while military specific items that had been stockpiled, like ammunition and motor vehicles, would yield results only a year after effective strikes. Each segment of Soviet industry was assigned a priority based on its "impact group" and targeting done accordingly.[64] This yielded targeting priorities weighted to produce rapid effects. There was general agreement that the 1952 target system include "Soviet liquid fuels, atomic energy, aero-engines industries, and government control centers," but more argument over the relative priority of those targets that would yield slower results, especially the relative merits of targeting the scattered electrical industry against several sets of heavier industry.[65] LeMay argued against adopting isolated electrical plants as targets, which would lose the potential bonus effect of hitting industry in urban areas. In asking for cancellation of an Air Staff directive to target the electrical industry, he cited the Tokyo fire raids as evidence that bonus damage could eliminate production even if the physical plant was salvageable.[66] Vandenberg granted his request, in the process reinforcing the de facto authority of SAC. Notably, operations chief, Lt. Gen. Idwal Edwards, complained to LeMay that the Air Staff had been hampered because only SAC headquarters in Omaha had full data about targets and weapons effects. Had SAC provided the information, it would have saved a year's effort and "some embarrassment to us."[67]

A 1954 lecture to the Air War College showed a gradual evolution in thinking about Delta. According to the briefer, SAC's capacity had reached the point where it had no great need to discern which particular target systems to destroy. Since there were no "Achilles' Heels" in the Soviet economy, an attack on only a few industries might not work. Hence, SAC planned a broad-based assault on "many industries." This aim was not dramatically different from the 1951 plans, which also identified many industries for simultaneous attack, not a single critical one. Nonetheless, the quantitative and qualitative improvement of SAC meant that more targets could and would be struck. "An attack on government controls, and other strengths . . . would add greatly to the effectiveness of an attack on the economy. The availability of more and bigger weapons now makes possible attack on these strengths in addition to the industrial and therefore could increase the likelihood of the attainment of the Delta Objective."[68]

The effort put into disruption increased from 200 designated ground zeroes in 104 cities in 1951, to 700 targets during 1956.[69] In 1953, LeMay still characterized Delta at a NATO conference as "a first priority target."[70] Delta remained important, yet in the thermonuclear and missile age, enemy industry grew less attractive. As late air-atomic thought concluded that war would be decided in days or hours, the destruction of few industrial target systems could provide a measurable benefit to the war effort. The change in the time factor reduced the value of attacking targets whose effects would be felt only months later.[71]

The fundamental targeting change from early to late air-atomic thinking was the displacement of disruption by blunting. Although both target types remained important, by 1950 LeMay argued that SUSAC must be attacked first. This operationalized the offensive-defense. He urged Air Force Secretary Thomas Finletter to expand SAC so it could "include a counter-weapon offensive. The present force is inadequate to absorb this additional mission."[72] Finletter expressed his agreement with LeMay when he told Chief of Staff Hoyt Vandenberg,

> It is obvious that the foregoing situation requires a radically different SAC in 1954 than in 1950. The 1954 SAC must be different in two respects: (a) Since the purpose is to silence the Soviet attack or, in other words, to stop the bombardment of American cities, a very safe margin of error in the first striking force for this purpose must be allowed for. (b) The SAC force must be such so that in phase two (D plus 3 - D plus 18, say) it must be able to carry out what is now the first mission but in

> 1954 will be the second, namely the attack on Soviet economic centers if the Soviets do not stop the war on the defeat of their strategic air force.[73]

Unlike Delta, Bravo was not a continuation of past experience and planning. It came into being with the new Soviet threat and grew with emphasis on the offensive-defense. It also was a less stable target set than disruption, because SAC's effort had to evolve with the growth of SUSAC, which changed rapidly, was difficult to fathom, and actively frustrated SAC. Moreover, the targets were hard to find. In 1952, the JCS noted that "adequate detailed information needs for operational accomplishment of certain of the objectives stated in the study is not currently available" for blunting.[74] A 1954 discussion of Bravo targets identified the Soviet atomic stockpile as the only single target whose destruction could achieve the objective. Since that target was unlocated, SAC must, just as against the disruption set, expansively assault LRA. Aircraft, POL, and known atomic-energy installations would all be struck in two phases.[75] The first phase would hit advanced staging bases with surface bursts, and all fully equipped and probable home bomber bases with airbursts (to damage the aircraft) as well as LRA command and control and logistic centers. If successful, this strike would deny staging facilities for attacks against North America, destroy bombers and personnel, force undamaged bombers to regroup at poorly prepared alternate airfields, and disrupt command and control when it was needed most. A second attack wave, following "swiftly and relentlessly" to take advantage of confusion caused by the first wave would aim at the regrouped parked bombers where they were found.[76]

Swift technological change and growing Soviet capability even redefined the meaning of Bravo. Initially, it was defined as "to destroy the military, logistic, and control strengths of the Soviet Bloc that enable the enemy to deliver air weapons against friendly forces and installations and to resist penetration of his airspace." By 1958, the time factor entered its meaning. The first goal in the basic strategic concept became to "*immediately* stop atomic attacks against the United States, our allies, and our military forces abroad" (emphasis added).[77]

Planning for Survival

SAC's ideal aim was to smash SUSAC before it killed many Americans, and so to make the USSR surrender before SAC had to kill many Soviets. That aim, however, was hard to achieve. SAC's tactical focus through the 1950s became to survive a SUSAC attack and inflict damage rapidly enough to make blunting effective. For aircraft, this produced three shifts: to reduce dependence on overseas bases, disperse aircraft in the continental United States (CONUS), and place aircraft on alert. Each shift was driven by the growing immediacy of the Soviet threat.

The limited range of SAC's medium bombers required overseas bases. An unrefueled B-47E could only reach targets 2,050 nautical miles (NM) away, forcing a dependence on forward bases.[78] In 1952, SAC assigned UK-based aircraft 79 percent of the EWP effort.[79] Emerging Soviet strategic power, however, led to studies that concluded that forward bases were too vulnerable. RAND (in a study led by Albert Wohlstetter) quantified the problem in terms of maximum "safe occupancy time" hours, between when bombers could arrive at overseas bases and Soviet aircraft could attack them. Aircraft at UK bases could face Soviet fighter-bomber attack in 3.5 hours and medium bomber attack in 6 hours.[80] Similar figures for bases in North Africa, Greenland, Alaska, and Japan prompted RAND to recommend major changes, including using overseas bases solely for refueling.[81] Although the Air Force did not adopt RAND's recommendations wholesale, SAC strove to reduce its dependence on non-CONUS bases through increased tanker use and the development of longer-range aircraft. By 1958, the only aircraft at overseas bases rotated in under the "Reflex Action" program, "cocked" and ready to execute their EWP missions instantly.[82]

As Soviet reach increased, even CONUS bases became threatened. The Air Force response, once again, was to move the aircraft. Rather than harden bases, SAC planned to disperse the bombers. A Soviet attack would be frustrated if it could not find their targets. A 1952 RAND study recommended scattering B-36 wings, but identified the major problem in the program—cost. SAC agreed with the dispersion idea, but disagreed with RAND's recommendation to place every B-36 squadron at different bases, because of the expense. The goal of one heavy bomber squadron per base remained the ideal solution, but by 1959, thirty-three squadrons operated out of eighteen bases. Medium bombers were similarly concentrated with twenty-eight wings on eighteen bases. SAC had sixty-five bases.[83] One year later, thirty-five heavy bomber squadrons operated from twenty-six bases and twenty-six medium bomber wings from nineteen bases. The total number of bases had climbed to sixty-six. Additionally, SAC had plans in place to disperse medium bombers to non-SAC military and civil airfields during crises.[84] Although dispersal was far better by 1960 than in 1953, when most SAC bombers operated from a few large bases, high cost prevented a fully realized program.

By the late 1950s, alert procedures dovetailed with the dispersal program. Like dispersion, an effective alert program would complicate a Soviet attack by placing SAC out of harm's way, and possibly en route to the target. SAC widely publicized its alert procedures to maximize their deterrent power. In a 1954 test with 1,544 aircraft, however, only 6 percent scrambled during the first hour, 57 percent by the end of three hours, reaching a low peak of 71 percent eleven hours into the exercise.[85] LeMay's displeasure with this result was evident during the 1955 SAC Commander's Conference. He directed his subordinates to improve indoctrination and training so the first aircraft from every unit would be in the air within one hour of an order to scramble.[86] In February 1956, Twining told Congress that SAC was being readied for an around-the-clock ground alert.[87]

As the Soviets added ICBMs to their arsenal, SAC commanders became restless. A 1957 Air Force study showed that if the Soviets launched six missiles at each SAC base and missile site, only 10 to 15 percent of the bomber force and 10 percent of the missile force would be available for launch within four hours for a retaliatory attack.[88] In October 1958, Power urgently requested an airborne alert (a small force of armed bombers actually flying, rather than ready for short-notice takeoff) capability because "an adequate airborne alert force offers our best solution to the problem of maintaining our deterrent posture in a no warning situation, and until the [USAF] ICBM is a reality."[89] The Air Staff, although supporting the effort in principle, told Omaha there was not enough money for a maximum airborne alert and other key programs in the Air Force budget, including upgrades to SAC's offensive force. Beyond the $1 billion added expense, the proposal would reduce Air Force readiness, increase crew fatigue, and produce only a limited penetration capacity with sixty to eighty bombers.[90]

Nonetheless, by April 1959 SAC developed an "emergency capability" for airborne alert. The point of dispute became not whether airborne alert was necessary, but what fraction of the force should be indefinitely sustainable on it. SAC wanted an "optimum capability" for one-fourth of the force, while the Air Staff supported an "on the shelf" program for one-eighth of its strength. By late 1960, SAC anticipated having enough spares to fly sixty sorties per day by April 1961 and requested funding to support twice that number. In addition, one-third of SAC was on fifteen-minute ground alert by May 1960, while the introduction of "minimum interval takeoff" (MITO) in 1958 reduced the time between aircraft takeoffs from one minute to fifteen seconds.[91]

A second procedural change introduced the same year was "positive control," more popularly known as "fail-safe." As described by the SAC historian, "Strikes are launched with a briefed 'Go' code. When the strike is ordered executed, the 'Go' code is . . . broadcast . . . continuously until the force is beyond all Fail Safe Points. If the 'Go' code is not received by the aircraft . . . [they] Fail Safe at their radius of action and return to their operating bases."[92] This procedure increased SAC's effectiveness by separating a launch decision from a strike decision. This reduced potential hesitation and bought time for analysis of ambiguous warning and contemplative national decision making, while, it was hoped, preserving enough of the offensive force to achieve SAC's goals.

All these measures—the withdrawal from overseas bases, dispersal within CONUS, ground alert, airborne alert, and positive control—were reactions to the time factor. Every one sought to preserve an increasingly vulnerable bomber force, allow time for an attack decision, and posture SAC to attack. This aided not only the "survival force" but also the peacetime "deterrent force." These publicized programs reduced the chance that SAC could be put out of action by a surprise attack, and so made it unlikely that the Soviets would try.

As tactics for aircraft matured, those about missiles were born. SAC began integrating ICBMs into its plans as the first weapons approached service. These missiles were to carry out two basic tasks: direct attack, and to clear the way for penetration by manned aircraft. SAC's objectives for missiles were similar to those for bombers. Every missile must be maintained on alert and have a short reaction time (with an eventual objective being to launch all missiles within fifteen minutes).[93] By 1959, SAC established a "basic concept" for the missile force. Unlike bombers using positive control, missile launch depended on an "unequivocal national decision." Given the time needed for that decision and the inability to recall them once fired, they must "ride out" an attack. Once SAC received a launch order, plans called for firing the missiles in a "ripple," as opposed to one "salvo," to "avoid exposure of secure and hardened systems."[94] Presumably, readying first-generation liquid-fuelled missiles for launch would require exposure of support personnel and equipment. During this preparation period, SAC wanted to avoid exposing the support equipment necessary for launching missiles to attack. By firing the missiles in a "ripple," a Soviet attack could only catch a fraction of the missiles and support equipment in the open. As with aircraft tactics, technical reality prevented a realization of the ideal program.

As a whole, these tactical programs focused on one part of the mission, getting SAC airborne. The second part of the mission, penetrating to targets, also became increasingly difficult. Soviet defenses grew thornier as Moscow deployed more effective interceptors and new surface-to-air (SAM) missiles. During the 1950s, Soviet designers engineered dramatically more effective air defense weapons. A first-line interceptor in 1950, the MiG-15, could attack with guns or unguided rockets from at most half a NM away, and reach 50,000 feet and 585 knots.[95] Even when specially adapted for interception, first-generation jet aircraft like the MiG-15 could not intercept targets without ground controllers.[96] By 1960, second-generation fighter aircraft like the MiG-21 and purpose-built interceptors such as the Su-9 had entered the Air Defense Forces (PVO) inventory. Having detected enemy aircraft with onboard radar, they could attack targets more than two miles away using passive air-to-air missiles, reach 60,000 feet and 1,200 knots.[97]

The same technology that made air interceptors more potent increased the lethality of ground based antiaircraft fire, through the introduction of SAMs. The Soviets deployed their first system, the SA-1, around Moscow in 1955. It could intercept targets up to sixty thousand feet and twenty-five NM away. In 1957, the Soviets emplaced a second defensive missile, the SA-2, around major industrial centers. It was effective up to ninety thousand feet and (in an upgraded version fielded in 1960) twenty-seven NM.[98]

The combination of such missile systems and second-generation interceptors posed substantial problems for SAC, but penetrating them was essential. Piercing the systems became so complex that it briefly, in mid-decade, became coequal with Delta, Romeo, and Bravo—the Alpha task. A 1954 Air War College lecturer defined Alpha as the effort "to neutralize the enemy strength to prevent unacceptable interference with the penetration of enemy air space by allied forces in pursuit of the Bravo and Delta objectives."[99] Unlike other air campaign objectives, Alpha did not directly contribute to Soviet defeat, but it did enable objectives that would. The most pessimistic attrition estimates at the start of the decade fell into a range of 30–55 percent percent of aircraft destroyed during the entire campaign. LeMay rejected these figures as too high, estimating numbers around 10 percent.[100] In 1954, when RAND advocated low-level attack tactics because they predicted a loss rate of 79 percent, LeMay violently disagreed, saying that they grossly overestimated Soviet ability.[101]

The tipping point came in the middle of the decade, as new Soviet technology entered service. In 1954, a study thought the strengths of Soviet defenses, including high-performance daytime interceptors, an extensive early warning network, a large-scale training program, ample heavy AAA, many airfields, and a well-developed aircraft industry, were balanced by weaknesses, like lack of all-weather interceptors, shortage of air-to-ground communications for fighters, too few technical personnel in the electronics field, the inability of AAA to hit above forty thousand feet, and lack of operational guided rockets. Atomic weapons were not necessary to penetrate air defenses, but they soon might be. Even a small increase in Soviet competence could unacceptably boost attrition. Hence, although not singled out for attack in 1954, the air defense system by 1956 was targeted to keep losses at an acceptable level.[102] This posed a particular problem for a sizable fraction of SAC's forces, the B-36. In 1955, one estimate stated that "in the USSR under conditions of good visibility, day or night, the B-36 will have little chance of survival."[103]

Between 1954 and 1959, the new Soviet defenses forced wholesale changes on SAC tactics. High-level bombing was supplemented by low-level attack, which minimized exposure to ground-based AAA and most radar coverage, complicated the job of ground observers, and added an element of surprise. Such attacks were not without cost, as LeMay's earlier rejection of the idea implies. They shortened the range of jet aircraft, because fuel consumption was four times as fast as at forty thousand feet, and the speed of B-47s was limited to 425 knots compared to 495 knots at forty thousand feet.[104] These facts, together with complications in navigating and heavier stress on airframes (shortening their service lives), made low-altitude attack a necessary evil. Old techniques that used large groups of aircraft were replaced by strikes with one or two bombers. Early attacks would clear "corridors" 100–150 miles in width of Soviet defenses, so high-altitude B-52s and B-58s could penetrate for follow-on attacks against blunting and disruption targets. By 1959, air-to-surface missiles were being developed to destroy defenses from a distance.[105]

The growth of Soviet defenses, and the USAF reaction to it, had two important implications. First, it became yet another reason for the uncontrolled increase in strategic forces. The penetration of thicker defenses demanded more weapons and aircraft. As with blunting, Soviet actions, not just American intentions, determined the growth rate. Second, the greater complexity of corridor tactics, both in the interaction of US and Soviet weapon systems and the timing of follow-on strikes, all compressed into the shortest possible times, reinforced the need and desire for centralized command and control.

Compressed Timelines

That centralized effort aimed to launch an increasingly rapid and tightly coordinated offensive. Over the decade, the speed of that reaction increased while the expected length of the campaign decreased. By 1959, chairman of the Joint Chiefs Nathan Twining told the NSC, without recorded opposition, that the goal of the campaign was to "shoot the works," without any plan for incremental application of power "degree by degree."[106] This goal, present in preatomic and early air-atomic plans, was articulated by LeMay in 1951 who described it as the ability

> to destroy sufficient important enemy targets in as short a time as possible; to insure decisive destruction, and damage beyond the capacity of the enemy to recuperate. I would like to explain that in simple terms. Let's say a certain industrial area can be completely destroyed with 1,000 tons of explosives. We could drop that much at the rate of 10 tons a day over a period of 3 months and in all probability that area would keep right on producing. But if we smothered the area with 1,000 tons within

> the space of an hour or less, it would be through. Instead of contributing, it would become a burden on the economy of the nation. For us to achieve decisive results against a whole nation, we should be able to carry out this type of operation against not one but simultaneously against many such targets.[107]

At that point, the offensive was timed to start only after six days during which bombers deployed from CONUS to overseas bases, and aimed for victory in ninety days.[108] LeMay thought these targets too slow and worked hard to hasten the stopwatch. "Our goal is to deliver in a minimum of time intervals sufficient atomic bombs to create a decisive result."[109] By 1956, SAC could shift from normal operations to launching its first strike within twenty-four hours, with succeeding waves following at twelve-hour intervals.[110]

SAC's improved capacity led to a compression in the phasing of the campaign. Faith in a decisive first phase remained even as the time expected to conduct it shortened. Even in 1955, Air Force documents discussed an air campaign lasting three months during which "the basic decisive action of the war will occur. The minimum objective in this phase will be to protect our vital areas and facilities and inflict decisive damage on the Soviet existing and potential military and industrial structure." A six-month "exploitation phase" would follow, with the goal of smashing Soviet resistance. A final "surveillance phase" would extend indefinitely to prevent a resurgence of Soviet power, while Allied powers negotiated the orderly surrender of surviving Soviet authority.[111]

A 1956 JCS document, however, showed that the number of phases had fallen to two: a short initial phase (of unspecified length), followed by an indefinite subsequent one, aimed to conduct whatever operations were necessary to secure allied war objectives. All the destruction of the first two periods under old plans was compressed into one.[112] The 1960 Joint Strategic Objectives Plan (JSOP, which projected a war in 1963) reinforced this vision, with a first phase "characterized by an intensive exchange of nuclear blows and the initiation of operations and deployments by Army, Naval, and Air Force forces." The "governing principle in the employment of nuclear weapons for the initial phase is that the United States must emerge from an initial exchange of weapons with the residual over-all advantage." These forces would "be designed to destroy the Sino-Soviet will and ability to wage war, while minimizing the damage to the United States and its Allies." The next phase was even less well foreseen than it had been in the 1956 plan, but frightening. Recovery, reconstitution, and continued nuclear operations would occur, but only "to the extent that the communications and control structure will permit." There was little optimism that the national command structure would survive. Commanders were directed to "be prepared to conduct operations, including nuclear operations, in the subsequent phase based upon over-all United States objectives and their own analysis of initial phase operations."[113]

SAC matched the compressed timeline with an intensified scale of effort. The 1951 war plan intended to hit 200 ground zeros in 104 urban areas with 231 95 KT and 24 120 KT weapons.[114] Two years later, in planning for a war with the blunting mission ascendant, the number of targets and weapons jumped sharply. Planners assigned 261 weapons to destroy Soviet air capability, 43 more to secure sea lines of communications, and 1,226 to "collapsing" the Soviet war economy. Tactical aircraft would suppress Soviet air defenses with another 150 weapons.[115] This was a sixfold increase in warheads in only a few years, although most of the mission still was directed against Soviet industry. By 1960, the list doubled again. SAC then assigned 360 weapons to blunting atomic attack against the United States, 825 more to halt similar attacks on US forces overseas and allies, 1,395 to control Soviet airspace, 735 to retard Soviet land and sea operations, and 245 to disrupt the Soviet warmaking economy. All told, SAC would place 3,560 weapons on 1,450 designated ground zeros.[116] At that time, LeMay estimated that by 1970, 2,475 weapons would be needed for blunting attack on CONUS with another 975 on overseas targets, 765 to retard the Soviet conventional offensive, 390 on Soviet industry, and 2,350 to penetrate air defenses—a staggering total of 6,955 weapons delivered on 3,800 ground zeros. The 1960 attack was fifteen times larger than that of 1951. By 1970 it would be nearly thirty times larger. An equally dramatic shift emerged in targets. The ascendance of the blunting objective over disruption was stark, as was the inseparable problem of penetrating air defenses. Again, the size of both efforts depended on Soviet actions, not American. Once the USAF set blunting SUSAC as its first objective, with the prerequisite of penetrating air defenses, Soviet actions determined the scale of American effort.

This amplified scale of SAC's mission was matched by the growth in its resources. In 1951, Vandenberg expressed dismay over the command's marginal ability to carry out its mission. "In fact, if we are successful, in my opinion it will be another year and a half . . . before we can do any policing after we have destroyed it, because it will take out the last airplane."[117] A 1952 internal examination, the Alness study, concluded that "sufficient mass" entailed not being outnumbered by Soviet fighters by more than 4:1. Even so, it estimated at least 40 percent losses in the early days of the war. To reduce such losses demanded a larger attacking force, and the stage was set for malignant growth.

By 1955, LeMay's efforts to expand SAC were paying dividends. He proudly told his colleagues, "We started 1953 with 22 ZI bases, 37 wings, 17 air refueling squadrons, and a total of 165,000 personnel. By January 1956, SAC had expanded to 39 ZI bases, 50 wings, 38 air refueling squadrons, and 198,000 assigned personnel." This translated into a 340 percent increase in bomb-carrying aircraft dedicated to the EWP, over 75 percent of them jet-equipped (compared with only 10 percent in 1953).[118] By 1960, SAC had 43 strategic bomber wings containing 1,890 jet aircraft with 65 missiles approaching operational status, supplemented by 57 air refueling squadrons.[119] It flew 2,992 aircraft with 266,000 personnel, up from 1,186 aircraft flown by 145,000 men in 1951.[120] Both target lists and strategic air forces bloated during the late air-atomic age, spurred by the time factor.

The prominence of the blunting mission, the ever more difficult task of penetrating air defenses, and the unrestrained growth of targets and resources had several effects on strategic air plans. First, as became evident during the writing of the first integrated operations plan in 1960, was "overkill." The need to disable SUSAC with a high degree of assurance, combined with incomplete intelligence and the potentially high attrition of attackers, led conservative planners to assign many weapons against individual targets. In 1958, the Net Evaluation Subcommittee informed Eisenhower that SAC targeted Moscow with 100 MT of weapons—5,000 Hiroshima equivalents: two-thirds of which were expected to reach the city.[121]

A further consequence was pressure to preempt. The razor-thin margin between success and failure in the blunting mission, with the difference measured in megadeaths, fueled already existing desires to strike as soon possible. As operations chief Frank Everest told the Air Force Commanders Conference in 1955, a recent Air Staff study assumed "the United States will not deliberately provoke a general war. This assumption does not preclude attempting to strike the first blow."[122] Air planning rode the line between the logical extreme of preventive war, banned by national policy and nearly absent from recorded discussion, and preemption, which, if done too slowly, would find empty Soviet airfields and missile launch pads, a homeland about to be devastated, and a war to be lost.

Preemption was the logical endpoint of late air-atomic thought. Early air-atomic strategy, before the "fantastic compression of time," desired rapid action against sources of potential enemy strength to ensure victory, but 1950s strategy demanded immediate action to avoid devastation. Although not as conspicuously absent from the record as its morally repugnant cousin, preventive war, preemption nonetheless was rarely discussed openly. Instead, euphemisms like "initiative" abound. The goal of preemption, or "initiative," remains clear nonetheless. In a perfectly executed—and unattainable—form, all Soviet strategic offensive forces would be destroyed after clear and unmistakable warning of their hostile intent, but before launching. However, the reality that preemption could never achieve perfect results did not mean that it was an invalid goal. Imperfect preemption would still catch some Soviet aircraft and missiles at their bases and utterly disrupt Soviet follow-on forces. In a context that defines victory as relative, destroying Soviet forces allows them to be more easily coerced into a favorable settlement. The potential of saving perhaps tens of millions of lives from attacks by the weapons which imperfect preemption destroyed would make the effort worthwhile. Preemption required resolute national leadership. So long as there was a president who the Soviets believed might launch SAC preemptively, a preemptive policy generated substantial deterrent force.

The tight coordination and the corridor tactics needed for the blunting campaign, so to maximize the destructive potential of the attack through concentrating it in time and space while avoiding fratricide reinforced the tendency toward Air Force autonomy, manifested as a need to control all strategic attack assets. This desire grew more important as the Navy began to field systems with real potential for strategic attack from the mid-1950s. The ability (or inability) to integrate forces into plans varied with whether these were measured in hours or in months. When a 1959 joint exercise in the Pacific revealed that Air Force units "across the board" achieved earlier times on target, it meant more than it would have in 1949.[123] So too, in 1949, Navy carriers might have been able to get into position to launch strikes against Soviet targets in time to make a measurable contribution to a campaign. Ten years later, the decisive phase might be over long before they could sail within range.

"Better" Weapons

The tightening of the time factor also shaped SAC's future requirements. As its targeting expectations for 1970 show, the USAF expected future war to be an incremental extension of its present expectations, including the need to blunt SUSAC and gain a meaningful victory. Because acquisition programs for new weapon systems took five to ten years from first discussion to operational use, the drawing boards of 1960 illuminate the Air Force vision of war in 1970.

The Air Force view of weapon systems was teleological, progressing from the earliest days of the low and slow Jenny to ever faster and higher-flying bombers carrying greater weapons over longer ranges. A graph used by Kuter in 1956 shows this movement along all three axes. What it does not show is also notable: survivability. Similar patterns emerge in other documents comparing aircraft characteristics during the decade. For example, a 1955 Air Staff intelligence study put Soviet and American models side-by-side, comparing wingspan, length, engine thrust, weight, combat radius, bomb load, maximum speed, maximum altitude, target speed, target altitude, and combat ceiling. In an age where the time factor was shifting definitions of an "effective" weapon, these traditional measures ignored key variables like the ability to perform at low altitudes, and penetration aids.[124]

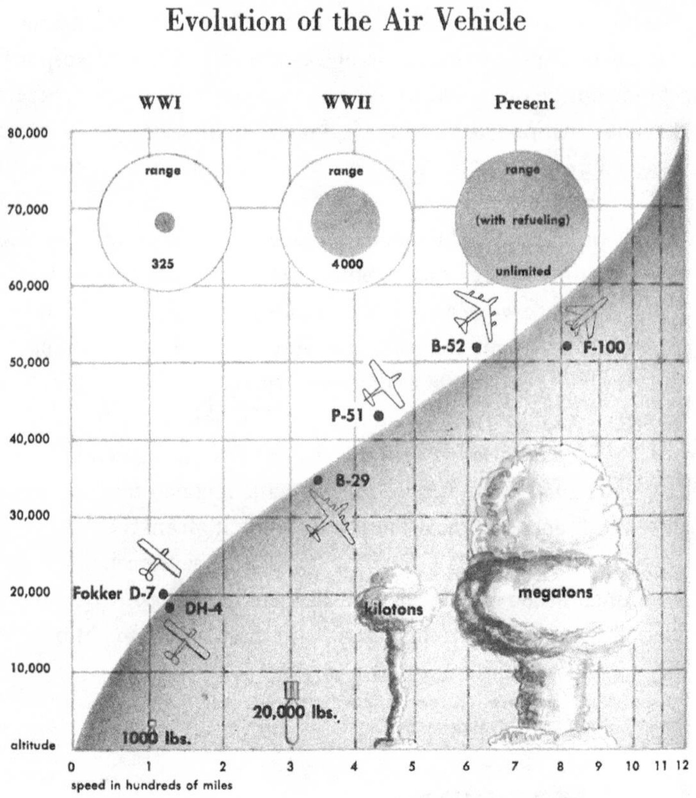

Figure 1. (Teleological) evolution of the air vehicle

Source: Gen. Laurence Kuter, "An Air Perspective in the Jetomic Age," *Air University Quarterly Review* 8.2 (spring 1956).

This was akin to measuring naval effectiveness in 1945 by comparing the number of sixteen-inch guns in opposing fleets and ignoring aircraft carriers.

The desired characteristics for a future bomber, which reflected the vision of combat to come, are mirrored in the medium and heavy bombers under development by 1960. The B-58, successor to the B-47, could carry out most of its mission at Mach 2 while flying at nearly sixty thousand feet. The B-70, around which controversy swirled in the Kennedy administration, would have reached seventy thousand feet at Mach 3. Both aircraft were designed to carry only one or two large weapons to targets.[125] They were fast, flew high, and would carry a few large weapons—more advanced tools for the same tactics. As technically impressive as the new aircraft were, they were clearly the lineal descendants of prewar and wartime aircraft, using altitude and speed to overcome enemy defenses.

By 1960, aircraft further along this curve were on the drawing board along with other weapon systems that fit this definition of improvement—missiles and manned space systems. Former deputy chief of staff for development, Lt. Gen. (Ret) Donald Putt, warned Congress that qualitative superiority was critical.

> If we are to maintain the required qualitative deterrent Air Force in-being we must always stay ahead through the development of tomorrow's weapons yesterday. World War III is being fought on today's drawing boards and in scientific laboratories. We could lose the next showdown if proper emphasis is not being placed on tomorrow's weapons today![126]

Besides these "better" (i.e., higher and faster) conventional weapons, two further categories of programs under development reflected the air defense environment projected for the 1960s. The first were "penetration aids," designed to defeat Soviet defenses directly. Decoy drones such as Quail and improved electronic countermeasures, complicated the interception of SAC bombers by jamming and deception. A 1957 study showed that for the cost of ten B-52s, $230 million, the Air Force could buy two thousand decoys. While the ten bombers would increase "total strike effectiveness from 10 percent to 11 percent," the decoys would boost it to 70 percent.[127] A complementary series of programs sought to extend the offensive range of existing bombers—air-to-surface missiles (ASM). The Hound Dog, a supersonic, turbojet powered cruise missile designed for external carriage on the B-52, could travel up to Mach 2 and strike targets 250 miles away with a nuclear warhead.[128] This let B-52s engage SAM sites from well outside their effective range, clearing the way for later strikes, or else to directly attack defended targets. Gen. Thomas White told the secretary of the air force that the Hound Dog would be essential against Soviet air defenses by 1961, otherwise B-52 attrition would be "unacceptable."[129]

Collectively, these programs for new and improved manned weapons were aimed to make war in the 1960s an intensified version of that in the 1950s. These aircraft still would reach their targets by clearing corridors through evolving air defenses, and their key characteristics remained essentially those since the earliest days of flight—speed, altitude, range, and payload.

By these standards, missiles should have been welcomed as improvements to existing capabilities. So they were. SAC often is seen as a classic example of an institution focused on one type of weapon, and so resistant to a better one. In fact, it strongly supported the role of missiles, but in the proper place—as an adjunct to bombers. The primary obstacle to their acceptance was the unreliability of novel technology. LeMay summarized both parts of this position in 1955 when he wrote

> As the long-range objective, I consider an intercontinental ballistic missile with a capability of instantaneous launch and with acceptable reliability,

> accuracy, and yield to be the ultimate weapon in the strategic inventory. During the interim and until these capabilities are proven, we must establish initial objectives and utilize demonstrably effective weapons systems.[130]

Twining too answered critics who viewed resistance to missiles as Luddism from pilots seeking to protect the man in the cockpit. In 1956, he told an Air War College audience that opposition to missiles had to be grounded in sensible operational reasons, not from fear of "technological unemployment." "When these changes are resisted, progress is slowed. We do not move ahead as rapidly and as objectively as we should. As a result, we get less effective defense. We perpetuate old weapons and with them old methods."[131]

Concerns over reliability also were evinced about manned aircraft. In 1952, LeMay told a group of aircraft designers that the complexity of modern bombers and atomic bombs could undermine SAC's effectiveness. "The malfunction of a single small vacuum tube in a bombing system can cause a 92-ton atomic bomb with the destructive potential of hundreds of World War II planes, to miss the target."[132] His concern that a "50-cent tube" might disable a bomber over Soviet territory shaped a conservative attitude toward the new missiles. The latter had undeniable promise, but a strategy that demanded close coordination and reliable performance was bound to be skeptical about the utility of first-generation weapons, which suffered embarrassing setbacks in tests.

A 1952 SAC paper gave voice to those doubts. Given the nature of the missile, with "several major elements all operating in series," including items such as guidance and propulsion, if just one part failed, so might the entire system. Unlike a human-directed bomber, if a missile malfunctioned, that failure might not even be discovered. Aggravating the problem were novel operational challenges. Unlike existing strategic weapons, a missile must spend "95 percent of its lifetime in a container" requiring specialized maintenance equipment sophisticated enough to guarantee a successful mission, yet be suited for maintenance by an enlisted airman with a high school education.[133]

In 1958, as the first generation of missiles approached operational status, Power reiterated his concerns about their effectiveness in the *Air University Quarterly Review*. Comparatively low accuracy, reliability, limited payload, and difficult maintainability hampered their capability. While speed and quick reaction were a major benefit, a system which could not be recalled or retargeted after launch posed tactical problems. Specific challenges SAC had identified included human error in keying guidance instructions, geographic error in target location or missile origin, misinformation about the target, inaccurate trajectory calculation, unknown or unexpected environmental conditions affecting the trajectory, and malfunction in flight.[134]

The inherent limits of the first guided missiles combined with long research and development cycles, also made them compete with more advanced weapons. For example, the Rascal air-to-surface missile began development in April 1946 based on a requirement of July 1945. Six years later, SAC requested that the missile's performance be upgraded to deal with new Soviet weapons. The program continued but, in 1956, LeMay told White

> The 90-mile range of the Rascal is completely inadequate when employed against the Soviet defenses expected to exist when the Rascal could be operational. The reduction in bomber attrition that may be expected through employment of the Rascal is insufficient to compensate for the degradation in bombing efficiency which will result from the inferior yield, and lack of reliability of this ASM.[135]

The Air Force canceled Rascal in 1958.[136]

Similar problems plagued the Snark cruise missile. This weapon flew at Mach 0.9 for five thousand NM. Difficulty in developing the guidance system and terminal dive maneuver added six years to development, making the weapon obsolete when finally deployed in 1959 for less than one year at Presque Isle Air Force Base in Maine.[137] While still an active program, however, it hampered other more viable weapons. In 1956, with the Snark already four years late, LeMay complained that it "is actually competing with the B-52 and more specifically with B-52 penetration systems. Operating in the same defensive environment at the same speed and altitude as the B-52, but unmanned and ill-equipped defensively, having poorer CEP [accuracy] yield and reliability, the Snark is relatively impotent when compared with the B-52."[138]

SAC approved of missiles but less wholeheartedly than did thinkers not responsible for their employment, and for good reason. SAC looked not at weapons whose reliability was assumed or abstracted, but real ones. Their promise was tempered by problems shared with existing weapons, and by novel ones whose resolution demanded work. As such, missiles shared the top of SAC's priority list with bombers, but did not displace them. The top four projects on the March 1957 priority list were an improved B-52, the B-70, the Navaho intercontinental cruise missile, and the ICBM.[139] In 1960, a similar list at the Air Force level placed ten programs in "Category I" including Atlas, Titan, Minuteman, the B-70, and Hound Dog.[140] SAC cannot fairly be accused of ignoring missiles, but certainly it did not believe they could overturn its idea of war.

SAC advocated programs that could create the "mixed force." In doing so, they incrementally added potentially revolutionary weapons as a new component in conservative tactics. As early as 1951, the primary strength of the missile—speed—was seen as a valuable addition to the strategic force. Maj. Gen. Gordon

Saville, deputy chief of staff for development, told the Commander's Conference of the idea behind the Snark missile (representing the Air Force's attitude toward all such systems):

> In an attempt to reduce the time period between the time of a go-ahead for an attack—strategic offensive—and the time that that attack can be launched against known targets, a gimmick like this appears to be extremely useful . . . that this can some day, if we can make it work, take on a part of the thing that we call the "strategic offensive" or the immediate retaliatory attack against known and fixed targets.[141]
>
> A major weakness of missiles was that they could only strike targets in known locations.

As the inaccuracy of first-generation systems meant that hardened targets would be difficult to kill reliably, these missile could attack only a limited subset of targets. As Lindsay wrote in 1956, a fact of "present . . . guided missiles is the lack of pinpoint guidance accuracy, [so] the intercontinental and the medium-range strategic missiles will be used against the relatively large fixed target complex or the war-making capability of the enemy."[142]

These strengths and weaknesses of missiles meshed well with the qualities of bombers. Aircraft could hit imprecisely located targets and those needing further attention after an initial strike. In 1953, Gen. Clarence Irvine of Air Material Command told LeMay "we need an airplane like the B-58 to hit those highly defended targets on which our intelligence is not good enough to fire [a missile] from 300 miles out."[143] The strategic force of the 1960s, built around second-generation missiles and supersonic bombers, would be well designed for launching a devastating and rapid attack. It could clear corridors to reach the most heavily defended Soviet targets and place overwhelming firepower on them. Notably, SAC envisaged the use of missiles as the fix to one of its key immediate problems, the power of Soviet air defense systems. The mixed force was the best one available to meet the key demands of the late air-atomic period, an effective deterrent force that derived its credibility from war winning, that is, from being able to dictate terms to an opponent while still surviving as a society.

In the larger picture of the air-atomic strategy, the projections of combat for the 1960s were an incremental change to conventional ideas of the 1950s, which in turn grew from the early air-atomic ideas. The consistencies are more striking than the differences. The strategy still centered on victory and shock. Intrawar deterrence, gradual escalation, secure second-strike forces, and other ideas did not enter future projections.

The shift from the early period of air-atomic strategy to the late shows how institutions can cover great distances through small steps. Before 1914, European nations, seeking mass to overwhelm opposing armies, increased the size of their armies, which were integrated into existing plans with small changes, rather than driving a reconsideration of strategies. So too, year-on-year iterative change drove SAC in the 1950s, as the force grew in numbers of aircraft and targets, performance of weapon systems, and size of budget. Each year was just a small change from the last, and the Air Force did business the same way. By 1958 the Air Force had inched its way from the early to the late air-atomic period. SAC controlled a major portion of the military budget and created overkill, but gained little effectiveness from each additional increment of resources. Nonetheless, officers who believed in air-atomic ideas were locked in to them, given the organizational success, measured in budget and influence, that the ideas had brought. It won senior officers immense personal prestige and power. Only an unusual SAC general could have questioned such ideas.

The transition from the early to late air-atomic era had a fundamental cause—the tightening of the time factor. Air strategy shifted to meet the new Soviet threat and changing technology, but within the existing framework of air strategy, firmly rooted in historical experience. Broad thinking about airpower reemphasized the offensive-defensive and the changed nature of war. But those changes simply reflected the trends in early air-atomic thinking and can be traced to the prewar thinkers on airpower. The expectation that war would open with two air forces exchanging blows until one disabled its opponent was a return to the earliest abstract notions of Douhetan combat. The plans written during the period applied these broad ideas with some unexpected outcomes. The reality of thermonuclear weapons brought the definition of victory, a concept rarely discussed, into question. Also, the imperative to strike rapidly with a vulnerable force against a target whose size was determined by the enemy dislocated and distorted SAC. In the end, the time factor spurred incrementally adjusted thinking, not new conceptions of strategic warfare. Technology advanced and plans adapted but thinking continued along the same track, with the train hurtling along ever faster, barely under control.

5

TO KILL A NATION

In peacetime, the ultimate test of military policy lies in its interaction with national policy. Committed executive opposition can slow, stop, or even reverse the bureaucratic momentum behind military policy. Less vigorous opposition or neutrality leads to slowed movement in the same direction. Strong support at the national level pushes an idea, while suppressing competitors. During the 1950s, the USAF's transition from early to the late air-atomic strategy benefited from—indeed, rested on—the vigorous support of President Eisenhower. His administration carefully studied atomic weapons and their implications, and integrated them into national security policy. These reports presented clear and accurate information on growing Soviet power and its grim consequences. Given this knowledge, Eisenhower backed late air-atomic ideas with all of its terrors and rejected conflicting schools of thought, although in crises he steered clear from the danger of world war. Nonetheless, conscious decisions taken in the Oval Office created a friendly strategic niche that encouraged the growth of late air-atomic strategy over its competitors.

Through National Security Council (NSC) paper 162/2 and subsequent Basic National Security Policies (BNSP), Eisenhower articulated a clear declaratory policy, which the action policy—air-atomic strategy—suited well. Eisenhower sought to reduce military spending so to fuel economic growth for a long struggle with the USSR, balancing the "great equation" and avoiding a "garrison state."[1] His military strategy sought to provide unambiguous destructive potential at low cost. The air-atomic action policy did so.

Thinking the Unthinkable

The Eisenhower administration was characterized by its systematic and staff-centered formulation of national policy. It sought expert advice and detailed evaluation from throughout the government. The NSC worked as designed in national security matters, including basic decisions about general war, atomic weapons, and the Soviet threat. Governmental groups in the Weapon Systems Evaluation Group (WSEG) and the NSC examined the hazards of the late air-atomic age, as did special panels of outsiders.

Two such groups, working under the auspices of the Office of Defense Mobilization Science Advisory Committee, became known by the names of their chairmen—Massachusetts Institute of Technology president James Killian and RAND Corporation trustee Horace Gaither. Killian, which issued its report "Meeting the Threat of Surprise Attack" in February 1955, concluded at present that neither side could attack decisively. Once both sides developed deliverable multimegaton weapons, a technological stalemate might follow that could not be changed. The United States lead in weapon and delivery technology would hold until 1958, or at best 1960, when stalemate would set in. Killian concluded the United States must reduce SAC's vulnerability before the Soviets developed robust power or else face the threat of surprise attack, because strategic warning might not be forthcoming once Soviet delivery means improved.[2] In other words, the stability of the stalemate hinged on SAC's relative vulnerability, which meant it must be strengthened.[3] In principle, Killian's conclusion was inconsistent with air-atomic thinking, because it precluded the hopes of preserving a winning margin of superiority or victory, but its ideas of protecting the force and maintaining technological superiority matched Air Force strategy in the short term. These conclusions illuminate the developments of the next decade.

The Gaither report of November 1957 addressed the effects of rapid technological advance. It recognized that US security depended on SAC's offensive strength, which was vulnerable to a surprise attack. This required a program of "prompt remedial action." The bomber threat could be reduced through alert, improved tactical warning, and active surface-to-air missile defense of SAC bases. The Soviet Intercontinental Ballistic Missile (ICBM) threat, estimated to emerge by late 1959, could be mitigated by early warning radars to detect missiles, reducing alert reaction time to between seven and twenty-two minutes, dispersing bombers, building aircraft shelters, and developing missile defenses. The administration should increase SAC's offensive power by augmenting Intermediate Range Ballistic Missile (IRBM) in Europe, building six hundred first generation ICBMs (rather than eighty), accelerating Polaris, and hardening ICBM bases.[4] Like Killian, Gaither envisioned a technological stalemate after a period of continued

US superiority. The major difference between the reports was that Gaither feared the stalemate might be unstable, and if stalemate was impossible, only superiority remained.[5] Thus Gaither was more in line than Killian with air-atomic thinking. From a national policy perspective, the two reports with their similar and distinct conclusions demonstrate that Eisenhower based his decisions on comprehensive counsel.

Military leadership took these panels seriously, as shown by the JCS's reference of Gaither's conclusions to WSEG. The latter replied with hard-headed advice that did not follow anyone's prior agenda. WSEG rejected hardening of existing Atlas launch sites, but thought that to do so with future sites would double the missile's effectiveness. It also recommended increasing Titan procurement, tripling Polaris submarine orders, and speeding up their delivery.

For its part, WSEG continued studying the strategic air offensive during the 1950s, along with topics from continental defense to ICBM basing choices and biological warfare to limited war.[6] WSEG-12, published in 1955, examined how a contemporary air campaign would affect the USSR's ability to wage war—the disruption objective. It reached several pessimistic conclusions, despite assuming that SAC could deliver all its weapons as planned. Large stockpiles of war materiel might survive attack and meet essential needs for six months. Too few weapons were earmarked for retardation; the Red Army would be delayed only two months. Although the damage to Soviet population and infrastructure would "leave in serious question the ability of the Soviets to utilize" them, WSEG (as in earlier reports) refused to assess the effect of the campaign on the Soviet "will to war." That is, it refused to assume a knock out. It recommended aggressive tactics designed to "survive and gain superiority during the initial atomic phase and, at the same time, be prepared to exploit success." The authors hoped that the Soviets might surrender if they exhausted their stockpile before the United States.[7] Although hardly a resounding endorsement of the air campaign, this WSEG report shows the open discussion within Eisenhower's national security structure.

The Net Evaluation Subcommittee (NESC) of the National Security Council produced some of the most important and least examined studies on nuclear warfare in the 1950s. The annual "net evaluations" compared the effect of an exchange on both nations. Important variables changed each year, including the degree of surprise and weight of attack, but all were limited to an initial exchange. Before the advent of a Soviet strategic capability, this sort of study would have been nonsensical because an air campaign was inflicted, not endured. It was possible only in the late air-atomic age.

The Truman administration, coping with preatomic Soviet power, left few comparable studies. Only one, noted in the NSC-68 series, shows an effort to answer a similar question. Looking forward toward the "year of maximum danger," 1954, it foresaw a Soviet attack on 255 critical targets with only twelve minutes of warning. The authors predicted 1.5 million dead within one week (thirty thousand dead per bomb in a fifty-bomb attack), with a further 7 million Americans left homeless.[8]

The evolving Soviet threat and more formalized national security structure led to a systematic exploration of the problem. On 19 January 1953, the last day of the Truman administration, the NSC approved NSC-140, directing "the preparation of a summary evaluation of the USSR's net capability to inflict direct injury on the United States, to be submitted to the Council on or before 15 May 1953."[9] This order began almost a decade of annual studies until the subcommittee was closed in the mid-1960s.

The first NESC report, delivered on 13 May 1953, became generally known by the name of its chairman, USAF Lt. Gen. Idwal Edwards. It examined the effects of a Soviet surprise attack in 1955, with "a view of inflicting maximum direct injury on the continental United States, and on selected U.S. installations outside the United States of major importance to a U.S. air atomic counteroffensive during the initial phases of war." Essentially, this attack was a mirror image of the blunting offensive SAC planned to carry out. Three hundred air-delivered eighty kiloton (KT) weapons would strike, chiefly at bomber bases, with its remaining strength directed on major population centers, presumably to disrupt American mobilization. Edwards's study concluded that an attack could destroy 30 percent of SAC atomic counterair (blunting) capability and cause additional damage, restricting remaining aircraft to half the normal sortie rate. Isolated overseas bases would be put out of operation indefinitely, forcing SAC to rely on its remaining intercontinental capacity with heavy and refueled medium bombers. SAC could mitigate this damage by dispersal; two hours' warning would buy time to scatter 65 percent of SAC aircraft, six hours would save another 20 percent: these estimates were optimistic, given the later experience of SAC. Meanwhile, American industry and population centers would suffer up to 12.5 million casualties, one half fatal. Industry within the attacked areas—two-thirds of total US production—would be paralyzed. Potentially worse than the physical damage would be the psychological. "There would be morale and political problems of a magnitude which it is impossible to estimate, or even comprehend, on the basis of any presently available valid data."[10]

Despite these gloomy predictions of damage to American force-in-being and potential strength, Edwards predicted "the delivery of a powerful [US] initial retaliatory atomic air attack, the continuation of the air offensive, and the successful prosecution of the war."[11] Further, if the Soviets chose to attack any other target systems, less damage would occur. This first NESC report suggested two significant conclusions: damage would be measured in megadeaths, and the United

States would prevail anyway. This represented the Eisenhower administration's first look at the stark realities of a nuclear exchange. It shows the context within which the new administration embraced the late air-atomic strategy.

The next recorded NESC study, the 1955 George report, predicted ever greater destruction, with 25 million dead and 70 percent of the remainder needing hospitalization. On hearing the conclusions, Eisenhower told the JCS that a "long, difficult struggle and that might take one, two, five, or one hundred years" would follow the first exchange.[12] He also told the assembled officers that while he rejected the Air Force vision of a two-day war, the next war would be atomic and bombs must all be used at once. Eisenhower's fears were consistent with Air Force thinking; his remedy was the same. He differed principally in being less optimistic of an early decision, though that matter was significant.

Succeeding reports continued to reflect tightening of the time factor and its potential impact on Soviet capability and SAC's response. The 1956 NESC study examined two distinct situations, one with and one without strategic warning. The first scenario resulted in the delivery of 6,600 megatons (MT) on US targets, effectively eliminating the US government. SAC, despite losing 68 percent of its personnel, retaliated with more than 1,300 surviving aircraft. After the exchange, the Soviets retained only 10 percent of their stockpile, while the United States held 80 percent of its total weapons. The NESC concluded that this degree of superiority would compel a Soviet surrender.

The second situation granted the United States twenty days of strategic warning. Due to alert American defenses, the Soviet attack landed only 5,500 MT, and SAC retaliated with 2,051 aircraft. Once again, relative superiority translated into US victory. The real gain from warning was not to minimize the damage Soviet bombers inflicted on the United States, but to maximize the devastation SAC wrought on the USSR. The authors concluded the "general ineffectiveness of our air defense forces to prevent devastation of the United States, even under conditions of 'full alert' when they have been augmented by additional forces, is a significant product of this report."[13] This vocal reinforcement of Air Force theory on the primacy of offense over defense was matched by an unstated agreement that victory was what ultimately mattered. If devastation was unavoidable, as Eisenhower seemed to accept the year before, then it was best to be in a position to dictate terms.

The 1957 report expanded on the previous year's multiple scenarios by examining four combinations of target systems and degrees of alert in a hypothetical 1960 Soviet surprise attack against military and civil targets, with both high and low defense effectiveness; and purely military targets, with both low and high defense effectiveness. In the four conditions, the number of Soviet weapons reaching targets varied from 236 (1,085 MT) to 686 (4,449 MT), with many detonating off target but still inflicting casualties. Deaths (within one year of the attack) varied from 46 to 95 million, with another 12–14 million injured—one-third to two-thirds of the US population. The survivors would have to cope with losing up to 88 percent of industry, 89 percent of oil, and 79 percent of housing. The retaliatory SAC offensive would use all remaining undamaged aircraft, 600–1,200 bombers, supported by 800 tankers.

The report concluded that so long as SAC maintained any alert system, such a nuclear war would devastate both countries. It was the first report to conclude that, without a sufficiently dispersed and protected retaliatory SAC, the USSR could destroy the United States with impunity. Furthermore, no amount of American retaliation could prevent disaster to the United States. Unlike the 1956 report, the authors recommended that damage be mitigated by effective air defense and civil defense. Like contemporary studies from Gaither and civilian strategists, the report recommended hardening ICBMs and scattering the bomber force before a substantial Soviet ballistic missile threat emerged.[14]

The 1958 report looked at one scenario, maximum strategic surprise, in which 500 Soviet bombers and 50 submarines struck without detection. Supplemented by two clandestinely placed 8 MT weapons in the Soviet embassy in Washington and UN consulate in New York, 250 ICBMs, and follow-up attacks by the rest of Soviet nuclear forces, this attack would have wrecked fifty-one of fifty-six SAC bases by thirty hours into the attack. The Navy lost the bases for 25 percent of its surface ships and half its submarines, and a quarter of naval aircraft and ships. Blast caused structural damage to 4 percent (mostly urban) of the total land area of the continental United States, fires burned out 169,000 square miles (5.7 percent of total land area), and lethal radiation blanketed half the nation, persisting in some areas for up to 2 years. The assault killed 12 million Americans outright, and 38 million more by the end of one year, with another 9 million injured, from a starting population of 179 million. Long-term health effects included genetic defects in 2 million pregnancies and 800,000 live births, an overall reduced life expectancy of two to four years, 2 million cases of leukemia, and 5 million cases of bone cancer. The attack destroyed 20 percent of industry and rendered 60 percent unusable for up to one year. The federal government was wiped out, except for the vice president and secretary of the interior, but state governments survived and Congress could be reconstituted. Despite widespread carnage, "the survival of the United States as a nation appears highly probable. There will be drastic changes but with the material available the remaining population is capable of eventually attaining pre-attack standards under determined leadership."[15]

In this scenario, SAC ordered US retaliation to the surprise assault one minute after detecting the Soviet bombers, with the first aircraft taking off five minutes later. Thirty minutes after the beginning of the Soviet attack, 449 bombers and support aircraft with 311 tankers were flying to targets, supplemented by 5 of 10 alert ICBMs, 3 of which struck targets. Of 90 IRBMs launched from European bases, 41 arrived on target. Rather than neatly defined discrete waves of bombers, the follow-on SAC attack was a continuous rolling strike lasting 16 hours. With the loss of 367 aircraft, the American counterstrike eliminated Soviet nuclear forces within thirty hours, reduced Soviet GNP by 75 percent for a year after the attack and decreased that of the entire Sino-Soviet bloc by 56 percent. Although the USSR and PRC survived as nations, they did so only with changed governments. The PRC's nascent industry would be destroyed and the nation would revert to agrarianism.[16]

The report concluded after the attacks, the balance of strength would lie with the United States. Although a Soviet surprise attack would destroy one-third of the US population and one-fifth of its economy, retaliation would "virtually eliminate [the USSR] as a world power."[17] This conclusion hinged on SAC scrambling the alert force within fifteen minutes. If it failed to do so, "the balance of strength could be on the side of the USSR at the termination of the nuclear exchange."[18] The 1958 report highlighted several conclusions that had been consistent since the first NESC study. Since 1954, the reports stated that a surprise attack on the United States would disrupt its political, economic, and social structure. Starting in 1955, the group stated that a nuclear exchange would devastate both countries. From 1956, it recommended protecting the retaliatory force through alert procedures and improved air defense.[19] The NESC recognized the time factor and embraced the late air-atomic response to it.

The 1959 NESC report, the last thus far declassified, examined a war in 1962 with forty-eight hours warning. Despite this alert, in the attack SAC lost 85 of its 90 bases, 1,200 of 1,700 bombers, all missiles, and 85 percent of its manpower before they could be used. The attack damaged 30 percent of American homes, set fire to over 150,000 square miles (occupied by 28 percent of the population), and spewed lethal radiation over half the nation. Out of a preattack population of 185.5 million, 12.5 million were killed outright, with the number of dead reaching 60.6 million, with an additional 6 million sick and injured. The attack destroyed 13 percent of industry and make 22 percent unusable for up to a year. A major difference from the surprise attacks previously examined was that the federal government survived, greatly easing the task of reconstruction.[20]

The outcome is a snapshot of late air-atomic strategy and its consequences. The Soviet attack was expected to peak in the first thirty minutes, a sea change from one-sided offensives measured in weeks and months, let alone World War II campaigns measured in years. The NESC expected one-third of the damage from missiles. One-third of the American population dead (one-half from fallout) showed that the devastation had become shocking. Despite this, the report grimly concluded that "the result of the initial nuclear exchange in these circumstances would not necessarily determine the outcome of the war,"[21] because both nations could suffer crippling damage and yet still prosecute global military operations.

The massive casualties predicted by the NESC appalled Eisenhower, but he saw little prospect of limiting them once a nuclear conflict began. A retaliatory attack was "a force so terrible that one simply could not be meticulous as to the methods by which the force was brought to bear."[22] He saw the continued growth of strategic forces during the late air-atomic period as a problem less from the military perspective of overkill than as a waste of resources and an unbalancing of the "great equation" of defense and economic growth.[23] Eisenhower believed Clausewitz's essential point that war tended toward escalation fueled by irrational passion. The time to control nuclear war was in the crises leading up to it, not after. Once war began, it was too late. If the United States were driven to use nuclear weapons, Eisenhower saw little reason to use them with restraint. He did not "lack" control, because he knew that any notion of controlled nuclear war was illusory. Eisenhower recognized that the only switch that could work was a simple on-off. A dimmer would not only fail, it might be dangerous. Here, perhaps, he demonstrated doubt about the competence of his successors of either party and sought to limit its consequences.

The general trend of all the national studies, from Killian to the NESC, recognized the growing vulnerability of the United States in general and SAC in particular to Soviet attack. Even though the assessments provided ammunition for the enemies of SAC, they nonetheless all supported the air-atomic idea of victory: seeking the ability to coerce the Soviets after an exchange, with damage to the United States as a secondary consideration. These ideas, and full knowledge of the devastation which nuclear war would bring to the United States, shaped the national policy of the Eisenhower administration.

What Is to Be Done?

Like the Truman administration, the Eisenhower administration encapsulated its national security policies in a discrete set of documents. Of these, BNSPs and NSC papers on wartime objectives most directly addressed atomic warfare. These core policies easily could have limited or precluded the Air Force from acting on its ideas for general war. Instead, they let it flourish. So, too, NSC decisions on other issues, such as weapon custody, added to the practice of air-atomic warfare. Eisenhower adopted strategic airpower ideas and followed them throughout his administration, despite increasingly grim prospects.

Eisenhower opened his first term with a deliberate analytical examination of national security policies. The NSC process during the Eisenhower administration is a better indicator than in most presidencies of actual thinking at the highest of levels. His formal process drew out well-documented positions from major stakeholders. Nuclear policy was no exception.

He assembled three competing task forces of experts to develop courses of strategic policy and promote them to the NSC. During "Project Solarium," strong and articulate advocates of each position led the task forces through incrementally more aggressive strategies to cope with the Soviets: status quo, massive retaliation, and rollback.[24]

Task Force A, led by the author of the original containment plan, George Kennan, supported the least aggressive alternative, a continued status quo. It argued that the United States was powerful enough to contain Soviet aggression and to win a prolonged struggle short of general war. It rejected a "calculated risk of general war," which would be "full of risk, empty of calculation, and unwarrantedly hazardous to the continued existence of the US."[25] Recovery from general war would take more than two generations. In air-atomic terms, Task Force A stated that the issue of relative advantage after the exchange was not the sole measure of victory. Kennan's group summed up its solution, which proposed an expensive containment of the USSR until its eventual collapse from internal pressure as, "The United States can afford to survive."[26]

Task Force A's recommendation could coexist with an air-atomic strategy, up to a point. Its fundamental belief that the atomic deterrent could prevent general war paid tribute to strategic airpower, but it rejected key aspects of orthodox air-atomic theory. The latter grounded the strength of the deterrent in a "war winning" capability, which convinced opponents that aggression could prompt unrestricted retaliation. Even if Task Force A did not publicly articulate its hesitance to engage in atomic war, its silence spoke loudly. So, Task Force A's policies would have allowed the air-atomic strategy to continue, but might have curtailed its growth (not necessarily in an unfortunate way) while perhaps unintentionally undermining its deterrent utility.

Task Force B, led by USAF Maj. Gen. James McCormack, held a stance more like strategic air advocates. The idea of applying "full power—whenever, however, and wherever necessary to defeat the main enemy" in a conflict that "would not be a repetition of World War II, or anything closely resembling it" fits the notion that warfare had fundamentally changed.[27] It shared the faith in offensive capability. Although Task Force B suggested increasing air defense, if only to slow the day when the Soviet Union could calculate that it had achieved atomic plenty, "we cannot set aside the fact of today that means of offense can now be foreseen against which the means of defense cannot yet be visualized."[28] An invulnerable offensive force must be preserved so "regardless of the damage that might be done on this continent, the U.S.S.R. could not expect to escape an unacceptable counterblow. Thus the advantage to the U.S.S.R. of a surprise attack on the United States may largely be made to disappear."[29] An atomic war would be "terribly destructive even to the victor" (implicitly acknowledging there would be a victor), but shunning the new "atomic reality" would frighten away the Free World and create conditions that would make general war more likely.[30] Alternative B was the only way to make US military strength an "effective factor" in world politics. American conventional forces could never counter the Red Army, and the United States could not contain Soviet aggression through symmetrical means. "Uncertainty and despair can, however, be converted into assurance and hope if the United States makes it unmistakably clear that the full extent of its military power will be applied immediately against the Soviet Bloc in the event of armed aggression."[31] Task Force B's authors directly contrasted their approach with that of Task Force A. While A left open the question of US resort to general war until the last moment of a crisis, B stated categorically that any Soviet military attempt to expand communism beyond its present borders should risk general war. "Under both . . . threat of general war is the ultimate deterrent to Soviet aggression but 'B' makes that deterrent unmistakably clear."[32] By stating in advance that Soviet military action would be met with unrestricted use of force, they would overcome a "fatal moral and political dilemma" inherent in Task Force A's position: the need to decide which areas of the free world should be abandoned to Communist domination. Resort to general war was the "ultimate sanction," but if the Soviets took military action despite American nuclear superiority after being warned it would cause a general war, this indicated they would accept the risk of annihilation to achieve their world domination goals. Such leaders would not hesitate to start atomic war themselves if they perceived an advantage. Conversely, certainty over US intentions, capabilities, and rules of the game was the surest way of restraining aggression and ambitions—of really containing.[33]

Task Force B's position was not only compatible with a robust air-atomic force but required one. By relying on a threat of general war to curb Soviet military expansion, defining it as being inevitably atomic, and denying the possibility of deterring Soviet aggression though conventional force, Task Force B embraced the air-atomic position and placed SAC at the center of national security.

Task Force C supported the most aggressive position: rollback. It rejected the ideas of containment or equilibrium. Rather, it argued, the United States had lost ground in the Cold War and the growth of Soviet atomic capability threatened to wreck the West's staying power. American superiority would end, and the United States must act before the Soviets achieved "decisive stocks and delivery capabilities."[34] Neither the status quo nor indefinite reliance on the threat of general war would do. The only choice remaining was to "face up to the challenge posed by the Communist conspiracy and devote the necessary effort to the task of winning the cold war."[35] This required not only military threats, but a political offensive against the Soviet Bloc. The threat of Soviet atomic weapons set the timetable for rollback, which must be done under the aegis of US superiority.[36] The only limit on the rollback campaign's intensity was that it be conducted "without . . . initiating general war," a position the authors contrasted to stated NSC policy of reducing Soviet power "without unduly risking a general war."[37] It hoped this policy would "reduce Soviet power and influence to a point which no longer threatens our security, without initiating general war."[38] Yet this aggressive political campaign demanded a readiness to engage in general war. Task Force C, reasoning that "every impartial study" had failed to prove that tactical nuclear weapons would reduce the need for conventional weapons, recommended that traditional forces be augmented to meet D-day commitments. It also called for an accelerated improvement of continental air defense to meet Soviet nuclear forces and ensure "that our counter-air-strikes could be launched without any delay whatsoever."[39]

Alternative C's authors framed their proposals as being more active than A or B. Except for preventive war, every "means of action" was on the table. Its authors suggested plans consistent with late air-atomic ideas and explicitly required readiness for an immediate blunting offensive, but rejected the idea that strategic airpower could achieve its primary jobs either of deterring or war fighting. In effect, Team C actually doubted the air-atomic strategy and supported a more aggressive and militaristic policy than did SAC.

After these options were presented to the NSC in mid-July 1953, Eisenhower directed that national policy follow a line combining elements of each Task Force's approach, as John Lewis Gaddis concludes. Citing Kennan's claim that Solarium was a victory for his version of containment, Gaddis points out that Task Force A's "containment" is actually closer to NSC-68's robust formulation than that of the Long Telegram.[40] In the NSC's words, American policy would "build and maintain, at the lowest feasible cost, US capability for a strong retaliatory offensive, a base for mobilization, and continental defense." It would focus on creating strong regional alliances, determine areas where Soviet aggression would be considered the initiation of general war, examine taking "selected aggressive actions of a limited scope" to eliminate Soviet-dominated areas in the West, and take nonmilitary action to curtail indigenous Communist movements. The Solarium outcome briefing estimated that the risk of general war resulting from aggressive action against the Soviet bloc was "less grave" than Task Force A estimated, and that the United States should accept the "moderately increased risks of general war" by taking aggressive actions against Soviet satellites.[41] Despite this borrowing from Task Force C, wholesale rollback was dead from this early point in the Eisenhower administration. Brig. Gen. Andrew Goodpaster, Eisenhower's staff secretary, summed up Solarium as eliminating rollback. "It was finished as of that day.

It had been very much in the rhetoric of the campaign and, to some degree, in the early months of the Eisenhower administration. But he used this, and in my belief he did it very intentionally and deliberately, as a means of forging a single controlling idea that would dominate his administration."[42] Solarium was a tool to let those with opposing views on grand strategy have their say, feel that they had been heard out, and unequivocally understand the president's decision. Meanwhile, Solarium probed the implications of the nuclear balance, put it into a Cold War context, and placed late air-atomic strategy at the core of American policy.

The resulting official national security policy was encapsulated in NSC-162/2. To use Gaddis's term, the new BNSP embraced an "asymmetrical" approach, which matched American economic and nuclear strength against Soviet conventional power, where NSC-68 had tried to build up US military forces to meet the Soviets on the battlefield in the "year of maximum danger." NSC-162/2 held that the Cold War would be fought over a long, indefinite period. Eventual victory demanded a healthy American economy not weighed down by excessive military expenditure. This was a key step for US victory in the Cold War. Brent Scowcroft summarized the new policy direction as putting "us in shape for the long run. The Cold War was not an acute crisis that had to be solved today; it was something we had to learn to live with."[43]

The paper defined the basic problem of national security as twofold: "to meet the Soviet threat to US security" without "seriously weakening the US economy or undermining our fundamental values and institutions."[44] This required "a strong military posture, with emphasis on the capability of inflicting massive retaliatory damage by offensive striking power."[45] NSC-162/2, however, recognized that Soviet atomic capacity was growing and would soon be strengthened with fusion weapons. Soviet nuclear forces could inflict serious damage, while a surprise attack might deal a "crippling blow."[46] When both nations reached atomic plenty, the BNSP forecast that each side could cripple the other while neither could prevent major retaliation. This situation could create stalemate, with both countries "reluctant to initiate general warfare," but only if the Soviets understood that a surprise attack could not prevent US retaliation.[47] The policy aimed to keep Soviet leaders certain of American resolve and policy, and uncertain of their own ability ever to destroy US capabilities.

NSC-162/2 stated that in a crisis where any warning might provide an added deterrent, the United States would "make clear" to the Sino-Soviet bloc, either in "general terms or with reference to specific areas," what it would do militarily. Given the reliance placed on restructuring US military forces around atomic weapons, that is, in a crisis the United States would threaten nuclear use. To make the point direct, paragraph 39 (b) (1) specifies, "In the event of hostilities, the United States will consider nuclear weapons to be as available for use as other munitions."[48]

Paragraph 39 (b) (1) became the subject of intense discussion during the drafting of the BNSP, with State squaring off against the Department of Defense (DoD). Their positions and the resolution illustrate the White House position on atomic use, and by extension, the air-atomic strategy. DoD staked out its territory firmly within traditional airpower thinking. The entire policy expressed in 162/2 depended on strategic and tactical atomic weapons. They were the "principal deterrent to war and as a way by which adequate security may be maintained without a dangerous burden on the US economy." Unless the NSC made "a final and clear decision" that nuclear weapons would be used precisely as other munitions, it would be impossible to prepare adequately for conflict. In peripheral wars, nuclear weapons would be "available," but not at the whim of local commanders. Rather, if the president expanded hostilities against "the obvious sources of supply and support, even though these might be in Red China or in the USSR itself," then the military must be ready to use its "best weapons." Similarly, in general war, the issue should be whether to attack, not what types of weapons to use.[49]

By contrast, the State Department argued that the purpose of 39b was to let the military plan for nuclear use, and not to make a "present decision that atomic weapons will, in fact, be used in the event of any hostilities." The president could decide whether to use atomic weapons only in the diplomatic context of a crisis.[50] So too, the Atomic Energy Commission, stated that 39b only meant nuclear weapons were part of normal military equipment. They were not "generally available" nor could "their use be arbitrarily decided upon by a local commander."[51]

Eisenhower considered these differing interpretations and firmly adopted the DoD position on general war, while leaving his policy for limited conflict ambiguous. The paragraph let the military plan on the availability of nuclear weapons but did not make an advance decision on their use, except in certain cases—such as an atomic attack on the United States or Europe—where it would be automatic. He recognized that in many situations, particularly in limited war, the president must decide whether to use such weapons based on the existing circumstances; no decision could be taken in advance. General war was a different matter. "The use of atomic weapons for such retaliatory purposes is not in doubt."[52]

NSC-162/2's wording and presidential confirmation, however, make clear the unambiguous intent of the BNSP on the use of atomic weapons in general war. This reflected Eisenhower's conviction that "the nature of war had changed forever."[53] This belief, the dependence on atomic weapons, and the conviction that national defense policy must rest on the deterrent strength of retaliatory force, all put basic national security policy squarely in line with nuclear air strategy. Eisenhower rejected Army attempts to return to a mobilization-based defense. In 1955, he expressed his frustration with the Army in a letter to Secretary of Defense Charles Wilson. "It would be perfect rot to talk about shipping troops abroad when fifteen of our cities were in ruins. You would have disorder and almost complete chaos in the cities and in the roads around them. . . . That order is going to have to be restored by disciplined armed forces. . . . That's what our military is going to be doing in the first days of an all-out atomic attack."[54] When the JCS examined NSC-162/2, they concluded that it placed "emphasis upon the capability of inflicting massive damage upon the USSR by our retaliatory striking power as the major deterrent to aggression, and a vital element of any US strategy in the event of general war" and demanded "the maintenance of qualitative superiority of our armed forces."[55] This refinement further linked national policy and air-atomic strategy. NSC-162/2 asserted that action and declaratory policy were not just compatible, but indivisible.

The NSC routinely reviewed BNSPs through the 1950s. Each updated document reflected changes in the strategic situation, but all remained steadfast in their conclusions about general war. For example, NSC-5501 admitted that "Soviet air-atomic capabilities are rapidly increasing;" by 1960 the USSR "almost certainly" would develop the net capability to cripple the United States.[56] The number of weapons threatened a total war which would "bring about such extensive destruction as to threaten the survival of both Western civilization and the Soviet system."[57] Rather than shift policy, however, the growing threat reinforced the reliance on the nuclear deterrent. "This stress on deterrence is dictated by the disastrous character of total nuclear war . . . Communist rulers must be convinced that aggression will not serve their interests: that it will not pay."[58] Security continued to depend on "effective nuclear-air retaliatory power," secure from a surprise knockout blow. So long as the Soviets remained uncertain if they could knock out SAC, they would avoid actions with an "appreciable risk of general war."[59] The growing cost of general war would not deter the United States from resolute action in a crisis. "In the last analysis, if confronted by the choice of (a) acquiescing in communist aggression or (b) taking measures risking either general war or loss of allied support, the United States must be prepared to take these risks as necessary for its security."[60]

This firm stance extended to the end of the decade. The final Eisenhower BNSP, NSC-5906, embodied both the grim truth of Soviet nuclear ability and the administration's conviction that only the air-atomic strategy could counter it. NSC-5906 still declared that it was "the policy of the United States . . . to integrate nuclear weapons with other weapons in the Armed Forces . . . and to use them when required to meet the nation's war objectives." Deterring general war depended on the maintenance of a secure retaliatory force that kept Soviet leaders "uncertain of their ability to neutralize" it. The United States must oppose "aggression despite risk of general war and must make this determination clear. The United States must also make clear its determination to prevail if general war occurs."[61]

NSC-5906, like its predecessors, recognized Soviet power and yet still accepted the basics of late air-atomic strategy, including the idea that "prevailing" was possible.

Rejection of preventive war was a further consistency in the BNSPs. Although the record is circumspect, during Solarium, an "Alternative D" to consider an American attack was mooted. The "working committee" (Eisenhower advisor Walter Bedell Smith, CIA director Allen Dulles, and Special Assistant for National Security Affairs Robert Cutler) decided that once Task Forces A, B, and C had completed their work, the "best men on these Task Forces" should study Alternative D, defined as "the possibility that time is not working in our favor."[62] No evidence, however suggests that examining preventive war moved past this early planning stage. Most probably, the president halted further examination of the subject, and named General Goodpaster to Task Force C to ensure that it did not stray from studying rollback.[63]

Although Eisenhower often raised the issue during NSC meetings, these were little more than "abstract musings."[64] His real attitude probably is reflected in a letter of August 1954 from National Security Advisor Robert Cutler to the White House Chief of Staff, Sherman Adams. Cutler described a proposal from former Vermont governor Ernest Gibson, which advocated for preventive war. Cutler declared that it was "inconsistent with current US policy and my belief of what it is possible for a Christian nation to do." Apparently the president had received similar recommendations as Cutler complained that "presentations of this kind are baffling to deal with" because they came from "men of high principle and goodwill." Still, "it's one thing to talk about 'preventive war' from an ivory tower. It's quite different to put it into action as president of the United States, upon whose decision may hang 30,000,000 American lives and the whole future survival of our people."[65]

Eisenhower publicized his thoughts during an August 1954 press conference, when NBC correspondent Ray Scherer asked him to address the "increasing suggestions that we should embark on a preventive war." Eisenhower replied that the hypothetical example of action against Hitler to prevent the outbreak of the Second World War shaped his definition of preventive war. The idea was to "wage some sort of quick police action, in order that you might avoid a terrific cataclysm of destruction later." In the nuclear age, however, preventive war was impossible by this definition. With Solarium, NSC-162/2, and NESC no doubt fresh in his mind, he asked Scherer "How could you have one, if one of its features would be several cities lying in ruins, several cities where many, many thousands of people would be dead and injured and mangled, and transportation systems destroyed, sanitation, implements and systems all gone? That is not preventive war. That is war. . . . I wouldn't even listen to anyone, seriously, that came in talking about such a thing."[66] Eisenhower's rejection of preventive war, both in internal policy discussions and public, set a limit to a driving force behind late air-atomic thought. The Air Force's reaction to the tightened time factor had been strike as soon as possible after the outbreak of conflict. The success of blunting depended on catching Soviet weapons on the ground. The logical conclusion would be to strike LRA by surprise in exactly the kind of attack SAC feared. However, just like Truman, Eisenhower ruled preventive war out as an alternative. Mark Trachtenberg writes that American strength with respect to the USSR in the first years of Eisenhower's administration influenced it to take a hard line, as Germany did in 1914, not actively seeking a showdown with Moscow, but not fearing the risk of war. But there is an important difference between risking war and beginning it.[67]

Ironically, under Eisenhower's administration, SAC was well suited to a preemptive attack, which would have demolished Soviet nuclear capabilities for few US lives and not many Soviet ones. Even as contemporary technology made a surprise attack possible, national policy ruled it out.

Other documents translated the BNSPs into specific wartime goals. The first set of Eisenhower era objectives, NSC-5410, built on NSC-162/2's primary mission of "insuring the survival of the United States as a free nation and the continuation of its free institutions in the post-war world." In wartime, that demanded reducing by "military and other measures the capabilities of the USSR to the point where it has lost its will or ability to wage war against the United States and its allies." This meant "rendering ineffective" the military and political mechanisms which the USSR and PRC used to control their satellites. Once these operations succeeded, the United States would insure that postwar regimes were not totalitarian or aggressive (but not insist that they be friendly or democratic). Whatever the form of the new bloc governments, they would not be allowed to develop military power sufficient to threaten the United States again. Eventually, the defeated nations would be integrated into a "just and peaceful" international order.[68]

Strategic airpower easily could accomplish these general objectives. Destroying or isolating the major communist regimes would not require their occupation. Nuclear airpower could destroy their "will or ability to wage war." Not surprisingly, the Air Force supported implementation of the draft version of 5410 without change. The Army and Navy, however, asked the secretary of defense to include more specific objectives and tie the wartime objectives more closely to a desired political end. They aimed directly at the air-atomic mechanism for reaching the postwar environment. The older services contended "full exploitation of our nuclear capability might so damage the governmental organization, the industrial and communications systems, and the social structure of the USSR as to produce total collapse." With "wide-spread chaos and human misery . . . on a scale unknown in Europe since the end of the Thirty Years' War," Army and Navy planners thought it impossible for the United States to rebuild a shattered global economy for the third time in forty years. Neither the secretary of defense nor the NSC found these arguments compelling, as the NSC adopted 5410 without change, embracing objectives permitting an unfettered air-atomic strategy.[69]

Just like the successive BNSPs, so too did the supporting wartime objectives reflect shifts in military power and technology. The final set approved by Eisenhower, NSC-5904, were bleak, but still supported late air-atomic thinking. The primary wartime US objective was to "prevail, and survive as a nation capable of controlling its own destiny." Military and "other measures" must undermine the USSR and PRC's will and ability to wage war, and sever their links to the satellites. Even though it counseled restraint against nonparticipants, the NSC directed the use of "all requisite force against selected targets in the USSR—and as necessary in Communist China, European Bloc and non-European Bloc."[70] The striking continuity between the first and last wartime objective statements of the decade displays the White House's commitment to an air-atomic strategy despite a growing Soviet threat.

National policy also covered a spectrum of issues, essential to the deterrent, such as weapon custody. In April 1953, the Defense Department asked the AEC to give it custody of atomic weapons, as the weapons were only one part of a larger system and their "effective application" required integration with associated military units. Consolidation would allow "more intelligent and progressive" planning and budgeting, and remove a potential block to rapidly launching an air offensive.[71]

While State agreed with Defense, the AEC dissented.[72] Framing the requested change as a "radical" reversal, Commissioner Henry Smyth told the NSC that the proposed arrangements would raise "grave problems" for maintaining and upgrading the weapons. He rejected the JCS assertion that divided responsibility for the weapons endangered security.[73] In a decision representative of many Eisenhower made over the decade, he generally affirmed the Defense position. The Pentagon would assume responsibility for the manufacture, production, acquisition, and custody of nonnuclear parts of implosion weapons, and of the nuclear systems of gun-type devices. Although this verdict left exceptions, it mainly supported the DoD position and enabled faster launching of the offensive.[74]

National security policy during the 1950s placed the nuclear air campaign at the heart of American security. After consciously considering the alternatives, Eisenhower selected one relying on the strategic air offensive, because it fit his conception of modern war, even as successive studies documented the devastation of a nuclear exchange. As he told McElroy in 1959, "If we get into an all-out war both sides would attack the population centers of the other."[75] Since a nuclear exchange would involve unrestricted violence, the deterrent must be perfected. "If we are going to fight a nuclear war, it was clear in [Eisenhower's] mind that we would attack cities and governmental concentrations. Invariably, the reasoning leads us back to perfecting the deterrent."[76] Eisenhower's desire to perfect the deterrent and SAC's apparent resignation to the possibility of war, which implies lack of confidence in deterrence, are compatible points of view, indeed, essential ones. The relationship can be compared to a man with a leashed pit bull. An aggressive dog, straining at its leash, prepared to fight for its owner, can be an excellent deterrent. It must be visibly ready to attack if it is to deter. So, too, the owner must convince a potential attacker that he would release the dog if he felt threatened. SAC derived much of its deterrent strength from the visible readiness of its crews to carry out their mission. A vital part of that credibility was mental preparedness to attack. That state of mind could be achieved only if SAC and its leaders believed conflict was a real possibility for which they must be prepared. Eisenhower had precisely the ideas, self-confidence, and expertise needed to keep SAC on its leash. Where Khrushchev distorted Soviet capability for war, Eisenhower exaggerated American desire for it. Eisenhower did not embrace the idea of nuclear war, but he regarded deterrence as unavoidable, which meant one must be able and willing to fight. In effect, he executed the strategy which Thomas Schelling later described as "chicken": when two drivers drive head on toward each other, and one ostentatiously throws his steering wheel out the window, so to force the other to abandon the competition.

Eisenhower's strategy for avoiding general war hinged on the horror of thermonuclear combat. Eisenhower became convinced by the middle of his first term that the only way to avoid nuclear war with the Soviet Union was to avoid war with it altogether. He denied that any conflict with the USSR could be contained. Gaddis points to Eisenhower's reading of Clausewitz's dictum that war always moves toward greater violence and escalation.[77] In the thermonuclear era, as NESC reports clearly showed, such escalation could lead only to national destruction. By clearly defining general war as the unrestricted use of force against the Soviet Union, and rejecting any illusions that such a war could remain limited, Eisenhower deliberately reduced crisis alternatives. A decision maker must opt either for political resolution or general war. And the way to do this was to persuade everyone involved in the making of decisions that (a) limited options did not exist, (b) in the event of war the president will push every button, and (c) the war will kill hundreds of millions and destroy American society. By contriving such a stark dichotomy, a strong leader could resist the pressure of those heretofore determined to wage war rather than conciliate.[78]

This policy was fully compatible with late air-atomic strategy. Indeed, had SAC not existed, Eisenhower would have had to invent it. Its overwhelming deterrent power (flowing from its visible war-fighting ability) was the one indispensable element in his strategy.

Limits of the Pit Bull's Leash

Soon after the Korean armistice, the question of using atomic weapons arose again. In 1954, an Air Force position paper on national policy categorized Russian and Chinese intervention in Indochina as a major danger. The threat of "massive retaliatory damage is today deterring Chinese and Russian intervention in Indochina" just as it "deterred Russia from intervening openly in Korea."[79] During May 1954, in the shadow of Dien Bien Phu, the JCS recommended to Secretary of Defense Wilson that "the United States should adopt the concept of offensive actions against the "military power of the aggressor," in this instance Communist China, rather than the concept of "reaction locally at the point of attack."[80] Should an atomic attack have become necessary, SAC probably would have carried out its plan for renewed war in Korea. It would deploy an augmentation force to the advanced operating areas to be prepared for general war if a local war escalated.[81] The national intelligence community concluded that an atomic offensive against selected Chinese targets would make the PRC believe the United States was ready for unrestricted war. The actions would make them negotiate a withdrawal from Indochina, but if that failed, the PRC would accept unlimited war. Notably, while the National Intelligence Estimate (NIE) stated that due to the attacks the Chinese "might eventually" negotiate, the Air Force intelligence director suggested using the words "would probably."[82]

Twining later bemoaned that the United States had shied away from using atomic weapons in Indochina. He told Air Force commanders in May 1954, "We have got to educate the peoples of the world about this atomic bomb."[83] The weapons were no more inhumane than napalm, they "just kill a few more people. . . . certainly if we ever depart from the fact that this is another munition, purely, we are going to use it when it is to the best interests of the United States to use it, we have lost this one."[84] Although he was referring to tactical use of nuclear weapons, the sentiment clearly applies to strategic issues as well: the atomic weapon was just another tool to be used when militarily profitable. A nuclear taboo that might hamper their employment could not be allowed to develop. Twining was to be disappointed.

The two crises over the Quemoy and Matsu islands in 1955 and 1958 show the continued problems with the application of an air-atomic centered national policy short of war. The Quemoy and Matsu islands remained in Nationalist Chinese hands after the 1949 revolution, despite being only a few miles off the mainland coast. The islands remained a major source of tension between the rival Chinese governments. A Communist commando raid on Quemoy in late August 1954 was followed by daily large-scale artillery bombardments starting 3 September. While the United States considered if its security guarantee to Taiwan should cover the offshore islands, the Communists expanded the crisis. They launched air attacks on the Tachen Islands on 1 November, while building up land and air forces opposite the islands. Occasional air and steady artillery attacks continued over the next few months. Four thousand troops took the island of Ichang on 18 January.[85] In the face of this carefully calibrated Chinese challenge, the United States considered a policy based on NSC-162/2. Admiral Radford, chairman of the Joint Chiefs, told Wilson in September 1954 that the local commander needed authority to strike when and where necessary to defeat an invasion of the islands.[86]

As the crisis ground on into the spring, and local Communist land and air strength grew, JCS plans firmed up. In mid-March 1955, Admiral Felix Stump, the Pacific Fleet commander, identified Chinese Communist air strength as the key measure of their capability and the trigger for American action. United States intervention would be necessary only if the Communists moved substantial airpower into the operational area, otherwise Nationalist forces could contain the threat alone. "If, however, the CHICOMS [Chinese Communists] move air forces in strength into the area, the U.S. would have to be prepared to employ atomic weapons before or as soon as the CHICOMS employ their air against CHINAT [Chinese Nationalist] forces or U.S. fleet elements."[87] When the JCS considered the use of atomic weapons, the Army believed the Communists would try to seize the offshore islands even if they believed the United States would intervene. It also thought there was a "greater than slight" danger that using nuclear weapons against China could trigger a retaliation, presumably by the Communist Bloc against regional bases such as Japan. The other services thought that danger "slight."[88]

On 31 March 1955, the JCS recommended warning Beijing and Moscow through diplomatic channels that the United States would defend Quemoy and Matsu, and deployment of SAC bomber wings to East Asia. The JCS thought danger very likely, signaled by Chinese improvements of nearby airfields to support jet aircraft, stockpiled fuel and other essentials, and preparation for amphibious invasion. If that came to pass, the United States must strike all airfields with assets able to reach the combat area (so to avoid a repetition of the Manchurian sanctuaries), and immediately use atomic weapons against airbases and POL storage sites close to the islands, progressively extending to more distant airfields. The first atomic targets included at least six airfields and POL storage locations at Shanghai and Canton. SAC would provide whatever support was requested and prepare for extended operations against the PRC. If the Communists broadened hostilities, the United States should launch further air attacks, establish a blockade, and conduct offensive mining.[89] The intelligence community, however, thought the chances of Chinese horizontal escalation were low. A special NIE concluded that the PRC was unlikely to "undertake courses of action which it considers might involve substantial risk of provoking unlimited war," although the USAF intelligence director dissented, stating, "Communist China's courses of action [are] dangerously unpredictable under outside pressure of any appreciable magnitude."[90]

After Chou En-Lai announced on 20 April that the PRC had no wish to fight the United States, the crisis tailed off. This followed a four-week period in which Eisenhower publicly stated that the use of atomic weapons was under consideration and a leaked off-the-record statement by the chief of naval operations predicted a Chinese attack and a robust US response.[91] Probably, the threat of horizontal and vertical escalation shaped the Chinese decision to defuse the crisis. Plans to blunt the Chinese Air Force and halt an invasion were well developed and dependent on atomic weapons. Although, strictly speaking, the initial atomic use was tactical (it was not preparing the way to attack industrial targets), to strike the enemy's force-in-being first was consistent with strategic air doctrine.

Yet the underlying political issues remained. On 23 August 1958, Communist shore batteries bombarded Quemoy and Matsu, firing fifty thousand shells on the first day alone and continuing at the same intensity through 4 September. Until 7 September, when the US Navy began escorting Nationalist convoys to the islands, they were cut off from resupply. After an initial period of indecision, the US government assessed the situation as critical, fearing that Quemoy could be the first in a series of dominoes (leading to Tokyo) whose fall would undermine Western security in Asia.[92] After Eisenhower loosely tied defense of the offshore islands to Taiwan during a press conference, Dulles implied strongly that US forces would meet an invasion of Quemoy with nuclear weapons. The Chinese shelling continued through September, although Beijing did not attempt an invasion. United States Navy convoys supplied the isolated islands by 21 September, and the crisis subsided with a 6 October cease-fire announced by the Communists.[93]

The JCS considered military action during this crisis much as it had done in 1955. While an invasion of the offshore islands could be handled with conventional weapons, an invasion of Taiwan would require the use of atomic weapons.[94] On 29 August, Eisenhower discussed these plans and considered approving the use of atomic weapons even to defend the islands, although it might "outrage world opinion."[95] Later, the British foreign minister and ambassador told him "that there would be no doubt that if the United States used nuclear weapons in that area, then there was 'going to be hell to pay.' "[96] In the end, Eisenhower declined to delegate authority to use atomic weapons at any stage.[97]

Despite hesitancy at the White House, the JCS concluded, as in 1955, that atomic weapons must be used if war broke out. Although atomic weapons would be efficient and decisive in stopping Communist attacks on the islands, Twining thought it likely that the United States initially would use only conventional weapons. If that failed, however, "it is most probable that we will have to use atomic weapons against air bases and perhaps against other targets on the Chinese mainland."[98] The initial attack would hit only five coastal airfields with seven 16 KT airbursts (because ground bursts would create too much fallout), each with a lethal area of three to four miles, after which the United States would "stop to observe the effect on communist intentions." Twining believed the bombs would take out the aircraft and ground facilities, but leave the runways intact.[99] He informed the secretary of defense that planning had commenced for the Navy to assist the Nationalists with either conventional or atomic weapons, while a SAC medium bomber squadron on Guam could hit mainland targets with thirty hours notice. Any SAC support beyond the medium bombers already in the theater would be flown from North America, under SAC control.[100]

At the height of the crisis, the Joint Chiefs bluntly said,

> This presents in concrete terms the whole question of whether we can use our best weapons in "limited war"—that is, in any eventuality except a major retaliation against the Soviet Union itself. Such an issue could indeed arise anywhere in the world.
>
> This issue in turn poses this dilemma; are we to risk loss of US prestige and influence in the world, through loss of the Offshore Islands occasioned by failure to exert a maximum defense; or are we to risk loss of prestige and influence, [redacted]
>
> It was the consensus that we should take the second risk. If we were to decide not to, we would have to recast our whole philosophy of defense planning. If we do not decide to take the second risk, each succeeding crisis and its concomitant decision will become increasingly difficult for us.[101]

The after-action assessments for the 1958 Taiwan Straits Crisis illustrate the limits of an air-atomic force in peripheral war. The JCS report, written in December, concluded that while Communist bombardment had been "clearly prevented only by CHICOM fear of US retaliation," American national interests would "not always permit the use of nuclear weapons, at least not initially."[102] So too, an NSC analysis stated that conventional weapons provided a vital time cushion for diplomacy.[103]

The Pacific Air Forces (PACAF) commander, Gen. Lawrence Kuter, presented his assessment to a Zone of the Interior Commanders Conference in November. Although he thought the crisis was well handled, he was

> surprised and dismayed on receiving guidance that we must initially use iron bombs. . . . Our US and particularly USAF planning for the last ten

> years has been predicated on nuclear warfare . . . to thwart the massive manpower and quantities of materiel available to the Communist Bloc. To date, we have apparently failed to convince our own government that to counter the Chinese Communist threat nuclear weapons must be used. We saw as recently that nuclear warfare is necessary to stop the Chinese Communists. To compound our situation, we cannot avoid the fact that we are not prepared to conduct [conventional] operations to any significant degree. . . . I fully recognize the political machinations surrounding the use of nuclear weapons but we must be realistic and convincing to our leaders that the only way we can stop the Communists is through the use of nuclear weapons.[104]

In other words, the nature of war had changed but the White House did not understand it. White praised Kuter's presentation as the best he had heard in years and agreed "strongly with [Kuter's] views on use of nuclear weapons and the public information problem."[105]

The 1958 Quemoy crisis exemplified the problems faced in applying the air-atomic ideas to limited war. The plans for using nuclear weapons relied on the late air-atomic idea of attacking the enemy's airpower first, in the hope that air superiority would coerce the enemy to halt aggression, and then to prepare for rapid horizontal escalation. The diplomatic limitations, problems with domestic support, and fear of escalation, however, all contributed to strengthening the atomic taboo first seen in Korea. Air-atomic power proved an excellent deterrent time and again, but when forced to look over the precipice, national leadership grasped for ways to buy time before using them, preferring first to exhaust the power of conventional forces. The threat of an atomic offensive was powerful, but the cost of executing one was daunting. Despite all the rhetoric of massive retaliation, politicians were unwilling to press forward and even planning did not get very far.

Late air-atomic strategy proved unstable in a crisis, but its deterrent effect sobered enemies and curbed their choices. Khrushchev was acutely sensitive to the balance of strategic forces and fearful of nuclear war, as two examples attest. In 1958, he waited until Soviet ballistic missiles capable of striking London and Paris were in place to issue his ultimatum on Berlin.[106] Four years later, a powerful motivation for his attempted placement of missiles in Cuba was to offset SAC's overwhelming strength. During that crisis, his rambling letter to Kennedy on 26 October in which he wrote of the "catastrophe of nuclear war," speaks to his fear of the devastation that SAC could wreak.[107] The vast imbalance in favor of SAC and its unquestionable ability to destroy the USSR was a constant backdrop to the crises of the 1950s and 1960s. Khrushchev tried to right that balance through building—and deliberately exaggerating the strength of—Soviet nuclear forces, and by desperate maneuvers such as placing them in Cuba. American air-atomic forces molded the strategic environment in which Khrushchev operated, shaped his choices, and curbed his adventurism.

Eisenhower's goal was to avoid crises altogether, and through all the instruments at his disposal, where his only options were military and air-atomic. The structure of the strategy, with its dependence on maximum violence in minimum time and a "go/no-go" command and control system, met Eisenhower's purposes. His only decision in military crises was to keep the air-atomic switch off. His success in doing so challenges prominent accounts of this period, which portray LeMay and his contemporaries as barely restrained, pointing to aggressive intelligence gathering and plans to transfer weapons to military custody in an atomic attack in which communication with Washington was cut. The record of actual behavior in crises, where provocation of the enemy could have been arranged had senior officers truly wanted war, should temper these accusations. This point, drawn from negative evidence, is reinforced by one case where positive evidence exists. Air Force deliberations after Eisenhower's actions in 1958 speak of educating the president and the public about the realities of contemporary conflict. These are the discussions of frustrated officers wishing to educate their commander in chief, not ones conspiring to undermine him.

Eisenhower had civil-military dynamics under control. Part of his success came from process. The NSC's formal mechanism for considering the positions of all stakeholders gave uniformed and civilian officials alike assurance that their concerns were heard in the White House. Eisenhower's control also stemmed from personal competence in military affairs. No military officer could claim knowledge superior to him. After bitter lessons in 1944–45, Eisenhower had learned to stop fundamental dissent from any officer. He did not spare his former service, as his fiery relationships with Army chiefs of staff Generals Matthew Ridgeway and Maxwell Taylor demonstrate.[108] Another sign of Eisenhower's confidence was his selecting secretaries of defense with managerial, rather than military, experience. Their task was to find the efficiencies the American economy needed in defense, not set strategic policy.[109]

National policy overall during the 1950s was narrowly tailored, but it strongly supported late air-atomic ideas. That policy was set in place by a White House fully aware of the growing dangers of a nuclear exchange. Its policies focused on general war where it accepted a near certainty of atomic use with maximum speed and violence. Although the realistic limitation of depending on such weapons reduced flexibility during crises throughout the decade, national policy remained unchanged. The power of a sympathetic White House gave the late air-atomic idea the room to flourish. Yet what the Oval Office gave, it also could take away.

6

STALEMATE, FINITE DETERRENCE, POLARIS, AND SIOP-62

The B-36 hearings did not resolve the interservice rivalry over placing the Air Force within the national security structure and displacing the Navy as the first line of national defense. Although the Air Force and its air-atomic ideas were secure from immediate threat, the other services continued their struggle against it. Some attempts to seize slices of the Air Force mission and budget, like the fight over tactical airpower, were rooted outside strategic airpower. However, the senior services also attacked strategic air theory to provide leverage in other skirmishes. At the start of the 1950s, the Navy continued using the aircraft carrier to restore its lost status. Here, it accepted the principles of strategic air theory and only sought a place for the carrier within it. The Navy's transition to advocacy of finite deterrence began in mid-decade, with the Martin XP6M Sea Master seaplane and culminated in the Polaris submarine-launched ballistic missile (SLBM). The place of finite deterrence, tailored to the strengths and weaknesses of the SLBM, sharply opposed air-atomic theory. Similarly, the Army challenged the theoretical basis of SAC's predominance by claiming that Soviet nuclear power would cause stalemate—reviving the need for Army limited war forces. These theories became possible because of the characteristics of the air-atomic idea and the size and success of SAC. The interservice disputes also reflected the influence of the civilian strategic community, which emerged as an entity during the 1950s. It affected the debate, but only when a service adopted their arguments. The services used civilian ideas about stalemate and finite deterrence when it suited their purpose—to gain a larger share of the budget. That was the prize.

Limited War and Stalemate

The Army's crusade for limited war forces burned slowly but steadily throughout the decade. The concept of a form of warfare other than globe-spanning industrial conflict rejected recent experience. Generally speaking, American definitions of general war involved ideas of unrestricted use of force against the Sino-Soviet bloc, while those about limited war hedged restrictions regarding the degree of force or geographic boundaries of its application. Slowly, however, distinguishing "limited war" from "general war" became an important part of the interservice struggle. By 1959, all four services had refined their own competing definitions.

To the Air Force, general war was "armed conflict directed by competent political authority between the USSR and the United States."[1] To the Army, "the only power which now possesses the capability to threaten the national survival of the United States is the USSR. There is, accordingly . . . a unique condition which exists in respect to a formally declared state of war between the United States and the USSR. This unique condition is recognized as general war."[2] To the Army, the only war that threatened national survival was general war. To the Air Force, any war with the USSR fit this bill.

Limited war to the Air Force was "overt armed conflict that may be characterized by limitations on locale, weapons, forces, participants or objectives . . . [against] an enemy other than the Soviet Union."[3] The Army's more baroque definition called limited war

> overt armed conflict which may be characterized by limitations on locale, weapons, forces, participants or objectives. . . . in which a Free World Nation is actively engaged in military conflict with a member of the Sino-Soviet Bloc. . . . The US . . . must always be ready to provide whatever assistance its Allies or the Free World may require. While this assistance may vary in degree, from advice and the furnishing of material to active support by US forces, there must be no doubt that it will be forthcoming.[4]

Telling differences between the two services' definitions reflect their agendas and underlying ideas about the nature of modern conflict. The Air Force definitions, clearer cut, stem from notions of a "pure" form of war with unrestricted violence and maximum speed. There was general and then progressively more restricted war, but limited war was just a diluted variant of the pure form. To the Army, general war meant only the narrow case of conflict to the death between the superpowers. Limited war covered every other case, in which the Army was the service chiefly concerned. The example of a Warsaw Pact invasion of Western Europe clarifies the distance between the two positions. Since this involved direct conflict between the superpowers, that would be a general war to the Air Force, implying it should take the lead role against it. To the Army, since a conventional invasion of Europe did not directly threaten American survival, it constituted limited war, and so was the Army's task. These were not empty semantic games. Rather, these subtle differences would direct primary responsibility to different services to handle major conventional conflict, with budgetary implications.

From the perspective of strategic air advocates, the Army argument focused on the idea of stalemate. The Army claimed that SAC sooner or later would lose its ability to deter or localize Soviet aggression, because of the reciprocal Soviet threat. The Soviets could expand in areas where diplomatic obstacles would prevent the United States from applying unrestricted force. This could be restrained only by "discriminating" forces. The United States must have not only a nuclear deterrent, but also the ability "to intercede quickly and effectively in military conflicts short of general war when US national interests or commitments require."[5] There was a direct line from the idea of strategic stalemate to increases in conventional war forces.

General Maxwell Taylor, Army Chief of Staff during the middle of the decade, summarized the Army's case for limited war forces in his 1960 book, *The Uncertain Trumpet*. He argued that the loss of technological superiority and the lack of an antiballistic missile undermined massive retaliation, which, more generally, suffered from the "Great Fallacy" that general war forces could assure national security. The United States was unlikely to use massive retaliation in ambiguous situations because of stalemate. This new reality reversed the roles of atomic and conventional forces.

> Initially, the concept had been that ground forces in Europe and the Far East were the shield behind which the US could deliver the devastating blows of its atomic sword. Now the role was being reversed. The atomic retaliatory forces had become the shield of protection warding off the threat of hostile atomic attack, while the forces of limited war provided the flexible sword for parry, riposte, and attack.[6]

In Korea, US atomic threats had not secured victory.[7] Taylor denied that nuclear weapons could win even a general war in a meaningful sense. Rather, after the first exchange there would be a long struggle, similar to what the British referred to as "broken backed" war. He proposed restructuring American security policy around "Flexible Response," which would stress meeting Soviet threats with equal forces, rather than threatening horizontal or vertical escalation.[8] More generally, he and the Army both stated that nuclear weapons could not solve key problems of important local wars.

A 1957 Air Force study noted other implications of the Army position on limited war. First, quick reaction to local conflicts required mobile ground forces prepositioned in flashpoint areas and supported by mobile reserves in the United States. These required air and sealift to get into position, relegating most air assets to a subordinate logistic role. Second, the Army thought that in limited war the enemy's center of gravity was his armed forces. The only objective would be to destroy those armed forces within the affected area and "restore its geographical and political integrity." This ran counter to the thrust of air-atomic thinking, because it was the least efficient use of force. Finally, the Army assumed that decision could be gained only by ground forces "and depreciate[d] somewhat the effectiveness of the Air Force and the Navy in limited war situations."[9]

The limited war debate also featured arguments from the emerging strategic studies community, especially Harvard professor Henry Kissinger in his 1957 book, *Nuclear Weapons and Foreign Policy*. No effort, Kissinger claimed, had been made to address the fundamental shifts that nuclear weapons created in power politics, only piecemeal attempts to fit new weapons in old contexts. The limits to this approach became plain when the United States failed to make all the limited gains it could have in Korea, because it allowed only for absolute victory with unrestricted force, or no gain at all. Power, policy, and strategy were not linked. Thus nuclear weapons were effectively useless in foreign policy. Strategic doctrine had been paralyzed by planning for maximum power, which was vulnerable to chipping away by small aggressions. Kissinger identified the primary strategic problem: maximum force and maximum willingness to act could no longer occur simultaneously. Having only the option of unrestricted use of nuclear weapons might stay a president's hand in a crisis. Like Taylor, he recommended a spectrum of capabilities to resist Soviet challenges, reemphasizing conventional forces, but also using diplomacy to limit conflicts. A new concept of tactical nuclear war might emerge in which states did not pursue total victory, so reducing pressure for escalation.

In effect, Kissinger wished to return war, including nuclear weapons, to the realm of possible diplomatic options, as in the time of Metternich, the subject of his first book, *A World Restored*. His arguments however reached the public only after several years of Army efforts to promote its own solution. Taylor and Kissinger had similar prescriptions but different agendas. Kissinger envisioned a radically altered force structure wielded for aggressive diplomacy in pursuit of limited objectives. Taylor was more backward looking, seeking to reverse the "disastrous demobilization of 1945" and restore the Army to its predominance of the World War II era.[10] In the end, whatever influence Kissinger's arguments had on the debate over massive retaliation was felt only through its influence in official channels. His book probably would have received little notoriety had it not overlapped with persistent Army lobbying to change the status quo. The Air Force responded to Army arguments as expressed in JCS planning and budget documents, but did not engage in a public debate with Kissinger. Kissinger's arguments, like those of other strategists and Maxwell Taylor, may have weakened SAC's case in the public domain, with long-term repercussions, but perhaps his greatest influence lay after air-atomic ideas had been beaten.

The Air Force worked to rebut the Army's arguments, especially by advancing three main ideas about limited war. It argued that the concept of stalemate was false and dangerous, while limited wars were unimportant and could be deterred or fought with general war forces.

As part of annual budget wrangling with the other services, the Air Force wrote specific briefs on major issues, including limited war. In 1956, it summarized the Army positions and offered rebuttals on "weapons selectivity." The Army argued that it could prevail through less destructive land campaigns while the Air Force, with an unwavering fixation on mass destruction, would be ineffectual without nuclear weapons. The Air Force retorted that it was the only service that could use weapons of any lethality, ranging from pamphlets to cannons, and napalm to nuclear weapons. Land warfare was not inherently humane. Modern warfare devastates nation-sized battlefields, while armies had destroyed cities as thoroughly through the centuries as modern airpower. The key difference between the two methods was that the Air Force offered victory with the fewest Americans in harm's way.

The Air Force also rejected Army claims to be the "decisive force" that had won all past victories. German leaders from the Second World War cited airpower first among reasons for defeat, Japan surrendered with 1.3 million men left in its army. In Korea, by 6 November 1950 airpower had inflicted 47 percent of the ground casualties on the enemy, destroyed 74 percent of its armor, 81 percent of its trucks, and 72 percent of its artillery while suffering only 241 casualties. In the modern age, the United States could not absorb a massive nuclear attack and still mobilize a decisive ground force. In late air-atomic language, the Air Staff stated that war had changed and moved past the Army.[11]

Fundamentally, it denied that nuclear plenty automatically caused nuclear stalemate. Restructuring of Soviet armed forces around nuclear weapons increased the probability they would be used in general war.[12] As LeMay said in 1958, mutual deterrence was a myth that provided false and dangerous security. SAC's visible preparedness and the grim resolve of its leaders to execute its war plan made them a powerful tool in the hands of a skilled statesman like Eisenhower. The Communist Bloc was unlike the Free World when it came to aggression as an instrument of national policy. "We did not aggress while possessing nuclear monopoly nor with clear superiority; they are under no such moral restraint should they achieve nuclear superiority."[13] Moreover, at a gut level, the Air Force dismissed limited wars. "Little wars" like Korea, LeMay told an audience, did not threaten American existence. The priority must be meeting the only existential threat, Soviet nuclear forces.[14]

Should limited wars break out, the USAF argued after 1955, general war forces could handle them. As one saying put it, "The dog we keep to lick the cat can lick the kittens too." This idea, inseparable from the changed nature of war, became the primary argument against the Army. In a 1957 lecture to the Air War College, the Air Force plans chief, Maj. Gen. John Cary, outlined the service position. The basic objective in local war was to deter one, and if that failed, to prevent the outbreak of general war. "The Air Force feels strongly that the best way to accomplish this is to end the local war quickly and decisively and this opinion is reflected in national policy." The only force that could tamp down aggression as it began was airpower, because sea and land power required several days before intervention. There were no distinct "local" and "general" war forces. Atomic weapons should be used in local wars. Cary rejected the idea that general war forces would cause excessive military and civilian casualties. Pointing to Korea as an example of a conventional war, most casualties occurred in the last two years. Had the war ended in days or weeks, casualties would have been lower, regardless of the weapons employed. "And had it been announced beforehand that the United States would intervene immediately in Korea, with the most modern weapons in its arsenal, probably the Korean war would not have occurred."[15] An Air University study raised a related point about deterrent credibility in local war. A potential aggressor had to be sure both of the means for atomic use and certain of the political will to use it.[16] The author recommended a surprise demonstration of nuclear airpower against a Chinese Communist offshore island. Such a move "could be decisive in the efforts of the Free World to deter limited aggression."[17]

SAC, of course, was well suited to such a role in limited war. As Chief of Staff Thomas White said during a DoD filmed interview in 1957, SAC could put a bomb of any size on any target, meaning there was no "upper or lower limit to SAC's capability." SAC could be effective in a war of any size. If ordered only to drop leaflets, it could do that. If it was to use conventional weapons, it could. SAC was a general use force with sufficient flexibility to operate anywhere on the spectrum of conflict. The military and political objectives dictated the only limits.[18]

In an internal letter to staff, SAC elaborated on how such a war would be fought. A few long-range strategic aircraft could finish a "brush war" (a suitable and dismissive term) quickly. The United States could issue an ultimatum before attacking so that civilians could be evacuated. If communist aggression continued, additional targets could be attacked until the enemy was unwilling or unable to continue.[19]

In 1958, SAC discussed the semantics of limited war. Col. Reade Tilley, the chief of public information, claimed that the preferred Army term, *small war*, had a particular meaning in the public mind which gave the Army the dominant role. Tilley recommended that SAC "create a new symbol in opposition to the existing one" which would be associated only with the Air Force. His recommended idea, Limited Air War (LAW), would have advantages of, "Less Cost, Quick Decision, Decisive Ending, Infinitely Less American Bloodshed, Less Damage to Enemy Country, More Humane, and will not contribute to already almost unbearable burden of cost of Veterans support."[20]

A 1960 article by Vice Chief of Staff Frederic Smith suggested yet another way to use atomic weapons in limited wars. Nuclear weapons could reshape the landscape in which insurgent forces were operating, by clearing swaths of rain forests, blocking mountain defiles, and aiding western forces in close-contact siege. Just as the United States had expressed its determination to use nuclear weapons in general war, so it must "speak out with equal clarity in affirming that we can and will use nuclear weapons in limited war when such weapons best serve our broad interests and meet the demands of the tactical military situation."[21] Smith, like other Air Force officers, sought to use forces built for general war as tools to win other types of conflict. Limited war (or LAW, or brush fire war) was only a special case of general war, requiring nothing more than political will and the rapid application of overwhelming force.

This position assumed that escalation was controllable. In the Air Force conception of limited war, one could use unrestricted force while controlling the risks the conflict would expand beyond desirable boundaries, while the United States retained overwhelming force at any level of escalation that would deter an opponent from expanding his aggression. In this benign view of escalation, fear of the effects of atomic weapons would not prevent national leaders from ordering their use. Quemoy seems to have been tailor made for testing this idea. The strict limits on using atomic weapons from the outset, combined with the months-long timeline for resolving the crises (both concluded by unilateral Communist announcement) show weaknesses in the Air Force argument. Political will was affected when presented with alternatives involving conventional forces that were less escalatory. Again, the Air Force held that unrestricted force, applied as rapidly as possible, improves the chances of victory. Beyond the diplomatic cost of using grossly disproportionate force—atomic weapons against barefoot guerrillas—was the premise there will be suitable targets for atomic weapons. In Quemoy, Communist airfields and artillery emplacements were reasonable targets, because they constituted the threatening enemy force-in-being. Destroying them, by whatever means, would affect the crisis. Less conventional forces, such as the Viet Minh, would present fewer

TABLE 2 Army and Air Force budget and manpower, FY 1953–59

FY	ARMY BUDGET (MILLIONS)	ARMY MANPOWER (THOUSANDS)	AIR FORCE BUDGET (MILLIONS)	AIR FORCE MANPOWER (THOUSANDS)
1953	16,249	1,534	15,137	978
1954	12,828	1,405	15,588	948
1955	8,788	1,109	16,227	960
1956	8,588	1,026	16,613	910
1957	8,972	998	18,235	920
1958	9,131	899	18,411	871
1959	9,533	862	19,249	840

Source: DoD Budget FY 07 Green Book, available at DoD Comptroller web site, http://comptroller.defense.gov/Portals/45/Documents/defbudget/Docs/fy2007_greenbook.pdf, 141, 221.

viable targets. The challenge in fighting insurgents would likely be finding targets, not firepower.

For all its weaknesses, the Air Force's ideas of placing general war forces first in national security planning and using them in limited war won the day. If budget and major force elements are used as a scorecard—as the services themselves incessantly did—that fact becomes clear.

Army manpower and budget share decreased dramatically over the decade, admittedly in part because the Korean War ended. Army ideas about limited war, grounded in the belief that nuclear stalemate made atomic war too dangerous and Soviet aggression more probable, were rejected by national leadership. During a 1956 conference with the president, Taylor made his case for redeveloping limited war forces. Eisenhower responded that in local wars, the tactical use of atomic weapons against military targets "would be no more likely to trigger off a big war than the use of twenty-ton "block busters," while local security forces must carry the major weight of conventional combat. Although it might put in a few battalions at "truly critical points" the United States would not "deploy and tie down our forces around the Soviet periphery in small wars."[22] Eisenhower's strategy for local war supported Air Force ideas and suppressed the Army alternative. He paid for a pit bull, which reduced the costs needed to maintain the rest of the pack, so reducing the drain of the dogs on the national economy.

Carrier Redux

Where the limited war debate shifted focus away from general war, most interservice disputes of the 1950s simply sought to change how it would be fought. Within these struggles, the Navy remained the principal rival to the Air Force. Just as during the 1940s, the Navy sought to reclaim its position at the head of American national defense. Although the "Revolt of the Admirals" failed dramatically, leading to the ouster of the chief of naval operations, the Navy continued to fight. During the 1950s, it promoted two major weapon systems—the carrier and the seaplane—which worked within the accepted air-atomic assumption that strategic airpower could achieve a decisive result in general war. The Navy advanced another new weapon system, the Polaris SLBM, using very different ideas of finite deterrence. The emergence of Polaris combined with a separate, long simmering, targeting fight to create a showdown over control of the new missile and the targeting process.

The Navy entered the 1950s still using the carrier as a means to regain its influence. Senior Air Force generals saw the fight over the carrier in terms of budgetary control. If the Navy could claim a major portion of the strategic mission, then it could take resources from SAC to carry it out. In July 1952, Vice Chief of Staff Thomas White told LeMay "eventually that battle (Navy versus AF) is going to have to be fought to a finish." The Navy was preparing to "wage all-out war for a bigger share of the responsibilities in warplans."[23] A contemporary Air Staff paper warned that expansion of carrier aviation forces was a "serious menace to retention of Air Force functions as presently assigned. The Navy is already achieving a significant capability for strategic air warfare which must be contained."[24]

White was particularly exercised over what he saw as brazen Navy tactics in funding the Forrestal-class carriers. He believed the Navy had slipped the ships into the budget within the executive branch and then portrayed the draft as already approved before the Congress. "The Congress that authorized this expenditure did so without knowledge that three of the four members of the Joint Chiefs of Staff do not believe that this is a wise expenditure of public funds or that the weapon produced by the expenditure will have a military use comparable to other weapons (Naval, Air or Army) that could be bought with the same money."[25]

In this area, the Navy made few novel arguments, generally recycling its points from 1949. The basic issue remained unchanged, "whether carrier bases are more suitable than land bases for the projection of air power."[26] A 1955 Air Force budget document examined the issue in detail. The Navy claimed that modern direction-finding radar could not find a carrier task force, able to travel five hundred miles in twenty-four hours and so escape surveillance, and that this carrier mobility reduced their vulnerability compared to land bases. The Air Force retorted that two B-36s with proper equipment could sweep the entire North Atlantic in twenty-four hours and locate a ship to within eleven miles. Far more nuclear weapons would be needed to destroy the 580 air bases worldwide able to service heavy bombers than to destroy the forty-three aircraft carriers in existence. A carrier task group scattered to avoid nuclear attack was vulnerable to submarines, while destroying just a few carriers would render a task force ineffective for offensive missions. The Navy continued to claim, as it had in 1949, that carrier-based aircraft could strike vital Soviet targets. By the mid-1950s however, although equipment had improved, carrier aircraft still were limited to a radius of 1,500 miles. This restricted the targets they could hit and their operating areas. The Navy held that it was independent of overseas bases, important if fearful allies or enemy action denied their use. The Air Force retorted that the United States had built an extensive series of overseas naval bases since the end of World War II, presumably because they were necessary for support, while the Navy ignored the growing number of intercontinental range forces in CONUS.[27]

Cost efficiency remained a hot point of contention. One Air Force study estimated that four Essex-class carriers cost twice as much to support as did four overseas bases of conventionally armed equivalent USAF aircraft, or two atomic aircraft bases. The basic four carrier task group cost 1.6 times as much to operate as did conventional USAF units (4 fighter squadrons, 2 B-50 squadrons, 1 B-47 squadron) and support, and three times that of equivalent atomic units (1 fighter squadron, 1 B-47 squadron) and support.[28] Another USAF cost study used Navy data from the Korean War to estimate that 115 USAF aircraft could have carried out the total offensive effort achieved in FY 52 by the 249 aircraft in the Navy's Task Force 77 (TF 77). Given the low sortie rate achieved by the carriers, their periodic absence from combat for refueling, and required defensive sorties, TF 77 needed 117 percent more aircraft to deliver the same offensive punch as equivalent USAF aircraft. USAF land-based aircraft could carry out the same offensive effort with only 46 percent of the aircraft.[29]

Korean War data also fueled debate over the accuracy of a WSEG study on the offensive potential of carrier battle groups in general war. According to the Air Staff, the WSEG study failed to account for several limits to TF 77 operations. WSEG estimated that four carriers could provide close air support for four divisions simultaneously. TF 77 data showed that this figure was only 1.5 divisions, while if enemy forces threatened the fleet, support would be withdrawn to protect the carriers. The TF 77 commander had reported, "Diversions such as supporting the Air Force or Army effort must be subordinated to a category of 'as feasible.'"[30] The report underestimated the efficiency of Soviet C2 in air defense and the superiority of the Mig-15, which had hindered a TF 77 attack near the Siberian border. WSEG credited carrier forces with a four hundred mile range, while TF 77 had strained to send aircraft two hundred miles. WSEG ignored the mining threat to the carriers and the mobile replenishment force, which had diverted the TF 77 commander from his offensive mission.[31] Unlike earlier examinations of the strategic air offensive, which analyzed actual plans and tactics, the WSEG carrier study only used a few abstract scenarios to evaluate carrier effectiveness. "The failure of the Study to consider specific operations and campaigns constitutes a failure of the Study to accomplish some of the most important of its potential objectives."[32]

The predictable result of rehashing old arguments was the Navy's failure to take any substantial portion of the strategic mission from SAC (though it still managed to achieve its primary aim, which was to build new carriers and keep the concept respectable for other reasons). In 1956 testimony to the Senate, Chief of Staff Nathan Twining summarized the carrier's status. Although they had nuclear attack capability, that was limited by the size of their defensive and support complement, and the "priority naval tasks," which might take precedence in a crisis. Carriers might not be in the right place to attack when hostilities began, particularly in the event of strategic surprise. Even if carriers could sail into position during a crisis, it might not be "strategically sound" to put them in close waters, vulnerable to submarine and air attack.[33]

This conclusion was unavoidable given the time factor. There was little guarantee that carriers could be in place when hostilities began, nor reach it in time. This would have been hard at the start of the decade when operations began six days after the beginning of hostilities. In the missile age when strikes had to be launched in minutes and carefully coordinated to avoid fratricide, carriers could not be integrated into the EWP. The Navy hunger for command independence—an essential element of naval self-identity—conflicted directly with the Air Force need for tight control. As long as they remained naval assets, outside SAC's control and dedicated to roles other than strategic air attack, naval nuclear-armed planes could only be "plus-value." The time factor, as much as Air Force recalcitrance, kept the carrier from winning back part of the strategic mission. From the perspective of air strategy, the mid-1950s carrier was a limited weapon with few clear advantages and many disadvantages.

Seaplane Origins of Assured Destruction

The same could not be said of the second system the Navy promoted for a strategic role during the 1950s. The Martin XP6M Seamaster combined the carrier's mobility and elusiveness with range and performance similar to the B-47. The jet powered aircraft promised 0.9 Mach flight at low-level, flying from coastal inlets. The Navy justified the aircraft with a synthesis of the arguments made for carriers and original ones. Its mobility combined with its small footprint to make more realistic the carrier's promise of invulnerability through stealth. Although B-36s could find a carrier task group in the North Atlantic and track it, the XP6M was almost impossible to track. Thus it could weather any surprise attack and then guarantee retaliation. This feature was a materially different justification than that used for carrier task forces or in air-atomic thinking, where deterrent power was defined by the ability to place more bombs on target in the shortest time. The Sea Master, while as effective as contemporary Air Force medium bombers, promised a different kind of deterrent power. Whereas the Air Force strained to outrun surprise attack, the Sea Master could evade one and constitute a second-strike force. Its deterrent potential stemmed from invulnerability, not only destructive power. A Navy justification for the program declared, "The way to prevent a nuclear war is to have absolute capability to deliver retaliatory nuclear attacks."[34] "No rational enemy would initiate a nuclear war unless he had a reasonable chance to win. Certainly he would hesitate if destruction of his country was assured."[35] Here, ignored by historians and strategists, lay the birth of arguments about second-strike capacity and Assured Destruction. The seaplane promised another advantage. Because it operated at sea, any Soviet surprise attack would at worst destroy the aircraft in open ocean. A similar attack on SAC would hit not only the bases but inflict grave civilian casualties, even if the aircraft survived. The base system, which formed SAC's "Achilles Heel," could be reduced or eliminated by adopting the seaplane, because the "vast seaplane operating areas are available on a year round basis, require no rights or agreements, no construction coats, no large air and land forces to defend, are indestructible, and, contrasted to land bases, do not invite attack."[36]

The Air Force, guided by years of planning and experience, retorted that these operations were more complex that the Navy assumed. While a lone aircraft in the middle of the ocean might be secure, still it required a large and vulnerable command, control, and logistic network. The Air Force also questioned whether the design actually could work, that is, perform in high-sea states while maintaining the performance characteristics needed to penetrate Soviet airspace.[37] Despite their dismissive arguments, however, the XP6M alarmed most generals. In 1954, as the aircraft advanced toward its first flight, White told the Deputy for Operations, "I am concerned about the Navy's development of a water-based jet bomber. It seems to me that an airplane of this type, provided performance can compare to land-based jet bombers, presents a much greater threat to the Air Force mission than any number of carriers."[38] Organizationally, the Sea Master represented a dangerous Navy attempt to use "R and D" to wedge its way into the Air Force mission. If the Navy could develop identifiably naval platforms with undeniable potential for the strategic mission, they might seize part of the budget.

The Air Staff solution to the XP6M was to absorb it. An October 1955 study outlined the problem. The XP6M compared favorably with the B-47, was faster than the B-52, could deliver a multimegaton weapon anywhere in the Soviet Union, and had excellent growth potential. Although the concept had not yet been fully developed, and would doubtlessly need more support than the Navy publicly stated, the requirements would not be crippling. The defense budget was too small for a duplication of major roles, and the Air Force had primary responsibility for strategic air warfare and therefore had proprietary interest in any development relevant to that field. The study recommended the Air Force announce a proprietary interest in all aspects of air development, openly implying a degree of ownership over the Sea Master. The study concluded,

> If this type aircraft proves reasonably successful, its inclusion in the Navy inventory will have a definite impact upon the USAF. The Navy undoubtedly will use this aircraft in its strategic bomber configuration. Success in this application by the Navy could lead to division of the strategic air role responsibility, with resulting duplication, dissipation of critical resources, and increased national defense expenditures or reduced Air Force budget.[39]

Concern over the XP6M, however, was not universal. At the 1956 Commanders' Conference, Gen. Orval Cook, deputy commander of European Command, expressed disdain. "All of this story about 75 per cent of the Earth's surface being water, and that seaplanes are very economical and easy to operate, in my opinion is just so much undiluted crap."[40] In mid-1955, as the Air Staff furiously worked out its strategy, LeMay urged calm, saying that "the subject is being given disproportionate emphasis." The Sea Master might have the performance of the B-47, but it would not be operational until 1960, when the B-47 would be approaching obsolescence, in the process of being replaced by the B-58. It would be worthless for the Navy to buy even a few XP-6Ms for experimentation because they would serve no useful purpose when ready for action. LeMay dismissed the idea that the Air Force should declare an active interest in water-based aircraft, which would only encourage the Navy to reciprocate by taking more active interest in land-based aircraft. Rather, the Air Force should plan for centralized control of all airborne strategic weapons.[41]

In the end, LeMay proved right. The Navy publicly announced the Sea Master in November 1955. The test program went smoothly until the first prototype crashed on 7 December. After a redesign, test flights resumed in May 1956, and abruptly halted when the second prototype crashed on 9 November. Flight testing resumed in January 1958—the Navy pushed the program hard, training crews and setting up a development unit in Hawaii, which had three production aircraft with all-Navy crews in August 1959 when the Navy finally canceled the program. Although the XP6M achieved its design goals and was a remarkably advanced aircraft, it fell victim to the same Soviet defenses that pressured Air Force bomber development.[42] The Sea Master's longer-term significance lies in the arguments the Navy tested out in its justification. The notion that deterrence flows from an invulnerable Assured Destruction force was a key departure from the Navy's rationale for carriers, and air-atomic thinking. This rejected the orthodox position that the role of atomic weapons was to destroy an enemy's force-in-being or military potential, and substituted for it a hazily defined punishment. This new conception of deterrence bridges the decade of Navy advocacy for carriers with that for Polaris.

Change by Fiat

Meanwhile, interservice friction continued around the issue of targeting, the heart of air strategy—indeed, in Colin Gray's sarcastic words, "the strategic world-view of the airperson is very much that of the earth as a dartboard. 'Aerial strategy' reduces to choices in targeting."[43] During the 1950s the Navy and Air Force (and to a lesser extent, the Army) struggled to control the targeting process and its output. From an air-atomic standpoint, the stakes were high. Without power over target selection, and the timing for striking them, the possibility of achieving the blunting and disruption missions, and even of victory through airpower, was imperiled.

The first question, who selects targets, had two answers. The de jure answer from 1944 was that strategic target selection fell under joint control. Until 1960, however, the de facto answer was the Air Force, and mostly SAC. Throughout the 1950s, the Air Force resisted joint influence on targeting. While it allowed for an appearance of jointness, the reality always was a drive toward control at SAC headquarters at Offutt Air Force Base in Omaha. The Navy tried to flesh out the paper arrangement and influence targeting through the JCS, while not letting Navy resources fall under joint or Air Force influence, preferring unified commanders—admirals commanding naval forces in the Pacific (CINCPAC) and in the Atlantic (CINCLANT)—to exercise operational control.

On paper, targeting arrangements between the services were cooperative. On 5 February 1944, Chief of Naval Operations Ernest King and Army chief of staff George Marshall directed their services to coordinate Japanese air intelligence through an ad hoc committee. JCS 1020/3 generalized the joint arrangement for air intelligence in October 1945, and JCS 1020/4 in December created a group with equal Navy and Air Force membership. After unification, the secretary of defense directed that the joint arrangement continue.[44]

As long as all strategic air assets remained in the Air Force, the other services had little leverage to shake SAC control. By 1952, however, the Navy began fielding atomic-capable carrier strike aircraft. An ad hoc JCS committee found compelling reasons to centralize control of weapon allocation in the JCS. That would avoid fratricide between atomic attacks, maximize the effect of weapon delivery, avoid overkill, and ensure critical targets were not ignored. The committee recommended a "jointly staffed war room annex," through which the JCS could supervise planning and execution of atomic plans. "They [JCS] must ensure that in the heat of conflict our atomic resources are not wasted or withheld through ignorance."[45]

The JCS directed the intelligence chiefs of the three services to formalize a "mutually acceptable arrangement" for air intelligence and targeting within the existing Air Force Intelligence organization. Roughly 160 Army and 300 Naval personnel would be integrated into the Air Staff's intelligence branch to "participate actively in the studies, evaluations of and recommendations as to targets and target systems which could be destroyed in support of current war plans, including the preparation of hypotheses for these studies and such other studies as may be agreed upon."[46]

This paper arrangement never reached fruition. By September, after months of wrangling, the chief of naval operations complained to the JCS that Air Force intelligence had unilaterally reorganized itself so to freeze naval personnel out of targeting. All major positions had been assigned to USAF personnel, and the other services marginalized.[47] Twining responded that the paper arrangement undermined service identity and damaged the intelligence directorate's ability to "respond directly to Air Force needs." To fulfill the sharing arrangement would "force Air Force abandonment of its primary responsibility and dominant interest in the area of air intelligence."[48] Core beliefs about service identity, strong in a service less than a decade old, overrode embryonic cooperation, and direct orders from the JCS.

That failure led to the establishment of Joint Coordination Centers (JCC) in the European and Pacific theaters. These bodies served only to sort out the wartime activities of the different military branches, not prewar planning. Early exercises highlighted the weakness of this approach. In 1954, the JCS directed each theater commander to send a target list ("atomic annex") to SAC for coordination. In 1955, SAC hosted a conference to find a common "*modus operandi* for the defeat of communist air power." This effort failed to do anything but recommend periodic coordination of atomic war plans. Subsequently, until 1958, SAC hosted annual World Wide Coordination Conferences where the commands agreed on rough target lists.[49]

The distance between the ideal and the reality of targeting is clear. In June 1955, Twining scolded LeMay for not making even a token effort at keeping the JCS informed of his operational plans. The most recent SAC plan available to the JCS dated from December 1951 and contained few details. Hence, other commands could not determine the support they should offer SAC or appreciate its atomic offensive.[50] SAC plans were an opaque black box to anyone else, whether outside the USAF, or in it.

The recalcitrance went both ways. When questioned in 1954 about Navy coordination, LeMay vented his frustration. In the Mediterranean, for example,

> I have yet to be able to pin down one definite target that the Navy is going to hit . . . [I] don't know where the fleet is going to be. . . . I have a vague idea by talking to people that they will be operating around some place, but I haven't been able to get together to get a communications plan whereby we can pass information . . . All the Navy plans I have read are so general that they are worthless.[51]

The coordination conferences did little to help this situation. The 1956 meeting ended because the commands were unable to agree even about how to coordinate their atomic strike plans. Air Force–dominated joint commands wanted centralized simultaneous analysis at a single location, presumably Offutt, because of its available expertise, while others favored differing degrees of theater control.[52]

Change by Argument

Through 1958, each command sought to maintain autonomy in targeting. Since most assets remained in SAC, Offutt kept primary control of the process and its output. Neither the theaters nor SAC sought coordination between commands. Service definitions of targets remained parochial. The Army pushed for more retardation targets in the early 1950s, the Air Force focused ever more narrowly on blunting, and the Navy gradually shifted to finite deterrence. Eventually, the Army and Navy cooperated in the "alternative undertaking," their last attempt to change the basis of strategic targeting before the SIOP. Finite deterrence and the alternative undertaking also moved outside the boundaries of air-atomic theory.

In 1952, as the Korean War stagnated, the Army pushed for strengthened retardation planning for Europe. An Army study forwarded to the JCS complained that attacking Delta targets, except POL, would not slow a Red Army offensive, because the Soviets had enough equipment reserves for a year of operations. Even with shattered POL production, an offensive could continue for six months during which the Soviets could seize Europe. The only acceptable course was to "develop a target system that will . . . retard the Soviet advance into Western Europe."[53] The Army organizational interest in the retardation targets is plain, because it enabled an Army victory and deemphasized strategic airpower. Still, this attempt to project Army interests into the strategic targeting lists fell within the broad scope of the air-atomic idea. It used airpower to enable decisive victory.

The same cannot be said of the finite deterrence theory that underlay the Army and Navy efforts later in the decade. That theory was distinct from, but complementary to, the stalemate ideas that underlay arguments about limited war. The policy recommendation arising from stalemate was to build forces for limited war, which would provide a viable deterrent at any level of conflict. So too, finite deterrence proposed that past a certain number of weapons, one or both sides would have a secure second-strike capability. That is, even after the most disastrous surprise attack, retaliation could inflict unacceptable damage on an aggressor. Here, deterrent power grew from the ability to inflict an unspecified amount of damage, rather than to destroy the enemy's military potential or force-in-being. This strategy fell outside the air-atomic tradition—and arguably, of orthodox military thought—because it aimed for sufficiency or stalemate, not victory. In the "minimum deterrent" variant of finite deterrence, any weapon over the number needed to inflict unacceptable retaliatory damage was a waste of national resources. The more general theory of finite deterrence was less stringent on the number of weapons, but found diminishing returns past an identifiable point. For the Army and Navy advocates of finite deterrence, this approach played to the accepted strategic principle of containing the drain of military spending on the economy, and it held an added linguistic advantage. "Finite" deterrence implies that its opposite, presumably the basis of Air Force thinking, was "infinite" deterrence, replete with reckless and ruinous spending. The USAF replied by describing finite deterrence as city destruction.

As with limited war, some civilian strategists discussed finite deterrence, albeit with less self-interest than their uniformed counterparts. Bernard Brodie, the most prominent strategist to discuss the arguments behind finite deterrence, was also one of the most articulate. His 1959 article, "The Anatomy of Deterrence," contained a succinct discussion of the finite deterrent position. Brodie separated "deterrence strategies" from "win-the-war strategies," neatly differentiating the service positions. So long as there was even a small chance of war, the United States must be concerned with the outcome.

> But what seems very difficult to grasp is that [the opponent's] gain cannot be measured simply in terms of damage to us, or vice versa, even though such damage may indeed provoke an act or condition (i.e., surrender or military obliteration) which he legitimately considers a great gain because it terminates a threat. But damage to an opponent, however large, which for one reason or another fails to have such an effect is no strategic gain at all.[54]

He followed this seeming rejection of any ideas about the arbitrary destruction of some proportion of Soviet industry and population with other points that could be taken as support of the finite deterrent. Brodie embraced the idea of a "hard-core" retaliatory force invulnerable to enemy attack, a description almost tailored to Polaris, and examined the problems of targeting during a retaliatory strike. Mirroring the arguments made by the Navy and Army against the attacks, Brodie said that blunting would be hampered because it would be mounted by a weakened force (thanks to Soviet initiative) through alert air defenses, against possibly empty Soviet atomic bases. Conversely, a publicly announced policy of targeting cities presents the dilemma that the United States would be initiating city destruction.[55]

Brodie cannot be put firmly into either the finite deterrent or air-atomic camps. He makes arguments that appear in the internal debates and public pronouncements from both sides of the service divide, and integrated them in original ways. Whether the services cribbed their debate points from Brodie or reached them independently is less important than the fact that his nuanced arguments were detached from any particular agenda. Like Kissinger's advocacy of limited war, it existed in the new parallel universe of strategic studies. Any direct influence on the debates came about only to the degree that the services adopted them, although they could shape public views in the long run, and did so from 1961.

To the Air Force, the organizational motive behind finite deterrence was obvious. "Its purpose is directly and simply to reduce Air Force programs, specifically programs which support SAC, so that Department of Defense funds which are currently so programmed, would become available to them for their forces." Finite deterrence was a sham to paint SAC as excessive and seize its budget.[56]

The Army presented a finite deterrent argument in the 1959 budget cycle. In a memorandum to the secretary of defense, the Army promoted an "adequate deterrent" force able to survive a Soviet attack and retaliate against around 200 "critical enemy targets [that] would, in conjunction with other operations, destroy the Soviet will and ability to continue the war."[57] The Navy, in support of Polaris, made more elaborate arguments. In a memorandum for all flag officers, Burke established a Navy line on finite deterrence. He argued that several technological developments required reexamination of retaliatory power: the vulnerability of US bombers and land-based missiles, the improbability of finding Soviet missile sites, and the increased cost of strategic weapons (with its impact on other military programs). In these conditions, the United States must have enough retaliatory strength to convince an enemy he risked destruction by starting general war. Blunting required preemption and perfect intelligence on targets, still risked ending civilization, and entailed an open-ended number of military targets.

> We believe that it is not necessary to have the capability to inflict multi-megaton destruction on hundreds of major Soviet military targets and on countless other military targets in order to provide adequate deterrence.

> The concept of destroying the enemy capability to attack in a large scale nuclear exchange has progressively lost effectiveness, and becomes unrealistic when the enemy possesses numbers of dispersed missiles in mobile or fixed locations unknown to us.

He proposed a finite deterrent aimed at the Soviet government, party controls, industry, and war-making capacity. To attack them would be simple compared to blunting, because damage would be cumulative (not depending on any single target's destruction) and less time-sensitive. Only an invulnerable force could carry out such a strategy. Bombers needed a prohibitively expensive system with tankers, dispersed bases, standoff weapons, and airborne alert. "Invulnerability will exist only when the enemy does not know the location of our deterrent forces. This can only be achieved by true concealment and mobility."[58] Burke had just such a platform in mind. He also claimed that massive retaliation lacked credibility because the threat was disproportionate. "You don't knock out a hundred million people or whatever because they send forty people into Iraq to subvert the country. . . . The punishment must fit the crime. The counteraction must fit the action."[59] An invulnerable finite deterrent force would, conversely, buy time for reflection, instead of being on a "hair-trigger."[60]

In a 1959 speech, SAC commander Thomas Power summarized the Air Force rebuttal to finite deterrence. The ability to inflict "unacceptable" damage on an enemy depended on knowing what that enemy defined as unacceptable. No one, except the Soviet leadership, could know for certain what degree of destruction would be unacceptable in pursuit of their goals. "And even Khrushchev may not know from one day to the other what will deter him, because he may be willing to accept more punishment today than he would accept tomorrow or vice versa."[61]

The Air Force Long Range Plans branch voiced a more detailed position on finite deterrence. Brig. Gen. Robert Richardson III identified the key factors distinguishing the other services proposals from strategic air theory. A force designed only to deter war, so satisfying the requirements of finite deterrence, would not necessarily be able to fight one. By comparison, "a credible or obvious war winning capability under any circumstances provides an optimum deterrent to war." The finite deterrent theory failed because it had no war-winning capacity and did not deter limited aggression. It was fundamentally irrational in the modern age because the threatened destruction of cities would matter only if post D-day production contributed to the outcome. Cities had no military value because industrial capacity would not shape the outcome of the war. The capacity to produce large conventional forces at some point in the future would not defeat an enemy with a powerful nuclear force-in-being. Finite deterrence therefore violated two basic principles: the only rational military objectives are enemy forces or the targets that affect them, and destruction that does not affect the outcome is unjustifiable. Nor could a finite deterrence force ever take the initiative. If the enemy launched general war, it could not respond rationally. In the face of an overwhelmingly superior enemy nuclear force, the holder of a finite deterrent could only initiate city destruction. Because there would be no prospect of destroying the enemy's offensive forces, it was tantamount to national suicide. "A Twilight of the Gods philosophy is not part of our heritage."[62]

Richardson also attacked the ideas of stalemate and mutual deterrence. Stability depended on almost complete equality in weapons technology, delivery capability, force survival measures, and equally ineffectual active defenses. Technical advances would make any stalemate temporary as one side would eventually research past it. Emerging nuclear powers would also destabilize the balance, because one could gain a narrow advantage in some area, or more likely, be inferior and tempted to lash out if threatened. Richardson labeled all ideas outside traditional air-atomic victory-seeking behavior as fatally flawed because they abandoned the "only valid military objective," which was successfully defending the nation in wartime. "Concepts of 'minimum [finite] deterrence,' 'stalemate,' 'mutual deterrence,' 'stable deterrence,' etc., are little more than rationalizations for reducing the cost of national defense, or elements thereof, by gambling on enemy intentions and the ability to prevent general atomic war at the expense of accepting defeat or annihilation if the gamble fails."[63]

Unlike their previous attempts to reduce Air Force budgetary dominance, the other services presented a coherent alternative theory by the late 1950s. The Navy had attacked air-atomic ideas during the Revolt of the Admirals with little beyond a repetition of the Pacific campaign as an alternative theory. Finite deterrence theory, by contrast, recognized the changes in strategic reality wrought by new technology, provided plausible grounds to reconfigure every aspect of nuclear policy, and appeared fresher than strategic air theory. For the first time in its history, the Air Force found itself defending the status quo.

Alternative Undertaking

The finite deterrence theories first entered JCS war planning in the struggle over the "alternative undertaking." The Army and Navy successfully incorporated the idea into the JSCP guidance approved in early 1958. As a result, the atomic annex to the draft Joint Strategic Operations Plan (JSOP-63) provided for a "primary undertaking," with the primary targets essentially military if the United States held the initiative, and "alternative undertakings," if it had lost the initiative, devoted toward population and the enemy atomic delivery capability.[64] The guidance assumed that only 25 percent of US forces would be available for employment, Soviet delivery capability would not be profitably targetable because it already was spent, while governmental control and population centers would be the primary targets.[65] Late air-atomic thinking underlay the primary undertaking while the alternative undertaking focus reflected finite deterrence.

How far this debate affected SAC war plans is unclear. The official SAC history states that "SAC had one target system and one strike plan, but a multitude of timing variations or options to fit any condition that might arise. There were two basic modes of execution."[66] That is, the list did not change, but execution, and therefore priority, did. A 1960 long-range plans study confirmed that view: "If we strike first, SAC will use an "Alpha" (Counterforce) target priority. If we strike second, SAC will use a "Bravo" (city-busting) target system which requires only a small number of weapons on target."[67] White clarified the gap between the two positions—one target list or two—in 1959. "We do not necessarily plan to hit 'cities' *per se*, under conditions of last resort; instead we will hit the most critical and lucrative complexes of the enemy's military strength within our available capability, even under those extreme circumstances. In essence, this would probably be the enemy's military control system."[68] SAC was admitting that it could be struck first and had to plan accordingly. Still, the targets chosen for attack would just be the most efficient at degrading remaining Soviet capability—not chosen specifically for terror or unrestrained destruction.

Whatever the impact on plans, at the JCS the services squared off predictably. The Army and Navy pushed to "give greatly increased stature to the alternative undertaking" which the Air Force opposed. White feared the other services were trying to make the alternative undertaking the "sole objective of nuclear offensive forces" and strategic programs.[69] White restated Air Force dogma that American strikes must focus on enemy military strength no matter which side had the initiative.

> U.S. delivery forces must be adequate to deter the Soviet Union from direct attack on the United States. This requires that in the event of strategic warning there be an established and recognized U.S. capability to neutralize that military strength which is a threat to the U.S. It requires, too, that there be a similarly recognized U.S. capability, even after an attack with little or no warning, to destroy any remaining Soviet offensive strength still a threat to the U.S., as well as the Soviet control structure and basic national strengths which allow for further concerted Soviet effort.[70]

When the Army and Navy pressed for more forces for limited war and less for general war, the White House refused to act without determining the minimum requirements for effective deterrence.[71] The president had been surprised at the three services' inability to agree on targets. When he asked them to draft terms of reference for the targeting study, they failed to agree, and instead gave him three separate papers.[72] Finally, in February 1959, Eisenhower directed the Net Evaluation Subcommittee (NESC) of the NSC to consider "the relative merits, from the point of view of effective deterrence, of alternative retaliatory efforts directed toward: (1) primarily a military target system, or (2) an optimum mix of a combined military-urban industrial target system."[73]

The study produced in response to this directive became known as the Hickey Committee report, or NESC 2009. After considering three alternative targeting concepts (mostly military, mostly city-industrial, and an "optimum mix"), in February 1960 Army lieutenant general Thomas Hickey's NESC report concluded that the optimum-mix was best. This effectively rejected the finite deterrence position.[74] According to Twining, this decision had several ramifications. A finite deterrence retaliatory force based on destroying urban targets was an inadequate military posture. The existing strategic force, developed during the period of Soviet weakness, was "in the right ball park," while the weapon stockpile (and its number of high-yield weapons) was "about right."[75] After the initial setback of having to consider the alternative undertaking, the Hickey Committee proved to be an Air Force victory. It confirmed Air Force policy since 1945 and its ideas about strategic airpower, while rejecting the novel ideas presented by the other services. In the interservice struggle over who did the targeting and what they were, the Air Force had won another round.

Single? Integrated? Operational Plan

Nonetheless, this question of the optimum mix, combined with the introduction of a new weapon, immediately began a related dispute. The combination of Polaris with the ongoing debate on targeting created the first major changes in the mechanisms of air-atomic practice since 1945. The SLBM itself was a curious mixture of strengths and weaknesses, well tailored to finite deterrence. In its initial A-1 form, Polaris had a range of 1,000 miles, although the 1,500 mile A-2 was in advanced development by 1959. It was relatively inaccurate and had a smaller warhead than land-based weapons, but could be fired underwater, perfectly suited to a finite deterrent. Because a retaliatory attack could be launched against Soviet cities without a tight timeframe, even slow command and communications procedures were acceptable. Inaccurate and low-yield missiles, too imprecise for a blunting mission or even perhaps for disruption, could destroy cities. For the Air Force, the stakes in this next round of interservice fighting were much higher than ever before. The Navy threatened not only to gain a piece of the strategic attack mission but also to redefine the requirements of deterrence. If deterrence came to hinge on invulnerable forces—which only the Navy could provide—then the Air Force would be hard pressed to find a satisfactory substitute. For the first time, another service threatened to combine new ideas and weapons and displace the Air Force from its dominating position. At its most basic, the question was simple: Is the goal of nuclear warfare victory or vengeance? The air-atomic strategy implausibly promised the former, and the Polaris-armed finite deterrence advocates offered the latter.

The place of Polaris in national strategy became the heart of interservice battle. Past targeting fights had been abstract and did not challenge SAC's de facto control. However, several questions had to be resolved about Polaris. Who would own the system? Who would operate the weapons in wartime? Who would decide the targets? Would it be integrated with other nuclear assets or function independently? The final product of the long debate over these questions was the Single Integrated Operational Plan for FY 62 (SIOP-62). The degree to which it embodied air-atomic or finite deterrence ideas, and divided responsibility between the services, acts as a final scorecard for the atomic strategy debates of the 1950s.

The services assumed familiar stances. The Navy angled to keep Polaris under its command while retaining maximum decentralization in all issues from control and targeting to execution. The theater commanders would control and target Polaris, which would remain an operational naval asset. The Air Force strove for maximum centralization, consistent with the existing placement of all strategic assets in SAC. LeMay also made a typical efficiency argument, with echoes of airpower's progressive roots, when he claimed that it cost seven times as much for the same destructive effect on targets using Polaris as opposed to land-based missiles.[76] As the issue of the integration of Polaris heated up in mid-1959, there was a temporary split in the Air Force position. Power wanted direct SAC control of Polaris, but Chief of Staff Thomas White overruled him and pushed for a unified Strategic Command, with an airborne component absorbing SAC and a naval component for the SLBM.[77] In itself, this marked a recognition that the USAF could not win as thorough a victory as before.

To force a consensus on the services about targeting and Polaris, Secretary of Defense Thomas Gates and JCS chairman Twining directed them to answer "18 Questions" in August 1959.[78] The questions ranged widely from the policy for developing a national strategic target system to the need for a single integrated operational plan to means to coordinate operational forces. The services could not reach a consensus on the issues and presented their conflicting viewpoints to Gates in May 1960. Each service's answers to the 18 Questions illustrates their views on strategic bombardment.

The Army chief of staff Lyman Lemnitzer, outlined a position close to that of the Navy. He supported a strategic target list based on the Hickey study, abandoning the idea of an "alternative undertaking." Targeting would be carried out under the authority of the Joint Chiefs, as opposed to a single unified commander (e.g., CINCSAC). Lemnitzer rejected a Single Integrated Operational Plan, since no single commander should be responsible for executing the entire strategic war plan. That would place one "superior commander" over the other unified commands, interfere with their performance of their responsibilities, undermine the JCS's authority for strategic direction of general war, and be too rigid to handle command and control after an attack. Polaris would remain under the control of the unified or specified commander (e.g., CINCLANT, CINCPAC) to whom it was assigned. Targeting would be coordinated with the commander for the area into which the weapon would be fired (e.g., CINCEUR would approve a strike by a CINCLANT Polaris). Those area commanders would be responsible for preplanning targets on the National Strategic Target List (NSTL) that fell within their areas. Under this system, SAC would retain control of attacks within the USSR and most of China, but other CINCs would gain responsibility for NSTL targets (and other targets to support their mission) within their area of operations.

Chief of Naval Operations Arleigh Burke wrote that the Navy saw "only one fundamental issue involved," whether a single command should develop and execute an integrated attack plan, or if the unified and specified commands should plan and conduct attacks on target systems developed by the JCS. The second view was the only correct one. The JCS could not "divorce" itself from the development of the NSTL because that was a topic too central to delegate. Instead, the JCS should select and maintain a list of targets which would be the NSTL and direct coordinated execution of the strategic offensive by all relevant commanders. Burke opposed a unified STRATCOM because it would deny unified commanders the choice of immediately striking critical enemy targets in their theater if they also were targets in an integrated plan. At the same time, during the moment of greatest danger, STRATCOM would withdraw forces able to strike targets within a theater to attack targets on the national list. The idea of withdrawing nuclear strike platforms like carriers from a unified commander, just as war broke out, and giving operational control to STRATCOM was "highly confusing and militarily unacceptable." A centralized strategic command was an illusion grounded in nostalgia for a dead era when homogenous forces under one command could conduct the offensive. The diversity of modern strategic platforms and their dispersion throughout the forces made centralized control unworkable. A centralized STRATCOM would require major revisions of unified and specified command responsibilities (effectively making them local area commanders), make a decapitating strike on US nuclear capabilities easier, complicate command and control of local nuclear forces in a postattack environment, risk leaving potent local assets, such as carriers, idle while slower CONUS-based weapons like bombers attacked, and fail to integrate growing Allied nuclear forces. In the Navy's scheme, Polaris would be assigned to unified commanders of major naval forces, who alone could handle key issues (e.g., coordination with antisubmarine forces, establishment of "safety havens," coordination of changes in patrol areas). "With the sole exception of target assignment the coordination problems are naval operational ones." Coordination needed improvement, but the Joint Chiefs could effect the necessary changes. Neither SAC nor a new STRATCOM was required to do so.[79]

White agreed the NSTL should be based on NESC 2009, but that because of its unique expertise SAC should create it. In writing a national target list, SAC would be performing the same role for the JCS as a subordinate did for a unified commander when writing a theater atomic strike plan. The national plan should be a Single Integrated Operational Plan (SIOP), because successful attack on the NSTL targets would be critical to a general war. It demanded "positive control of planning and assured unity in execution." Because the operations were global and overlapped many geographical areas of responsibility, targets might require assets assigned to more than area commander, and maximum concentration of effort without conflict or duplication required it. The JCS could not write the SIOP because it was not organized for detailed planning. Instead, SAC should write the plan for JCS approval. White urged the creation of a unified strategic command to which both SAC bombers and missiles and Polaris should be assigned. If STRATCOM were not set up, Polaris still must be under centralized control, preferably through the mechanism of a SIOP.[80]

Gates met the Chiefs on 30 June 1960 to hash out their answers to the 18 Questions. He pointed out that they had all agreed the JCS should have a written target policy and a unified NSTL, but disagreed on who should develop it. The secretary thought only the Air Force had a clearly defined idea of an "integrated" plan, while the other services had "fuzzed up" the definition so to cover what was only a "coordinated" plan. Earle Wheeler, director of the Joint Staff, clarified that the Air Force wished to build a detailed plan on the model currently used at SAC, while the other services wanted the JCS to issue a basic plan to be fleshed out by the Unified Commanders. Furthermore, the Air Force would develop the NSTL concurrently with the operations plan, while the other services would develop it first and the rest of the plan subsequently. Burke agreed with that view and said that "if CINCSAC were given the job of developing the plan that the Unified Commanders would be put in the position of wing commanders." After more discussion, Gates proposed that the JCS write a target policy. Then, CINCSAC, acting as an agent of the JCS, would prepare the NSTL and SIOP, with the resulting plan carried out under JCS direction. After more discussion, in which Burke argued for sequential targeting and planning under the JCS, Gates concluded the JCS must reach a consensus on target planning. If they failed, "non-professional" people (that is, himself) would have to determine these matters. "It makes my position very interesting but it is not a very good way to run the country."[81]

When Gates met the Chiefs a week later, they had not budged. Lemnitzer restated the Army position that the JCS should develop the target policy and resulting list. CINCSAC would then take the list and develop an outline plan, assigning targets to the unified commanders. He expected the total to include four hundred to five hundred complexes.[82] Burke outlined an almost identical position, adding that the unified commander plans would be coordinated at the JCS to resolve conflicts. His proposal would result in "much tighter policy than we [have] now."[83] LeMay, sitting in for White, outlined the Air Force position. The JCS should not try to establish the NSTL but only define the percentage of target categories to be destroyed. On that guidance, field commanders would draw up plans and assign forces. Exactly which targets must be struck to achieve these outcomes depended on tactical and operational questions that only CINCSAC had the resources to answer; hence, he must prepare the plan. The Joint Staff did not have the information or experience to devise the target list, let alone the detailed plan. Twining agreed that "the Joint Staff does not have the know-how" to prepare the NSTL.[84] He grew emotional, stating that if the JCS made up the target list they "would cut SAC down to 50 targets. Service pressure would be terrific." He feared that once he left the chairman's billet, only the Air Force would be left to fight for SAC's survival. The depth of interservice dissension became clear in the exchange that followed:

> LEMNITZER: I have no knowledge of anyone wanting to carve up SAC.
> TWINING: I did not mean you.
> BURKE: Did you mean me, Nate? (Burke repeated this)
> TWINING: Apparently started to answer but did not.[85]

Gates decided the JCS would develop a policy, while there would be no unified strategic command. He also declared he had decided how the plan would be developed, although he did not say how at the meeting.[86] Gates ordered that the JCS provide targeting guidance and damage criteria to CINCSAC, who, acting as an agent of the JCS as the "Director, Joint Strategic Planning Staff," would oversee a joint team at Omaha developing a NSTL and SIOP. The SIOP would include all forces, including Polaris.

The JCS directed the creation of a detailed SIOP, using the Air Force plan as the model. The plan to be written in Omaha would satisfy several objectives that only an intensive effort could do. Forces would be mutually supporting to exploit mass, "crossing tracks, ECM, and enemy defensive degradation." Routes and times over target would be coordinated to avoid fratricide. Although the eventual plan would not reflect it, the guidance urged economy of effort. The target list would be an optimum-mix on the model of NESC 2009, "which considers targets of primary importance in event of either an initiative or retaliatory execution."[87] Reflecting the impact of the time factor, the plan would cover only the first strikes, not even the full first phase of the war.[88] From plans in 1950 outlining actions spanning years of a potential war, the most important war plan in 1960 was measured in hours.

Struggling to SIOP

Although the Navy had won few of its points before the JCS, it still saw the chance to carve up SAC. The interservice battle was not over, it had just changed venues. At the Chief of Naval Operations Deputies Conference on 18 August 1960, the assembled admirals nodded in agreement when one said, "We've got to make SAC honest for the good of the country." Another responded, "This is the best opportunity we've had in 15 years to do it. We've been fighting it a long time. It's an opportunity, Admiral."[89] Burke thought it essential that the plan at Omaha be "done right." If not, the result would be two war plans, one on paper, another for fighting. In an astonishing statement of service independence, Burke said, "When the war comes we will not use SAC's plan if it is improper."[90] If events went well, however, the Navy could gain. "So I think that if we are good enough we can take over this SAC—not over the whole SAC, but we can take over this targeting . . . in about two years."[91] With the stakes so high, the Navy feared underhanded Air Force maneuvering. Burke directed his representatives at Offutt to set up secure Navy-only communications back to Washington, safe from interception by the real enemy, the USAF.[92] His deep-seated distrust of SAC and the Air Force showed itself on 22 August 1960, when he spoke with a senior deputy assigned to work on the JSTPS.

> BURKE: They're dishonest. Not all of them are dishonest. Some of them are dishonest to hurt their souls. They know it.
>
> [CAPT. FREDERIC] BARDSHAR: Well, their tactics are basically Communist tactics.
>
> BURKE: Exactly.[93]

Feelings also ran hot at Offutt, as years of work came under intense interservice scrutiny. The senior Navy officer at Offutt told Burke that Power and his staff were reluctant to accept criticism of the SIOP, not surprisingly, as the SAC intelligence director had spent eight years building up the procedures. The interservice stakes were high. Both sides were painfully aware of it.[94]

Over the months of writing, several interservice differences became constant irritants. Only SAC had the detailed intelligence to perform targeting for a detailed SIOP plan, and it also claimed to have the only expertise and resources to wargame the resulting plan. Burke, however, insisted that the JCS be given the first draft of the SIOP.[95] Power resented the "fact that SAC is analyzed and scrutinized endlessly, while other commands seem to have acquired a degree of immunity to this sort of thing."[96]

Despite the service quarreling, the overall process produced a new plan by December 1960. It was huge. As briefed to the incoming administration, the NSTL had been developed from a potential list of more than 80,000 targets in the "Bombing Encyclopedia." The final list had 3,729 installations, many co-located, so reducing the final number of Designated Ground Zeroes (DGZs) to 1,060.[97] Tactically, the SIOP had two phases lifted directly from existing EWP tactics: "penetration," which created corridors for "delivery."[98] The plan had "options," but only in the sense of altering timing, not targets. Option one designated execution with alert forces only, options two through thirteen were based on preparation times of fourteen hours, and option fourteen was the "strategic warning option." Under option one (surprise attack), 1,004 delivery systems with 1,685 weapons were capable of immediate launch. One hour of preparation would give time to ready an additional 95 platforms, six hours would provide for a total of 1,658. Strategic warning would allow 2,244 systems to be readied with 3,267 weapons.[99] Kennedy's briefer stressed that the SIOP, while flexible with respect to warning time, was "designed for execution as a whole."

> A fundamental characteristic of the current SIOP is that it provides for attack of an Optimum-Mix Target System. This follows the conclusions and the Presidential decision relative to Study No. 2009 that an optimum-mix of both military and urban-industrial targets must he successfully attacked in order for the United States ultimately to prevail. Consequently, the SIOP is designed for the accomplishment of this total essential task. This embraces such things as timing and routing of attacks so that the maximum mutual support of the attacking forces is achieved. For example, tactics of follow-on forces relate directly to results expected to be achieved by earlier-arriving forces.[100]

The "flexible features" of the plan included execution as a total plan either in retaliation for a Soviet strike on the United States (option one) or as an entirely preemptive measure (option 14), and covered the contingency of "withholding" against targets in any combination of the Satellites, except for "defensive targets."[101]

Given the size of weapons involved and the arrangement of Bloc defenses, it is hard to imagine that strikes only on defensive targets would have been meaningfully less destructive than full attacks. That, however, was the limit of the plan's flexibility, because "exclusion of attack on any category or categories of targets" would make it unworkable. "There is no effective mechanism for rapid re-work of the plan, after order for its execution, for a different set of conditions than for which it way prepared."[102]

Flawed but Acceptable

Despite years of responsibility for developing US nuclear forces, both Gates and Eisenhower were shocked by aspects of SIOP-62. Gates ordered that future versions of the NSTL must be reduced; there were simply too many targets on the list. The base of intelligence must be broadened beyond just SAC to exploit joint assets. A third issue, overkill, usually is treated as a symbol for the irrationality and inhumanity of SAC's thinking. In fact, it arose from the search for certainty in a strategy of victory. It stemmed from the assurance and damage criteria included in the JCS instructions. The directive demanded a 75 percent overall assurance of delivery at each bomb release line. The question was what the assurance factor should be at particular targets, especially high-value ones. The issue was not that higher priority targets required more weapons, which everyone agreed. Rather, "if you have got 90 percent assurance of knocking out a target with say ten weapons, is it worthwhile to add four more weapons in order to get 95 percent or would it be better to use those four weapons on other less important targets?"[103] The actual assurance factor on most targets reached roughly 90 percent, with up to eight sorties against very high priority targets, raising them to an average of 97 percent.[104] Meanwhile, damage criteria demanded 90 percent probability of severe damage to half of Soviet industrial floor space, far more than had been inflicted at Hiroshima. The methods of computing such damage also were questionable, with only blast being used, and the effect of firestorms ignored. Multiplying high-assurance factors and damage criteria created overkill. Eisenhower complained to his naval aide about this "times 10 business." Overkill was bound to upset a president dedicated to maintaining US economic strength as the foundation of eventual Cold War victory. The aide reported to Burke, "He said POLARIS may be the solution to this whole thing, he said what we can do is take the POLARIS boats and say 'alright, you're the back-up' and we will let everybody just have one whack - not ten whacks and then we will get a [reconnaissance] report [and] we can go and tell the POLARISES to clean up."[105] Eisenhower also criticized the plan's inflexibility, particularly with Polaris employment.[106]

TABLE 3 Service total obligational authority, FY 1951–60 (current dollars in millions)

FISCAL YEAR	ARMY	NAVY	AIR FORCE
FY 51	17,453	12,212	15,102
FY 52	21,685	15,147	19,989
FY 53	13,475	11,762	18,650
FY 54	9,892	8,080	12,029
FY 55	10,813	9,993	10,615
FY 56	9,901	10,615	16,997
FY 57	9,919	10,805	18,449
FY 58	9,757	11,550	19,158
FY 59	9,555	12,148	19,599
FY 60	9,867	11,727	17,662

Source: Department of Defense Comptroller, "National Defense Budget Estimates for Fiscal Year 2007," available at http://comptroller.defense.gov/Portals/45/Documents/defbudget/Docs/fy2007_greenbook.pdf, 7, 74–75.

Despite its evident weaknesses, the JCS and White House accepted SIOP as national policy. What is most remarkable is not how revolutionary the SIOP was in incorporating land- and sea-based missiles, but that it did so fully within the framework of late air-atomic ideas. It had one target set whose destruction would let the United States "win." Alternative notions of finite or minimum deterrence had failed to dent the traditional plan. Any concept of pauses, target set withholding, intrawar deterrence, or other alien notions had been excluded. The scale, structure, and organization of SIOP-62 were a decisive victory for the Air Force notion of strategic warfare: the last.

Short of conflict, the budget is the ultimate scorecard for interservice rivalry. The budgetary picture over the course of the 1950s is clear.

After the end of the Korean War, the Air Force maintained dominance in the budget, easily eclipsing the other services. The Navy made an uneven recovery through the middle of the decade, while the Army budget share remained small and static. These budget figures reflect the acceptance of service ideas within the government. Fear of nuclear stalemate, desire for limited war forces, and notions of finite deterrence had some appeal for the nascent strategic studies community and general public, but little support at the policy level. Attacks on Air Force predominance based within the air-atomic idea, such as carriers, and those outside it, like finite deterrence did not change national policy. White House support during the Eisenhower years was firm and rarely questioned the ideas at the heart of strategic air doctrine. Those years ended on 20 January 1961.

7

NEW SHERIFF IN TOWN

Truman and Eisenhower held different beliefs on the role of atomic weapons in national security. Still, Truman's NSC-20 and NSC-68 left comfortable niches for air-atomic strategy, while Eisenhower's NSC-162/2 created an environment in which it flourished. Each administration entered office with distinct views on the role of nuclear weapons and gave the Air Force support ranging from tepid to overwhelming. In 1961, this situation changed. The Kennedy administration brought new personalities to power whose ideas about nuclear warfare threatened air-atomic strategy.

New Leaders with New Ideas

The new administration presided over a diverse intellectual opposition to air-atomic ideas. Advocates of finite deterrence seeking everything from nuclear submarines to special forces stood shoulder to shoulder with civilian strategists trying to return to Metternichian limited war. All these camps needed a healthy share of the budget for their programs, and all had to defeat the air-atomic status quo and its defenders. The USAF had to overcome each challenger's strongest arguments, while the contenders could cooperate to attack it from many directions simultaneously. None accepted SAC's argument that atomic weapons should be treated as just another bomb, for use when militarily justifiable. But they rejected that fundamental position for different reasons, based on diverse ideas about nuclear weapons and warfare. They could afford to cooperate long enough to defeat the air-atomic stranglehold on the budget and worry later about which alternative program would become dominant in its stead. They were all embarrassed by Eisenhower's pit bull, some by its crudity, others by its aggression, all by its existence. Whether to buy another dog, or learn judo, was another question that could be addressed later.

The central idea was that general war could not be won. As an essential conclusion of his seven years in the Pentagon, Secretary of Defense Robert McNamara emphasized "that although our strategic nuclear capability is absolutely vital to our security and to that of our allies, its only realistic role is deterrence of all-out nuclear or non-nuclear attacks since it is now impossible for either the United States or the Soviet Union to achieve a meaningful victory over the other in a strategic nuclear exchange."[1] This truth lay at the center of reasons for civilian distrust of the military and especially air-atomic ideas. Even administration civilians without much formal involvement in nuclear thinking probably agreed that nuclear weapons were unusable for achieving meaningful "victory."

The new administration, and particularly the new defense secretary, regarded the grim prospect of atomic war as an inherited problem that demanded resolution. They also viewed their predecessors' work with disdain. It is clear in the sweeping changes they made to the National Security Council (NSC) after Kennedy's inauguration. On 24 January 1961, after reviewing standing NSC policy papers, National Security Advisor McGeorge Bundy wrote to President Kennedy that although some of the papers that were important and guided Pentagon policy demanded rewriting, many "are fairly useless exercises . . . [which] can be ignored for now."[2] Eisenhower had handled national security through a civilianized version of joint military decision-making systems. The Kennedy administration replaced it with managerial models. From the perspective of systems analysis, SAC appeared to be extremely expensive while producing little usable force. The new administration soon resented the lack of options that a force structured around air-atomic ideas provided in crises. The public perception stemming from the Cuban crisis of a Kennedy administration aversion to nuclear weapons is inaccurate. They sought usable nuclear options in ways that Eisenhower had not. They considered first use and preemption in crises and preventive war against the Chinese nuclear program.[3] The New Frontiersmen were ready to clash with Eisenhower-sanctioned ideas and their supporters and to impose radical change in national security policy.

Another flashpoint between this new leadership and the Pentagon was social. The new president had won the election with an image of youthful vigor and a promise of generational change. Dynamism was an electoral asset but a liability in dealing with military leaders who had been senior officers in World War II. Eisenhower, with rank superior to all his Joint Chiefs, had been an untrumpable authority on military matters. In this area, the youth of Kennedy and his senior officials worked against him. Gen. Lauris Norstad, Supreme Allied Commander Europe (SACEUR), later recalled the shift: "Every new Administration brings in with it young, brilliant, eager, and ignorant people. The only difference in the Kennedy Administration was that they were younger, more eager, possibly more brilliant, but also clearly more ignorant."[4]

The new president lacked the expertise and credibility that had let his predecessor impose personal judgment on a fractious military. For example, in a 1956 White House conference, the Army chief of staff Maxwell Taylor outlined his theory of nuclear stalemate and the need for limited war forces. Eisenhower simply rejected the idea, replying that if general war came, nuclear weapons would be used "at once, and in full force. . . . it was fatuous to think that the US and USSR would be locked into a life and death struggle without using such weapons."[5] Kennedy lacked the gravitas to so handle a senior soldier. Youth and vigor could not substitute for this resource, and his prestige in the Pentagon soon was sapped by his failures in the Bay of Pigs and the summit with Khrushchev. In turn, Kennedy and his advisors quickly grew to distrust the advice of their senior military advisors, seeing them as out of touch with reality, their counsel of questionable value following the Bay of Pigs, and their air-atomic ideas as too narrowly confining in crises.

Analytical Expertise

What could and did substitute for authority was analysis, derived from the strategic studies community. Some of the most prominent civilian strategists gained influential positions in the White House and Pentagon. Charles Hitch, author of a 1960 book that applied an economic approach to defense problems, became the DoD Comptroller. Alain Enthoven, a prominent systems analyst, entered the systems analysis office, while Carl Rowen and Daniel Ellsberg found positions in the Pentagon. Although nuclear strategists William Kaufmann, Thomas Schelling, and Henry Kissinger did not take permanent positions, all three advised the administration.[6] When these civilian strategists had exerted influence before, they had done so from outside the government. They were successful only to the degree that the services adopted their arguments for use in budgetary battles. From 1961, they could directly influence budgetary decisions through their positions in the Office of the Secretary of Defense (OSD), with or without service concurrence.

The most important figure for the civilian strategists to influence was their master, Robert McNamara. Whereas Eisenhower had made the key national security decisions and used his secretaries of defense (Charles Wilson, Neil McElroy, and Thomas Gates) to implement them, Kennedy and McNamara had a different relationship. Although the evidence is scant, there are few presidential fingerprints on key nuclear strategy decisions. On some issues, such as the Limited Test Ban Treaty, which had a substantial diplomatic component, Kennedy's speeches outlined new policy directions. On issues of procurement and basic nuclear strategy, however, such as no-cities and Assured Destruction, McNamara appears to have been the driving force. The fundamental battle was fought in the Pentagon, as the White House steadfastly supported its civilian secretary against critics in the military, public, and Congress.

McNamara and his "whiz kids," as they became known, supplemented, or supplanted, traditional military expertise as the basis for decision making with an alternative: systems analysis. This approach linked strategy and expenditure by seeking the "most bang for the buck" through comparison of alternative programs for a given problem. Systems analysis recast military decisions as economic ones. As Hitch wrote in 1960, "Strategy and cost are as interdependent as the front and rear sights of a rifle."[7] This new system gave McNamara an alternative to relying on military expertise grudgingly offered by hostile generals and admirals. Mastery of the tactical and operational characteristics of weapons was subordinate in a system in which "models of one type or another are required to trace the relations between inputs and outputs, resources and objectives, for each of the systems to be compared, so that we can predict the relevant consequences of choosing any system."[8] Maxwell Taylor, returned to active duty by the new administration first as an advisor and then as chairman of the Joint Chiefs, complemented the new "rational basis" for fixing the size of general war forces. "To my knowledge it is the first time an effort has been made in the formulation of the Budget to answer the question, "How much is enough?"[9] Or, as McNamara told the House Armed Services Committee, "The relevant question is not only 'Do we want the very best for our military force?' but also, 'Is the additional capability truly required and, if so, is this the least costly way of attaining it?' "[10]

On assuming control in the Pentagon, McNamara quickly imposed his new analytical order. His office reviewed the FY 61 and FY 62 budgets approved by the previous administration, applying a new process, the Planning, Programming, and Budgeting System (PPBS), for the FY 63 budget and forward. Part of the review process involved wholesale reexaminations of strategy and force structure, the so-called "99 projects."[11] On this list were at least two wide-ranging considerations of nuclear strategy. Project 12, which aimed to "develop a statement of quantitative requirements for delivery vehicles for strategic nuclear weapons, based on appropriate target analyses and survivability factors . . . [and to] split the total strategic requirements among the available delivery vehicles, and state the long range requirements for each, including Polaris," was completed in November 1961.[12] Project 47, submitted the following year, appraised the "adequacy of the strategic nuclear delivery force."[13] Both reports used intensive analysis to reexamine fundamental questions and compare weapon effectiveness across services.

This approach was far from alien to the Air Force. Operations research received a major boost from the Air Force's Second World War interest in assessing strategic bombing, in which McNamara had participated. In the late 1940s, the Air Force established RAND, home to the abstract analytical approach to nuclear strategy. The Air Force's attacks on carrier effectiveness hinged on mathematical comparisons of the effectiveness of alternative sea- and land-based offensives. It made greater use of these techniques than any other fighting service in the 1950s. The key differences between those disputes and the 99 Projects were the subject matter and the stakes. Deciding whether carriers and bombers were the most efficient offensive tool was different from deciding if the offensive itself should be carried out. Systems analysis probed underlying strategies, and the stakes were high. Air Force and Navy studies of the previous decade, conversely, had not threatened the existence of either service's main weapon systems nor their undergirding strategies.

The Air Force was the leading target of this approach and the number and diversity of the reports initially overwhelmed the Air Staff. The Air Council, charged with running the day-to-day operations of the Air Force, identified the problem as early as April 1961, advising White that the Air Staff had the analytical support needed to answer DoD projects, but was using it ineffectively.[14] The situation was little better the next summer when LeMay lamented to Power that OSD had created fifty-eight new projects, many examining major questions of force structure and strategy.[15] By 1964, the Air Staff considered major reorganization to cope with OSD demands. The USAF had failed to promote programs and courses of action because it had "not fulfilled the OSD requirement for information in appropriate detail and scope." This failure had undermined confidence in Air Force studies and threatened the "long-term credibility of Air Force views in defense planning." This had occurred despite dedicating 1,400 people to the OSD studies, at a cost of over $30 million a year, and damaged other staff work, as officers were detailed for longer and longer periods on new OSD requirements.[16]

Beyond ad hoc studies, the analytic mindset also reshaped the budget process. What previously had been the major battleground for interservice fighting now featured OSD not only as a mediator between the services, but as a major player. From its first days in office, the new administration dedicated itself to reforming the defense budget. Only one week after the inauguration, Bundy's staff outlined critical flaws in the old system. Plans and budget were weakly linked. The JCS's Joint Strategic Objectives Plan, the closest thing to a link between plans and the budget, was "not wholly approved" by the secretary of defense or supported by the budget. Underlying the dysfunction was a lack of common assumptions and doctrine among the services. "The underlying strategic doctrines of the three services are different, which means that plans and budget are aimed at different objectives. (Air Force: 'counter force deterrent'; Navy: 'finite deterrent'; Army: 'credible deterrent')." The budget machinery, built around the annual budget and congressional schedule, failed to take a long-range perspective.[17]

The PPBS system sought to address these flaws. Rather than address programs individually, and submit separate service budgets, OSD would compile the budget in functionally separate areas including strategic offensive forces (also called central war offensive forces and strategic retaliatory forces), general purpose forces, and continental air and missile defense forces. This structure placed similar weapons in direct competition for the same budgetary dollars. Polaris and B-70 fought for strategic offensive dollars rather than being artificially stove-piped into Air Force and Navy budgets. Enthoven and Wayne Smith, central figures in the radical budget changes, identified several fundamental ideas underlying the new system: open and clear analysis, active use of an analytical staff, decision making based on explicit criteria of the national interest in defense programs, consideration of military needs and costs together, explicit consideration of alternatives at the top decision level, and a multiyear force and financial plan. The primary vehicle for integrating forces into each mission area was an overarching "Five-Year Defense Program." The debate between the services and OSD took place in the Draft Presidential Memorandum (DPM), whose final form became the basis for the budget.[18] OSD wrote the draft, received service comments, redrafted, and received additional comments in an iterative process. The new system embedded OSD power and the analytical approach into the budget, and so into the fundamental decisions about weapon systems and strategies. Matters that had previously been left to the services to fight out, with the secretary of defense acting as a referee and the president as CEO, now were replaced by active OSD leadership and micromanagement, with systems analysis providing an alternative to military expertise as the basis for decision making.[19]

This shift from military advice caused problems for a USAF leadership accustomed to basing its decisions on personal experience. Such expertise did provide a foundation for judgment, but was almost impossible to quantify. For example, the Air Staff supported the B-70 by arguing that its high speed and altitude complicated the Soviet defensive problem. On its own, the weapon might not guarantee effective assault, but when combined with low-level penetration aircraft, ICBMs, medium-range missiles launched from Europe, SLBMs, and carrier-based aircraft, it would overwhelm untried Soviet defenses. No matter how intelligent and desperate, Soviet defense commanders were bound to make mistakes that would fatally favor SAC. This recommendation stemmed from the wartime experience of commanders like LeMay, who faced the problem of insufficient mass in attacking Axis air defenses. The air defenses of those nations learned from mistakes made in earlier, poorly planned strikes and mounted better defenses. LeMay and his generation held that confronting an inexperienced enemy defense with the most complex problem possible from the outset would compel its catastrophic failure. A Mach 3 bomber operating at seventy thousand feet promised to be central to such an assault. The problem lay in quantifying its importance relative to the other parts of the attack and to alternative force mixes. Such issues, qualitative judgments based on operational experience, resisted quantitative systems analysis. They also strained professional and personal relationships. LeMay spoke for many of his uniformed contemporaries when he wrote of his resentment of McNamara's analysts setting "themselves up as military experts" when canceling programs.[20]

The services eventually did learn to use systems analysis against OSD and one another, but took several years to gain the expertise. LeMay quickly recognized that the Air Force needed officers with advanced degrees in systems analysis and began training a cadre.[21] A similar approach is evident in Project Forecast, a 1963–64 study conducted by Gen. Bernard Schriever, who had overseen Air Force ballistic missile development in the 1950s. Forecast, a reaction to the programmatic defeats the Air Force suffered under the new administration, asked basic questions about how to integrate emerging technology into the Air Force. Gen. David Burchinal, who led the group examining strategic forces, presented those conclusions to McNamara. When the secretary challenged him to support his evaluation with quantitative data, Burchinal provided detailed studies produced by his team, the national nuclear labs, and industry. His conclusions challenged many of McNamara's, supporting a continued manned bomber force and the construction of high-yield weapons to support Assured Destruction. Although the effort failed to convince McNamara to support counterforce or high-yield weapons, it shows that the Air Force could adopt systems analysis and rigorous quantification.[22]

Muzzling

Meanwhile, McNamara is alleged to have "muzzled" the USAF's established organs to justify policy. The Long Range Plans (LR) and Policy Coordination branches of the Air Staff, under Brig. Gen. Robert Richardson and Col. Noel Parrish, had been producing service positions on strategic issues since the late 1950s. According to Parrish, McNamara manufactured allegations that LR had leaked classified information to justify closing the branch and making an example of its leaders to other officers. Parrish asserted that they had been guilty not of publishing classified information but simply of embarrassing civilian officials with well-argued positions opposing administration policy.[23] Richardson, writing several years later, identified his office as "the Air Staff focal point for the development of the Air Force position on strategy and national security questions such as deterrence, counterforce, nuclear policy, etc. We formulated the Air Force position and General Parrish's office—Policy Coordination—saw to it that it was disseminated and followed."[24] Supposedly, the removal of Parrish and Richardson from Washington (the former to Alabama, the latter to Europe) eased McNamara's task by silencing articulate Air Force voices on strategy. Even if Parrish and Richardson exerted less influence over policy than they imagined, their removal was bound to create pain when Air Force planning and strategy was under pressure. Certainly, the Air Force lost some of its capacity to make compelling arguments to the public through the press and its congressional allies, and McNamara did try to prevent any of the services from openly disagreeing with his policies.

As though being unprepared for systems analysis and losing some senior thinkers was not enough, the interpersonal relationships between the new administration and the Air Force (as well as other services) created additional friction. In any organization, the strengths and weaknesses of interpersonal relationships shape the efficiency and quality of work. The new civilian leadership in the Department of Defense developed a particularly poor rapport with their senior officers. Oral histories from military and civilian participants are filled with anecdotes of bureaucratic infighting amplified by bad feeling.

Personal Friction

McNamara is the central figure in many of these stories. He came to the Pentagon from Ford Motor Company with limited wartime experience. He had entered the Army Air Force in 1942 as a captain, analyzed strategic air operations, and finished the war as a lieutenant colonel aiding LeMay's offensive in the Pacific.[25] McNamara's formative exposure to airpower was through statistics, not flying. He participated in the same operations as the senior Air Force officers whom he later would lead, but viewed these engagements through a different conceptual lens. McNamara's postwar experience took him from military affairs but immersed him in mathematical analysis of complex operations. His great success at Ford, crowned by appointment as the company's president after only fourteen years of service, attested to his managerial skill. While at Ford, he left contemporary military affairs behind. McNamara later claimed to have read only a single book on nuclear strategy (Oskar Morgenstern's *The Question of National Defense*) before joining the Kennedy administration.[26] He watched the transformation of strategic airpower from the Pacific theater through the early and late air-atomic eras as a member of the public.

While another secretary of defense might have relied on the counsel of the Joint Chiefs, McNamara's difficult relationship with senior officers became legendary. As Norstad's quote suggests, the military leadership perceived him, and the staff they derisively nicknamed the "whiz kids," as having inadequate respect for military experience and advice. The partisan *Air Force* magazine editorialized in 1963 that "the Secretary of Defense is substituting the judgment of a handful of men for the carefully weighed decision of a small army of experts."[27] Not just the judgment, but also the way that it was rendered, bred hostility. A Navy "Source Y" who worked in the secretary's office, reported several instances of boorish behavior from senior civilians. The source asserted that Harold Brown, assistant secretary of defense for Research and Development, told an Air Force major general, "If you had any sense or were capable of doing anything else, you wouldn't be in uniform."[28] Adam Yarmolinksy allegedly said "at a dinner party in response to a question as to 'what do you do' that his job was 'to make and break admirals and generals.' "[29]

The uniformed military returned this hostility. According to an observer of a 1964 Pentagon briefing presented to senior officers and civilians, Power "was obviously extremely bitter that recommendations by civilian advisers (computer-type minds) to the President and Secretary of Defense prevailed over those of the military. He closed the session by saying these types, i.e. civilian 'computer types who were making defense policy don't know their ass from a hole in the ground.' "[30] Many officers believed that, beyond denigrating military advice, McNamara sought to control dissemination of their views, particularly to Congress. For example, in 1961, when the *New York Times* reported that the Air Force was preparing a "vigorous appeal to Congress" to support manned bomber programs, McNamara told Air Force Secretary Eugene Zuckert that he was "shocked and embarrassed." He directed Zuckert to ensure that every civilian and military leader in the Air Force understood that he expected public support for his—and the president's—decision. Zuckert later claimed that McNamara intentionally kept the Air Force off balance to control its powerful influence with Congress and the public. "He wanted the Air Force to know at all times who was the boss."[31] Moreover, of all military programs, the Air Force strategic mission seemed most amenable to systems analysis. For the service with the greatest proportion of the budget and the perceived leading role in national defense, led by a general renowned for lack of tact and more spit than polish, it was a recipe for disaster.

On several occasions, McNamara believed LeMay was disingenuous or dishonest. During the Berlin Crisis, the secretary was present at a meeting with the president in which LeMay claimed that US tactical aircraft in Europe were outnumbered by ten or thirteen to one. McNamara recorded this "is not true" but did not "dispute the point at the meeting."[32] This tact crumbled over the next few years. In December 1963, as the executive branch scrambled to educate Lyndon Johnson on his new position, LeMay briefed him on strategic force programs, which had run strongly against Air Force recommendations. McNamara heatedly complained that his statement "contains a number of inaccurate and misleading statements. . . . Please review the paper and the accompanying charts and discuss with me the action you plan to take to avoid misrepresentation of our strategic force programs vs. those of the Soviet Union."[33] At one point, during the TFX source selection furor (when the USAF and USN recommended adopting a Boeing design, but McNamara awarded the contract to General Dynamics), a Navy officer reported that McNamara lectured LeMay on "honesty, honor, and integrity," in front of a group of flag officers.[34] LeMay reciprocated the disrespect. At one point, he privately asked a colleague, "Would things be much worse if Khrushchev were Secretary of Defense?"[35] Gen. David Jones, then a junior general officer, recalled a contemporary story of LeMay chasing McNamara around the latter's desk in an attempt to "flatten him" during the extended struggle over the B-70. Although Jones acknowledged the tale was apocryphal, that such a story could be taken as credible testifies to the strain between the two.[36]

LeMay and the Air Force had a troubled relationship not only with McNamara, but even more damagingly, with the president. Since Eisenhower had been the protector and enabler for Air Force strategy, Kennedy's hostility was disastrous. Soon after the inauguration, the president and his closest advisors attended a firepower demonstration at Eglin Air Force Base in Florida. The Air Force assembled nearly every aircraft in the inventory from single-propeller spotter planes to B-52s, for a series of flyovers and strikes. An observer escorting several cabinet members reported that they showed uneasiness at the entire demonstration, seemed to "deplore" it. Bundy refused to enter a hangar with a display of nuclear weapons. Even if the observer misinterpreted Kennedy and his party's reactions to the display, he was certainly correct to note that "the Air Force was not really in tune" with the new administration.[37]

The president also had a dysfunctional relationship with LeMay. Deputy Secretary of Defense Ross Gilpatric recalled that Kennedy would be "in a fit" after any meeting with LeMay, because the general could not or would not listen and made "outrageous proposals." Kennedy avoided any but the most minimal contact with LeMay, and after these few meetings was "choleric."[38] Again, LeMay returned the distaste shown by his superior. Consistent with the overall impression of senior officers that the administration was filled with inexperienced men with dangerous ideas, LeMay complained about Kennedy's resolve, or the lack of it.

During the Berlin crisis, he told a staff meeting, the use of nuclear weapons was "apparently not acceptable to the administration—and that no one seems to have the guts to use atomic weapons." To LeMay, Kennedy's problem was his lack of resolution to avoid defeat and misunderstanding of the relationship of strength and deterrence.[39] LeMay did not change his opinion as the New Frontiersmen gained experience. In August 1964, after a briefing on the SIOP, he lamented that the major problem in every practice execution of the plan had been tardy decision making.[40] To a man convinced that success demanded the fastest possible application of overwhelming force, indecision, especially presidential indecision, was intolerable.

As Norstad said, any new administration brings new people into positions of influence over strategy, many of them inexperienced. When the Kennedy administration brought in such people, they sought to substitute analytical talent for absent experience. While ultimate authority had resided in the White House during previous administrations, the services had kept considerable autonomy over programs, force structure, and even strategy. In the new decade, the OSD's analytical approach eroded that autonomy. From the service perspective, this development was a maddening and dangerous intervention by amateur outsiders. From the OSD perspective, rational scrutiny finally had been brought to bear on previously intractable disputes and resolute leadership had made hard decisions. Such irreconcilable worldviews generated tension, intensified by the foul chemistry between the major actors. While good personal rapport might have smoothed over difficulties, its lack aggravated them.

The most important arena in the struggle between the services and the administration was the familiar one of nuclear strategy. Although arguments in this sphere had taken place continuously since 1945, two two-term presidents, who supported a central role for nuclear weapons in US strategy, had provided environments ranging from neutral to friendly for air-atomic thinking. The Kennedy administration's approach marked a major change which could—and did—threaten the viability of the strategic niche which nourished the air-atomic idea.

New Strategy

Thinking about nuclear strategy went through three major changes during the early part of the decade. The first iteration introduced the theme of controlled and deliberate nuclear war, closely followed by city avoidance. The final mature strategy of the Kennedy administration, and the end of the air-atomic strategy, were the twin concepts of Assured Destruction and Damage Limitation. Meanwhile, the Air Force consistently promoted a single theme, counterforce, which was an incremental refinement of earlier ideas, especially blunting. The failure of counterforce and the success of Assured Destruction fundamentally changed nuclear strategy and shifted the locus of nuclear strategy formulation away from the uniformed services—all of them, not just the USAF.

The Kennedy administration's first ideas about nuclear strategy were articulated as a critique of late air-atomic beliefs. The body of thought that the McNamara OSD confronted had developed substantially but incrementally since 1945. At its core was the conviction that general war with the USSR was the greatest threat. Limited war was a distant second, which could be faced down, if necessary, with well-developed general war forces. If war occurred with the USSR, there would be a single goal: to put the United States in a position to dictate terms at the end of an exchange. The exchange itself would involve striking a single "optimum-mix" of targets as swiftly and powerfully as possible. That massive attack would saturate inexperienced Soviet air defenses and destroy the most time-sensitive targets for blunting the Soviet force-in-being and disrupting its potential military strength. Carrying out this attack and acquiring the requisite qualitative edge, demanded the maximum attainable technological and quantitative superiority. All of this demanded constant progress because Soviet achievements showed worrisome scientific and engineering skill. Maintaining visibly superior forces prepared to launch a devastating attack provided the strongest possible deterrent threat. This air-atomic argument demanded all these elements simultaneously. For example, without superiority, the offensive force would not penetrate defenses and smash the Soviet military. A piecemeal attack would squander the initiative and let Soviet defenses devise countermeasures to SAC tactics. Focusing on limited war forces to the exclusion of general war forces would sap resources for general war and raise doubts about US commitment to use nuclear weapons. In the end, the air-atomic strategy was a brittle set of interdependent premises. If one fell, all would be in jeopardy.

First Thesis—Choice

Given its preference for radical change, the new administration was bound to collide head-on with such rigid concepts. On taking office, Kennedy directed a review of the FY 61 and FY 62 budgets. In February 1961, Bundy provided a snapshot of the president's thinking to guide this reexamination. It embraced four requirements. First, US military capability had to be powerful enough to prevent an intentional Soviet nuclear attack. In itself, this was consistent with existing Air Force ideas.[41]

Second, the capacity to act with conventional weapons in situations short of atomic attack must be "substantially increased." Inherent in this argument, which drew heavily on the ideas of Maxwell Taylor, was the concept of nuclear stalemate and the need to have forces for all intensities of conflict. Kennedy's early ideas on nuclear strategy, limited war forces, and stalemate sounded as though they had been written by the former Army chief of staff, which, Parrish later stated was no coincidence because they had been. He claimed that Taylor wrote most of Kennedy's campaign speeches on the subject and, along with retired lieutenant general James Gavin, often visited Kennedy's home in Hyannis Port and stayed during the weekends.[42] Whatever its origin, the idea of increased conventional forces was not incompatible with Air Force thinking. Although it opposed the Air Force position that general war forces should be used in limited wars, with a sufficiently large budget, large air-atomic and conventional forces could coexist, as envisioned, for example, by the authors of NSC-68.

The most important change from the Air Force perspective was the third identified in Bundy's memo. Should nuclear war occur, the US must "retain the capability to act rationally to advance the national interest by exerting pressure and offering choices to the enemy." This was the core of the first set of changes to nuclear strategy introduced by the Kennedy administration. In his review of the 1961 and 1962 budgets, McNamara explained that the US wanted to avoid what he termed "spasm war" and embrace a flexible posture "permitting more endurance in the face of attack, more control, flexible and selectivity, and toward more capability to limit damage to ourselves and to terminate a war."[43] The new posture would be possible only with survivable forces, improved C2, and "strategies at the highest level for a wide range of general war contingencies." Only then could the United States avoid being forced to commit forces reflexively, possibly making catastrophic errors in the process.[44] By increasing stability and the safety of forces, and by not forcing them to react immediately on indefinite information from fear of destruction, the chance of accidental war would be reduced. The United States would not have to take "crash" actions to protect forces which might be misinterpreted as an attack, and so provoke one. Furthermore, in a hint of what would become official policy a year later, McNamara declared that effective American use of nuclear force in a "careful and discriminating way" might induce the Soviets not to launch a wholesale attack on American cities.[45, 46]

Fourth and finally, Bundy said, the president reaffirmed that he did not want to create forces for preventive or preemptive war; such an attack was "not the policy of the US Government." Furthermore, the United States would continue to seek limitation and control of armaments.[47] These stipulations on nuclear strategy also directly conflicted with contemporary Air Force thinking. To act "rationally" in the midst of an atomic campaign carried the risk of failing to act at all.

Time lost in deciding the identity of targets and the sequence of attacks in an effort to "signal" the USSR could shred the tightly woven attack, dividing its effect and permitting a more powerful Soviet strike. The air-atomic strategy, which sought to reduce the time between a decision to strike and its moment of maximum intensity, ran directly against the new policy, as did its tendency to blur preventive and preemptive war. Under the new administration, the decision to strike threatened to be only the first of many high-level interventions in conducting a campaign. This line of argument rejected the idea that there was a single best way to fight. Fifteen years of building the air offensive force had focused on inflicting maximum shock on the Soviet Union, which now was derided as "spasm war." This centerpiece of administration strategy rewrote both strategic ends and operational means, and these politicians were doing something they had never done before: interfering in the way the USAF handled details.

The approach unsettled LeMay, who complained that elements of defining military objectives for forces and weapons systems "defy precise calculation." Because of that irreducible uncertainty, the requested Air Force programs were the minimum needed for national security, and even then carried an element of risk. "A posture of lesser quantity, quality and readiness would cast serious doubt on both the determination and the ability of this nation to continue to deter general war."[48] In a general sense, the air-atomic position always had recognized that Clausewitizan friction in operations produced requirements for forces and strategy that defied precise quantification through rational analysis. Overwhelming strength and blunt plans left the least up to chance. This approach was in peril. Here, in principle, he was more right than McNamara, though not in practice.

The first round of changes in nuclear strategy under the Kennedy administration shaped the reworking of the FY 61 and 62 budgets, and molded FY 63. The programmatic effects (to be discussed in the next chapter) involved cancellation of manned bomber systems and increased reliance on Minuteman and Polaris deployments. Other than the running fight over the B-70, the Air Force had little success in pushing back the changes in force structure and strategy.

Second Thesis—No Cities

After a year in office and the wholesale shift in budgeting, the administration put forth its second shift in nuclear strategy—"no-cities." This policy was first voiced at a NATO meeting in Athens in May 1962, but became publicly known at the Ann Arbor commencement in June. McNamara told the assembled graduates that strategy in a nuclear war had to be reoriented toward a traditional model, which focused on destroying enemy military forces, not his society. Because United States and Allied forces were strong enough to retain the striking power to destroy Soviet society, even after a surprise attack, the United States could restrain itself. By publicly announcing as policy that the United States would not attack Soviet cities in a first strike, he hoped that the USSR would reciprocate. "We are giving a possible opponent the strongest imaginable incentive to refrain from striking our own cities."[49]

In essence, the no-cities idea was an extension of the first round of strategies. That first year of changes focused on the rational and flexible execution of nuclear war. The "no-cities" idea simply defined the preferred American option. A war carried out under the ideas of the Ann Arbor speech would necessarily focus on military targets, but this carried with it collateral dangers. Rear echelon military targets were tempting, but as they might be close to population areas, attacks on them could be misinterpreted. Similarly, there would be a strong incentive to attack hardened and protected Soviet nuclear forces, yet that might be seen as an attempt to "win" by disarming as opposed to "damage limitation." Intrawar bargaining and signaling, so tempting in theory, might be unrealistic in practice.

The great flaw in the no-cities strategy, however, was that it depended on Soviet cooperation. In effect, Moscow must agree to limit the damage it would inflict on the United States, to avoid cities even if they contained important military targets, as part of a tacit agreement with the United States, one defined precisely as American weapons were devastating the USSR, reducing the size and strength of the Soviet arsenal, reducing its future options, and killing its citizens. The "no-cities" idea used an unworkable mechanism to pursue a commendable goal.[50] While no-cities was a policy failure, it did help lay the intellectual ground for Assured Destruction. It was an important, perhaps essential, intermediate step toward that far more enduring strategic change.

Antithesis—Counterforce

The Air Force's principal response to the 1961 and 1962 iterations of nuclear strategy was counterforce. Although the term first appeared in Air Force discussions during 1959–60, when Parrish oversaw a study to develop the idea, a 1963 document lays out the most developed case for it. Counterforce, an incremental extension of late air-atomic thought, added a degree of discrimination and control to the blunting mission, while still seeking to make the enemy surrender on American terms. Echoing McNamara's rhetoric about the no-cities idea, the Air Force promoted counterforce as an old-fashioned strategy. To target cities as promoted by finite deterrent advocates and even by the "no-cities" school as the final sanction, was a "desperate and illogical attempt to achieve deterrence through the threat of destroying organized society rather than achieving deterrence through the clear ability to gain military victory."[51] Rather, the proper targets for destruction were the enemy's aerospace forces. Their defeat would expose all other enemy assets. That vulnerability would enable the United States to end the war on its terms.

Adopting McNamara's rhetoric from 1961, the strategy would use "discriminating" weapons and limit reliance on bonus effects in nonmilitary areas. Counterforce advocates argued that improved guidance systems could allow nuclear attacks whose intent was easily discernible. A low-yield (for example, 1 KT) weapon delivered with high accuracy would be sufficient (by generating 1,000 psi) to destroy any military target but not damage frame or brick residential structures more than two thousand feet from the blast. With such weapons, the Soviets could discern American intent from the targets actually attacked, not a prewar promise of what would not be attacked.[52] The intent of these attacks on military targets with these discriminating weapons would be clear and not generate a reflexive counter-city reaction.

In response to critics of Air Force planning who stated that counterforce (or blunting) could not find Soviet bombers at their bases or ICBMs on their launch pads, promoters of counterforce predicted the Soviets would withhold some offensive forces so to strike at surviving American nuclear capability. For the Soviets to fire their entire force in a first strike would leave them "at the mercy of the opponents' forces which survive that attack."[53] Nor would the Soviets resort to destroying cities with that remaining force. At this point in a strategic nuclear exchange, when the USSR lacked a counterforce alternative of its own (because reconnaissance over the United States to find remaining military targets would be impossible), the Kremlin could either commit suicide by attacking US cities and inviting retaliation, or attempt to negotiate better terms. The latter course, ending the war on the most favorable terms to the USSR, would require retention of its weapons as a bargaining chip.[54] So, to destroy these forces was to win whatever victory was possible in such a war.

In peacetime, the counterforce doctrine would provide the greatest possible increment of deterrent power. Any strategy that held Soviet cities hostage, as both finite deterrence and "no-cities" did, lacked credibility because it put the onus for opening a counter-city campaign on the United States. Since the USSR would have an identical "terror" capacity, counterforce advocates thought, the Soviets would find such a threat incredible and not be deterred by it. By contrast, if the Soviets were credibly threatened with the loss of their own military forces and therefore of the war they started, they "will be deterred to the greatest degree."[55]

At first glance, counterforce can be difficult to distinguish from no-cities because both focus on destroying enemy military forces. Interestingly, Freedman claims that the Air Force's advocacy of counterforce as a complementary strategy to "no-cities" was an important reason for McNamara's subsequent shift to Assured Destruction. However, the two have fundamentally different underlying mechanisms. No-cities relied on a tacit Soviet agreement to avoid the destruction of civil society. Counterforce sought the same goal by destroying Soviet weapons and compelling a favorable political settlement. No-cities relied on Soviet cooperation, while counterforce removed their ability to cause harm. Another subtler difference is that no-cities was essentially a negative strategy; it directed how not to conduct nuclear operations. Counterforce provided positive guidance on which targets to strike. The difference between the two becomes clear when examining a hypothetical military airbase near a major Soviet city. No-cities would ban the strike because it might signal that attacks on cities were permissible and so invite retaliation. Counterforce would consider the base a legitimate target if a sufficiently discriminating method could be devised. LeMay highlighted a related difference in the contrasting role of the American military. In no-cities, the military's primary role is to hold Soviet lives hostage; in counterforce it is to preserve American ones. "What must be remembered is this—the primary task of the US Armed Forces is not to destroy the Soviet population but to protect and save American lives and property."[56] Finally, the greatest contrast between the two strategies is that no-cities starts with the assumption that victory in nuclear war was impossible. To counterforce advocates, a postwar world under Soviet or Chinese domination was worse than one under democratic government. Any strategy that reduced the chance of the American form of government surviving in its present form was unworthy of consideration.

USAF ideas about counterforce in the early 1960s were driven by engrained modes of thinking about war. The Air Force retained an unshaken belief in the feasibility of military victory. Senior officers emphasized the need for a visible numerical and technological superiority to deter war, and if deterrence failed, to prevail. They feared threats to the professional standing of the Air Force. If the service lost control of when and what aircraft struck, it had lost its defining function. For senior officers who had struggled for Air Force independence based on the concept of strategic airpower as co-equal with land and seapower, to lose command of its most important functions threatened the identity of the service, and their own as professionals. Moreover, they resented meddling in their professional function by civilian outsiders. LeMay later wrote that a leader should stay out of the way after telling people what he wanted done.[57] Civilian control of nuclear operations directly contradicted this deep-seated belief.

The administration judged counterforce impossible. McNamara claimed that the Air Force was seeking a "full first-strike capability" which would enable the United States to so reduce Soviet retaliatory power that it could not unacceptably damage US population and industry. The secretary rejected counterforce as a policy alternative to no-cities and the later policy of Assured Destruction. Unless the Soviets were extremely foolish, they were bound to protect their forces as well as the United States did its own. Taylor, by 1963 the chairman of the Joint Chiefs, further rejected the counterforce assertion that a residual Soviet missile force could be found and struck. To destroy any single Soviet weapon would require an excessive number of American aircraft and missiles, most of which would attack empty bases and missile sites. "Clearly, at some point it will become futile to attempt to destroy the Soviet missile system either in preemption or in retaliation."[58] Even if counterforce were possible, it was unnecessary and "not particularly useful," because for twenty years the credible threat of a US first strike had failed to deter limited aggression. As such, it would still be necessary to build up substantial conventional forces.[59] Whether or not the counterforce strategy was feasible with contemporary technology, the defense budget cancelled weapons like the RS-70 and abandoned the superiority to carry counterforce out in the long run.

Nemesis—Assured Destruction

In its place, McNamara proposed the final nuclear strategy of the Kennedy administration, introducing the ideas that underlay American policy for the rest of the Cold War. The failure of no-cities and the impossibility of counterforce demanded a new framework for understanding nuclear warfare. From the FY 64 budget through to FY 70, the United States had two nuclear war objectives. The first, Assured Destruction, formalized the arguments made by finite deterrent advocates since the 1950s. A sufficient deterrent could be fashioned from a secure retaliatory force that could ride out the most powerful surprise Soviet attack and then inflict unacceptable damage on the USSR. In the 1965 Draft Presidential Memorandum, McNamara arbitrarily quantified that degree of destruction as 30 percent of the Soviet population, 50 percent of industrial capacity, and 150 cities. An Assured Destruction force would deter any "calculated deliberate Soviet nuclear attack." By comparison, the JCS anticipated that the full SIOP-62 would kill 108 million Soviets, or 54 percent of the population.[60] Notably, this estimate would have been based on blast damage alone. Fire damage would have killed even more.

Any forces beyond the number of secure systems needed for Assured Destruction would be for "Damage Limiting." They would be purchased if they could "further reduce the damage to the United States in the event of a Soviet attack by an amount sufficient to justify their added costs." Damage Limitation systems would destroy some Soviet weapons and disrupt others, essentially pursuing a limited form of blunting or counterforce. However, unlike those missions, its size was limited by cost efficiency. A blunting or counterforce mission that demanded the expenditure of ten American weapons to destroy one Soviet missile might be a valid mission, but would be frowned on as Damage Limitation.[61] A force designed without regard for cost efficiency in a Damage Limitation mission would constitute a "full first-strike."

Assured Destruction differed from the earlier no-cities strategy in several ways. It was blunter. No-cities hoped to protect American (and Soviet) civilians from unnecessary suffering through agreement and intrawar bargaining. Assured Destruction pursued the same goal through the threat of destroying cities. Still, it was the clear intellectual successor to no-cities, with the added benefit of separating the counterforce-like elements of no-cities out into Damage Limitation.

Damage Limitation was much like counterforce in means, but not its ends. Blunting and counterforce disarmed the enemy and coerced him to a favorable political settlement by denying him the means to achieve his ends. Damage Limitation simply reduced the potential for damage to the United States without being tied directly to a political end, outside support of deterrence. Bargaining presumably would be going on throughout an exchange, but Damage Limitation did not assume that the best strikes would be those that left a disarmed enemy, because a force powerful enough to do so would constitute a "full first-strike" force, which, in McNamara's reckoning, was an impossible goal.

During the late Kennedy and early Johnson years, the Air Force offered no program in response to Assured Destruction and Damage Limitation beyond counterforce. However, General Bruce Holloway, Air Force vice chief of staff and then commander of SAC during the late 1960s, later critiqued Assured Destruction as an unrealistic "bum policy." Reflecting similar arguments of the previous decade against finite deterrence, he said that an Assured Destruction threat made by the United States was not credible. The idea of the United States beginning a city-exchange was implausible and therefore an incredible deterrent. Even if the Soviets believed the United States might carry out Assured Destruction, their ideology did not value citizens beyond what they produced for the state. It might be willing to lose comparatively "unimportant" farmers and workers if "key people" are unharmed. "So these are the two cardinal points to me. First, they probably don't believe it, and second, to the degree they do believe it, it doesn't deter." Assured Destruction had any deterrent credibility only because it was devised in a period where the United States had sufficient overall superiority to destroy whatever the Soviets valued. In other words, the declining remains of the air-atomic force deterred Soviet aggression, not the secure second strike power of Assured Destruction. Holloway emphasized that what deterred the Soviets was known only to them, and American survival should not rest on such a shaky foundation.[62]

Assured Destruction also abandoned twenty years of reliance on the offensive-defensive. Throughout the 1950s the key solution to growing Soviet capability had been to compress the time necessary for a decisive attack. The faster SAC could arrive over Soviet bases, the more American lives would be saved. This ingrained principle led airmen to an intuitive rejection of Assured Destruction. The new strategy abandoned any possibility of preserving American lives by active measures against the enemy military, relying instead on passive (and distastefully explicit) threats against his civilians. And indeed, in the middle term, McNamara's strategy did mean more Americans would die in a nuclear exchange than SAC's strategy would allow.

Carrying out Assured Destruction also gave civilians detailed control of military operations. Since the earliest days of SAC, LeMay had sought autonomy in executing his plans. At the 1947 Dualism conference, he pled with the vice chief of staff to protect that autonomy from service rivals, let alone civilians. In turn, Vandenberg confirmed that the most basic principle of delivering an atomic attack "in the greatest possible mass after the outbreak of war with the USSR to enhance the psychological and perhaps decisive effect which will be produced by great destruction in a very short period of time."[63] The delays inherent in Assured Destruction and fine-grained control of retaliation guaranteed that principle was no longer practicable.

More generally, Assured Destruction was troublesome from the air-atomic perspective, because it eschewed victory as the objective of war. It left the decision for terminating a nuclear war in Soviet hands rather than using American forces to compel a conclusion. To air-atomic advocates, the only acceptable victory came by knockout, not decision. Traditional air-atomic thinking and the McNamara nuclear strategies, culminating in Assured Destruction and Damage Limitation, were irreconcilable. To air-atomic strategy, the conventional end of war—victory—can be won by unfettered means. Skillful use of unrestricted force lets a nation dictate victorious terms to its opponent, but the use of the force itself is not a political negotiation. Air-atomic strategy fights and then talks. Assured Destruction and Damage Limitation, as well as the earlier iterations of Kennedy-era strategy, interweave political ends and military means. Nuclear operations are not military in the traditional sense, and traditional victory is unattainable. "Winning" means little if the nation is mortally wounded. Instead, nuclear operations are an abstract form of direct communication between national leaders. As such, national leaders must control the conduct of wartime nuclear operations and cannot leave the execution of plans to military officers.

Nuclear strategy and operations, as defined by the Kennedy administration, were inextricably intertwined. In turn, this led the administration to try to micromanage matters that USAF officers believed should be their concern alone. Since nuclear war with unrestrained force would have led, perhaps by the early 1960s and definitely by the late 1960s as the Soviets reached parity, to the deaths of hundreds of millions, McNamara's prognosis was right. Victory was unattainable in any meaningful sense in the nuclear world of the 1960s—which was not true even only five years before. Whether Assured Destruction was the right answer to the question McNamara posed is less clear. He had properly diagnosed the illness sapping the strength of American nuclear strategy, but the surgery never fully healed the patient. The Kennedy administration's ideas of abstract bargaining and deliberate action using nuclear weapons ignores the unpredictable and emotional conduct of war. To expect Soviet (or American) leaders to coolly accept the deaths of a few millions of their citizens, instead of hoping that an attack could end the carnage and bring victory, is too much to expect. Revenge is a powerful motivator in daily life. In the midst of nuclear war only inhuman self-control could inhibit it.

Competition between concepts about nuclear war had occurred since the beginning of the atomic age. The Air Force's historically derived air-atomic ideas integrated new weapons into old ideas. Until 1961, it had defended control of nuclear war planning and strategy against interservice rivals. Changes in national declaratory strategy had always left enough room for strategic air advocates and their air-atomic action policy to survive and generally to flourish. The Kennedy administration, however, introduced new approaches to military problems and forced them on the USAF. It decided that pit bulls were too embarrassing to breed, so it fixed the one it had and put it on a tighter leash, while adding a pack of Dobermans—quiescent until commanded. Thus the Air Force, and the military, lost control of nuclear operations. In a real sense, nuclear strategy, by rejecting victory as a goal, left the realm of traditional military thought and became an independent entity.

What had changed was the strategic environment. Air Force strategy, building incrementally from its previous experience, was unable to shift quickly and decisively enough to handle the competition and thrive in its strategic niche. Even had there been better ideas for prosecuting a nuclear war than Assured Destruction and Damage Limitation, the Air Force was not mentally prepared to make the leap. Rather, the age of hardened missile silos, submarines, and vulnerable bombers called for changes they could not make.

Advocates of air-atomic ideas and their opponents fought over more than weapon systems, budget share, or strategy—they fought over identity. John Lynn proposes a framework for understanding thinking about war in terms of belief systems.[64] Any military, or subset of the military, shares a vision of warfare's purpose and proper conduct, which provides an identity. Belief systems can be close to the reality of warfare in a period, or at odds with it. The two most common reactions to a gap between a belief system and the reality of war are to try to force reality to conform to expectations, or more rarely to adapt beliefs to changing facts. By proposing counterforce, air-atomic advocates tried to draw the reality of nuclear combat closer to their belief system, which claimed that victory was possible. McNamara rejected their belief system in favor of Assured Destruction, which rejected the possibility of victory. The result was a loss of identity for air-atomic advocates, and of influence for them in the Air Force and for the latter as a service. The USAF moved from the center of national security to the periphery, or at most to being one among equals. Within the nuclear mission, the manned bomber, workhorse of air-atomic strategy, became displaced by missiles. Air-atomic advocates, primarily the bomber pilots, lost their dominance of the Air Force, which eventually passed to fighter pilots.

McNamara's ideas, with all their potential flaws, squarely faced the realities of 1960. If nothing else, he grasped the absurdity of calling a situation where hundreds of millions lay dead in their burned-out homes a "victory." Nuclear strategy needed something new. The Kennedy administration delivered it.

8

END OF AN ERA

During the one thousand days of the Kennedy administration, the Air Force and administration not only clashed in the realm of strategic concepts, they also interacted with the real world. The collision played out in contemporary crises and future plans. For the first time since 1945, ideas at the national level directly opposed those at the service level. In the past, support or acceptance of Air Force thought produced crisis decisions consistent with it (if not at the service's desired speed and intensity) and support for future weapons. The new administration's ideas about discriminate nuclear weapon use, no-cities, and Assured Destruction radically changed crisis management and procurement. The distance between concepts produced chasms between air-atomic advocates and their opponents.

The most direct collision between these ideas and reality occurred during the intense crises of the early 1960s. The limits of abstract strategy became plain when real issues were at stake. These crises also reflected other changes in the national security structure, most importantly, a shift from seeking the counsel of uniformed advisors and toward detached civilian analysis; and they also show how hard it was to apply the ideas generated by academics to the real world. While crises such as Laos hold instructive lessons in evolving civil-military relations, two examples best exemplify this change: Berlin and the Cuban Missile Crisis.

Berlin

Kennedy inherited the Berlin crisis from his predecessor. On 10 November 1957, Khrushchev set a six-month deadline for the Western powers to withdraw from Berlin and agree to make it an open city. If the West balked, the Soviets threatened to give the East German government control of access to the city. However, when the three allied powers stood firm at a foreign ministers conference in 1959, the ultimatum lapsed. Although the conference did not resolve the future of Berlin, it relaxed tension and opened the way for Khrushchev's 1959 visit to Camp David. The Kremlin agreed to postpone further discussion of Berlin until the 1960 Paris summit.[1]

The cancellation of that summit and the election of a new president led the Kremlin to reopen the issue. Even before Kennedy's inauguration, the Soviets hinted that they wanted to settle Berlin's fate. At the end of the Vienna summit in June 1961 (where Kennedy was widely thought to have performed poorly), Khrushchev renewed the crisis. He threatened to sign a separate peace with East Germany that would end guaranteed Western access to Berlin. A Soviet aide-mémoire declared that the two German states should negotiate reunification terms by the end of the year. On 17 July, Kennedy expressed a willingness to talk but reaffirmed Western rights in the city. Simultaneously he accelerated an ongoing buildup of conventional forces in Europe, winning congressional authority to call up reserves, increase taxes, and impose economic sanctions on Warsaw Pact countries. On 13 August, East German authorities began erecting the Berlin Wall, but the crisis continued. The height of direct confrontation occurred in October as Soviet and American tanks squared off at Checkpoint Charlie between the Soviet and American zones of the city. Formal meetings between Secretary of State Dean Rusk and Soviet Foreign Minister Andrei Gromyko, and informal contacts between Kennedy and Khrushchev, finally led to the lifting of the deadline and the petering out of the crisis by the end of the year.[2]

The Kennedy administration viewed the role of nuclear weapons in that crisis differently than its predecessor had done. Eisenhower saw the use of nuclear weapons at Berlin as he did in other contexts. They were, for better or worse, fundamental to modern general war. Should the Berlin crisis lead to conflict with the USSR, it could not remain conventional. In fact, the structure of American conventional forces made use of some nuclear weapons almost unavoidable. These beliefs were reflected in Eisenhower's NSC policy papers. When Bundy's staff reviewed NSC-5906/1, Eisenhower's final basic national security paper, they found provisions inconsistent with Kennedy's thinking. The 20 July analysis specified two paragraphs which referred to "prevailing" in general war, as "inconsistent with our present Berlin planning." The paper also placed "main but not sole reliance" on nuclear weapons, another major inconsistency with the new administration. As a result of these disagreements in strategy, Kennedy cancelled NSC-5906/1.[3]

Canceling Eisenhower's guidance proved easier than crafting new directions for the use of nuclear weapons. In this process, Kennedy leaned heavily on civilian advisors in and out of government. Thus Thomas Schelling, the prominent civilian nuclear strategist, examined options in July as the crisis accelerated. He counseled that nuclear weapons should be used to "pose a higher level of risk to the enemy," rather than as part of a "grand nuclear campaign," as presumably would have been the Eisenhower plan if war occurred. The United States should localize the conflict. The most important use of nuclear weapons in a limited war would be to signal the Soviet leadership that their actions might cause a general war, even if that was not Moscow's intent. Signaling meant that tactical nuclear weapons would be used primarily not to destroy military targets, but to influence Soviet decision makers. They must be convinced that the risk of escalation outweighed their tactical objectives, without tempting the Soviets to preempt. Destruction of a target would be "incidental to the message" sent to Soviet leadership. Targets must be chosen based on "what the Soviet leadership perceives about the character of the war and about our intent, not for tactical importance." Strikes in the Soviet Union were important because they were in the USSR, not because of their relationship to the European battlefield. Destruction of a target amounted to a " 'proposal' that must be responded to." The United States must prepare detailed plans matching targets and the messages that would be sent by destroying them. "The concept of selective, strategic bargaining use is not enough; there must be plans for how to do this."[4]

Schelling's paper has several remarkable features. There is no record of such civilian strategic advice being sought or given in the Eisenhower administration. Records of discussions about the use of nuclear weapons only show serious consideration by the NSC, with frequent participation from the Joint Chiefs. Although civilian strategists might have contributed to such deliberations, there is no surviving record that they did, not even Brodie, the strategist treated most seriously by the services in that era. The only civilian strategists to have any influence over policy were in government service. They, and those in RAND, shaped the details of operations, not strategy. Again, Schelling coolly abstracted bargaining by nuclear detonation from the military effects of the weapons. Discussion of the use of nuclear weapons during crises in the 1950s revolved around the question of when to use them, not why. Should they be needed, tactical weapons would strike those targets that helped achieve military objectives, so the United States could control and favorably terminate the crisis. Schelling short-circuited this process. He sought to use the weapons as a diplomatic tool in their own right, though his proposals seem rather too elaborate to be executed. His counsel, received at the highest levels of the US national security hierarchy, show that civilian leadership was open to considering direct control of nuclear operations.

Not just outsiders took this approach to nuclear weapons. Administration insiders took similar positions, including NSC staffer Robert Komer. In a 20 July paper to Bundy, he recommended using overtly political demonstrations with nuclear weapons to signal intent to the USSR. He posited a situation where NATO forces were losing a conventional fight in Germany. As such a situation could occur only if the Soviets already thought the United States would not use nuclear weapons, deterrence would already have failed. Hence nuclear weapons must be used on a small or symbolic scale to reinvigorate the deterrent without triggering a general nuclear exchange. Despite the great danger of escalation, or of the Soviets employing the same tactics, he urged contingency planning to postpone an alternative between conventional defeat and general nuclear exchange. Like Schelling, Komer separated the military from the political effects of nuclear use. Absent from his discussion was what would have been on the mind of any air-atomic advocate: that piecemeal use of nuclear weapons would lack sufficient shock and tip the Soviets to American nuclear tactics, training them to more effectively withstand SIOP.[5]

JCS advice over the Berlin crisis proposed a series of escalatory steps, from small demonstrations to large conventional attacks along lines of communication to the isolated city. Lemnitzer advised that if those efforts failed and the Soviets threatened to defeat NATO conventional forces, only two choices would remain: to use tactical nuclear weapons or proceed direct to general war. Although the decision could not be made in advance, the JCS chairman (and Army general) urged planning "to afford us the maximum opportunity to pre-emptively use our power—both nuclear and nonnuclear."[6] This implied that there would be a single agonizing decision to begin the use of nuclear weapons, which would be used for conventional military purposes—to stave off defeat and move toward victory.

Following the debate, the administration sent instructions to NATO commander Gen. Lauris Norstad in August. Nuclear weapons would be used only if the Soviets used them first, to avoid defeat of major operations, or if a specific political decision were made to employ them "to demonstrate the will and ability of the Alliance to use them."[7] Norstad, upset by the negative wording, retorted that the United States should use nuclear weapons "to insure the success of major military operations," not just to prevent their defeat.[8] He returned to Washington in October to consult with Kennedy and his cabinet. Before the meeting, Bundy warned the president that Norstad would be difficult to deal with on the nuclear issue. The adversarial distance between the civilian administration and its military advisors is evident in Bundy's caution that "at root [Norstad] is a nuclear war man, and all his preferences move accordingly." Bundy and Taylor urged Kennedy to confront Norstad, making sure the general knew "you are in charge and that your views will govern."[9] It is difficult to imagine Eisenhower receiving similar advice, or requiring it. Indeed, part of the problem of civil-military relationships under the Kennedy administration occurred precisely because Eisenhower had been confident enough to appoint strong officers to run commands, whom his successors found hard to master. Ultimately, Norstad retired after prolonged tension with senior figures in the Kennedy administration, notably Rusk and McNamara. He later recalled a conversation at NATO headquarters in Paris with the two secretaries where he was asked, "'Just to whom do you feel your obligation, your commitment?' I said, 'Do you mean between the United States and NATO?'" The indignant Norstad felt his integrity had been questioned.[10]

The argument between Norstad and the administration revolved around tactical nuclear weapons, but existing strategic plans also came under scrutiny. Another civilian strategist brought in as a consultant, Henry Kissinger, weighed in on SIOP-62. He urged Bundy to educate the president on his options and have the Department of Defense plan for "graduated nuclear responses even if the Joint Chiefs do not consider it the optimum strategy."[11] Bundy forwarded Kissinger's suggestions to Kennedy with the comment that the entire NSC staff thought SIOP-62 "dangerously rigid." It would leave the president few choices in "the moment of thermonuclear truth."[12]

The NSC staff summarized SIOP-62's limitations and recommended an alternative tailored to the Berlin crisis. Beyond the rigidity that disturbed Bundy and Kissinger, it was inappropriate for Berlin because it was a second-strike plan and could support attacks only against the single "optimum-mix" target set. The NSC writers thought SIOP rigid because the military believed the USSR must strike American cities and therefore ignored the need to plan for American restraint. More important, the military believed "that winning general war means coming out relatively better than the USSR, regardless of magnitude of losses." Meanwhile, a false alarm would degrade SAC's ability to implement SIOP for eight hours as scrambled aircraft returned to their bases.[13]

The NSC staff urged consideration of a first-strike alternative to address the situation around Berlin, by destroying all Soviet long-range nuclear offensive capability while minimizing other damage. The alternative, sketched out by NSC staffer Carl Kaysen, ruled out missiles as too unreliable for a minimum-warning attack. Instead, fifty-five bombers could attack eighty-eight ground zeros. Using

1 megaton airbursts, fewer than 1 million Soviets would become casualties, and probably only 500,000 (or as Gen. Buck Turgidson of *Dr. Strangelove* might have said, "tops, depending on the breaks").[14]

The NSC staff, aided by outside civilian strategists, not only rejected SIOP-62 but even created a full first-strike proposal of their own, one far more belligerent and less realistic than anything SAC ever produced. As with other changes during the Kennedy administration, the proposal involved not just a shift in nuclear strategy, but in nuclear operations. Kaysen, an economics professor, argued that just fifty-five bombers could launch a disarming first strike. Although there is no recorded military reaction to Kaysen's plan, undoubtedly there would have been raised eyebrows over the small size of the force and the realism of the plan. Every NESC study over the preceding decade had projected casualties in a nuclear war of tens of millions in both superpowers, yet Kaysen believed the minuscule strike causing little other damage could disarm the Soviet Union. No doubt, air-atomic advocates would have thought the plan implausible.

While these criticisms of the SIOP and discussion of alternatives occurred at the NSC, civilian analytical practices entered another aspect of crisis management. The administration used gamelike decision-making exercises for senior officials to examine political and military options in the crisis. According to Nitze, who organized one such game, the emphasis was on bargaining between the adversaries and communicating "intent by actions and to design actions accordingly, and to interpret the other side's intent." Although military actions probably would become dominant, the purpose was not to examine the "tactical implications" of military actions, but instead to aid political decisions.[15] This description of the game implied a focus on bargaining through military actions and saw, as Schelling did, nuclear operations simply as a means of communication.

According to Kaysen, writing after the exercise's conclusion, the game reinforced the desire for more flexibility in "the process of continuous bargaining," which involved not only shows of force but the "real application of force in a carefully graded and controlled manner." The game also showed the "dominant influence of the overhanging threat of general war and the state and conduct of strategic forces." A localized crisis like Berlin required that SAC's actions be as carefully calibrated as were local forces.[16]

The exercise provides another glimpse of how the Kennedy administration viewed the role of military force, in crisis and war. All forms of force were potentially communication, with a political content that could override military considerations. The administration was ready to micromanage military operations in order to send desired signals. No doubt, the Kennedy administration would have seriously considered actions that might have sent strong signals about SAC's readiness, even if they complicated the implementation of the SIOP.

The Berlin crisis demonstrated dramatic changes from Eisenhower's practices. Civilian strategists shaped American diplomatic and military plans. Viewing force as communication and crisis as bargaining became official policy. The desired flexibility to communicate, combined with the rigid inflexibility of SIOP-62, led to unrealistic and desperate contingency planning. During the Eisenhower years, such crises had caused heated debate in the NSC but centered on decisions to use military force and when to apply nuclear weapons, not their "meaning." Meaning, such as firm resolution, might have been inferred from their use, but the use itself would not have been devoid of military utility. Wholesale rejection of the standing war plan and substitution of a hastily designed one would have been inconceivable. Berlin set the pattern for future crises in the Kennedy administration. Close civilian control of military operations and horror at the inflexibility of nuclear options combined with interpersonal tension, produced conflict over the use of nuclear weapons and even their very purpose.

Cuba

Nuclear weapons had a similar role in the Cuban Missile Crisis. The crisis began in April 1962 when Khrushchev decided to deploy medium- and intermediate-range ballistic missiles to Cuba. Recent scholarship places his motivation in a complex of Soviet strategic inferiority and romantic attachment to defending the Cuban revolution.[17] However, to the Kennedy administration, the bold Soviet move was a direct challenge to the American deterrent and a personal insult to the young president, redoubled by the fact the Soviets lied about their actions. After Castro agreed to receive the weapons, in July Soviet cargo ships began to deliver forty ballistic missiles, IL-28 medium bombers, MiG-21 fighters, tactical nuclear weapons, and forty thousand troops.[18] On 14 October, U-2s located the partially installed missiles. Two days later Kennedy assembled a subset of the NSC, the Executive Committee, or ExCom, to consider a response. He rejected calls for an immediate air strike on the missile sites and instead, on 19 October, opted for a blockade ("quarantine") of the island. On 22 October he publicly announced his decision, imposed the blockade, and placed US forces worldwide on heightened readiness (DEFCON 3). This speech included a general threat of retaliation against the USSR for any attack on the United States. This blanked massive retaliation threat was at odds with standing administration policy and was never really mooted. Soviet ships carrying additional missiles ultimately turned around. On 28 October, Khrushchev agreed to remove the installed missiles, in return for a secret guarantee of Cuban security and a promise to remove American missiles from Turkey and Italy.[19]

In deciding on the blockade, Kennedy considered and rejected the idea of immediate airstrikes on the missile sites, either alone or in combination with an invasion. Airstrikes and invasion were nonnuclear choices, from the US perspective, but not to the Soviets, who probably would have used tactical nuclear weapons against an invasion. The administration's approach to deciding between these options suggests its broader attitude toward the use of military force. At the first ExCom meeting on the sixteenth, the group examined the range of airstrikes they could launch, from a narrow surgical strike targeting only missiles to larger attacks, including both SAMs and airfields.[20] Although the initial debate was confused, both McNamara and Kennedy took these ideas seriously. Over the next days, strike plans expanded to suppress newly identified Soviet defenses. By the twentieth, the minimum number of sorties needed stood at eight hundred. McNamara thought airstrikes on that scale would inevitably cause major Soviet retaliation, potentially intensifying to general war.[21] Although Rusk joined McNamara in urging restraint, they were opposed by Bundy (the airstrikes were even referred to as the "Bundy plan" at one point) and the Joint Chiefs, including Taylor. On the nineteenth, Kennedy met with the Chiefs who urged immediate military action. LeMay feared that blockade would allow the Soviets time to move the missiles into better defensive positions. He predicted that the Soviets would not react to a US strike with a move in Berlin, or elsewhere. The greater threat was to "gradually drift into a war under conditions that are at great disadvantage to us, with missiles staring us in the face, that can knock out our airfields in the southeastern portion [of the United States]."[22]

For Kennedy, the deciding factor appears to have been the prospect that no air strike could guarantee destruction of all the missiles. General Sweeney, commander of Tactical Air Command (TAC), told the president that he could assure the destruction of 98 percent of all the missiles with the first wave of strikes, which follow up attacks within ten minutes would raise above 99 percent. After a pause, Sweeney added, "That is, all we know about." Kennedy replied, "Aye, that's the rub." Sweeney, so he later said, knew at that point the airstrikes were unviable.[23]

The discussion of airstrikes and alternatives illuminates the differences between the administration and the military on the use of forces—differences that suggest their possible behavior in a nuclear crisis. The military generally, and LeMay specifically, operated on the belief that deterrent strength flowed from superior force. That led to the conclusion that the Soviets would not escalate in Berlin from fear of American nuclear superiority. Fear for preserving that superiority also drove the recommendations to attack the missiles before they were an active threat to American strategic forces. Strategic superiority was a bulwark against Soviet adventurism that must be protected. A second long-standing belief, that victory lay in dictating political terms from a position of relative superiority after an exchange, also informed military advice. The military unanimously urged action based on their best plan for destroying known missiles, followed by aggressive pursuit of the remaining forces, if necessary with a ground invasion. The United States could not afford to squander the initiative, and delayed action would only make a later attack harder. The same pressures would have operated in considering a nuclear attack.

Kennedy, conversely, wanted to delay resorting to force. To lose the initiative was less important than retaining the future ability to decide. Fear of losing control over events underlay much of the ExCom discussions. Kennedy also held a different conception of victory. To him, even one missile fired at the United States was a catastrophe, no matter the outcome. Relative victory and the ability to dictate terms would not substitute for US lives. In this crisis, that attitude was reasonable, but it had limits as a general rule, and certainly it undercut all previous ideas for behavior during a nuclear crisis.

Although tactical air strikes dominated discussions about airpower in the Cuban Missile Crisis, Strategic Air Command also played a role. As players in the Berlin war game noted, every action taken during the crisis occurred against the background of strategic war forces. At a JCS meeting during the first days, Power recommended that SAC assume a higher state of readiness (DEFCON 2) than other US forces, disperse bombers to civilian airfields, and maximize the airborne alert.[24] SAC moved rapidly from a peacetime posture to heightened alert. On 19 October, half of its force was on 15-minute ground alert, with 12 B-52s conducting airborne alert training sorties. Within one week, SAC evacuated its bombers from Florida to make room for tactical forces, placed one eighth (66) of the B-52s on airborne alert (by 23 October), and scattered 183 B-47s to thirty-three military bases and civilian airports. This dispersal, made when McNamara was promoting the no-cities doctrine, would have forced the Soviets to attack civilian airports (and the surrounding cities) in the event of war. Hence, the dispersal mechanism undermined the declared nuclear strategy.[25] Within one day of receiving JCS direction, 95 percent of SAC, 1,436 bombers and 916 tankers, was "in a fully combat ready posture."[26] SAC maintained an elevated alert well into November.

Unlike TAC, SAC did not have an immediately planned role in the crisis. Its increased alert exerted significant, if unquantifiable, influence. Beyond this role, SAC did not go and, according to later accounts, would never have gone. McNamara later claimed the administration never considered executing SIOP. He told a conference of Cuban Missile Crisis participants and scholars that the existing nuclear war plan "was absolutely useless. Under no circumstances would I have used it. And, as you know, I said to both President Kennedy and to President Johnson that I couldn't imagine any circumstances in which I would recommend they initiate the use of nuclear weapons."[27] Instead, McNamara had in place alternative plans for "withholding" weapons which, he admitted "would have given the military a fit."[28] Incredibly, McNamara said, "We never even talked about [carrying out the SIOP] . . . we never discussed it. We should have, but we didn't."[29] To the Kennedy administration, SAC's role in this crisis never rose beyond the symbolic. Had the confrontation reached a point where the execution of SIOP would have been considered, to predict what might have happened is hard. Whether McNamara would have acted as he later claimed is unclear, while had he done so, the effect of his intervention would have had a less clear effect than he seemed to believe. A SAC that had prepared for a decade to follow a rigid plan once given a single go-ahead command might have been flummoxed by an ad hoc substitute. SAC would have tried to do what it was told, but probably could not have done as asked, which would have crippled its ability to do anything at all. At a minimum, there would have been substantial confusion and friction, if not outright failure, or even a disaster.

Continued civil-military friction was another continuity with the Berlin crisis. At the 19 October meeting, LeMay showed his tactlessness twice. At one point, he compared a refusal to immediately attack the missiles to Munich, unsubtly evoking the president's father, with his reputation as an appeaser. The uncomfortable silence on the tapes hints at the discomfort in the room. Later, the general told Kennedy that, "you're in a pretty bad fix at the present time." The president, who had let the Munich remark go unchallenged, replied "you're in there with me."[30]

Friction was not limited to Air Force officers. Admiral Anderson had a similarly tense encounter with McNamara. While reviewing the rules of engagement governing the blockade, the secretary clashed with the CNO, telling him that not one shot was to be fired at a Soviet ship without the secretary's permission. When Anderson replied that the Navy had been conducting blockades since the days of John Paul Jones, McNamara acidly retorted that it was not a blockade, but a form of communication between Kennedy and Khrushchev. Later that day, McNamara told an associate that Anderson had lost his confidence; the admiral was removed within a year.[31]

McNamara's disagreement with Anderson stemmed from the same root as those with LeMay and the Air Force. The secretary saw the role of operations as fundamentally different from the way service chiefs did. Just as a nuclear exchange was not intended to use unrestricted violence in order to gain a position to dictate political terms, so a blockade was not aimed to prevent contraband from reaching an enemy port. Instead, both actions were forms of communication between national leaders. This signal required calibration of operational and even tactical details by national leaders, even if it meant pushing aside senior military officers who defended service autonomy.

Divergent interpretations of the Cuban Missile Crisis reflect this disagreement over the role of military force. Senior officers viewed strategic airpower as having the central role in the Soviet defeat, while McNamara thought its role less critical. OSD denied permission when SAC proposed releasing four brief accounts of its actions during the crisis. Power appealed to McNamara to reverse the decision, citing the command's central role. "The chances of a global conflict resulting from the President's Cuban declaration was lessened in direct proportion to the Soviets' assessment of US capability to inflict unacceptable punishment upon the Soviet Union were that action not kept confined."[32] A week later, Power told interviewers that although only Khrushchev knew how SAC's going to DEFCON 2 had affected Soviet decision making, he believed it had hurried the Soviet capitulation.[33] LeMay took a similar line. In a speech reproduced as talking points for all Air Force commanders, he flatly stated that there was no substitute for strategic superiority and the Cuban crisis was proof. "The ace of spades in the deterrence deck is clearly superior strategic strength." In a thinly veiled dig at the secretary of defense, he added another lesson from Cuba: "Military airpower must be designed and operated by people who have spent their lives operating airplanes and who are dedicated professionals."[34] In an interview immediately before his retirement in 1965, LeMay said the "hard language worked because it was backed up by strategic airpower."[35]

McNamara's interpretation of these events diverged in essential ways. In January 1963, he told the House Armed Services committee there were three "salient points" about Cuba. First, the United States must have the power to deter or defeat significant Soviet moves. In this case, deterrence had failed, but the United States defeated the aggression. Implicitly, the nuclear deterrent failed to operate and would only have succeeded had it prevented the Soviet move in the first instance. Second, McNamara said, nuclear and conventional forces played essential roles and trying to parse which was preeminent was "like trying to argue about which blade of the scissors really cut the paper." The danger of a nuclear exchange restrained Soviet countermoves elsewhere in the world, but "our unmistakable conventional superiority in the Caribbean, and our unmistakable intent to use it" forced the Soviets to back down. That is, the risk of nuclear exchange, not any meaningful superiority, prevented escalation, while conventional superiority carried the day. Finally, the crisis showed the inseparability of the political and military strands of national policy. Its resolution demanded "that control be held firmly in the hands of the man pre-eminently responsible for national security; that is, in the hands of the President."[36] The outcome of the crisis, in McNamara's mind, validated close civilian control of operations. That point is obvious, and indeed had been followed by Eisenhower in earlier crises, but McNamara's general view of why the Soviets had surrendered (and also had gone to Cuba at all) underrated the role of SAC.

To assign credit for the outcome of the Cuban Missile Crisis is difficult. The conventional narrative is not far from the truth as revealed in the post–Cold War roundtables at Key West, Cambridge, and Moscow. Kennedy did steer a course that kept war from breaking out. The dangers of that conflict were even greater than previously thought, with tactical nuclear weapons under local Soviet commanders' control and intense pressure from Castro to launch a nuclear attack on the United States. These points, clear only in retrospect, indicate that a more militant approach as promoted by air-atomic advocates would have risked global war. LeMay might have made a hash of things. Equally, conventional narratives of the crisis devalue the deterrent power of SAC. Marc Trachtenberg concludes that McNamara underestimated the utility of nuclear weapons in the crisis. The open debates in the United States over nuclear strategy convinced Khrushchev that the United States took nuclear war seriously, and so he intentionally kept the USSR's nuclear forces demobilized to avoid provoking American preemption.[37] Khrushchev's first letter of 26 October with its talk of the destruction of war and his resistance to Castro's demands for armageddon imply that the specter of war with the United States motivated the Soviet leader's climb down. These acts reflect the importance of the force that threatened that destruction—and the air-atomic ideas behind it. Any explanation for the outcome of the missile crisis must give more credit to SAC than the conventional narrative, even if less than LeMay and Power would have wished.

Taken together, the Berlin and Cuban Missile crises illustrate the Kennedy administration's view of nuclear weapons, that of their senior military advisors, and the gulf between them. The crises reinforced both groups' conviction that their beliefs were correct. From McNamara's perspective, particularly, both crises had revolved around buying time for additional decisions and negotiations. Soviet actions did enough to ratchet up the tension; there was no need for Air Force policies to increase them even more. SAC's hair-trigger vulnerability was undesirable and avoidable. Interpersonal friction widened the gap between the camps. Statements by both civilian and military leaders carry more than a hint of disagreement for the sake of disagreeing with the other side, not just certainty in their own ideas. And, as in policymaking, the crises show the dominance of civilian leadership over even the most resistant and senior military officers.

As with Quemoy and Berlin in the 1950s, the crises of the Kennedy administration showed the limits of air-atomic military power. The Eisenhower administration tolerated the lack of options, but the New Frontiersmen wanted usable ones. Their frustration with air-atomic forces for not providing them was a strong impetus behind the push to Flexible Response, Assured Destruction, options in the SIOP, and the civilian control of nuclear operations.

Attacking the SIOP

Harsh criticism of the SIOP during these crises and rapidly evolving ideas about nuclear strategy combined to force decisive changes in nuclear war plans. SIOP-62 had emerged at the end of the Eisenhower years out of a bitter interservice fight that pitted late air-atomic concepts for "spasm war" against Army and Navy ideas framed around finite deterrence. It integrated Polaris into a single plan that embodied late air-atomic ideas, not those of its competitors. SIOP-62 struck at a single target set (based on the NESC 2009 "optimum-mix") with no options beyond adjusting for different levels of tactical and strategic warning. Strikes against satellites, however, could be withheld, except for those directed at "defensive" targets. SIOP-62 was designed for execution as a "total plan" either in retaliation for a Soviet strike or in preemption.[38] It embodied traditional Air Force planning to inflict maximum damage with unrestrained force in minimum time, so to blunt Soviet offensive power and compel a favorable political settlement.

Kaysen summarized the plan's weaknesses during the Berlin crisis. He traced SIOP-62's rigidity to four causes. Planners expected that a Soviet first or second strike would attack a mix of American targets comparable to the "optimum-mix" on which SIOP-62 was based. This gave no incentive to be selective about targets in the USSR. If the Soviets were going to maximize the damage they would inflict, then US restraint served no purpose. SIOP-62 also assumed that the Soviets would launch a significant number of weapons against the United States. Its blunting mission would never be completely successful, and thus the Soviets could attack an optimum-mix target set. Taken together, these two assumptions drove a US attack on a composite target system. "Nowhere is any real consideration given to the possibility that there may be an interaction between our targeting philosophy and that of the Soviet Union." Kaysen also accused the SIOP planners of believing that prevailing in general war "means coming out relatively ahead of the enemy. . . . If the US has lost 20% of its industrial capacity and 30% of its people, but the Sino-Soviet Bloc has lost 40% of its industrial capacity and 60% of its people, then the US, somehow or other, has won the war."

Kaysen identified underlying reasons for Air Force resistance to introducing flexibility into the SIOP. A surprise attack might cripple a smaller offensive force, leaving residual forces in the intolerable position of having only the alternatives of starting a city-exchange or surrender. It also could leave surviving forces uncertain about which plan to carry out, unless there was only a unified plan like SIOP-62. Greater flexibility, should it become known to the Soviets, might prompt an attack in the hope that American leaders would be paralyzed by their choices.[39]

His first two criticisms of the SIOP are consistent with the evidence, as is his analysis of the Air Force position on flexibility, but his third critique misses the point. Advocates of air-atomic strategy, the basis of SIOP-62, considered a favorable political outcome to be the objective of unrestricted force. Causing more damage to Soviet targets than the Soviets could inflict on American ones was a by-product of the superiority needed to coerce the USSR. Fixation on relative percentages of damage, by contrast, was a property of civilian nuclear strategists within and without the administration.

On entering office, even before the Berlin crisis brought SIOP-62 under scrutiny, McNamara outlined displeasure with it. He directed the JCS to "prepare a doctrine which, if accepted, would permit controlled response and negotiating pauses in the event of thermonuclear war."[40] The JCS response, predictably, was split along service lines. The Army and Navy suddenly had an advocate at the highest level. As Burke gleefully told a colleague on hearing McNamara's initial instructions, "much of what is proposed reflects Navy concepts."[41] The JCS told the secretary that the Army, Navy, and Marine Corps "consider that the essential national task must and can be finitely dimensioned in terms of its objectives and the weight of effort required against these objectives." To minimize the likelihood of nuclear war was the most important military requirement the nation faced, but, these three services argued—as they had for years—a finite force combined with large conventional forces could respond "to aggression in all its diverse forms," and so best deter any war. A SIOP that demanded too large a nuclear force would starve conventional units and tempt Soviet nonnuclear aggression.[42]

The Air Force, alone on the JCS, proposed that "strategic offensive plans be calculated to achieve maximum US strategic advantage in any of the circumstances under which deterrence may fail."[43] The chief of staff wrote that he knew of no study that could justify the reduction of strategic offensive forces without creating unacceptable risk. Rather, only an attack on the composite system identified by NESC 2009 could provide a "reasonable assurance of success on the basis of reasonable estimates of enemy strength." If the majority view prevailed, an exchange could occur in which the Soviets could retain a force that "could be brought to bear in subsequent operations to effect systematic destruction of the US." American strategy could not be based on the idea of wartime Soviet cooperation in minimizing damage. "We can expect no comparable generosity from the enemy in his planning for attacks on the US."[44]

The split was little different from those before the initial SIOP. What had changed was who adjudicated, and that made all the difference. What is known of SIOP-63 and its 1960s successors shows a reversal of the Air Force triumph in SIOP-62 and the defeat of the air-atomic strategy. The JCS guidance for SIOP-63 delineates five attack options, any of which US strategic forces had to execute on direction. Each option (I–V) involved some combination of three tasks (I–III), under different degrees of warning.[45] Although the available SIOP-63 instructions do not specify Tasks I–III, Nixon-era reconsideration of the plans does consider the contemporary SIOP Tasks A–C, which probably were parallel. Task Alpha was defined as destroying Sino-Soviet strategic nuclear capability outside urban areas—essentially, a city-avoidance target set. It also included the "highest Soviet and Chinese political and military control centers" which would be attacked by specially designated "Moscow-Peking Missile Packages" (MPMP). Task Bravo involved destruction of Sino-Soviet military forces and resources not included in Alpha and outside major urban centers. Task Charlie aimed at destruction of remaining military forces and resources (including those in urban areas) and at least 70 percent of the "urban-industrial bases" of the USSR and PRC. Like SIOP-63, the plan examined in 1969 combined these three tasks into five options. "The smallest attack, a pre-emptive strike on the ALPHA targets, would involve 58 percent of our SIOP committed forces. Roughly 1,750 weapons would be expected to arrive on or near their targets in the USSR." The remaining options, including flexible "withholds" of individual tasks or the MPMP portion of Task Alpha, were designed both for preemption and retaliation. Kissinger's staff reported that other "withhold elements" permitted up to ninety subvariants of the five main attack options.[46] Even if the approved SIOP-63 had fewer variants and options, Power recognized it as fundamentally different from SIOP-62. "As you know, the SIOP-62 was finalized basically as a single plan whereas SIOP-63 guidance and planning provided, in effect, three plans."[47]

The contrast between SIOP-62 and its successors is stark. The former's underlying strategy was much more like that of the USAF Emergency War Plans of the 1950s than anything that followed. The first SIOP, based on major shock against one target set, anticipated a single decision to attack after which the strategic offensive machine would move, returning for additional direction only after completing the initial strike. SIOP-63, at a minimum, demanded not a decision only to launch a nuclear offensive, but also an operational one about how to do so. Options and withholds, even if not as well developed as by 1969, demanded that national leadership decide on the spot how to fight a nuclear war. The new plans embodied the Kennedy administration's fondness for detailed control of operational matters, shown so clearly during the Berlin and Cuban crises. Not only would a decision to initiate be required, and another on how to best fight, but potentially also decisions for follow-on actions, all in the midst of a strategic nuclear exchange. Although not spelled out in the available SIOP-63 information, nuclear combat was intended to become a form of tacit bargaining, which demanded finely tuned control from national leadership. The air-atomic strategy, which crudely sought to inflict maximum damage so to disarm and compel the enemy, had been replaced. No plan that demanded so many decisions in such short time under such intense pressure could hope to generate the same shock as one plan waiting for a single implementation order. Beginning with SIOP-63, there was more than one way to fight a nuclear war, and more than one mechanism to achieve its ends, which were undefined in advance.

Ironically, the more flexible plans would likely have failed to achieve the greater flexibility in crisis that the Kennedy administration desired. One analysis of command and control written two decades later cited the organizational complexity of contemporary plans as making the careful orchestration of options in nuclear war nearly impossible. In the emotionally charged and information starved fog of nuclear war, the options of the 1980s plans—let alone the 1960s versions supported by more primitive command and control—would have been nearly impossible to orchestrate. Chaos would have reigned.

Civilian ideas of nuclear strategy affected not only contemporary plans, but also future ones, through programmatic decisions. Plans and programs shape future strategy by altering force structure. Decisions taken during the Kennedy administration ended the air-atomic era by eliminating the weapon systems, investments, research and concepts needed to continue it. Canceling several manned weapons foreclosed the possibility of a reconnaissance-strike, bomber-centered counterforce and slowed the pace of technological advance, while the Limited Test Ban Treaty made qualitative superiority difficult to maintain in the long run.

Bomber of Diminishing Returns?

Although the B-70, as a replacement for the B-52, had a troubled development even before the Kennedy administration, it was only one weapon. The national leadership had never seriously questioned the future of manned weapons as a whole. Bombers, with deep historical roots in the Air Force, were the basis of its strength in the early 1960s. It is easy to see why the service fought to keep them, from an organizational behavior perspective. They were proven systems that the Air Force saw no compelling reason to abandon. They were a flexible tool that could perform their mission—in general or limited war—despite Soviet defenses because of the crew's adaptability. From a systems analysis perspective, however, the bomber was an expensive and vulnerable weapon ill-fitted to the missile age.

The desired amount of destruction could be purchased more cheaply without the B-70. The B-70 fight also involved a healthy dose of personal antagonism. To the Air Force, missiles were a promising but still unreliable complement to the bomber. Underlying its argument was unease with a wholesale change not only in strategy but also the physical symbol of their service.

The next generation of strategic bomber, as envisaged by its requirements writers in the 1950s, was to be a huge, six-engined aircraft using a specially designed "high energy fuel." It would fly at up to Mach 3 at seventy thousand feet, carrying one or two large ("Class A" or "Class B") nuclear weapons, relying on high speed and altitude to penetrate Soviet defenses.[48] These characteristics place the B-70 firmly in the teleological progression of aircraft performance. To Air Force officers who had moved in a career from twin-engined bombers like the B-10 to the B-52, it was the next logical, upward, step.

The Air Force published the first B-70 requirement in October 1954. Three years later, North American won the design competition. The service soon accelerated the program, advancing the aircraft's initial operating capability date to 1964. Then, the program started running into the problems that would kill it. They were an unavoidable aspect of designing aircraft at the leading edge of aeronautical and material science. The B-70 would have to perform reliably at speeds and altitudes that only experimental aircraft had approached. Solving these problems proved to be difficult. In the summer of 1959, the "high energy fuel" program was cancelled as was the F-108 fighter, which was intended to use the same engine as the B-70. In December 1959, the Eisenhower administration briefly downgraded the "weapon system" program to a "prototype," but in January 1960 reinstated a reduced development plan.[49]

When the new administration came into office, the Air Force pushed hard to strengthen the faltering program. While accepting the growing importance of missiles as a strategic weapon, it strongly argued for manned bombers and the B-70. Bombers were capable of "discriminate target selection" because they were more accurate than unmanned systems. Their combination of accuracy and high-yield weapons made them ideal to attack hardened targets. These advantages made manned weapon systems a valid requirement for the immediate future. With all its flaws, the B-70 was the only bomber in development and had to be supported. And, in a reversal of what normally was considered a strength of missiles, the Air Force promoted the bomber as a hedge against missile vulnerability. Missiles would have to ride out an attack and could not launch on warning as could a bomber under positive control.[50]

Beyond these general advantages of bombers, the B-70 had characteristics that made it attractive to SAC and the Air Force, the most obvious being performance. A contemporary SAC history placed the new aircraft's speed in the context of the

Quemoy crisis. A Chinese Communist invasion fleet sailing at ten knots on the hundred mile journey to Taiwan could be intercepted halfway to its destination by a B-70 scrambling from San Francisco one hour after the fleet left port.[51] High speed would act with high altitude to make the B-70 effectively invulnerable to most Soviet defenses, at least as they were foreseen when the original requirement was written. Finally, the B-70 was purpose-designed for the missile age in that it could take off with only a three minute warning of impending attack.[52]

The new administration, however, inherited its predecessor's skepticism about the new bomber, and in early 1961, the Air Force was not prepared to sell the B-70 with systems analysis. When LeMay was scheduled for a July 1961 meeting with Dr. Brown, the deputy secretary of defense for Research and Development, the Air Staff advised him that OSD doubted the B-70 could penetrate Soviet defenses. Rather than equip the chief of staff with a quantitative study, as they would know how to do a few years later, he was told to use World War II experience to show how Soviet defenses could be overcome.[53]

Anecdotal evidence did not convince McNamara that the B-70 program should be continued. As the B-70 proposal sputtered in 1961–62, he argued against bombers generally and the B-70 specifically. At that point, bomber vulnerability on the ground was a major problem. The best solution devised so far, alert, was prohibitively expensive. Only half the bomber force could be kept on ground alert indefinitely, and air alert cost far more. Even if alert worked as intended and moved bombers out of the way of impending attack, a false alarm could find the reconstituting force at reduced readiness when a second, real attack came. Further, if the bomber force had to attack, the requirement that corridors be cleared of Soviet air defenses prevented carefully calibrated and discriminate attacks. To an administration fixated on increasing control of operations, this was a serious flaw. Missiles were a viable alternative to strike most targets that a bomber might attack. They could reach military targets faster, and so had a better chance of catching Soviet weapons on the ground, while Polaris could wait in reserve to launch city attacks for days, granting time for negotiation.

McNamara also argued that the B-70 duplicated the ICBM, but only managed to be a less capable "manned missile," not a truly complementary weapon. It still needed missiles to reach the target and so could not operate independently, unlike missiles. Finally (in the B-70 configuration as opposed to the RS-70), it was not equipped to search for targets as some of its supporters claimed.[54]

These arguments reflected different analytical frameworks. The Air Force views had a presumptive teleological element, simply assuming the need for a new bomber, which must be "better"—that is, flying faster and higher—than what it replaced, combined with an unquantifiable sense, probably with merit, that the bomber could overcome Soviet defenses. The service's conviction was based in the personal experience of senior officers who knew the challenges of facing a well-trained and equipped defense, and believed that the human element of that defense could be defeated.

McNamara countered with a cool analysis of alternative weapon systems. He was not "pro-missile" or "antibomber," but rationally compared the advantages of the two systems. In almost every case, the bomber was a more expensive way to inflict damage. Even more, the necessary tactics for employing bombers crippled the all-important goal of controlling the execution of nuclear operations. Both sides in the B-70 debate made persuasive arguments, but only to listeners who shared their conceptual framework. Conflict was guaranteed when neither side could convince the other that it was fundamentally correct.

When McNamara tried to reduce the program in the FY 63 budget, Air Force congressional allies not only restored funding, but "ordered, required, directed, and mandated" that $491 million be spent on the B-70. Congress called on the Air Force to brief the House appropriations committee, but McNamara initially forbade any military personnel from testifying. When threatened with a contempt citation, he sent a single briefer, without any support—even to carry his charts.[55] Kennedy resolved the showdown during a walk in the Rose Garden with Senator Vinson, when he promised to continue the B-70 program at a lower funding level.[56]

To preserve the B-70, and to answer the criticism that it was unsuited to deliberate nuclear attack, the Air Force updated the B-70 concept into the "reconnaissance/strike," or RS-70. While the B-70 had been a "manned missile" attacking preplanned targets, the RS-70 would carry an onboard radar, enabling it to hit preplanned targets or to seek new, imprecisely located ones. "The most important single characteristic of this system will be its capability to place man with adequate equipment over enemy territory so that he can observe, evaluate, exercise judgment, act on this judgment within the limits of previously assigned authority, locate and destroy assigned targets, and report his observations and actions." This mission combined the Air Force's desired "man-in-the-loop" with discriminate attack.[57]

LeMay outlined the new system's advantages for the new secretary of the Air Force Eugene Zuckert in July 1962. Unlike the B-70, the RS-70 fit into national strategy. "The capabilities represented by the RS-70 weapon system are essential to our strategic forces if these forces are to support a military strategy of controlled, informed, discriminate and deliberate response." The RS-70, like the B-70, was a technological advance that would render current Soviet defenses ineffectual. Keeping an advanced US bomber in the force mix rather than depending purely on missiles maximized the Soviet defensive problem—to cancel the RS-70, and so advanced manned bombers, from US offensive forces would let the Soviets reallocate bomber defense funds to ABM programs. The RS-70 would complement missiles by attacking targets they had missed or could not hit in the first place. It also was a hedge against Soviet ABMs. Furthermore, the RS-70, entering service in the mid-1960s, would gain new technological capabilities to be integrated into its advanced airframe. LeMay concluded by reiterating his long-held belief, and central principle of air-atomic strategy, that superiority was the root of deterrent strength.

> I firmly believe we can continue to hold the line for the Free World only so long as we maintain strategic forces clearly superior to those of the Communist Bloc. This means continued modernization and constant improvement in both the manned and unmanned elements of strategic air power. The RS-70, in my view, represents such modernization.[58]

McNamara outlined his case against the RS-70 to the president in November 1962. His first target was the novel RS-70 idea of transattack reconnaissance and strike, which he claimed Indirect Battle Damage Assessment (IBDA) could do as effectively and faster. OSD studies had shown that postattack reconnaissance could be done better with a different aircraft or mix of them. By the time the RS-70 was fully integrated into the offensive force, satellite reconnaissance probably would have found all targets of interest anyway, making it redundant. By the early 1970s, there would be few stationary but imprecisely located targets (which the RS-70 would excel at finding) left to locate.[59]

The second half of the RS-70's new mission, strike, was also was a nonstarter. After a Soviet attack, the Soviet forces able to destroy American cities and therefore influence the conflict would be submarines, not land-based systems. The RS-70 could not limit damage, because it could not strike anything worthwhile. McNamara also rejected the Air Force claim that the RS-70, by its nature as a manned system, could be discriminating. By the 1970s, missile accuracy should have improved to the point where they could provide comparable precision. All told, the RS-70 had the same technical and fiscal weaknesses as the B-70 without providing offsetting advantages. There was nothing the RS-70 could do that could not be done cheaper or better by missiles.

As with the B-70, the Air Force and OSD argued from different conceptual frameworks. The Air Force promoted the weapon with "fuzzy" arguments. The system's strength lay in the intangible—it would use human ingenuity and judgment to overcome the problems bound to occur during early strikes. Weapons fail to reach their targets, warheads misfire, targets move—friction happens. The RS-70 was a concept based in operational experience and limited confidence in new technology. Its role is reminiscent of the command and control aircraft

LeMay used during Second World War raids. In one memorable attack, Power acted as the on-scene commander during the 9 March Tokyo raid. Such a role could not have been far from either general's mind when pitching the RS-70. McNamara retorted that finely honed operational expertise, such as a successful RS-70 could provide, was futile. Even if the RS-70 could be developed, an unlikely prospect given the state of the art in airborne radar, it would be ineffective against submarine-based weapons. The Air Force argued about operational means and the secretary about strategic ends.

McNamara convinced the president to cancel the program, and the Air Force's congressional allies did not reverse the verdict. The RS-70 program was formally rejected in mid-1962, with a token $50 million approved for sensor component development. North American built two experimental XB-70s, the first one flying in September 1964. Following the crash of the second airframe in 1966, the Air Force transferred the remaining prototype to NASA.[60]

The sputtering failure of the B-70 and RS-70 was assured from the day the Kennedy administration took office. Only congressional resistance, and the threat of a constitutional showdown over budgetary discretion, slowed the process. The failure was certain because the B-70, and the air-atomic strategy it emerged from, were at odds with the new administration's ideas. The arguments made by the two sides show different questions being asked and answered in distinct analytical frameworks. The Air Force advanced an incrementally better aircraft to pursue the same victory-seeking strategy and justified it by experience. The secretary of defense compared the B-70 to competitor systems and found it inefficient at producing the desired outcome. The cancellation of the B-70 broke the teleological progress that had begun fifty years earlier. McNamara was right to deny the underlying idea that "higher and faster" conferred higher survivability and correct to predict that improvements in imagery and guidance systems would improve the accuracy of missiles. Despite that, the RS-70 probably had more promise than he gave it. Although the technological hurdles in designing an imaging radar were too much for the 1960s, future advances likely would have made it feasible in the long run. An RS-70 could have hunted mobile missiles during a nuclear exchange and have contributed on other battlefields in a role like the combination of airborne ground surveillance radar (such as the E-8 JSTARS) and modern strike aircraft.

Skybolt

While the B-70 struggle continued, another Air Force plan for extending the utility of manned bombers came under fire, the Skybolt air-launched ballistic missile.

This joint US-UK project aimed at a two-stage, solid-propellant air-to-surface missile, designed for launch from the B-52 (or British V-bomber) at forty thousand feet. Where contemporary systems like the Hound Dog reached their targets by flying through the atmosphere, the Skybolt would use a ballistic flight path rendering it immune, it was hoped, to interception after launch from the carrier aircraft.[61]

The development of Skybolt began in early 1958. The Air Force established a formal requirement in January 1959, and Secretary Gates approved development in February 1960. Soon, a Memorandum of Understanding and a technical agreement solidified the arrangement: the United States would develop the weapon and ensure compatibility with British systems, while the British would buy at least a hundred missiles.[62]

Shortly after taking office, McNamara assured his British counterpart the arrangement would continue.[63] However, Skybolt was not holding up well to scrutiny in the new OSD. In May 1961, Brown reported its justification was slight and no production seemed warranted. The program's difficulties deepened in September when McNamara visited the primary contractor, Douglas, and left disenchanted with the program management. He warily continued the program, but repeated test failures plagued Skybolt. The first powered flight in April 1962 suffered a second-stage failure, and the second guided launch in June had a first-stage failure. OSD threatened to withdraw funding in July, but restored it, only to see two more failures in September. By the time a generator malfunction botched a November test, McNamara had removed Skybolt from the draft FY 64 budget request.[64]

OSD's reasons for cancellation and the USAF responses again outline their divergent perspectives. McNamara's decision followed several years of studies during the Eisenhower and Kennedy administrations. In July 1959, the Fletcher Committee reviewed the program and recommended that it not be approved, although Gates still did so.[65] A year later, the Strategic Weapons Panel of the President's Scientific Advisory Committee concluded the original technical requirement unrealistic. The only feasible missile would have one-third the desired accuracy, one-half the range, carry a smaller warhead, and take a year longer to develop. Although that weapon would be well suited for corridor clearing because it would be easier to coordinate with other bomber strikes, Skybolt could do little other weapons could not do more cheaply.[66]

In his justification for the FY 64 cancellation, McNamara argued that Skybolt, beyond its shaky track record, was a poor weapon. Because it had to be launched from a manned bomber, it shared the aircraft's vulnerability to first strikes and slow speed in reaching a launching position. Then, when launched, the weapon was comparatively inaccurate. Even if the technical challenge of launching from a airborne platform could be solved, Skybolt would be no more accurate than other contemporary missiles. The system combined the vulnerability of the bomber with the inaccuracy of the missile. He rejected the argument that Skybolt would extend the service life of the B-52. From the system analytical perspective, the objective of defense spending was not to extend the life of any system, but to destroy targets for the lowest cost. Anyway, other systems in development, like the air-breathing Hound Dog missile, would extend the B-52's life.[67]

Although the JCS supported Skybolt, Maxwell Taylor, by November 1962 chairman of the Joint Chiefs, supported the secretary's decision. In his dissent, he told the secretary there was no compelling case for the Skybolt. The chiefs' primary reason for supporting the weapon, extending the life of the B-52, was insufficient because missiles could attack most of the target set assigned to bombers. "My lukewarmness for spending any substantial sum for a new standoff missile for the B-52s results from my own doubt as to the long-term effectiveness of the manned bomber in the strategic mission." Skybolt was just another excessive weapon that magnified overkill.[68]

LeMay outlined the Air Force arguments in a futile attempt to save Skybolt. Operationally, as claimed earlier about the B-70 and RS-70, diverse attack methods complicated the Soviet defensive problem. Stopping Skybolt would leave 40 percent of the B-52 force without air-to-surface missiles, degrading the effectiveness of the bomber force. Air Force studies calculated that hard and "super-hard targets (Nuclear Storage)" could not be economically attacked by ICBMs, while the B-52-Skybolt combination could destroy them cheaply. LeMay noted, with a hint of exasperation, that "further, it has other advantages which are not amenable to pure cost effectiveness comparisons."[69] In a covering memorandum, Zuckert added that a small expenditure on the Skybolt would extend the usefulness of the $14.5 billion already spent on the B-52 by letting them operate through the late 1960s.[70]

Air Force arguments made no headway. McNamara met his British counterpart in December to prepare the ground for cancellation. Despite British protests that it would "tear the heart out" of their defense position, McNamara stood firm. Skybolt might be technically possible, but it "was impossible to achieve the objectives which had been set for the program in the time period planned."[71] When Kennedy met Prime Minister Macmillan at Key West at the end of the month, they finalized cancellation. The British turned down an offer to continue the program on changed terms but accepted an offer of Polaris missiles as a substitute.[72]

The day after the two leaders publicly announced the end of Skybolt, the Air Force issued a press release celebrating a successful guided test during which the missile "flew its full mission range under its own power to a point more than 800 miles down the Atlantic Missile Range."[73] McNamara was furious about the press release, which he saw as intentional undermining of the president's decision. When newspaper stories about the Air Force release appeared quoting angry but anonymous DoD sources, LeMay complained to McNamara that one story implied that he had been disloyal. LeMay protested that OSD had approved the wording for a previous test.[74] McNamara replied that he retained "complete confidence in the military departments, in their leaders and never questioned their loyalty, devotion or motivation," but defended the anonymous press statements.[75] This petty argument between the secretary of defense and the Air Force chief of staff over a press release shows the decay in working relationships by 1963.

Nearing his retirement in 1965, LeMay tartly remarked that the cancellation of Skybolt would have been a good decision only if the superpowers never went to war. "If we fight, it was a bad error." The weapon was technically feasible and could have extended the life of the B-52. Test failures had been "random," rather than systematic. The final test and the ensuing argument over the press release was galling. LeMay thought the test success had embarrassed the administration, and so OSD had issued "a misleading press release which stated Skybolt didn't land in the target area. . . . But the shot was successful, since it accomplished what it set out to do."[76] LeMay's bitter account reflects the two constant themes of Air Force arguments during the period: operational focus on diverse weaponry and difficult interpersonal relationships. Unlike the B-70, Skybolt seemed to have overcome its technical problems, and LeMay thought the weapon was killed just as it became viable. As test failures were mostly in propulsion and other conventional systems, not advanced ones like guidance, the general's position seems justified in a way that it is not with the B-70. In the end, the Air Force used the cancellation of Skybolt to justify increasing the inventory of Hound Dog and Minuteman.[77]

Beyond the B-70

Canceling Skybolt threatened the future of the B-52. Cancelling the B-70 killed the next generation manned bomber. A third cancellation—Dynasoar—blocked the Air Force efforts to move military man into space. Where the B-70 represented an incremental improvement along the higher-and-faster curve, space systems would have been a major jump. Several Air Force programs in place by 1961 sought to expand traditional air-atomic strategy beyond the atmosphere. Brig. Gen. Robert Richardson, a key author of Air Force long-range plans, justified the space systems by connecting them to historical Air Force experience. "It was only by gaining advantage in range, speed, and altitude that we defeated the Luftwaffe and the Japanese Air Forces, gained air superiority and won the war."[78]

They were a technological leap, but a logical one to make for those who believed in maintaining technological superiority. The 1959 revision of Air Force Manual 1-2 introduced the term *aerospace* to show the indivisibility of the Air Force's current and future media. Freedom to operate in aerospace was of "vital military significance." The nation that predominates in space "will have the means to prevail in conflict."[79]

In 1960, LeMay outlined the required space operational capabilities the Air Force should seek. Targeting and surveillance, programs already well underway by then in the Corona program, topped the list. Other, more advanced capabilities included counterspace neutralization of space vehicles, and space-based ballistic missile defense (intercepting during boost and mid-course). Two goals specific to strategic airpower included "earth target strikes" and "space alternate command posts." Space was to be the perfect "high ground."[80]

Naturally, SAC viewed space as the next arena for strategic airpower. In August 1958, Power outlined a command position on space. The ultimate objective was a system that would seamlessly "expand the airpower of today into the space power of tomorrow." SAC would need a space reconnaissance capability, followed eventually by offensive weapons, so achieving a true melding of the missile and manned aircraft.[81] A 1960 Air Staff document described the "aerospaceplane" as carrying a thirty-thousand-pound payload in a three hundred NM circular orbit, or twice that payload within the atmosphere at a speed of up to Mach 6 to a range of eight thousand miles.[82]

Essential to Air Force and SAC plans were a series of programs, of which Dynasoar (from "Dynamic Soaring") was the most directly identifiable with strategic airpower and the aerospaceplane. Dynasoar, later termed the X-20, combined several disparate earlier efforts into one experimental program with three phases.[83] The first requirement in 1955 was updated in 1959 to demand "a global, hypersonic strategic bombardment weapon system." The immediate objective, Phase I of Dynasoar, was to be a manned atmospheric test system to explore the flight regime at near-orbital velocity. The results of Phase I would settle the parameters for a follow-on operational system. It would attempt a series of milestones ranging from a crewless launch in mid-1962 to a first "global" manned launch by mid-1965.[84] Phase II would examine orbital flight and controlled reentry, while Phase III would develop military hardware based on the technological lessons learned.[85] Dynasoar's goal was to push the outer boundaries of performance, not immediately to produce a functional weapon. However, the B-70's son, or grandson, could depend on the fruits of Dynasoar.

The available evidence on Dynasoar's short life is thin, but seemingly it found the same fate as other Air Force strategic manned programs. During an October 1963 program review with McNamara, Air Force officials failed to answer critical questions he had posed at an earlier meeting, which boiled down to a single one: "What does the Air Force really want to do in space and why?" He felt the Dynasoar contractors and Air Force managers were too concerned with the technical problems of getting into and out of orbit, and not enough with what was to be done while there. One billion dollars per vehicle was too much for a nonoperational craft. The Air Force tried to recast the X-20/Dynasoar as a part of a military space station program that used the aircraft as a resupply vehicle (in a role similar to the eventual Space Shuttle program and International Space Station). However, this last gasp effort failed. McNamara terminated the program in December 1963.[86] This did not mark the end of American civilian or military efforts in space, as the Gemini, Apollo, Corona, and Strategic Defense Initiative programs show, but the idea of waging traditional strategic air warfare in a new medium seems to have ended by 1963. The program, like other manned programs, simply did not buy enough security for the dollar.

Dynasoar's fate, when combined with the B-70, RS-70, and Skybolt, show the threat to manned bomber systems by the mid-1960s. Traditional ideas involving diverse attacking forces, with experienced airmen agilely shifting tactics, were a thing of the past. The cancellations halted the "upward" march of progress, defined traditionally (perhaps unconsciously) as "faster and higher." Although there would be future manned strategic systems (FB-111, B-1, B-2), their "improvement" involved low-altitude penetration, stealth, and precision, not brute force performance. To the traditional air-atomic promoters in the early 1960s, raw power was the means to overcome defenses and perform a mission. For the foreseeable future, that route to superiority, ideas from which their deterrence and warfighting flowed, was shut.

Technological Malaise

The end of manned bomber superiority merged with another development during the Kennedy administration to alarm air-atomic advocates about prospects for progress: the Limited Test Ban Treaty (LTBT). Testing was important in air-atomic strategy because it was the mechanism by which the United States maintained technological superiority. Atmospheric tests had underwritten every major innovation in atomic weapons since 1945. By the early 1960s, areas of inquiry for testing included (but were not limited to) missile reliability and accuracy, silo hardening, ballistic missile defense, and "very large" yield devices. Progress in such areas was critical when American strategy aimed at preserving superiority.[87]

The treaty, signed in the summer of 1963 and ratified by the end of the year, banned testing in the atmosphere, underwater, and in outer space. It did not have provisions for on-site inspections, which had been the main obstacle to earlier negotiations. Rather, it depended on newly available "national technical means." Any signatory could withdraw from the treaty with notice of three months. The United States, USSR, and Britain were the only three initial parties. Although other nations eventually joined, France and the PRC did not. The former had become a nuclear power by the time of the signing, as the latter would within a year.[88]

The twisted path leading to the LTBT began in 1954 when public awareness of the dangers of fallout grew with the irradiation of a Japanese fishing trawler (the "Lucky Dragon") during the Castle tests in the South Pacific. The UN disarmament committee began formally discussing an atmospheric test ban in 1955. Separate negotiations between the existing nuclear powers, the United States, UK, and USSR, began in October 1958. The technical sticking point, on-site inspections, pointed to a larger issue of mutual mistrust. United States military leaders consistently cited Soviet untrustworthiness and record of treaty-breaking as reasons to oppose a test ban.[89]

Although the negotiations of the late 1950s did not produce a formal agreement, the three nuclear powers entered an informal test moratorium from 1958 to 1961. United States military leaders, however, believed the Soviets would break the moratorium when it suited their needs. Twining told the NSC, including Eisenhower, that to stop testing—and the progress of American arms essential to air-atomic strategy—was a "bad mistake."[90] Critics felt vindicated on 30 August 1961 when, in the middle of the Berlin crisis, the Soviets (citing French testing) unilaterally broke the moratorium by launching three tests in a week. The series included the largest test ever conducted, a 58 MT air-dropped weapon. The rapidity of the Soviet tests demonstrated to many that they had only been waiting for a moment of American political vulnerability and had used the moratorium to pull ahead in high-yield weapons. Twining lamented three years of lost "technology time."[91]

The United States resumed an aggressive test program and negotiations on a test ban faded into the background until after the Cuban Missile Crisis. That event rekindled interest in arms control. Kennedy sent Rusk to Moscow in the summer of 1963. He returned with the signed test ban treaty. The arguments between its supporters and advocates of superiority played out in Senate ratification hearings.

Rusk's testimony outlined the broad advantages of the treaty for the United States. The country would benefit when the slackening arms race reduced tensions. This agreement (combined with the Hot Line) would lead to future agreements. The secretary even claimed the treaty held military advantages, as the United States had a lead in low- and medium-yield weapons that would survive longer than if unrestricted testing continued. The Soviet lead in high-yield weapons was inconsequential, because there was no military requirement for them.[92] Kennedy's formal message transmitting the treaty to the Senate enumerated the same advantages and assured critics that US military strength would not be affected.[93]

The administration also requested the Joint Staff to study the treaty and determine the military advantages that could accrue from it. The officers who prepared the report replied that the LTBT's primary advantages were political, not military. Its military advantages were not quantifiable, while the losses and risks were concrete. Nonetheless, there were positive benefits from the LTBT. It could increase trust and confidence—if the USSR refrained from cheating—and so ease world tension, slow the arms race, and constrain proliferation. It might reduce defense costs and increase tension between the USSR and PRC, because the latter was pushing to become a nuclear power.[94]

Undoubtedly, the administration sought this list of military advantages because it feared the chiefs would openly oppose the treaty or work with senators who did. The JCS had largely been left out of the negotiations. Rusk had gone to Moscow without any member of the body. The president consulted the Joint Chiefs on the issue only once as a whole, and met each chief once individually.

As the administration's effort for a test ban quickened in the spring of 1963, Congress asked the chiefs to testify. In June 1963, LeMay testified against the idea of a test ban, reflecting both the JCS's overall opinion and an opposition based in traditional air-atomic strategy. Testing to understand weapon effects was the only way to preserve superiority and to develop new techniques. A ban would cause the rapid decay of American testing capability. While an autocratic Soviet state could maintain indefinitely the personnel and equipment to resume testing when it wished, American scientists and technical personnel would move to more lucrative and rewarding jobs. LeMay cited the Soviet resumption of testing that ended the moratorium as evidence of this Soviet capacity. Those Soviet tests, moreover, had given them a lead in high-yield weapons and ballistic missile research. He rejected the administration's claim that there was no need for high-yield weapons, as certain hardened targets demanded them and they also provided a psychological edge. LeMay disparaged the main driving force of the treaty, the danger of fallout. That threat had been overrated, as all tests performed through December 1962 had produced only one-twentieth of the normally occurring background radiation. Nor could the Soviets be trusted to abide by the treaty. When Senator Thurmond asked whether the Soviets had strayed from their goals of "world domination and enslavement," LeMay flatly stated that Moscow had never done so and would cheat. To LeMay, a Soviet Union with nuclear superiority was a far greater danger than fallout.[95]

When LeMay appeared before the Senate a second time in August, he and the Joint Chiefs understood the political reality that the treaty was signed and would be ratified. Thus he outlined four conditions on which the chiefs, and he, would agree to it. The United States must vigorously develop national technical means for enforcing the LTBT's terms and maintain a program of vigorous underground testing and continue to support research at the national labs (such as Los Alamos). These would preserve US superiority in low- and mid-yield weapons for as long as possible. LeMay also urged the senators to ensure that the United States was ready to restart atmospheric testing if the Soviets violated the treaty.[96] For his part, when the Senate called Power to testify, the SAC commander broke with the JCS and recommended rejection of the treaty. United States strategic superiority must be preserved, and that required further testing. In particular, it was needed to meet the Soviet lead in high-yield weapons and the lack of a US end-to-end ICBM test.[97]

In the end, the Senate accepted the LTBT and doing so weakened the foundation of traditional air-atomic strategy. By denying unrestricted technological progress, which depended on unrestrained testing, the treaty envisaged a world where both superpowers would reach parity in weapons technology. By seeking a sufficient level of technology, rather than continuously chasing a receding goal of superiority, the test ban was the diplomatic counterpart of Assured Destruction. It prized stability and a slowed arms race above superiority, assumed the current level of technology could provide an adequate deterrent, and rejected any notion that stability arose from superiority. Like the cancellation of manned bombers, the LTBT widened the gap between the administration and the Air Force.

The Final Score

Collectively, the changes to the SIOP, the cancellation of manned bomber programs, and the LTBT, profoundly altered the structure of US strategic forces by 1970. SAC shrank by almost 40 percent, from more than one-quarter million personnel to just over 150,000. The retirement of the B-47, B-58, and older B-52s eviscerated the manned bomber force. Missiles, central to Assured Destruction, entered service in large numbers. Overall, there were fewer weapons, bombers had little better performance than they did at the start of the decade, and missiles assumed a major role. In 1969 SAC was a force designed for Assured Destruction and a margin of Damage Limitation, not a "full first-strike." The forces were weighted toward survivability and were not the fast, accurate, and vulnerable systems that would have been needed for counterforce in the old air-atomic mold.

SAC's eclipse had a clear effect on the budgetary balance between the services. As the table below shows, even after the Vietnam War, the USAF failed to regain the predominant budgetary share it had enjoyed in the air-atomic years. The

TABLE 4 SAC force levels, 1960–69

YEAR	TOTAL SAC PERSONNEL	BOMBERS	MISSILES
1960	266,788	B–47: 1,178 B–52: 538 B–58: 19 Total: 1,735	Snark: 30 Atlas: 12 Total: 42
1961	280,582	B–47: 889 B–52: 571 B–58: 66 Total: 1,526	Atlas: 62 Titan: 1 Total: 63
1962	282,723	B–47: 880 B–52: 639 B–58: 76 Total: 1,595	Atlas: 142 Titan: 62 Minuteman: 20 Total: 224
1963	271,672	B–47: 613 B–52: 636 B–58: 86 Total: 1,335	Atlas: 140 Titan: 119 Minuteman: 372 Total: 631
1964	259,871	B–47: 391 B–52: 626 B–58: 94 Total: 1,111	Atlas: 138 Titan: 114 Minuteman: 698 Total: 950
1965	216,681	B–47: 114 B–52: 600 B–58: 93 Total: 807	Titan: 59 Minuteman: 821 Total: 880
1966	196,887	B–52: 591 B–58: 83 Total: 674	Titan: 60 Minuteman: 908 Total: 968
1967	191,305	B–52: 588 B–58: 81 Total: 669	Titan: 63 Minuteman: 973 Total: 1,036
1968	168,500	B–52: 579 B–58: 76 Total: 655	Titan: 54 Minuteman: 1,000 Total: 1,054
1969	164,328	B–52: 505 B–58: 41 FB–111: 3 Total: 549	Titan: 60 Minuteman: 1,005 Total: 1,065

Source: J. C. Hopkins, *The Development of Strategic Air Command, 1946–1981 (A Chronological History)* (Omaha, NE: Office of the Historian, Headquarters Strategic Air Command, 1986).

overall defense pie was larger, but the Air Force share had shrunk. The big winner was the Navy.

The markedly different strategic forces of 1959 and 1969 prove the subordination of service culture—and its central strategic ideas—to national policy. Given strong national leadership, as provided by McNamara, the greatest shifts can be effected over service resistance. Decisions in declaratory policy enforced changes

TABLE 5 Service budgets, FY 1957–78 (in millions of contemporary dollars)

FISCAL YEAR	ARMY	NAVY	AIR FORCE	ARMY % TOTAL	NAVY % TOTAL	AF % TOTAL
57	8,972	10,318	18,235	23.9	27.5	48.6
58	9,131	11,009	18,411	23.7	28.6	47.8
59	9,533	11,835	19,249	23.5	29.1	47.4
60	9,453	11,726	19,289	23.4	29.0	47.7
61	10,145	12,234	19,804	24.0	29.0	46.9
62	11,248	13,191	20,790	24.9	29.2	46.0
63	11,476	13,973	20,610	24.9	30.3	44.7
64	12,011	14,466	20,456	25.6	30.8	43.6
65	11,552	13,339	18,146	26.8	31.0	42.2
66	14,732	15,962	20,065	29.0	31.4	39.5
67	20,958	19,246	22,912	33.2	30.5	36.3
68	25,222	22,072	25,734	34.5	30.2	35.2
69	25,033	22,505	25,892	34.1	30.6	35.3
70	24,749	22,505	24,867	34.3	31.2	34.5
71	23,077	22,051	23,778	33.5	32.0	34.5
72	22,596	22,336	23,999	32.8	32.4	34.8
73	20,185	22,470	23,627	30.5	33.9	35.6
74	21,395	23,984	23,928	30.9	34.6	34.5
75	21,920	27,393	25,042	29.5	36.8	33.7
76	21,398	28,462	26,446	28.0	37.3	34.7
77	23,919	30,775	27,915	29.0	37.3	33.8
78	26,019	33,524	29,217	29.3	37.8	32.9

Source: Department of Defense Comptroller, "National Defense Budget Estimates for Fiscal Year 2007," available at http://comptroller.defense.gov/Portals/45/Documents/defbudget/Docs/fy2007_greenbook.pdf, 141–42.

in action policy through the mechanisms of centralized planning and budgeting. The Air Force's view that nuclear warfare was still a form of traditional conflict that sought victory was replaced by one that saw the grim prospect of stalemate as the best outcome. Nuclear doctrine shifted from victory to sufficiency. Rather than seeking a single goal, there would be many ways to fight and many potential outcomes. Compelling an enemy into victory by brute force became only one potential alternative, to be determined not in advance, but depending on the situation at the moment of conflict, and the temperament of national leaders. The maximum attainable superiority in quantity and quality ceased to be an operational asset or source of deterrence, replaced by secure second-strike forces, embodied in the nuclear triad. Military operational control gave way to detailed civilian direction. To the displaced uniformed strategists, this outcome seemed like dangerous meddling, but in fact it also reestablished the connection between military and political objectives in the actual conduct of war, not just its beginning. Whatever view an observer takes of the viability of the strategy, it demonstrated the supremacy of civilian control. The air-atomic strategy, incrementally built from prewar and World War II experience, was decisively rejected—the military, of any uniform, never regained full control of nuclear strategy or operations. The Air Force's identity, forged in strategic airpower that had become air-atomic strategy, shattered into two separate streams. With atomic strategy under civilian control and seeking sufficiency, and the main focus of destruction, missiles, no longer controlled by pilots, air strategy sought a separate identity. The service faced an arduous path in finding a way of seeking victory without resorting to unrestricted violence.

Assured Destruction was radical surgery to eliminate a threat to national security health, and McNamara was the surgeon. Like radical surgery, it was not a good option, simply a necessary one. It preserved, but radically altered, the patient's life. In the case of Assured Destruction, it constrained the growth of strategic forces, slowed the growth of overkill, and gave at least the appearance of usable options for military force. However, it left the national security patient with uncoordinated action and declaratory policies, and set its Air Force adrift. McNamara had properly diagnosed the problem and done what was possible but had not cured the condition.

A few months after the Senate ratified the Limited Test Ban Treaty, movie audiences around America filed into theaters to watch the new film, *Dr. Strangelove.* In response to an unbalanced SAC wing commander launching his wing on an unauthorized preemptive attack, the Air Force chief of staff, Gen. Buck Turgidson, lectures President Merkin Muffley on the importance of preemption. "It is necessary now to make a choice, to choose between two admittedly regrettable, but nevertheless, distinguishable post-war environments: one where you got twenty million people killed, and the other where you got a hundred and fifty million people killed. . . . Mr. President, I'm not saying we wouldn't get our hair mussed. But I do say . . . no more than ten to twenty million killed, tops. Uh . . . depending on the breaks."[98] Audiences either recoiled from Turgidson's cavalier sentiment or chuckled at its absurdity, but what few realized was that they were seeing a parody of an era that was already dying. Within a few years, Turgidson—and the air-atomic strategy he represented—would be firmly lodged in a forgotten past.

Conclusion

SURVIVE

It is a war of nuclear bargaining.

—Thomas Schelling, Nuclear Strategy in Berlin, 1961

The reorientation of general war away from the traditional goal of victory finally split air from atomic strategy.[1] Nuclear strategy and operations continued to develop throughout the Cold War, but under civilian direction. Through the 1960s, Assured Destruction remained the focus of US strategy, structuring forces to survive, not to prevail. Although later administrations sought to reinvigorate nuclear operations, most notably through James Schlesinger's Countervailing doctrine, there never was a return to the idea of air-atomic brute superiority and shock. Countervailing, like other more aggressive strategies, simply sought to ensure the United States could be marginally stronger than the USSR at any level of escalation. However, even that definition was fundamentally different than air-atomic thinking, which posited in general war one must inflict maximum damage in minimum time, with the aim of victory.

These developments freed air strategy from the problems of relying on unrestricted atomic force to gain its ends but also forced the USAF to redefine itself. Since 1947, Air Force identity had been based on air-atomic ideas. The latter had gained the service its independence and defined its primary mission. In redefining the goal of atomic strategy as sufficiency—indeed, recasting it as no longer being even military—the Air Force had to find new ways to seek victory through airpower alone. Vietnam became a testing ground for new strategic air ideas. Incrementalism, effectively a nonnuclear version of communication through military action, failed during Rolling Thunder. Although the brute force of Linebacker II, which harkened back to air-atomic roots with its relentless daily B-52 strikes, would be better remembered, Linebacker I's precision attacks had a longer-term impact on the USAF. Precision substituted for brute force and gave air strategy an acceptable way to achieve victory. Even so, the collapse of the air-atomic strategy cost the USAF its position of preeminence among the services and lost it perhaps 25 percent of its relative share of the military budgets between 1958 and 1978; and precision has yet to regain all of that status for the USAF.

With the manned bomber disappearing from the inventory and tactical aircraft now capable of strategic attack, the Air Force underwent a leadership change, "The Rise of the Fighter Generals" as dubbed by one historian. In 1960, ten general officers on the Air Staff (in addition to the CJCS) had bomber backgrounds, while only two had fighter backgrounds. Fifteen major commands were led by bomber generals and only two by fighter pilots. In 1990, eleven fighter and two bomber generals ran the Air Staff, while eight major commands were under fighter pilot control and just three under bomber control.[2]

Strategic Air Command, as an embodiment of the air-atomic strategy in the 1950s, became increasingly isolated in the new precision-oriented Air Force. After 1965, it was like Wylie E. Coyote in the Roadrunner cartoon, having run off a cliff but not yet aware it must fall. In 1992, SAC followed its Soviet enemy into history. In a special irony, a unified Strategic Command replaced SAC, but instead of signifying the total dominance of the air-atomic strategy as the Strategic Command proposal of 1960 would have done, this step signaled its final failure.

Several broader implications applying beyond the narrow realm of the Air Force and its identity follow from this study. SAC in the 1950s was not an aberration on an otherwise smooth road to precision in airpower, but instead the last stage on another path toward victory that became discredited when unrestricted force became unviable. It was a logical, unavoidable, inevitable stage in strategic bombing. Both precision and its air-atomic predecessor seek victory, only by different mechanisms. Nor was SAC just a part of the history of nuclear deterrence, or the lair of strategic cavemen: it demonstrated that the last stage in traditional strategic airpower and the first stage of the nuclear age were one and the same.

SAC in the age of unfettered force has become a forgotten, even a taboo, subject for airpower historians. The popular idea of its history stems from fiction and film. This occurs because some airpower historians simply write about what happened, rather than the deterrence of what could have happened. Still others may be avoiding discussion of the "dead end" that complicates their triumphalist tale of the march to precision. In fact, unlimited destruction matched precision as an element in airpower until quite recently: to write it out of that history is bad history. Whatever the reasons for avoiding the topic, SAC and the first twenty years of the atomic era are central to the development of airpower. The period established the relationship of airpower to the traditional military arms and its influence extended for decades after its end. Precision airpower theory was not developed in a vacuum but arose instead in an environment shaped by—and to a degree in opposition to—the original brute force form of postwar airpower. This conclusion should force a reevaluation of the Vietnam War's place in airpower. Failure in Vietnam did not spur a search during the 1970s for new ways to apply airpower; it was itself part of an already ongoing search. The fission of air and atomic strategy had already forced the exploration for a replacement. Vietnam was part of that pursuit, not its cause.

For students of bureaucratic politics, this study reinforces the importance of the early Cold War to civil-military relations and illustrates its nature. The services fought each other with little restraint in a ferocious free-for-all, each trying to claw its way to the top of the budget. However, they all remained loyal to the system of civilian control, even when they believed that system was run irresponsibly and dangerously by inexperienced men. Even in the face of civilian politicians with whom they strongly disagreed and whose ideas threatened the identity at the core of their service, USAF leaders remained fully subordinate. There were no *Seven Days in May*. The pit bull was perfectly obedient to its master, no matter the order. For their part, civilian leaders in the executive branch maintained firm control over national nuclear security policy and did not shy away from sweeping changes to impose their programs. The executive branch retained effective power over nuclear strategy and forces.

Again, histories of nuclear strategy, and many of their theories, underestimate the importance of routine. Although accidental nuclear war has been productively discussed from this point of view, the evolution of doctrine has not. Air-atomic strategy, rooted in prewar thought, refined by the perceived successes of the Second World War, and reinforced by the new atomic bomb whose power fit easily into the established framework, was a routine way of approaching the application of military power. The new weapon was used to extend established routines, not to challenge them. This situation created momentum for air-atomic strategy that could not be lightly batted aside by new and untested theories. It propelled the Air Force to dominate the defense budget, so reinforcing the perception that the air-atomic strategy was a winning idea for the organization.

This study has additional implications for the realm of strategic studies. It demonstrates that any examination of nuclear strategy and deterrence must consider the historical origins of strategic airpower theory, and understand its incremental development in the face of technology and Soviet power. The theories of the earliest nuclear strategists do not represent the earliest nuclear strategies, nor did they have any effect on the first twenty years of the nuclear age. Independent of their merits, these ideas only gradually seeped into practice. Furthermore, the conviction that nuclear war and atomic weapons always meant mutual destruction, and that Assured Destruction therefore always was and is a valid idea, the only valid idea, is common but false. After 1945, there was a long period of overwhelming American nuclear superiority, consciously and rationally preserved by national and military authorities, which served the national interest effectively in deterring Soviet adventurism during a time when fundamental parts of the world political system were collapsing and others being built. During this era, the air-atomic strategy actually was a better guide to the use of the forces that existed than any contemporary ideas of nuclear theorists. Indeed, when members of the Kennedy administration tried to apply these ideas to reality in 1961–63, they did not fare well, a hint of unfortunate consequences to come in the Vietnam War. Only by the later 1960s did these theories finally provide the best, and a good, guide to the use of nuclear forces. Meanwhile, strong presidents imposed clear limits on preemption and prevention. Neither the US government nor the USAF started a war against an enemy over whom they had superiority and whom they considered implacable and aggressive, and whom in fact they could have destroyed easily. There was no Jack D. Ripper. In hindsight, the remarkable thing is the restraint and responsibility with which American leaders handled their power.

This study suggests the need to modify significantly the standard interpretations of US strategy and power in the early Cold War. The starting point for reconsideration is the presumed relationship between national strategy and operational planning—between declaratory and action policy. A common, if unstated, assumption in the literature is the idea that changes to declared policy are the central element of national strategy, that the word of a national leader is directly translated into the deeds of military subordinates. This did not hold true in the realm of early nuclear strategy. Resistant (but not rebellious) subordinates in powerful military cultures that followed established standard operating procedures slowed strategic change. Eisenhower's dismay with the overkill of SIOP-62 did not lead to the immediate overhaul of the plan. Kennedy and McNamara's direction to alter the plans and introduce flexibility in their execution was at best partially successful even two administrations later, as Nixon administration records suggest. Such changes no doubt entered the evolving SIOP, but only as flexible command and control systems developed, most nuclear warheads were mounted on land- or sea-based missiles, and the Air Force grew to accept the new expectations—and those who could not retired. The changes were made in the end, but not instantaneously. The delay stemmed not from attempts by the machine to evade decisions but from the very way it worked.

This assessment also suggests that Kennedy era expectations for carrying out SIOP flexibly would have caused disaster. In both the Berlin and Cuba crises, high officials mooted ad hoc nuclear attacks. A system designed over twenty years for rapid and wholesale execution of the entire war plan, expending the entire arsenal as rapidly as possible, with procedures, technology, and training tuned to that end, would not have managed piecemeal implementation. The highest levels of government fundamentally misunderstood how military operations worked, and even more, how nimbly the military could enforce new policies, even those it accepted. They underestimated the immense work needed to overcome the inertia established by years of standard operating procedure. This situation created hidden but potentially disastrous problems in some of the most dangerous Cold War crises. Counterintuitively, one of the most dangerous moments in the Cold War was when the US government sought stability by abandoning SAC's traditional plans for victory and turned toward Assured Destruction, and for precisely that reason.

This book also reveals several implications for civil-military relations. The most commonly examined are connections between elected civilian leaders and military officers. Senior military figures of the 1950s and 1960s are portrayed commonly—*Seven Days in May* and *Thirteen Days* are representative examples—as barely under the control of civil authority, often straining at the leash to attack. The evidence suggests a different picture. Military leaders such as LeMay were inclined toward aggressive solutions to diplomatic problems, ready to use unrestricted force at the earliest moment. Yet precisely this attitude was essential to Eisenhower's national strategy. He required an undeniable and overwhelming offensive force in order to present a credible deterrent threat. A Strategic Air Command led by men who visibly shied away from military action would have encouraged Soviet aggression. That is, military leaders who publicly agreed with their commander-in-chief's actual hesitance to resort to nuclear combat would have made that outcome more likely. The visible difference in position was not a sign of civil-military friction, but instead was an essential lubrication to them. LeMay's willingness to fight a nuclear war was a significant reason why one never was fought.

Again, throughout the 1950s, USAF officers were baffled by Eisenhower's reluctance to use atomic weapons when a crisis seemed to demand it. What is most telling about the relationship between civilian and military leaders is their suggested solution: to educate the president on the realities of the nuclear age. They did not seek to undermine the president's authority, go around his directives, or defy him. Rather, they sought to change his mind. No General Ripper ordered the execution of "Plan R." The White House was not an enemy to be defeated (that verbiage and desire was reserved for the Navy) but instead the respected source of authority to be convinced. Even during the Kennedy administration, when White House and Pentagon civilians devalued military expertise, the Air Force fought only within accepted channels. It lobbied the Congress, encouraged public pressure, and used all its persuasive skills to reverse policy. In the end, the USAF failed to change the direction it was given from above, but it complied in the destruction of a policy it believed essential to American security, damaging its own self-interest in the process. Senior military leaders protected their services and visions of national security, but remained fully subordinate to civilian control.

Civil-military relations included those between civilian and uniformed strategic thinkers. The common conception, encouraged by the strategic studies literature, is that the ideas of civilian strategists like Brodie and Schelling automatically and immediately found their way into military practice. Closer study reveals that the path was not so simple. The ideas of civilian strategists, no matter how compelling or well argued, only influenced operational planning that flowed through government channels. Sometimes this influence was voluntary, as when the Air Force dispersed bombers as suggested by William Kaufmann's RAND studies. At other times, civilian arguments were used as ammunition in interservice budget fights, when services selectively drew from contemporary civilian studies. Only after 1961, when civilian strategists gained authority in the White House and Defense Department, did their ideas force their way into actual planning. Even so, it took years of effort and changes to the force structure to bring about major shifts, because the Air Force, and the other services, tenaciously protected their professional functions from interference by outside "amateurs." This happened even after 1964, when civilians dominated the development of nuclear strategy, displacing both the established master, the USAF, and the insurgent, the USN. The services then left civilians to dominate that domain and small parts of their forces, measured in numbers or funds, and returned to focus on the more practical realm of conventional war, where debate became reinvigorated and creative. In their traditional domain, military strategists maintained control in the decades that followed, and still pursued strategies of victory.

Morality mattered to the same extent and through the same mechanism as the ideas of civilian strategists: interservice fighting. Moral arguments influenced policy only when an organizational rival adopted them, as when the Navy argued against the B-36 in 1949, or the Army for more flexible forces in the 1950s. The other services objected to the morality of air-atomic strategy only when promoting their own agendas.

For those studying modern nuclear states, there is a further implication. The best predictor of how a new nuclear power may use its weapons will be found in which organization is responsible for them and how that organization has acted in the past. As important as the question of how the Iranian government approaches nuclear weapons is that of how the Iranian military approaches war. Abstract nuclear theory is only important to the degree that it is actively adopted by those whom it claims to govern. Deterrence is not the only valid way to think about nuclear forces: indeed it may only have been accepted by Western forces from 1963, not by anyone else who has possessed them, or might do so.

This account also matters for Cold War history. The early Cold War differed from the later Cold War, because for over a decade the United States held usable nuclear superiority. Had Truman, Eisenhower, or Kennedy wished, they could have obliterated Soviet nuclear forces and achieved meaningful victory, with plausibly manageable risk to American lives. This capability, which arose from SAC's viable first-strike capacity rooted in air-atomic strategy, remained unused, despite the fact that all these administrations feared Soviet intentions and knew the latter's capabilities were rising fast, and even though each knew that preventive war was, in the abstract, the simplest solution to their problems. Instead, they created stability and security through a combination of overwhelming superiority in capabilities with a defensive strategy. The USAF of the 1950s commonly is viewed as a paranoid, belligerent, and anti-Soviet institution, with some truth. Nonetheless, unlike civilian strategists such as Kaysen and public intellectuals like Bertrand Russell, it never openly advocated preventive war. It regarded nuclear war as winnable because, with incrementally diminishing probability, between 1950 and 1964, that was the case: the USAF would have failed its duty, and its country, not to develop that capability, or to make that power plain to presidents. Eisenhower, who understood the implications of nuclear weapons and the irresistible tendency toward escalation in war, inhibited not only himself, but also his successors from taking risks. He pursued a conscious defensive strategy, despite Soviet provocation, and alarming developments in its nuclear strength and in the Third World. He eschewed risky policies that in fact the United States might have been strong enough to pursue, such as rollback. While Eisenhower had the experience to manage levels of nuclear conflict short of unrestricted city exchange, he ensured that his successor would not have to do so. By structuring American nuclear forces so that they could be used only in a blunt and overwhelming assault, he made choices for his successors starker—and simpler. They would not have the choice to "show resolution" with a nuclear demonstration, an attempt as futile as becoming "just a little pregnant." As Craig argues, Eisenhower's strategy drove Kennedy's peaceful resolution of the 1961 Berlin confrontation, when his advisors advocated steps that might have led to war. After that crisis, the Cold War changed as American superiority waned. However, it was not just Soviet effort that brought this about, but a conscious American decision to give up its lead rather than to maintain it, which certainly they could have done for some time.

Individuals matter. Nuclear strategy is separate today from military strategy because of the interaction of leaders with strong ideas. Truman, Eisenhower, Kennedy, McNamara, Twining, Kuter, LeMay, and those who worked with them, thought long and hard about the requirements for national survival in the nuclear age. Their solutions, however imperfect, were grounded in their personal experiences and modes of thought. Just as it mattered whether Kaiser Wilhelm or

Bismarck determined Germany's foreign policy, so too it mattered whether Eisenhower or McNamara established national nuclear strategy, and if Kenney or LeMay carried it out.

SAC was a finely honed instrument for a specific purpose: to wreak maximum damage in minimum time. In 1950, it would have destroyed the USSR with little damage to the United States—victory as conventionally understood. Every year later, the potential damage to the United States grew incrementally, but air-atomic logic remained steady. The best outcome, other than deterring war altogether, was to destroy the enemy on the ground immediately. The costs of war, rising every year, were recognized, but air-atomic advocates saw the offensive-defense as the only way to contain them. Anything but an all-out air-atomic offensive aimed to impose American will on the USSR would invite attack and worsen its consequences. SAC knew only one way to deter. In the game of Chicken, they had already thrown out the steering wheel and could only stomp harder on the accelerator. The only air-atomic solution was to try harder as the problem worsened—the definition of Eden's path-dependency. As Soviet capability increased, the absurdity of the air-atomic strategy became increasingly apparent to those outside the USAF. By 1964, SAC was finely honed, for a strategy whose definition of victory no longer made sense for its political masters, or the larger public.

In the end, the system worked. Between 1945 and 1963, Americans made rational decisions about nuclear forces, which were well suited to their time and emerging trends. Responsible men made good decisions about hard issues. Even the least polished among them, such as LeMay, made policy only after deliberation and duly considering alternatives. They were not cavemen, and they were not wrong. They had grave responsibilities in a new era in which mistakes were measured in megadeaths. They did their duty by creating the most lethal military force in history. They succeeded because it never had to be used.

Key to Sources and Abbreviations

Sources are referred to by the abbreviations in the following table. I have abbreviated some collections and series, but folder titles are verbatim and denoted by quotations marks. To conserve space, the notes substitute for a bibliography. All NARA records are at NARA II in College Park, MD.

ABBREVIATION	SOURCE
A335	Series 335, RG 341, NARA
ABPR	Arleigh Burke Papers (Rosenberg MDR), Operational Archives Branch, Naval Historical Center, Washington, DC
ABPT	Drawer 4, Case 1457, CNOF-87, Burke Papers, Operational Archives Branch, Naval Historical Center, Washington, DC
ACSD59	Chief of Staff Decisions 1959–65, RG 341, NARA, College Park, MD
ADCOSI	Deputy Chief of Staff for Operations, Executive Office, Senate Investigations, Aug–Oct 1949, RG 341, NARA
AFA	US Air Force Academy Special Collections
AFC54	Air Force Council Commander's Conferences 1954–56, RG 341, NARA
AFPDF	Air Force Plans, Decimal File 1942–54, RG 341, NARA
AIC	Director of Intelligence, Intelligence Correspondence [1955], RG 341, NARA
AOA	Operations Analysis, RG 341, NARA, College Park, MD
AOPGF	Deputy Chief of Staff for Operations, Director of Plans, General File 1944–53, RG 341, NARA
AVTS	Vice Chief of Staff, TS Files 1950–65, RG 341, NARA
CL	Curtis E. LeMay Papers, Manuscript Division, Library of Congress, Washington, DC
CR	CREST (CIA) Database, NARA [Documents identified by CREST database ID]
CS	Papers of General Spaatz, Library of Congress, Washington, DC
DAECPC	Defense - Atomic Energy, Combined Policy Committee Files, RG 330, NARA
DASCCS	Office of the Administrative Secretary, Correspondence Control Section, House Armed Services Committee B-36 Hearings, RG 330, NARA
DDE	Dwight D. Eisenhower Library, Abilene, KS
DZ47	Double Zero - 1947–50, Operational Archives Branch, Naval Historical Center, Washington, DC
DZT60	Turnover Books 1960–65, Double Zero - 1966, Operational Archives Branch, Naval Historical Center, Washington, DC
EAWD	Ann Whitman Diary, Dwight D. Eisenhower Library, Abilene, KS
EDAW	DDE Diary, Ann Whitman, Dwight D. Eisenhower Library, Abilene, KS
EIAW	International Series, Ann Whitman, Dwight D. Eisenhower Library, Abilene, KS

(continued)

(continued)

ABBREVIATION	SOURCE
EINSCP	Intelligence Files, US National Security Council Presidential Records, Dwight D. Eisenhower Library, Abilene, KS
ENAW	NSC Series, Ann Whitman, Dwight D. Eisenhower Library, Abilene, KS
ENSSWS	NSC Series, Subject Subseries, White House Office, Office of the Special Assistant for National Security Affairs, Dwight D. Eisenhower Library, Abilene, KS
EPAW	Press Conference Series, Ann Whitman, Dwight D. Eisenhower Library, Abilene, KS
ERC	Reference Collection of Miscellaneous Declassified Documents, Dwight D. Eisenhower Library, Abilene, KS
ESSF	Executive Secretary Subject File, NSC Staff, Dwight D. Eisenhower Library, Abilene, KS
GCLG	General Correspondence, RG 200, Papers of General Groves, NARA
HAMG	Hap Arnold - Murray Green Collection, US Air Force Academy Special Collections
HRA	Air Force Historical Research Agency [Documents identified by IRIS number]
HV	Hoyt S. Vandenberg Papers, Manuscript Division, Library of Congress, Washington, DC
HVP	Hoyt S. Vandenberg Papers, Manuscript Division, Library of Congress, Washington, DC
JCDF	Central Decimal File 1946–47, RG 218, NARA
JCDF2	Central Decimal File 1951–53, RG 218, NARA
JCDF57	Central Decimal File 1957, RG 218, NARA
JCDF58	Central Decimal File 1958, RG 218, NARA
JCDF59	Central Decimal File 1959, RG 218, NARA
JCDF60	Central Decimal File 1960, RG 218, NARA
JCDF61	Central Decimal File 1961, RG 218, NARA
JCFGB	Chairman's File (General Bradley, 1949–53), RG 218, NARA
JGF51	Geographic File 1951–53, RG 218, NARA
JGF54	Geographic File 1954–56, RG 218, NARA
JNA	Agency File, National Security File, Lyndon B. Johnson Presidential Library, Austin, TX
JW	James Whisenand Papers, AFHRA
JGF57	Geographic File 1957, RG 218, NARA
KNC	Countries, National Security Files, John F. Kennedy Presidential Library, Boston, MA
KNDN	Departments and Agencies, National Security Files, John F. Kennedy Library, Boston, MA
KNMM	Meetings and Memoranda, National Security Files, John F. Kennedy Library, Boston, MA
LK	Kuter Papers, US Air Force Academy Special Collections
LNT	Nathan F. Twining Papers, Manuscript Division, Library of Congress, Washington, DC
LTW	Thomas D. White Papers, Manuscript Division, Library of Congress, Washington, DC

ABBREVIATION	SOURCE
MS18	Kuter Papers (MS 18), US Air Force Academy Special Collections
MS22	Nathan Twining Papers (MS 22), US Air Force Academy Special Collections
MS58	Reade Tilley (MS 58), US Air Force Academy Special Collections
NCFR	Chairman's File (Admiral Radford, 1953–57), RG 218, NARA, College Park, MD
NGA	George Anderson Papers (1917–76), Operational Archives Branch, Naval Historical Center, Washington, DC
NMP	Mill Papers, RG 273 (National Security Council), NARA, College Park, MD
NNIE	National Intelligence Estimates Concerning the Soviet Union 1950–61, Intelligence Publication File (HRP 92-4/001), RG 263 (Central Intelligence Agency), NARA
NOMM	Official Meeting Minutes, RG 273, NARA
NPP	Policy Papers, RG 273, NARA
NSAD	National Security Archive (Digital) [Documents identified by item number]
NSANH	US Nuclear History, National Security Archive (Digital) [Documents identified by item number]
OAP	Orvill Anderson Papers, Air Force Historical Research Agency
OSDISA	Office of Assistant Secretary of Defense (International Security Affairs) Coordinating Division, National Security Council Files of the Office of the Secretary of Defense 1947–61, RG 330, NARA
RM	Records of Robert S. McNamara, RG 200, NARA, College Park, MD
RR	Robert C. Richardson III Papers, AFHRA
RTP	Reade F. Tilley Papers (MS TBD), US Air Force Academy Special Collections
SMS649	Addendum 2, Series 7, Reade Tilley (SMS 649), US Air Force Academy Special Collections
TDAMC	Memoranda of Conversations, Papers of Dean Acheson, Harry S. Truman Library, Independence, MO
TDSKSR	Department of State (Korea Selected Records), Topical File, Staff Member and Office Files, Harry S. Truman Library, Independence, MO
TGF	General File, Harry S. Truman Library, Independence, MO
TPSNSC	Subject File, NSC Meetings, President's Secretary Files, Harry S. Truman Library, Independence, MO
WDPRTS	Public Relations Division General Records, Top Secret Correspondence 1944–46, RG 165 (War Department General and Special Staffs), NARA
XNS	National Security Council Files, Subject Files, Nixon Presidential Materials Project, NARA

Notes

INTRODUCTION

1. The epigraph by Brown comes from "Concepts of Strat Air War," 3 Dec 51, 483198, HRA, 15.

2. Kuter, Notes on Cdr's Conf, 20 Nov 58, "Quemoy," LK.

3. The most detailed and scholarly work on USAF air doctrine is Robert Futrell, *Ideas, Concepts, Doctrine* (Montgomery, AL: Air University Press, Maxwell AFB, 1974). Also see Phillip Meilinger, ed., *The Paths of Heaven* (Montgomery, AL: Air University Press, Maxwell AFB, 1997). The wartime development of airpower toward unrestrained violence is well documented in Michael Sherry, *The Rise of American Air Power* (New Haven, CT: Yale, 1987). Creating the early air-atomic force is the subject of Walton Moody, *Building a Strategic Air Force* (Washington, DC: Government Reprints, 2001). Typical of the broad overviews of airpower that neglect the air-atomic period is the otherwise admirable Tony Mason, *Air Power* (London: Brassey, 1994).

4. Mark Clodfelter, *The Limits of Air Power* (New York: Free Press, 1989).

5. The best overview of nuclear history is Lawrence Freedman, *The Evolution of Nuclear Strategy*, 3rd ed. (London: Palgrave, 2003). For Eisenhower's approach to national security, see Campbell Craig, *Destroying the Village* (New York: Columbia, 1998). An essential work is David Rosenberg, "The Origins of Overkill," *International Security* 7.4 (Spring 1983): 3–71, and his other articles on the period. Fred Kaplan, *The Wizards of Armageddon* (New York: Simon and Schuster, 1983), is important, although it portrays uniformed strategists in a particularly negative light, as does Richard Rhodes's work. Books that describe the development of nuclear strategy while advocating for contemporary policy changes include Gregg Herken, *The Winning Weapon* (New York: Knopf, 1980); and Paul Bracken, *The Command and Control of Nuclear Forces* (New Haven, CT: Yale University Press, 1983).

The intersection of intelligence and nuclear policy in the 1950s is examined in William Burrows, *By Any Means Necessary* (New York: Farrar, 2001). The evaluation of the Soviet threat is probed in the insightful John Prados, *The Soviet Estimate* (New York: Dial, 1982). The two best works on Soviet strategic forces are Pavel Podvig, ed., *Russian Strategic Nuclear Forces* (Cambridge, MA: MIT Press, 2001); and Steven Zaloga, *The Kremlin's Nuclear Sword* (Washington, DC: Smithsonian, 2002).

Representative early works of nuclear strategy that write from first principles include Thomas Schelling, *The Strategy of Conflict* (Cambridge, MA: Harvard, 1960); William Kaufmann, *Military Policy and National Security* (Princeton, NJ: Princeton University Press, 1956); and Albert Legault and George Lindsey, *The Dynamics of the Nuclear Balance* (Ithaca, NY: Cornell University Press, 1976). The nuclear strategist who best addressed its roots in airpower doctrine is Bernard Brodie, for example, in *Strategy in the Missile Age* (Princeton, NJ: Princeton University Press, 1959).

In Curtis LeMay, *Mission with LeMay* (Garden City, NY: Doubleday, 1965), postwar frustrations with the Kennedy administration come through clearly, and even more so in Thomas Power, *Design for Survival* (New York: Coward-McCann, 1965).

A recently published work with a promising new approach is Francis Gavin's *Nuclear Statecraft* (Ithaca, NY: Cornell University Press, 2012). Gavin judiciously uses the historical record to examine nuclear theory both historically and with respect to today's challenges.

6. Jeremy Stone, "The General Faces 'Reality,'" *New Republic*, 155 (29 Oct 66), 18, quoted in Bernard Brodie, *War and Politics* (New York: Macmillan, 1973), 495.

7. The best introduction to the period's national security strategies is John Gaddis, *Strategies of Containment* (New York: Oxford University Press, 1982). The essential study of deterrence during crises is Alexander George and Richard Smoke, *Deterrence in American Foreign Policy* (New York: Columbia University Press, 1974). For the Soviet perspective, using Soviet archival materials is Vladimir Zubok and Konstantin Pleshakov, *Inside the Kremlin's Cold War* (Cambridge, MA: Harvard University Press, 1996).

National security in the Truman administration is well documented. Recommended starting places are Melvyn Leffler, *A Preponderance of Power* (Stanford, CA: Stanford University Press, 1992), and Michael Hogan, *A Cross of Iron* (Cambridge: Cambridge University Press, 1998). Superb scholarship continues to be produced on the Eisenhower era, especially Robert Bowie and Richard Immerman, *Waging Peace* (New York: Oxford University Press, 1998). A useful overview of the Kennedy years is Lawrence Freedman, *Kennedy's Wars* (New York: Oxford University Press, 2000). Essential to understanding the Cuban Missile Crisis are Graham Allison and Philip Zelikow, *Essence of Decision*, 2nd ed. (New York: Longman, 1999); and Sheldon Stern, *Averting "The Final Failure"* (Stanford, CA: Stanford University Press, 2003). The analytical methods of McNamara's Pentagon are well documented in Alain Enthoven and K. Wayne Smith, *How Much Is Enough?* (New York: Harper, 1971).

8. Evan Thomas, *Ike's Bluff* (New York: Little, Brown, 2012), 15.

1. ANTECEDENTS

1. For clarity, I use "USAF" to refer to the US Air Force and its organizational predecessors.

2. Giulio Douhet, *Command of the Air* (New York: Coward-McCann, 1942), 34.

3. Ibid., 51.

4. Phillip Meilinger, "Giulio Douhet and the Origins of Airpower Theory," in *Paths of Heaven: The Evolution of Airpower Theory*, ed. Phillip Meilinger (Montgomery, AL: Air University Press, Maxwell AFB, 1997), 12.

5. Douhet, *Command*, 61.

6. Mark Clodfelter, "Molding Airpower Convictions," in *Paths*, 90.

7. Ibid., 98–99.

8. Mark Clodfelter, *Beneficial Bombing* (Lincoln: University of Nebraska Press, 2010).

9. Tami Davis Biddle, *Rhetoric and Reality in Air Warfare* (Princeton, NJ: Princeton University Press, 2002), 141. In "British and American Approaches to Strategic Bombing" ed. John Gooch, *Airpower* (New York: Routledge, 2013), Biddle cites George Brown for making this connection (see n83).

10. Peter Faber, "Interwar US Army Aviation and the Air Corps Tactical School," *Paths*, 215–19.

11. Ibid., 16–17.

12. Ibid., 20–32.

13. Gian Gentile, *How Effective Is Strategic Bombing?* (New York: NYU Press, 2001).

14. *The United States Strategic Bombing Survey, Over-all Report (European War)* (1945; reprint New York: Garland Press, 1976), 37–38.

15. Ibid.; ibid., 39; ibid., 39–40.

16. Speeches by Anderson to Civ Seminar, 1 Mar 47, 125818, OAP, 5.

17. Jodl, "A War between the Western Powers and the Soviet Union in the European Theater (A Strategic Study)," Aug 46, and "319.1 A War between the West Powers and USSR in Euro The," JCDF.

18. Interview of General Burchinal, 11 Apr 75, AFA, 73–74.

19. *The United States Strategic Bombing Survey: Summary Report (Pacific War)* (1946; Montgomery, AL: Air University Press, Maxwell AFB, 1987), 88; Curtis LeMay, *Mission with LeMay: My Story* (New York: Doubleday, 1965), 366.

20. *USSBS (P)*, 108–10.

21. Interview of Major General Montgomery, 1 May 84, 01105130, HRA, 73–74.

22. Interview of General Burchinal, 79.

23. Marshall to Spaatz, 8 Aug 45, "Top Secret File II 1945," WDPRTS.

24. Interview of generals LeMay, Leon Johnson, David Burchinal et al., 15 Jun 84, 1114855, HRA, 74–75.

25. *USSBS (P)*, 102.

26. Moody, *Building a Strategic Air Force*, 100; LeMay, *Mission*, 523.

27. Power to Eaker (Atch Brief), 1 Feb 47, "Folder - AAG File E-F-1 thru F-249," AOPGF, 4.

28. Colonel Dale Smith, "Operational Concepts for Modern War," *Air University Quarterly Review* 2.2 (Fall 1948): 6.

29. Power to Eaker, 6.

30. Kenney to Spaatz, 29 Jul 46, "AAG File E-500 thru E-749," AOPGF, 3; speeches by Anderson to Civ Seminar, 28.

31. Power to Eaker, 8.

32. Interview of General LeMay et al., 15 Jun 84, 153.

33. Testimony of General Vandenberg before HASC, "B-36 Investigation (File No. 1)," HV, 7–8.

34. Conrad Crane, *Bombs, Cities, and Civilians* (Lawrence: University of Kansas Press, 1993), 147.

35. LeMay, *Mission*, 381–82; Sahr Conway-Lanz, *Collateral Damage* (New York: Routledge, 2006).

36. Crane, *Bombs*, 147.

37. Moody, *Building a Strategic Air Force*, 138.

2. DECLARATION, ACTION, AND THE AIR-ATOMIC STRATEGY

1. Paul Nitze, "Atoms, Strategy, and Policy," *Foreign Affairs* 34.2 (January 1956): 187–98.

2. Interview of Thomas Finletter, 2 February 67, AFA, 36–37.

3. "JWPC 416/1 (Revised)," in Stephen Ross and David Rosenberg, *America's Plans for War against the Soviet Union*, vol. 1 (New York: Garland, 1990), app A to enc A, 5.

4. Ibid.

5. "JCS 1844/46," in Ross and Rosenberg, *America's Plans*, vol. 12, 350.

6. Ibid, 350–51.

7. Ibid.

8. Ibid., 353.

9. Ibid.

10. Ibid., 367.

11. Ibid., 406.

12. Ibid., 419–20.

13. Ibid., 424–26.

14. Moody, *Building a Strategic Air Force*, 140.

15. Min of 241st Mtg, 13 March 46, "334 Jt Staff Planners (3-6-46)," JCDF, 6.

16. Min of 252nd Mtg, 18 June 46, "334 Jt Staff Planners (3-6-46)," JCDF, 2.

17. Ibid.

18. "JIC 329," in Ross and Rosenberg, *America's Plans*, vol. 1, 1.
19. "JIC 329/1," in ibid., 1.
20. Harry Borowski, *A Hollow Threat* (Westport, CT: Greenwood, 1982), 105–7.
21. JIC 329, 4.
22. Ibid., 4–5.
23. Ibid., 5.
24. Ibid., 6.
25. "JPS 789/1," in Ross and Rosenberg, *America's Plans*, vol. 2, annex B, 19–20.
26. "JCS 1952/1," in Ross and Rosenberg, *America's Plans*, vol. 9, 10.
27. "JCS 2057/1," in Ross and Rosenberg, *America's Plans*, vol. 11, 1.
28. "JCS 1823/19," in ibid., 129.
29. "JCS 1952/11," in Ross and Rosenberg, *America's Plans*, vol. 13, 163.
30. Min of 240th Meeting, 6 March 46, "334 Jt Staff Planners (3-6-46)," JCDF, 5.
31. JWPC 416/1 (Revised), 20.
32. SAC History, 1947, vol. 1, 198535, HRA, 138–39.
33. "Preliminary Suggestions as to Information Needed for the Interim Study," OPD 385 (RAND) (5 Feb 48), AFPDF, 1.
34. Vandenberg to Symington, 23 August 48, "CAG File I-1 Thru I-1000," AOPGF, 1.
35. Intro to Intel by Gen. Charles Cabell, 1 November 48, 918245, HRA, 21.
36. Interview of Gen. George Kenney, 21 Aug 74, 1016279, HRA, 144.
37. Intel Est for War Plans, 2 Nov 48, 1005464, HRA, 4–5.
38. Commanding General's Daily Diary, 28 March 50, "LeMay Diary No. 1 1 Jan 50 to 30 Jun 50," CL, 3; LeMay Lecture to ACSC, 6 February 50, "LeMay Diary No. 1 1 Jan 50 to 30 Jun 50," CL, 4.
39. LeMay Lecture, 25 January 50, 1.
40. Power to Eaker, 1 Feb 47, AOPGF 8.
41. Capabilities and Limitations of SAC Given at the RAF Staff College, 7 June 51, 483197, HRA, 8.
42. CG Diary, 28 March 50, 2.
43. Interview of Gen. Curtis LeMay, 9 March 71, 904847, HRA, 48.
44. "AWC Lecture: Horizontal Approach to the S V of the USSR," 12 Dec 51, 1005746, HRA, 6.
45. Ibid., 4.
46. CG Daily Diary, 28 Mar 50, 3.
47. Notes for Discussion with Gen. Vandenberg, 4 Nov 48, "Diary, Box B-103," CL, 1.
48. LeMay to Norstad, 15 Dec 48, NH00183, NSANH, 2.
49. Vandenberg to Symington, 23 Aug 48, 1.
50. Min of 245th Mtg, 17 Apr 46, "334 Jt Staff Planners (3-6-46)," JCDF, 4.
51. LeMay 1971 Interview, 13.
52. Presentation, "Commander's Conference Dec 6–7, 1950, and Jan 22, 1951," CL, 1; Notes for Discussion with Gen. Vandenberg, 2; circular error probable (CEP): standard measurement of accuracy for munitions. It is the radius of an imaginary circle within which ½ of a given number of weapons will fall. Three thousand feet became the accepted minimum for atomic weapons.
53. Vandenberg to LeMay, 21 Sep 49, "Twining," CL, 1–2.
54. Interview of M. G. Yudkin, 15 Nov 77, 1053503, HRA, 143.
55. LeMay 1971 Interview, 34.
56. LeMay to Vandenberg, 15 Jul 49, "Twining," CL, 1.
57. LeMay to O'Donnell, 16 Jul 49, "Multiple Addressee," CL.
58. Excerpts from interview of LeMay by McNeil, Scripps-Howard Papers, 1015, 20 Oct 1950, "LeMay Diary No. 2, 1 Jul 50 to 30 Dec 50," CL, 1.

59. LeMay to Vandenberg, 11 Oct 49, "Twining," CL, 2.
60. Graphic Presentation, Wing Commanders Conf, Dec 50, 3–4.
61. LeMay to Old, c1950, "Unmarked," CL, 1–2.
62. Presentation, Wing Commanders Conf, Dec 50, 15.
63. LeMay to Norstad, 17 Feb 50, "Norstad," CL, 1.
64. AF Emergency War Plan 1-50 (AFEWP 1-50), A335, annex B, 5.
65. EWP 50, annex A, pt IV, 1.
66. Ibid.
67. Ibid.
68. Lt. Gen. Curtis LeMay, Discussion Period Following Lectures on the Mission and Organization of SAC, 13 Jun 50, 483139, HRA.
69. CG Daily Diary, 28 Mar 50, 1.
70. Anderson to Symington, 24 Feb 50, "PD 334.8 Air Policy Commission (7 Aug 47)," AFPDF, 4–5.
71. Lynn Eden, *Whole World on Fire* (Ithaca, NY: Cornell University Press, 2004), 119–21.
72. "JCS 1952/1," 21 Dec 48, in Ross and Rosenberg, *America's Plans*, vol. 9, encl, 5.
73. Ibid., 4.
74. Ibid., 6.
75. Ibid., 7–10.
76. Ibid., 20.
77. Ibid., 5a.
78. Steven Ross, *American War Plans, 1945–1950* (London: Cass, 1996), 107.
79. JCS 1953/1, 12 May 49, in Ross and Rosenberg, *America's Plans*, vol. 11, encl B, 5.
80. Ibid., 19–24.
81. JCS 1953, Ross and Rosenberg, *America's Plans*, vol. 11, 3.
82. Ibid., 30–31.
83. JCS 1953/1, 32.
84. Ibid., 6.
85. Ibid., 9–10.
86. JCS 1953/4, *America's Plans*, vol. 11, 279–82.
87. JCS 1953/5, 285.
88. Warner to Norstad, 15 Oct 49, "OPD 334.8 Research and Development Bd (3 Nov 47) Sec 2," AFPDF, 1–2.
89. JCS 1952/11, 163–64.
90. Ibid., 159.
91. Ibid.
92. Interview of Lt. Gen. Earl Barnes, 23 Jan 75, 1021489, HRA, 7; CG's Diary, 9 May 50, "LeMay Diary No. 1, 1 Jan 50 to 30 Jun 50," CL, 1.
93. John Gaddis, *Strategies of Containment* (New York: Oxford, 1982), chap. 2.
94. Kennan Expresses Views on Soviet Union, 20 Jun 46, "9.51," HAMG, 1.
95. NSC-20/1, 18 Aug 48, "OPD 381.02 (13 Jul 48) Section 1," A335, 31–34.
96. NSC-20/1, 35–41.
97. Some critics have stated that the blunt instrument of air-atomic attack that obliterated enemy cities would make a desired political settlement less likely. However, political settlement does not necessarily have to come from a meeting of the minds. An intact Soviet government compelled to do America's will is still a form of political settlement. See Gregg Herken, *The Winning Weapon* (New York: Knopf, 1980), 279–80.
98. NSC-20/1, 32.
99. Tentative Agenda for Meeting of the War Council on 8 Feb 49, 9 Feb 49, "OPD 334.8 (16 Sep 47), Armed Forces Policy Council (Minutes) Sec 1," AFPDF, exhibit 2b, 2.

100. Anderson to Symington, 15 Jun 48, "OPD 334.8 Mil Liaison Comte (16 Jan 47) Sec 2," AFPDF.

101. NSC-30, 10 Sep 48, "NSC-30 Series - US Policy on Atomic Warfare," OSDISA.

102. Gaddis, *Strategies*, chap. 4.

103. NSC-68, 14 Apr 50, "NSC-68 United States Objectives and Programs for National Security (Folder 2)," OSDISA, 38.

104. Ibid., 38–39.

105. Marc Trachtenberg, "A 'Wasting Asset,'" *International Security* 13.3 (December 1, 1988): 5–49; and Tami Davis-Biddle, "Handling the Soviet Threat," *Journal of Strategic Studies* 12.3 (1989): 273–302.

106. Trachtenberg, "Wasting," 40.

107. Untitled, 21 Sep 50, "Anderson - O," TGF.

108. LeMay, *Mission*, 482.

109. Richard Rhodes, *Dark Sun* (New York: Simon & Schuster, 1995), 438.

110. Anderson to Le Baron, 27 Dec 49, "Hydrogen Bomb," DAECPC, 1–3.

111. Military Implications of Thermonuclear Weapons, 9 Dec 49, "Hydrogen Bomb," DAECPC, 2–5.

112. Anderson to Le Baron, 28 Dec 49, "Hydrogen Bomb," DAEPC, 12.

113. Ibid., 2–4.

114. McMahon to Truman, 21 Nov 49, "Thermonuclear Weapons Program Miscellaneous," DAECPC.

115. Interview of Barnes, 23 Jan 75, 319.

116. Moody, *Strategic Air Force*, 394.

3. FINDING A PLACE

1. In Re: B-36 Investigation (Agenda Items 3 to 8) vol. 17, 11 Oct 49, DASCCS, 1891.

2. Colin Gray, *Airpower for Strategic Effect* (Montgomery, AL: Air University Press, Maxwell AFB, 2012), 67.

3. Anderson to CG of AAF, 16 Feb 47, AOPGF, 47.

4. Chronology of Changes, 7 Feb 58, "CCS (4-2-49) Bulky Package Key West Conference April 7-12 1949," JCDF2, 4–6.

5. Ibid., 9–10.

6. Doolittle before the Senate Military Affairs Cmte, "PD 020 (2 Nov 43) Sec. 2," A335, 6.

7. Arnold to CGs of the AAF, 6 Nov 45, "PD 020 (2 Nov 43) Sec. 2," A335.

8. Spaatz to the Senate Military Affairs Cmte, 15 Nov 45, "Unmarked Folder," CS.

9. Quoted in 'Speeches by General Anderson to Civilian Seminar,' 1 Mar 47, 125818, OAP, 24.

10. Presentation Given to Pres by Norstad, 'Postwar Military Establishment,' "Soviet - 1949," Box 63, HVP, 9.

11. Anderson speeches, 18.

12. Doolittle Senate Statement, 19.

13. Norstad to Arnold, 21 Jul 46, "9.41," HAMG, 2.

14. President's Air Policy Commission, *Survival in the Air Age* (Washington, DC: GPO: 1948), 12.

15. Ibid., 24–25.

16. Ibid., 33.

17. Ibid., 10. The number of aircraft in a group varies over time and by aircraft type. At the time of the Finletter Commission, a heavy bomber group included eighteen B-36s, and a medium bomber group had thirty B-29s or fifty B-50s (Air Force Statistical Digest

1948, HRA, 1). To further complicate matters, the USAF changed its basic organizational unit for force planning from the group to the wing in the early 1950s. Later discussions of force structure sometimes anachronistically refer to this program as the seventy-wing Air Force.

18. Samuel Huntington, *The Common Defense* (New York: Columbia, 1961), 35.

19. Ibid., 42–43.

20. Edward Kolodziej, *The Uncommon Defense and Congress, 1945–1963* (Columbus: Ohio State, 1966), 38.

21. Memo for DCNO (Air), 17 Dec 47, DZ47.

22. McDonald to Spaatz, 17 Oct 46, "Navy (1)," CS, 1.

23. McDonald to Spaatz, 18 Oct 48, "Navy (1)," CS, 1.

24. Memo for Spaatz, 25 Nov 46, "Navy (2)," CS, 1.

25. Using Airpower as a Diplomatic Weapon -1946, 10 Sep 46, "9.41," HAMG, 2.

26. Weapons of a Future War - 1947, "9.41," HAMG, 2.

27. Address by LeMay before the Automotive and Aircraft Museum, 14 Feb 49, "1," SMS649, 9.

28. John Norris, "Airpower in the Cold War," *Air Force* 31.9 (Sept 48): 24.

29. Navy Thinking on the Atomic Bomb, "Navy - Effects on (N- Z)," GCLG, 1.

30. The USSBS report specified 220 B-29s, but Brodie inexplicably used 210 in his example.

31. Compiler's Critique on US Navy Views, "Navy - Effects on (N- Z)," GCLG, 5.

32. Symington to Sullivan," 21 Jul 48, "Navy vs. Air Force," HVP.

33. Symington to Forrestal, 22 Nov 48, "Navy vs. Air Force," HVP.

34. Symington to Forrestal, 6 Oct 48, "Navy vs. Air Force," HVP.

35. Symington to Spaatz, 3 Aug 48, "Navy vs. Air Force," HVP.

36. "Oftsie to Navy and Marine Corps Members of the Naval Analysis Division," 16 Sep 45, quoted in David MacIsaac, *Strategic Bombing in World War Two* (New York: Garland, 1976), 124–25.

37. MacIsaac, *Strategic Bombing*, 126–33.

38. "AJ (A-2) Savage," GlobalSecurity.org, available at http://www.globalsecurity.org /military/systems/aircraft/aj.htm.

39. Using Airpower as a Diplomatic Weapon -1946, 10 Sep 46, "9.41," HAMG, 1.

40. JPS 247th Mtg (Minutes), 25 Apr 46, "PD 334.8 JPS (4 Jan 46) (234th mtg thru [blank])," AFPDF.

41. Minutes of 250th Mtg, 29 May 46, "334 Jt Staff Planners (3-6-46)," JCDF, 3.

42. "JSPG 500/2," 8 Mar 48, in Ross and Rosenberg, *Plans,* vol. 8 (New York: Garland, 1990).

43. Anderson to Vandenberg, 11 Mar 49, "OPD 381.02 (13 Jul 48) Section 2," A335.

44. Memo to Parrish, 13 Aug 51, "Correspondence 1951," MS22.

45. Discussion Pd Following Lectures on the Mission and Org of SAC, 13 Jun 50, 483139, HRA, 9.

46. Sherman to Bradley, 6 Apr 51, "CJCS 020 JCS 1951," JCFGB.

47. Government and Atomic Energy, 30 Sep 52, CL, 26.

48. Chief of Staff USAF to SecDef, "Organization of Atomic Energy Activities (AFSWP)," DAECPC.

49. Statement before the Sen Mil Affairs Cmte: Unification, 19 Oct 45, "Unification Oct-Dec 1945," CS, 7.

50. Symington to Forrestal, 16 Apr 48, "Secretary of the Air Force (2)," CS, 1.

51. Denfeld to Secretary of Defense, 22 Apr 49, "Navy vs. Air Force," HVP.

52. Vandenberg to Secretary of Defense, 23 Apr 49, "Navy vs. Air Force," HVP.

53. Francis Drake, "The Case for Land-Based Air Power," *Reader's Digest* (May 1949), 65.

54. "The Super-Carrier Decision," Apr 50, 125848, OAP, 20–24.

55. James Whisenand and Ahring."What's Wrong with the Air Force's Public Information Program," 125832, OAP, 3.

56. Ibid., 5–6.

57. Herman Wolk, "The Quiet Coup of 1949," *Air Force* 82 (Jul 1999): 76–81.

58. Whisenand, "What's Wrong," 10–12.

59. Analysis of Another Anonymous Attack on the Air Force and the Concept of Aerial Warfare Held by the JCS, "3-C-4," RTP.

60. Whisenand "What's Wrong," 18.

61. A study compiled by the Air Force in 1945 contrasted the USN claim of 6,700 tons dropped on Japan to the 147,000 tons dropped by the AAF. It also noted that the Navy could only operate the carriers for three days without resupply. Thornton to Spaatz, 15 Oct 45; "Unification Oct–Dec 1945," CS.

62. Ibid., 25.

63. Interview of Gen. Lauris Norstad, 25 Oct 79, 1077004, HRA, 219–20.

64. Norstad's suspicion that the Navy had stolen documents from his safe gains credibility in light of the events in the NSC in 1971. A White House investigation led by John Ehrlichman uncovered that Navy yeoman Radford had been copying Henry Kissinger's NSC documents and sending them to JCS chairman Admiral Thomas Moorer. On 24 Dec, Nixon opined that Moorer was part of a system that "goes back over years." *Foreign Relations of the United States 1969–1976*, vol. II, 337, available at http://www.fas.org/sgp/news/2007/03/radford.pdf; and John Ehrlichman, *Witness to Power* (New York: Simon & Schuster, 1982), 303–10.

65. Agenda of the B-36 Investigation, 9 Jun 49, "B-36 Investigation (File No. 1)," HVP, 1.

66. In Re: H. Res. 234, vol. 11, 25 Aug 49, DASCCS, 1459–60.

67. Navy Position, Oct 49, "1," ADCOSI.

68. In Re: H. Res. 234, vol. 17, 11 Oct 49, DASCCS, 1907–8.

69. Ibid., vol. 14, 1717.

70. Ibid., vol. 17, 1914.

71. "Navy Position," 1.

72. Testimony before the HASC, "B-36 Investigation (File No. 1)," HVP, 7–9.

73. In Re: H. Res. 234, vol. 22, 19 Oct 49, DASCCS, 2574.

74. Ibid., vol. 21, DASCCS, 2451.

75. Ibid., vol. 21, 2450.

76. Ibid., vol. 19, 2328–29.

77. Ibid., vol. 14, 1699–1700.

78. Ibid., vol. 22, 2567–70.

79. Ibid., vol. 17, 1914.

80. Topical Digest of Testimony before HASC during Hearings on the B-36 and Related Matters, Oct 49, Part III, "1," ADCOSI.

81. In Re: H. Res. 234 vol. 22, 2721.

82. Vandenberg Testimony, 6; "Topical Digest III."

83. Memo to Parrish, 2.

84. O'Donnell to Stratemeyer, 13 Aug 50, "Stratemeyer," Box B-59, CL.

85. Stratemeyer to O'Donnell, 15 Sep 50, "Stratemeyer," CL, 1–2.

86. History of SAC, Jul–Dec 50, vol. 1," Dec 50, 501938, HRA, 32.

87. Ibid., 9–12.

88. Report of Trip, 5 Oct 50, 908280, HRA.

89. Korean Evaluation Project, 16 Jan 51, 472470, HRA, Sec 8, 1–2.

90. Statements before Congress at MacArthur Hearings, 28 May 51, "General Vandenberg's Speeches - 1951," HVP.

91. Ibid.

92. Vandenberg to Stratemeyer, 3 Jul 50, "LeMay Diary No. 2 1 Jul 50 to 30 Dec 50," CL, 2.

93. O'Donnell to LeMay, 21 Jul 50, "LeMay Diary No. 2 1 Jul 50 to 30 Dec 50," CL, 2.

94. Memo of Conversation, 19 Dec 50, "24 Massive Chinese Communist Intervention and Allied Reactions," TDSKSR, 3.

95. LeMay to Stratemeyer, 6 Mar 51, "Stratemeyer," CL.

96. Stratemeyer to LeMay (w/attach memo LeMay to Montgomery)," 16 Feb 51, "Stratemeyer," CL.

97. LeMay to White, 12 Jun 52, "White, Thomas D," CL.

98. LeMay to Twining, 5 Jun 52, "Twining," CL.

99. Notes on Fear of Flying Policy, "LeMay Diary No. 4 1952," CL.

100. Transcript of phone conversation LeMay and Wetzel, 26 Mar 52, "LeMay Diary No. 4 1952," CL.

101. Acheson to Paul, 12 Jul 50, "July 1950," TDAMC, 1.

102. NSC 73, attach to Lay to Dennison, 1 Jul 50, "Meetings 63 (August 3, 1950)," TPSNSC, 7.

103. NSC 76, 21 Jul 50, "Meetings 62 (July 27, 1950)," TPSNSC, 2.

104. Study of Effectiveness of Action to Counter Chicom Aggression, 14 Dec 50, "Meetings 75 (December 14, 1950)," TPSNSC, 2.

105. Bevin to Franks, 11 Oct 50, "20 Efforts to Prevent Enlargement of Hostilities," TDSKSR.

106. White House Press and Radio News Conf, 30 Nov 50, "25 Allied Criticisms of the UN Commander," TDSKSR.

107. Acheson to Moscow et al., 30 Nov 50, "25 Reactions to President's Statement re Possible Use of Atom Bomb," TDSKSR.

108. NSC 93, 12 Dec 50, "Meetings 82 (February 1, 1951)," TPSNSC, 2.

109. SM-3038-50, 14 Dec 50, "CJCS 091 Korea 1950," JCFGB.

110. Remarks of Twining, Business Advisory Council, The Modern Air Weapon, 13 Mar 52, "Speeches—by Twining (1952)," MS22, 4.

111. JCS 1924/67, 24 Jul 52, "CCS 092 USSR (3-27-45) Sec. 62," JGF51.

112. Nichols to Pace, NH00049, NSANH, 2.

113. Transcript of Briefings, 30 Nov 52, "OPD 381 Korea (9 May 47) Sec 18," AFPDF, 18–20.

114. Possible Effects of Bombing in Manchuria, 31 Dec 52, "Current Hold Here for Gen Van," HV.

115. Interim Estimate of Types and Numbers of Targets for Accomplishing Specified Purposes in Far East, c Dec 52, "OPD 381 Korea (9 May 47) Sec 18," AFPDF.

116. Lee to Twining, 10 Feb 53, "OPD 381 Korea (9 May 47) Sec 20," AFPDF.

117. Thatcher to White (JCS 1776/354), 16 Feb 53, "OPD 381 Korea (9 May 47) Sec 20," AFPDF.

118. Ibid.

119. Air Force Flimsy, 22 Mar 53, "OPD 381 Korea (9 May 47) Sec 21," AFPDF, 2.

120. JCS 1776/367, 27 Mar 53, "OPD 381 Korea (9 May 47) Sec 22," AFPDF, 2236–40.

121. SE 41, 31 Mar 53, "139th Meeting," NOMM, 15.

122. Lee to USAF Chief of Staff, 11 May 53, "OPD 381 Korea (9 May 47) Sec 23," AFPDF.

123. Lee to DCSO, 30 Jun 53, "OPD 381 Korea (9 May 47) Sec 25," AFPDF, 1; Lee to Chief of Staff, 6 Jul 53, "OPD 381 Korea (9 May 47) Sec 25," AFPDF, 2.

124. Air Force Position on Questions Regarding the 'New Look," 1954, "National Security Policy 1948–1953, 1963," MS22.

125. William Stueck, *The Korean War* (Princeton, NJ: Princeton University Press, 1995), 329–30.

126. Young to Lee, 16 Sep 52, "OPD 385 (RAND) (5 Feb 48) Sec. 3," AFPDF.

127. Air Power in the Land Struggle for Europe, 31 Aug 51, "General Vandenberg's Speeches - 1951," HVP.

128. Col. Willis Carter, "Strategic Bombardment and National Objectives," *Air University Quarterly Review* 4.3 (Spring 1951): 8.

129. Remarks by LeMay at Naval War College, 20 Feb 58, "Cleared Copies Oct 1957–Sep 1958 (General LeMay)," CL, 16.

130. Interview of Twining, Nov 1965, 904883, HRA, 21.

4. THE FANTASTIC COMPRESSION OF TIME

1. CG's Diary, 25 Sep 50, "LeMay Diary No. 2 1 Jul 50 to 30 Dec 50," CL.

2. SE-10, 15 Sep 51, "17," NNIE, 1–3.

3. JCS 2081/1, 13 Feb 50, "CCS 471.6 (11-8-49) S. 2," JGF54, 12.

4. USAF Presentation to Senate Appropriations Cmte 4th Supplemental Estimates, FY 1951, "Speeches and Writings 1951," LNT, 1.

5. NSC 68/3 (Annexes), 8 Dec 50, "Meetings 75 (December 14, 1950)," TPSNSC, 2.

6. Steven Zaloga, *The Kremlin's Nuclear Sword* (Washington, DC: Smithsonian, 2002), 21.

7. Ibid., 22–31.

8. Richard Rhodes, *Arsenals of Folly* (New York: Vintage, 2008), 93.

9. John Prados, *The Soviet Estimate* (New York: Dial, 1982).

10. Ibid., 124–26.

11. Speech by Power to Missouri Bankers Association, 12 May 59, "1-B-16," MS58, 3.

12. Address by LeMay to the Annual Conference of Engineers, 6 May 55, "6," SMS649, 1.

13. Information Services Fact Sheet No. 3-56, 19 May 56, "Army-Navy-Air Force 'Inter-Service Rivalry,'" LNT, 6.

14. CG's Diary, 18 Apr 50, "LeMay Diary No. 1 1 Jan 50 to 30 Jun 50," CL, 1.

15. *A History of Strategic Arms Competition 1945–1972*, vol. 2, 1 Jan 76, 1012425, HRA, 113.

16. Ibid., 162.

17. SNIE 11-8-54, 14 Sep 54, "68," NNIE, 3.

18. NSC 5515/1, 1 Apr 55, "NSC 5515/1," NPP, 4–7.

19. NIE 11-6-55, 1 Jul 55, "80," NNIE, 2–4.

20. NIE 11-3-57, 18 Jun 57, "1," NNIE, 6.

21. CM-430-59, 20 Nov 59, "JCS Memoranda CM 1959 May–Dec," LNT, 1.

22. Donnelly to White, 25 Jan 60, "2–15 SAC," LTW, 1.

23. "Jet Strategic Bombardment-1952," *Air University Quarterly Review* 5.1 (Winter 1951–52): 19.

24. Concepts of Strategic Air Warfare, 3 Dec 51, 483198, HRA, 15.

25. Proceedings, 19 Jun 53, AFPDF, 15.

26. AFOPD to Assistant for Programming, 23 July 1951, "OPD 110.01 (27 Aug 47) Sec 19," A335, 3.

27. Views of the Chief of Staff USAF on US Program for National Security, "Nuclear Weapons 1952–61," MS22, 3.

28. Lt. Gen. Laurence Kuter, "No Room for Error," *Air Force* 37.11 (Nov 1954): 30.

29. Issues Underlying Service Differences of View in the JSCP, 25 Sep 53, "Nuclear Weapons 1952–61," MS22, 2.

30. AF Commanders Conf 24 May 1954 (verbatim proceedings), "Secretariat Air Force Council Commanders Conference 1955," AFC54, 67.

31. "Must Atomic Weapons Be Used?" Jun 60, 125985, RR, 10.

32. Commanders Conf, Ramey AFB, PR, 23-5 Jan 56 (Verbatim Transcript), vol. 1, 23 Jan 56, "Secretariat Air Force Council Commanders Conference 1956," AFC54, 31.

33. Lee to Asst Dep Chief of Staff for Ops, 27 Jan 53, "OPD 334.8 Objectives Comte (12 Jun 52)," AFPDF, 1.

34. AF Manual 1-2, Mar 53, Call No. K168.13001-2, HRA, 11.

35. Gen. Thomas White, "The Current Concept of American Military Strength," *Air University Quarterly Review* 7.1 (Spring 1954): 8.

36. "Some Reasons Behind the Views of the AF," 126254, JW, 7.

37. Col. Robert Richardson III, "Atomic Weapons and Theater Warfare (Parts 3 and 4)," *Air University Quarterly Review* 7.4 (Spring 1955): 94.

38. David Snead, *The Gaither Committee, Eisenhower, and the Cold War* (Columbus: Ohio State University Press, 1999), 33.

39. "The Security of the US from Air Attack in the Thermonuclear Age," vol. 1, Jul 1954, 480513, HRA, 86.

40. Presentation, FY 1953, 8 May 52, "FY53 Presentation to Approp Comm," HVP, 25.

41. Whitehead to Schoeppel, 18 Dec 57, "Congressional (M–Z)," LTW, 2.

42. Twining Rmks to Armed Forces Staff College, 9 Apr 56, "Speeches—by Twining (1956)," MS22, 15.

43. Q&A following LeMay address to Georgetown, 3 Dec 56, "7," SMS649, 2.

44. Address by LeMay to Harvard Adv Mgt Assoc," 6 Dec 55, "6," SMS649, 2.

45. Tilley to Cmd Sect, 26 Sep 56, "7-C-2," MS58, 2.

46. Security of US from Air Attack, vol. 1, 31.

47. Ibid., 39.

48. Address by Power to Chicago Assoc of Comm & Ind, 20 Mar 58, "7-C-2," MS58, 6.

49. Interview w/Price of AP, 5 Feb 60, "Speeches by General White (January Thru June 1960)," LTW, 7.

50. AF Manual 1-2, 1 Apr 55, 127266, HRA, 7.

51. Air Doctrine and the Realities of the Cold War World, Mar 55, "6," LK, 13.

52. Tami Davis Biddle, "Handling the Soviet Threat," *Journal of Strategic Studies* 12.3 (1989): 273–302; John Ferris, *Men, Money, and Diplomacy* (Ithaca, NY: Cornell University Press, 1989).

53. AF Manual 1-2 55, 1.

54. Air Doctrine, 11.

55. AF Objectives [Split], 1 Nov 57, "Split," LTW, 3.

56. Ibid., 8.

57. Ibid., 18.

58. Memo for Record: Commanders' Conf, 4–7 Nov 57, 19 Nov 57, "Conference 4 November 1957," TDW.

59. War Plans Digest, 20 Sep 51, "OPD 381 (24 Aug 51)," A335, 5–6.

60. Air Force Emergency War Plan 1-52 (AFEWP 1-52), vol. 1, "OPD 381 (2 May 50) Section 3," AFPDF, App A, Ann E, 1.

61. Air Power in an Overall Strategy, 23 May 51, 483196, HRA, 18.

62. LeMay's Diary, 6 Jul 51, "LeMay Diary No.3 1951," CL.

63. Strat Vuln of Sov Mil Strengths, 5 Feb 54, 918350, HRA, I-8.

64. Application of the Horizontal Approach to the S V of the USSR, 12 Dec 51, 1005746, HRA, 6–12.

65. Target System for FY52, "Notes for Commander's Conference 7 Nov 51," CL, 14.

66. CG Diary, 23 Jan 51, "LeMay Diary No. 3 1951," CL.

67. Edwards to LeMay, 18 May 51, "Edwards," CL, 1.

68. Strat Vuln, II-21.

69. Lee to CINCSAC, 2 Aug 55, "INT 4-1-1 Weapons Effect January–December 1955," Box 27, AIC.

70. CG Diary, 16 Mar 53, "LeMay Diary No. 5, 1953," CL.

71. A DGZ is the impact point for a single weapon and can be selected to damage more than one target. In this case, the increased weight of attack is still evident.

72. LeMay to Finletter, May 50, "LeMay Diary No. 1 1 Jan 50 to 30 Jun 50," CL, 5.

73. Finletter to Vandenberg, 12 May 50, "Memos SecAF to CS USAF," HV, 2.

74. JIC 439/47/D, 20 Nov 52, "CCS 373.11 (12-14-48) Sec. 9," JCDF2, 1; assessing SAC's success in gaining the intelligence it required for striking these targets would require access to unreleased target folders. Such a study would need to examine when sufficient information to strike a target—generally the acquisition of accurate location information, preferably with photographs and radar overlays—became available. The only two examinations of this question, William Burrows' *By Any Means Necessary* and John Farquhar's *A Need to Know*, do not address the issue from this angle. The former is largely anecdotal and the latter ends its coverage in 1953. Nonetheless, the push in the early 1960s for a "reconnaissance-strike" aircraft (i.e., RS-70) strongly implies that many targets, especially mobile strategic forces, were at best imperfectly located. Their general location might be known from intelligence means, but not well enough to preplan a strike. Instead, an aircraft with ground imaging radar would have to be sent to find and destroy them.

75. Strat Vuln, I-12.

76. Ibid., I-14-15.

77. Developments in Air Targeting, Spr 58, CIA-RDP78T03194A000100020001-2, CR, 14.

78. "A History of Strategic Arms Competition 1945–1972, Volume 2: A Handbook of Selected U.S. Weapon Systems," January 1, 1976, Iris No. 1012425, Air Force Historical Research Agency, Maxwell Air Force Base, Alabama, 95.

79. Anderson to LeMay, 3 Jan 52, "Anderson, S. E.," CL, 3.

80. Ahring to Dir of Intel, 25 Aug 53, "OPD 385 (RAND) (5 Feb 48) Sec. 4," AFPDF, 2.

81. Harris to Dir of Plans, 8 May 53, "OPD 385 (RAND) (5 Feb 48) Sec. 4," AFDPF.

82. DoD Rpt to NSC on Status of US Mil Pgms as of 30 Jun 58, 22 Sep 58, "OMM 388 (Folder 1 of 2)," NOMM, 3.

83. Memo for SecDef, 2 Oct 59, "Memos 1 OC 1959 Nos 405–10," LNT, 5.

84. Memo for SecDef, 18 Aug 60, "JCS Memoranda Aug 1960," LNT, app b, 8.

85. Alert and Evacuation Test Ops Order 10-53, 8 Feb 54, "LeMay Diary No. 6, 1954," CL.

86. SAC Cdrs Conf, 12 Apr 55, CL, 2.

87. Untitled: SAC's capability to penetrate Russia's defenses, 20 Feb 56, "Budget - Fiscal Year 1957 (Part II)," MS22, 2.

88. McConnell Rpt, 30 Sep 57, "McConnell Report," LTW, 9.

89. Power to White, 22 Oct 58, "1958 Top Secret File (4)," LTW, 1.

90. LeMay to Power, 12 Feb 59, "AFCCS Reading File Feb 1959," LTW, 1.

91. Airborne Alert, 26 Oct 60, "CCS 3340 Strategic Air and ICBM Opns (23 Jun 1960)," JCDF60, 3–8; SAC Hist Jul–Dec 59, vol. 6, 502050, HRA, 3.

92. SAC Hist Jul–Dec 59, vol. 5, 502049, HRA, 3–4.

93. SAC Participation in the Msl Pgm, 30 Mar 57, 1056920, HRA, 2–3.

94. Some Concepts for Retaliatory Employment of Msls, Jul 59, 1056937, HRA, 298.

95. NIE 11-3-64, 16 Dec 64, "18," NNIE, 25.

96. Pavel Podvig, ed., *Russian Strategic Nuclear Forces* (Cambridge, MA: MIT University Press, 2001), 409.

97. NIE 11-3-64, 25.

98. NIE 11-3-66, 7 Nov 66, "41," NNIE, 27.

99. Strat Vuln, I-17.

100. JCS 1952/11, in Ross and Rosenberg, *Plans*, vol. 13, 192; and CG's Diary, 28 Ma 50, "LeMay Diary No. 1 1 Jan 50 to 30 Jun 50," CL, 1.

101. CG's Diary, 9 Mar 51, "LeMay Diary No.3 1951," CL, 1.

102. Strat Vuln, I-18-20.

103. Schneider to Kincaid, 27 Dec 55, "INT 2-4 Capabilities January–December 1955," AIC, 3.

104. Everest to White, 6 Oct 55, "INT 2-2-2 Aircraft and Aircraft Engines July–December 1955," AIC, 1–2.

105. Memo for Record, 27 Jul 59, "16–30 Jul 1959," ABPR, 2.

106. Memo, 22 Jan 59, "394th Meeting of the NSC," ENAW, 10.

107. Address by LeMay to Chamber of Commerce in Columbus, 19 May 51, "2," SMS649, 6–7.

108. CG's Diary, 17 Jan 51, "LeMay Diary No. 3 1951," CL, 1; and C. Young, Application, 12 Dec 51, 1005746, HRA, 16.

109. Lt. Gen. Curtis LeMay, Tactics of Strategic Bombing, 28 Mar 51, 483265, HRA, 11.

110. SAC Targeting Concepts, Apr 59, "SAC Targets," ERC, 16.

111. Brothers to DCSO, 11 Aug 54, "TS No. 1031 Aircraft Attrition Rates Suggested by Operations Analysis for Use in WPB-58," AOA, 1.

112. SM 763-56, 19 Sep 56, "CCS 381 U.S. (1-31-50) Sec. 66," JCDF57, 1–2.

113. Memo for SecDef: JCSM-3-60, 8 Jan 60, "Memos 7-8 JA 1960 Nos 1–5," LNT, 15–17.

114. Application of the Horizontal Approach, 14.

115. Operations Analysis Special Technical Memo No. 18, 16 Sep 53, "TS No. 915 Operations Analysis Special Report No. 18," AOA, 2–3.

116. A single designated ground zero could contain several targets.

117. The AF—Present and Future, 25 May 51, "Hoyt S. Vandenberg - Future Speeches," HVP, 8–9.

118. Commanders Conf, Ramey AFB, 23-5 Jan 56 (Verbatim Transcript), vol. 1, "Secretariat Air Force Council Commanders Conference 1956," AFC54, 34–35.

119. USAF Statistical Digest, FY60, Call No. K134.11-6, AFHRA.

120. J Hopkins, Development of SAC, 1 Jul 82, 1129061, HRA, 87.

121. Smith to Dulles, 25 Nov 58, NH00377, NSANH, 1.

122. AF Commanders Conf 17-9 Jan 55 (verbatim proceedings), vol. 1, "Secretariat Air Force Council Commanders Conference 1955," AFC54, 10.

123. Burke to Felt, 14 Aug 59, "12–30 Sep 1959," ABPR, 1.

124. Samford to White, 18 May 55, "INT 2-2-2 Aircraft and Aircraft Engines January–June 1955," AIC.

125. Handbook, 162–63, 183–84.

126. Putt testimony before the Symington Subcommittee, 15 May 56, "1956 Symington Committee," LNT, 9.

127. White to SECAF, 2 Aug 57, "Secretary of the Air Force," LTW, 8.

128. Handbook, 296–97.

129. White to SECAF, 2 Aug 57, 9.

130. LeMay to Twining, 26 Nov 55, "1955 Command - Strategic Air Command," LNT, 1.

131. Remarks to Air War College, 6 Jun 56, "Speeches—by Twining (1956)," MS22, 13.

132. Address by LeMay to the Institute of Aeronautical Sciences, 15 Jul 53, "4," SMS649, 11.

133. History of SAC, Jan–Jun 52, vol. 2, 501950, HRA, 5–7.

134. Gen. Thomas S. Power, "SAC and the Ballistic Missile," *Air University Quarterly Review* 9.4 (Winter 1957–58): 11–16.

135. LeMay to Twining, 20 Jul 56, "1956 Command - Strategic Air," LNT, 2.

136. Handbook, 401–8.

137. Handbook, 452–58.

138. LeMay to Twining, 20 Jul 56, 2.

139. LeMay to Quarles, 5 Mar 57, "1957 Command - Strategic Air," LNT, 1.

140. LeMay to White, 5 Feb 60, "5-1 Air Force Council (Folder 1) Jan–June 1960 Correspondence," LTW, atch 1.

141. Commanders Conference, Headquarters USAF—The Pentagon, 22 Jan 51, CL, 36.

142. MG Richard Lindsay, "How the Air Force Will Use Its Missiles," *Air Force* 39.9 (Sept 1956): 100.

143. Irvine to LeMay, 11 Mar 53, "Irvine No. 2," CL, 3.

5. TO KILL A NATION

1. Robert Bowie and Richard Immerman, *Waging Peace* (New York: Oxford, 1998).

2. Lawrence Freedman, *The Evolution of Nuclear Strategy*, 3rd ed. (London: Palgrave, 2003), 149–50.

3. Report to the President on the Threat of Surprise Attack, 14 Mar 55, NH01319, NSANH, 1–2.

4. NSC 5724, 7 Nov 57, "NSC 5724," NPP, 5–7.

5. Freedman, *Evolution of Nuclear Strategy*, 151–52.

6. Index to WSEG Pubs, Apr 74, 1001083, HRA.

7. JCS 1953/22, "373 (10-23-48) B.P. Pt 3A," JGF54, 406–18.

8. Annex 3, NSC 68/3 (Annexes), 8 Dec 50, "Meetings 75 (December 14, 1950)," TP-SNSC, 2.

9. NSC 140, 19 Jan 53, "NSC 140," NPP, 1.

10. NSC 140/1, 18 May 53, "NSC 140/1," NPP.

11. Ibid., 7.

12. Memo for Record, 10 Feb 56, "Correspondence February 56," ABPR, 2.

13. Chairman's Staff Gp to Adm Radford, 1 Nov 56, "381 (Net Evaluation) (1956)," NCFR, 7.

14. 1957 Report of NESC, 15 Nov 57, "1957 Report of the Net Evaluation Subcommittee," EINSCP.

15. 1958 Report of NESC, 10 Nov 58, "1958 Report of the Net Evaluation Subcommittee," EINSCP, 9–15.

16. Other US forces were presumably destroyed.

17. Ibid., 23.

18. Ibid., 24.

19. Ibid., 26.

20. 1959 Report of NESC, c Nov 59, "1959 Report of the Net Evaluation Subcommittee," EINSCP, 8–10.

21. Ibid., 16.

22. Bowie and Immerman, *Waging Peace*, 194.

23. Evan Thomas, *Ike's Bluff* (New York: Little, Brown, 2012).

24. Solarium Project, 8 May 53, "Project Solarium (3)," ESSF, 1.

25. Solarium TF A Rpt, 16 Jul 53, "Project Solarium Report to NSC by Task Force A (3)," ENSSWS, 22.

26. Ibid., 56.

27. Solarium TF B Rpt, 16 Jul 53, "Project Solarium Report to NSC by Task Force B (1)," ENSSWS, 2.

28. Ibid., 4.

29. Ibid., 5.

30. Ibid., 12.

31. Ibid., 48.

32. Ibid., 1.

33. Ibid., 1–4.

34. Solarium TF C Rpt, 16 Jul 53, "Project Solarium Report to NSC by Task Force C (1)," ENSSWS, 3.

35. Ibid., 8.

36. Ibid., 13.

37. Ibid., 15–16.

38. Ibid., 85–91.

39. Ibid., 29.

40. John Gaddis, *Strategies of Containment* (New York: Oxford, 1982), 141–42.

41. Cutler to Smith, 31 Jul 53, "Special Assistant (Cutler) Memoranda 1953 (4)," ENSSWS.

42. Interview of Gen. Andrew Goodpaster, 10 Apr 82, DDE, 14.

43. Dennis Showalter, *Forging the Shield* (Chicago: Imprint, 2005), 212.

44. NSC-162/2, quoted in *Foreign Relations of the United States,* 1952–54, vol. 2 (Washington, DC: GPO, 1984), 578 (hereafter *FRUS*).

45. Ibid., 582.

46. Ibid., 579.

47. Ibid., 581.

48. Ibid., 593.

49. Meaning of Para 39b, as Understood by DoD, 1 Dec 53, "Policy re Use (File No. 1) (1)," ESSF, 2.

50. Smith to Eisenhower, 3 Dec 53, "Atomic Energy - The President (2)," ENSSWS.

51. Strauss to Cutler, 3 Dec 53, "Atomic Weapons Correspondence and Background for Presidential Approval (1)," ENSSWS.

52. Lay to Eisenhower, 31 Dec 53, "Atomic Weapons Correspondence and Background for Presidential Approval (1)," ENSSWS.

53. Showalter, *Forging the Shield,* 214.

54. Eisenhower to Wilson, 5 Jan 55, Box 27, Ridgway Papers, quoted in A. Bacevich, "The Paradox of Professionalism," *Journal of Military History* 61.2 (Apr 1997), 329–30.

55. JCS 2101/113," 10 Dec 53, "CCS 381 U.S (1-51-50) Sec. 32," JGF54, 1085.

56. NSC 5501, quoted in *FRUS,* 1955–57, vol. 19 (Washington: GPO, 1990), 25.

57. Ibid., 26.

58. Ibid., 32.

59. Ibid.

60. Ibid., 33. The mid-decade BNSPs did reflect a divergence of opinion between Eisenhower and his senior advisors, principally Dulles, about the role of nuclear weapons in limited war. According to Campbell Craig, Dulles sought to add "flexibility" to American policy in limited conflicts by expanding the role of conventional and tactical nuclear forces. This was a shift from his previous position of advocating general war in crisis situations. See Campbell Craig, *Destroying the Village* (New York: Columbia, 1998), 50–52.

61. NSC 5906/1, 5 Aug 59, "NSC 5906/1," NPP, 6–7.
62. Cutler to Eisenhower, 2 Jun 53, "155th Meeting," NOMM.
63. Bowie and Immerman, *Waging Peace*, 164.
64. Ibid.
65. Cutler to Adams, 2 Aug 54, "Special Assistant (Cutler) - Memoranda 1954 (8)," ESSF, 1–2.
66. Transcript of DDE Press Conf No. 48, 11 Aug 54, "Press Conference 8/11/54," EPAW.
67. Marc Trachtenberg, "Preventive War and U.S. Foreign Policy," *Security Studies* 16.1 (2007): 7.
68. NSC 5410, 19 Feb 54, "NSC 5410," NPP, 1–2.
69. JCS to SecDef, 15 Mar 54, "Background documents on NSC 5410," NPP.
70. NSC 5904, 19 Feb 59, "NSC 5904," NPP.
71. Statement by Acting SecDef on Transfer of Custody of Atomic Weapons, 28 Apr 53, "Defense Interest (6)," ESSF.
72. Lay to Eisenhower, 16 Dec 53, "Atomic Energy - The President (2)," ENSSWS.
73. Smyth to the NSC Exec Sec, 1 May 53, "Defense Interest (6)," ESSF.
74. Statement by Acting SecDef.
75. Memo of Conf w/President, 6 Nov 59, NH00681, NSANH.
76. Memo of Conf w/President, 2 Jan 60, NH00506, NSANH.
77. John Gaddis, *The Cold War* (New York: Penguin, 2005), 66–68.
78. Campbell Craig, *Glimmer of a New Leviathan* (New York: Columbia, 2003), 69.
79. AF Position on Questions Regarding 'New Look,' "National Security Policy 1948–1953," MS22.
80. JCS to SecDef, 21 May 54, "200th meeting," NOMM.
81. Status of SAC Far East Outline Plan 8-54, Feb 54, "LeMay Diary No. 6, 1954," CL.
82. SNIE 10-4-54, 15 Jun 54, "63," Box 2, NNIE, 5.
83. AF Cdrs Conf 24 May 54 (verbatim proceedings), "Secretariat Air Force Council Commanders Conference 1955," AF54, 66.
84. Ibid., 67.
85. Alexander George and Richard Smoke, *Deterrence in American Foreign Policy* (New York: Columbia, 1974), 279–91.
86. Radford to Wilson, 11 Sep 54, "091 China (Sep 54)," NCFR, 4.
87. Goodpaster to Cutler, 16 Mar 55, "240th Meeting," NOMM, 1.
88. Totten to CJCS, 16 Mar 55, "091 China (Feb-Mar 55)," NCFR.
89. US Military Courses of Action, 31 Mar 55, "091 China (Feb–Mar 55)," NCFR.
90. SNIE 11-5-54, 7 Jun 54, "62," NNIE, 2–3.
91. George and Smoke, *Deterrence*, 291–92.
92. Estimate of Factors, Sep 58, "Staff Notes Sep '58," EDAW.
93. George and Smoke, *Deterrence*, 361–67.
94. JCS to CINCPAC, 25 Aug 58, "Formosa [1958] (3)," EIAW, 5.
95. Conf w/President, 29 Aug 58, "Formosa [1958] (3)," EIAW.
96. Conversation between the President, Lloyd, and Caccia, 21 Sep 58, "Staff Notes Sep '58," EDAW.
97. Burke to Felt, 18 Sep 58, "Sep 1958," ABPR, 2.
98. Twining to SecDef, Sep 58, "Formosa [1958] (2)," EIAW, App 3–9; JCS 947046, 25 Aug 58, "CJCS (Radford) 091 China (1957) No 1," NCFR.
99. MemCon, 2 Sep 58, "Formosa [1958] (2)," EIAW, 5.
100. Sherrill to Goodpaster, 3 Sep 58, "Formosa [1958] (3)," EIAW. A May 1958 study named Sierra estimated that wider attacks on Chinese military targets with ground bursts would inflict 16.5 million casualties, but that the same effect could be produced less lethally with air bursts. See "Observations on Sierra Briefing," 1 May 58, DDE.

101. Taiwan Straits, 4 Sep 58, "Formosa [1958] (2)," EIAW, 3–4.

102. JCS 2295/1, 1 Dec 58, "CCS 319.1 (11-18-58)," JCDF58, 5–6.

103. Boggs to NSC Planning Board, 2 Mar 59, "Mill 200," NMP.

104. Report on Taiwan Straits Situation, Nov 58, "Quemoy Crisis," MS18, 10–11.

105. Notes on Commander's Conf, 20 Nov 58, "Quemoy Crisis," MS18, 5. General Dean, interviewed in 1975, however, doubted that using a few atomic bombs on the Chinese would have made a measurable difference. "China is so large, and they are so unindustrialized, we could have certainly caused discombobulation, but it's sort of like fighting feathers." Interview of Lt. Gen. Fred Dean, AFA.

106. Aleksandr Fursenko and Timothy Naftali, *Khrushchev's Cold War* (New York: Norton, 2010), 194.

107. *FRUS*, 1961–63, vol. 6, Doc 65.

108. Bacevich, "Paradox," 303–34.

109. Erin R Mahan and Jeffrey A Larsen, *Evolution of the Secretary of Defense in the Era of Massive Retaliation*, vol. 3, Special Studies (Washington, DC: Historical Office, Office of the Secretary of Defense, 2012) [OSD history].

6. STALEMATE, FINITE DETERRENCE, POLARIS, AND SIOP-62

1. CASFM 458–59, 15 Oct 59, "CCS 3120 JSCP (23 Mar 1959)," JCDF59.

2. Army Flimsy, 25 Sep 59, "CCS 3120 JSCP (23 Mar 1959)," JCDF59, 2–3.

3. CASFM 458–59.

4. Army Flimsy, 4.

5. Army Flimsy on JSPC 895/24, 16 Oct 57, "CCS 381 USSR (3-2-46) Sec. 73," JGF57, 1.

6. Maxwell Taylor, *The Uncertain Trumpet* (New York: Harper, 1960), 64.

7. Ibid., 14.

8. Ibid., 7.

9. McConnell Report, 30 Sep 57, "McConnell Report," LTW, 6.

10. Taylor, *Uncertain Trumpet*, 136.

11. Untitled doc: Army positions w/rebuttals, c1956, "Army-Navy-Air Force 'Inter-Service Rivalry'," LNT.

12. Ibid., 13.

13. Remarks by LeMay at Amer News Pub Assoc, 18 Apr 58, "Cleared Copies Oct 1957–Sep 1958 (General LeMay)," CL, 5.

14. Address by LeMay to the 50 Club, 31 Oct 55, "6," SMS649.

15. Maj. Gen. John Cary, AF View of Force in Limited War, 16 Apr 57, 918391, HRA, 6–8.

16. Col. W. Erwin, "Air Power, Political Realities, and the Cold War," Jun 56, 480318, HRA, 88.

17. Ibid.

18. Questions to Be Asked during DoD Interview, 12 Apr 17, "General White's Statements (Jan–Dec 1957)," LTW, 9.

19. Tilley to Cmd Sect, 26 Sep 56, "7-C-2," MS58.

20. Tilley to Power, 26 Aug 57, "7-B-11," MS58.

21. Gen. Frederic Smith, "Nuclear Weapons and Limited War," *Air University Quarterly Review* 12.1 (Spring 1960): 14–26.

22. Memcon w/President, 24 May 56, "May '56 Goodpaster," EAWD, 1–2.

23. Remarks during Telcon LeMay and White, 16 Jul 52, "LeMay Diary No. 4 1952," CL.

24. Roles and Missions of the Services, Dec 52, "Alness Comte Report Folder 1 of 12," AFPDF.

25. Memo for General White, 1 Aug 52, "Budget - FY 1953," MS22.

26. Sluman to Harris, 27 Feb 53, "OPD 385 (RAND) (5 Feb 48) Sec. 3," AFPDF, 1.

27. Untitled: Navy positions w/rebuttals, "Folder - Army-Navy-Air Force 'Inter-Service Rivalry,'" LNT.

28. Roles and Missions of the Services App I, c. Dec 52, "Alness Comte Report Folder 2 of 12," AFPDF.

29. Memo for Gen Vandenberg, 11 Mar 53, "Miscellaneous Actions and Policy Papers 1950–1951," LNT.

30. Potts to Vandenberg, 3 Apr 52, "Draft JCS Paper: Carrier Task Forces - SF 36-59 - 1952," AVTS, 2.

31. Ibid., 3–7.

32. Fast Carrier TF Study Could Have Been Related to Specific Plans, No. 2, Jun 52, "Draft JCS Paper: Carrier Task Forces - SF 36-59 - 1952," AVTS, 13.

33. Insert for Record, Page 180, SASC, "Budget - Fiscal Year 1957 (Part II)," MS22.

34. Lindsay to Twining, 15 Jan 55, "045 (22 Jan 48) Sect 1 A," A335, 1.

35. Ibid., 5.

36. Ibid., 7.

37. Lindsay to AFODC, 15 Jan 55, "1955 Organization," LNT.

38. White to DCS/O, 7 Dec 54, "1954 Organization (2)," LNT, 1.

39. Lindsay to Asst Vice Chief of Staff, 18 Oct 55, "045 (22 Jan 48) Sect 1 A," A335.

40. Commanders Conf, Ramey, vol. 1," 23 Jan 56, "Secretariat Air Force Council Commanders Conference 1956," AFC54, 26.

41. LeMay to Everest, 25 Jul 55, "Everest," CL.

42. John Pike, P6M, http://www.globalsecurity.org/military/systems/aircraft/p6m .htm.

43. Colin Gray, *Modern Strategy* (New York: Oxford, 1999), 237.

44. JCS 2056/35, 9 Sep 52, "CCS 373.11 (12-14-48) Sec. 9," JCDF2, 266–67.

45. JCS 2056/24, 21 Feb 52, "CCS 373 (10-23-48) Sec. 6," JCDF2, 195–203.

46. JCS 2056/29, 2 Jun 52, "CCS 373.11 (12-14-48) Sec. 7," JCDF2, 228–30.

47. JCS 2056/35, 9 Sep 52, "CCS 373.11 (12-14-48) Sec. 9," JCDF2.

48. JCS 2056/39, 10 Feb 53, "CCS 373.11 (12-14-48) Sec. 10," JCDF2, 292–93.

49. History of the JSTPS, NH00026, NSANH, 1–3.

50. Twining to LeMay, 9 Jun 55, "Twining," CL.

51. General Curtis LeMay, "The Strategic Air Command," 28 Jan 54, NH00482, NSANH, 6–7.

52. LeMay to Twining, 2 Jun 56, "Unmarked," Box 194 (Unsorted), CL.

53. JCS 1953/11, 26 May 52, "CCS 373 (10-23-48) Sec. 7," JCDF2, 310–11.

54. Bernard Brodie, "The Anatomy of Deterrence," *World Politics* 11.2 (Jan 1959): 179.

55. Ibid., 181–86.

56. Wheless to Westover, 12 May 59, "Command - SAC," LTW, 1.

57. Memo for SecDef, 8 Jun 59, "Memos 8 JE 1959 Nos 217," LNT, app b, 3.

58. Memo for All Flag Officers, 4 Mar 59, "3–9 Mar 59," Box 5, ABPR.

59. Address by Burke, 8 Oct 59, "Oct 1959," ABPR, 10.

60. "Dope," 2 Feb 60, "1–13 Feb 1960," ABPR.

61. Speech by Power to Missouri Bankers Assoc, 12 May 59, "1-B-16," MS58.

62. The terms *minimum* and *finite* deterrence were used freely within Air Force documents to refer to the same theory. The arguments made against one were replicated against the other.

63. Brig. Gen. Robert Richardson, Analysis of Deterrence and Related Concepts, 125964, RR; Richardson, Fallacy of the Concept of Minimum Deterrence, 125977, RR.

64. Kuter to White, 31 Dec 58, "Top Secret General 1959," LTW.

65. David Rosenberg, "The Origins of Overkill," *International Security* 7.4 (Spring 1983): 53–54.

66. SAC Targeting Concepts, Apr 59, "SAC Targets," ERC.
67. AF Position on Counterforce, 9 Jun 60, 1028551, HRA, 82.
68. White to Power, 11 May 59, "1959 Top Secret General File," LTW, 2.
69. White to Kuter, 3 Mar 59, "1959 Top Secret General File," LTW.
70. Ibid.
71. Rosenberg, "Origins of Overkill," 54.
72. Memo for Record: Mtg w/Pres, 18 Feb 59, NH00204, NSANH.
73. JCS 2056/121, 20 Feb 59, "CCS 3070 Grand Strategy (20 Feb 1959)," JCDF59.
74. Rosenberg, "Origins of Overkill," 55, 62.
75. CM-465-60, 22 Jan 60, NH00219, NSANH.
76. LeMay, *Mission*, 532.
77. Memo for SecDef, 6 May 60, "Memos 3-10 MY1960 Nos 184–195," LNT, 16–17.
78. Memo for SecDef, 6 May 60; "Memos 3-10 MY1960 Nos 184–195," LNT.
79. Ibid., App B.
80. Ibid., App C.
81. Memo for Record: JCS Mtg with SecDef, 30 Jun 60, "CNO 'Turn-Over' File," vol. 5, 7 Jan 60, DZT60.
82. Memo for Record: 18 Questions discussion, 7 Jul 60, "CNO 'Turn-Over' File," vol. 5, 7 Jan 60, DZT60, 2.
83. Ibid., 3.
84. Ibid., 6–7.
85. Ibid., 8.
86. Ibid., 10.
87. JCS 2056/181, 13 Sep 60, NH00251, NSANH, 1677–78.
88. Minutes of CNO Deputies' Conf, 18 Aug 60, "No. 19: Transcripts and Phonecons (NSTL)," ABPT, 17.
89. Ibid., 20.
90. Burke's instructions to Parker, 21 Aug 60, "No. 19: Transcripts and Phonecons (NSTL)," ABPT.
91. Burke's conversation w/Miller, 29 Aug 60, "No. 19: Transcripts and Phonecons (NSTL)," ABPT.
92. Burke's conversation w/Various Flag Officers, 17 Aug 60, "No. 19: Transcripts and Phonecons (NSTL)," ABPT.
93. Burke's Conversation w/Bardshar, 22 Aug 60, "No. 19: Transcripts and Phonecons (NSTL)," ABPT, 18.
94. Miller to Burke, 15 Nov 60, "Nov 1960," ABPR, 2.
95. Meeting of Admiral Burke w/ Op-06, et al., 2 Nov 60, "Nov 1960," ABPR.
96. White to Power, 26 Nov 60, "2-15 SAC," LTW.
97. Briefing for Pres by CJCS on SIOP-62, 13 Sep 61, NH00333, NSANH, 7.
98. Ibid., 12.
99. Ibid., 14.
100. Ibid., 15.
101. Ibid., 16.
102. Ibid., 17.
103. Special Edition Flag Officers Dope, 4 Dec 60, "1–5 Dec 1960," ABPR, 2–5.
104. Omaha to CINCPACFLT, 1 Nov 60, NH00270, NSANH.
105. Burke's Conversation w/Aurand, 25 Nov 60, "No. 19: Transcripts and Phonecons (NSTL)," ABPT.
106. Memo for Record, 28 Nov 60, "Nov 1960," ABPR.

7. NEW SHERIFF IN TOWN

1. Robert McNamara, *The Essence of Security* (New York: Harper, 1968), x.

2. Bundy to Kennedy, 24 Jan 61, "NSC, Organization and Administration, 1/1/61-1/25/61," KNDN, 4.

3. Marc Trachtenberg, "Preventive War and U.S. Foreign Policy," *Security Studies* 16.1 (2007): 9–10.

4. Interview of Gen. Lauris Norstad, 25 Oct 79, 1077004, HRA, 325.

5. Memo of Conf w/Pres, 24 May 56, "Goodpaster," EDAW, 2.

6. Freedman, *Evolution of Nuclear Strategy*, 218–19.

7. Charles Hitch and Roland McKean, *The Economics of Defense in the Nuclear Age* (Cambridge, MA: Harvard University Press, 1960), 3.

8. Ibid., 119.

9. Taylor to Kennedy, 14 Oct 61, "DoD, Defense Budget, FY 1963, 1/61- 10/61," KNDN, 1.

10. Statement by McNamara before HASC, 27 Jan 64, "Unclassified Statement," RM, 2.

11. Interview of Lt. Gen. Glen Martin, 10 Feb 78, 1028878, HRA, 431.

12. History of Directorate of Plans, vol. 22, 22, NSANH 81.

13. Project 47, 15 Sep 62, "JCS Strategic Nuclear Study Project 47," RM, cover letter, 1.

14. LeMay to White, 12 Apr 61, "Air Force Council," LTW.

15. LeMay to Power, 9 Jun 62, "13-10 SAC (Strategic Air Command) 1962," CL.

16. Collett to Vice Chief of Staff, 12 Dec 64, "5 - Memoranda for the Chief of Staff and Memoranda for Record 1964," ACSD59.

17. Bell to Bundy, 30 Jan 61, "NSC Meetings, 1961, No 475, 2/1/61," KNMM.

18. Enthoven and Smith, *How Much Is Enough?*

19. Although the specific wording changed as PPBS matured, it is interesting to note the linguistic switch from categorizing nuclear weapons as "general war forces" to "strategic offensive forces" while simultaneously renaming "limited war forces" as "general purpose forces." This change in language reflects a fundamental shift in the role of nuclear weapons.

20. LeMay, *Mission*, 8.

21. Interview of Brig. Gen. Cleo Bishop, 8 Jul 76, 1026127, HRA, 111.

22. Interview of Gen. David Burchinal, 11 Apr 75, AFA, 109–12.

23. Interview of Brig. Gen. Noel Parrish, 14 Jun 74, 1006743, HRA, 353–82.

24. Summary of the 1961 New Frontier "Muzzling," "Nuclear Weapons 1952–61," MS22.

25. Charles Stevenson, *SECDEF* (Washington, DC: Potomac, 2006), 25.

26. Freedman, *Evolution of Nuclear Strategy*, 218.

27. Claude Witze, "Is the Stage Being Set for a Political Power Grab in the Pentagon?" *Air Force* 46.5 (May 1963): 26.

28. 1730, 21 May 1963, "X File (2–20 May 1963)," NGA.

29. For the 'X' File, 7 May 1963, "X File (2–20 May 1963)," NGA.

30. Cassiday to AFESSMC, 7 Apr 64, "Defense, Dept of, 11/63, vol. 1," JNA, 2.

31. Interview of Eugene Zuckert, 9 Dec 86, 1000943, HRA, 3.

32. Meeting on Berlin, 18 Jul 61, "Germany (Berlin, General, 7/18/61)," KNC, 2.

33. Memo from McNamara, 31 Dec 63, "LeMay's Memo to President and JCS Views 1964," RM.

34. Memo for Anderson, 16 May 63, "X File (2–20 May 1963)," NGA.

35. Robert Dallek, *An Unfinished Life* (Boston: Little, Brown, 2003), 345.

36. Interview of Gen. David Jones, 14 Mar 86, 1105219, HRA, 70.

37. Interview of Lt. Gen. Glen Martin, 10 Feb 78, 1028878, HRA, 448–49.

38. Dallek, *Unfinished Life*, 345.

39. Chief of Staff's Staff Meeting 5 September 1961, "SAC Reflex Force - 342- 65 - 1961," AVTS, 4.

40. Memo from Jospehson, 21 Aug 64, 355, NSAD, 2.

41. Bundy to Sorenson, 13 Mar 61, "DoD, General, 3/61," KNDN.

42. Interview of Brig. Gen. Noel Parrish, 14 Jun 74, 1006743, HRA, 334–36.

43. Rvw of FY 61-2 Military Prog and Budgets, 21 Feb 61, "DoD Review of FY 61 and FY 62 Military Programs and Budgets, 2/21/61," KNDN, 23.

44. Ibid., 10.

45. Ibid., 3.

46. As Trachtenberg documents, this was not the reality of JFK's crisis management approach. His administration actively considered preventive war against China. See Trachtenberg, "Preventive War," 1–31.

47. Bundy to Sorenson, 13 Mar 61, "DoD, General, 3/61," KNDN.

48. LeMay to Zuckert, 3 Jul 61, "Defense, Secretary of 1961," CL.

49. Remarks of McNamara at Michigan, 7 Jun 62, "DoD, General, 6/62," KNDN, 11.

50. Freedman, *Evolution of Nuclear Strategy*, 222–31.

51. This is Counterforce, 28 Feb 63, 473130, HRA, 4.

52. Ibid., 11.

53. Ibid., 15.

54. Ibid., 18.

55. Ibid., 3.

56. LeMay to Calvin Bullock Forum, 7 Nov 63, "Statements and Articles, Cleared Copies 1963," CL.

57. LeMay, *Mission,* 132.

58. CM-524-63, 17 Apr 63, "JCS Views - FY 1965 Program April 1963," RM, 2.

59. McNamara to Kennedy, 21 Nov 62, "FY 1964 Budget Memos (1 of 3)," RM, 7–9.

60. McNamara to Johnson, 6 Dec 63, 448, NSAD, I-5. "U.S. War Plans Would Kill an Estimated 108 Million Soviets, 104 Million Chinese, and 2.3 Million Poles," *UNREDACTED*, available at http://nsarchive.wordpress.com/2011/11/08/u-s-war-plans-would-kill-an-estimated-108-million-soviets-104-million-chinese-and-2-3-million-poles-more-evidence-on-siop-62-and-the-origins-of-overkill/.

61. Ibid.

62. Interview of Gen. Bruce Holloway, 18 Aug 77, 1027429, HRA, 211–14.

63. Vandenberg to Symington, 23 Aug 48, "CAG File I-1 Thru I-1000," AOPGF, 1.

64. John Lynn, *Battle* (Cambridge: Basic, 2004).

8. END OF AN ERA

1. George and Smoke, *Deterrence*, 391.

2. Ibid., 414–16.

3. Kaysen to Bundy, 20 Jul 61, "Basic National Security Policy, 6/22/62 and Undated [Folder 1 of 2]," KNDN.

4. Thomas C Schelling, "Nuclear Strategy in the Berlin Crisis," 5 Jul 61; "Germany," KNC. Schelling, "Nuclear," 5 Jul 61, 5.

5. Komer to Bundy, 20 Jul 61, "Germany (Berlin, General, 7/19/61-7/22/61)," KNC, 3–4.

6. JCSM-508-61, 29 Jul 61, "Misc - 1961 (Berlin, Europe, Conversation with Eisenhower)," RM, 4–5.

7. Memo for Norstad, "Germany (Berlin, General, 8/29/61–8/31/61)," KNC, 4.

8. Taylor to Kennedy, 28 Aug 61, "Germany (Berlin, General, 9/23/61–9/30/61)," KNC.

9. Bundy to Kennedy, 3 Oct 61, "Germany (Berlin, General, 10/1/61–10/4/61)," KNC, 1–2.

10. Interview of Gen. Lauris Norstad, 25 Oct 79, 1077004, HRA.

11. Kissinger to Bundy, 7 Jul 61, "Germany (Berlin, General, 7/7/61–7/12/61)," KNC.

12. Ibid.

13. WYS to Taylor, 7 Sep 61, "Germany (Berlin, General, 9/7/61–9/8/61)," KNMM.

14. Kaysen to Taylor, 5 Sep 61, Electronic Briefing Book 56, NSAD.

15. Nitze to Bundy et al., 22 Aug 61, "Germany (Berlin, General, 8/23/61–8/24/61)," KNC.

16. Kaysen to Kennedy, 22 Sep 61, "Germany (Berlin, General, 9/17/61–9/22/61)," KNC, 1, 2, 19.

17. See, for example, A. Fursenko and Timothy Naftali, *One Hell of a Gamble* (New York: Norton, 1997); and Graham Allison and Philip Zelikow, *Essence of Decision*, 2nd ed. (New York: Longman, 1999).

18. James Nathan, *Anatomy of the Cuban Missile Crisis* (Westport, CT: Greenwood, 2001), xxiv.

19. Ibid., xxiii–xxvii.

20. Sheldon Stern, *Averting "The Final Failure"* (Stanford, CA: Stanford, 2003), 72.

21. NSC Record of Actions, 20 Oct 62, "NSC Meetings, 1962, No 505, 10/20/62," KNMM, 8.

22. Timothy Naftali, Philip Zelikow, and Ernest May, *The Presidential Recordings: John F. Kennedy*, vol. 2 (New York: Norton, 2001), 583.

23. Interview of Gen. Wilbur Creech, 1 Jun 92, 1114823, HRA, 66.

24. Interview of Gen. Thomas Power, 15 Nov 62, 1118537, HRA.

25. Freedman, *Evolution of Nuclear Strategy*, 231.

26. Statement by McNamara before HASC, 24 Jan 63, "Cuba Statement," RM, 14–15.

27. James Blight and David Welch, *On the Brink*, 2nd ed. (New York: Noonday, 1990), 63.

28. Ibid., 69.

29. Ibid., 195.

30. Naftali et al., *Presidential Recordings*, 583–88.

31. Stern, *Averting*, 233.

32. Power to McNamara, 7 Nov 62, "13-10 SAC (Strategic Air Command) 1962," CL.

33. Interview of Gen. Thomas Power, 15 Nov 62, 1118537, HRA, 2.

34. AF Info Policy Ltr for Cmdrs, 15 Dec 1962, "National Security Policy 1948–1953," MS22.

35. Interview of Gen. Curtis LeMay, Jan 1965, 1070780, HRA, 7.

36. McNamara before HASC, 24 Jan 63, 31–32.

37. Trachtenberg, "Influence."

38. Briefing for President by CJCS, 13 Sep 61, 15–16.

39. Kaysen to Taylor, 5 Sep 61, 12–14.

40. Burke to Felt et al., 19 May 61, 320, NSAD, 1.

41. Ibid., 2–3.

42. JCS 2056/274, 18 Aug 61, "CCS 3105 Plans (Jt. Planning) (20 Mar 1961)," JCDF61, 1–2.

43. Ibid., 2267.

44. Ibid., App B, 4.

45. JCSM 756-61, 26 Oct 61, "CCS 3105 Plans (Joint Planning) (8 Mar 1961) (3) Sec. 2," JCDF61.

46. Lynn to Kissinger, 8 Nov 69, "SIOP (Single Integrated Operations Plan) [May/June 1971]," XNS.

47. JSTPS to JCS, 24 Aug 62, "CCS 3105 Plans (Joint Planning) (8 Mar 1961) (3) Sec. 4," JCDF61.

48. Handbook Strat Arms, vol. 2, Jun 76, 1012425, HRA, 176–84.

49. Ibid., 177.

50. Power to White, 11 Aug 59, "Command - SAC," LTW.

51. SAC Hist Jan–Jun 1960, vol. 2, 1056962, HRA, 264.

52. Power to White, 11 Aug 59, 258–64.

53. Ellis to LeMay, 19 Jul 61, "Defense, Secretary of 1961," CL.

54. McNamara to Kennedy, 7 Oct 61, "DoD, General, 9/61–10/61," KNDN; McNamara to Kennedy, 20 Nov 62, "FY 1964 Budget Memos (1 of 3)," RM.

55. Interview of Gen. David Jones, 14 Mar 86, 1105219, HRA, 61.

56. Ibid., 64.

57. SOR 82 in SAC Hist 1 Jan–30 Jun 61, vol. 4, 1117971, HRA, 2–11.

58. LeMay to Zuckert, 26 Jul 62, "B-70 (1 of 2)," RM.

59. "The two main potential sources of IBDA data are postlaunch signals from the weapon systems and signals associated with the detonation of nuclear weapons (which can give evidence on whether the defense, if there was one, was penetrated successfully). Perhaps the simplest example of such a technique is the use of a "good guidance" signal from an ICBM. If an ICBM of sufficient accuracy is launched at an undefended target, and if the missile commander receives a signal from the missile that it successfully followed the initial portion of its programmed ballistic trajectory, he can draw the inference that, with a high probability, the target was destroyed. Identification of the nuclear burst with a specific warhead by correlation in position and time is still under investigation. If it proves practical, penetration of defended targets can be verified." (McNamara to Kennedy, 20 Nov 62, 18–19.)

60. Handbook, vol. 2, 179.

61. Handbook, vol. 2, 424.

62. Handbook, vol. 2, 426; Skybolt MoU, 6 Jun 60, "Skybolt (1 of 3) 1961–62," RM.

63. Skybolt MoU.

64. Handbook, vol. 2, 424–26.

65. Brown to McNamara, 21 Aug 62, "Skybolt - Studies and AF Press Releases on Test 8-21-62," RM.

66. Macauley to York, 5 Aug 60, "Skybolt 1960–62," RM.

67. McNamara to Kennedy, 21 Nov 62, FY 1964 Budget Memos (1 of 3)," RM, 19–22.

68. CM 128-62, 20 Nov 62, "RS-70 Skybolt," RM.

69. LeMay to Zuckert, 20 Nov 62, "JCS Views Sept–Nov 1962," RM, atch memo, 3.

70. Zuckert to McNamara, 20 Nov 62, "JCS Views Sept–Nov 1962," RM.

71. McNamara to Kennedy, 11 Dec 62, "Skybolt (1 of 3) 1961–62," RM.

72. Proposed US-UK, 17 Dec 62, "Skybolt (1 of 3) 1961–62," RM.

73. Untitled press release, 22 Dec 62, "Skybolt - Studies and AF Press Releases on Test 8- 21-62," RM.

74. LeMay to McNamara, 3 Jan 63, "Skybolt - Studies and AF Press Releases on Test 8-21-62," RM.

75. McNamara to LeMay, 5 Jan 63, "Skybolt - Studies and AF Press Releases on Test 8-21-62," RM.

76. Interview of LeMay, Jan 65, 9.

77. Hester to AFXDC, 20 Feb 63, "1 - Chief of Staff Decisions 1963," ACSD59.

78. USAF Briefing on Space, Pt I, 10 Feb 61, 125973, RR.

79. AFM 1-2, 1959, quoted in Fact Sheet on R&D, "vol. 5, Research and Development," RM.

80. LeMay to White, 16 Sep 60, "5-1 Air Force Council (Folder 2) Jul–Dec 1960 Correspondence," LTW.

81. Concepts, HRA, 301–8.

82. LeMay to White, 19 Oct 60, "3 - Memoranda for the Chief of Staff 1960," ACSD59.

83. Threshold of Space, Sep 60, 908185, HRA, 35.

84. Current Status Report: 620A, Feb 60, 1003000, HRA, 23–24.

85. AF in Space FY62, 472258, HRA, 26.

86. AF in Space FY64 1006199, HRA, 24–28.

87. The only end-to-end ballistic missile test with a live warhead ever performed by the US was of a Polaris A-1 in 1962. No land-based ICBM has ever had such a test.

88. Coit Blacker and Gloria Duffy, *International Arms Control*, 2nd ed. (Stanford, CA: Stanford, 1984), 130.

89. Albert Carnesale and Richard Haass, *Superpower Arms Control* (Cambridge, MA: Ballinger, 1987), 10–14.

90. Edward Kaplan, "Peace through Strength Alone," in *Milestones in Strategic Arms Control, 1945–2000* (Montgomery, AL: Air University Press, Maxwell AFB, 2002), 42.

91. Ibid.

92. Ibid.

93. Special Message to the Senate, 8 Aug 63, "ACDA (Disarmament, Subjects, Nuclear Test Ban Treaty, President's Message to Congress 8/8/63)," KNDN.

94. Treaty, 25 Jul 63, "ACDA (Disarmament, Subjects, Nuclear Test Ban Treaty, Communique and Treaty 8/27/63-7/25/63 [*sic*])," KNDN.

95. Kaplan, "Peace through Strength," 45.

96. Ibid.

97. Ibid., 46.

98. *Dr. Strangelove*, DVD, directed by Stanley Kubrick (1964, Columbia).

CONCLUSION

1. The epigraph of this chapter is from the Schelling memo, Nuclear Strategy in Berlin, 5 Jul 61, "Germany (Berlin, General, 7/1/61–7/6/61)," KNC.

2. R. Michael Worden, *Rise of the Fighter Generals* (Montgomery, AL: Air University Press, Maxwell AFB, 1998), 243–46.

Index

CPSIA information can be obtained
at www.ICGtesting.com
Printed in the USA
LVHW041933210723
752907LV00005B/121

9 781501 752049